D1391350

# ON
# AND
# OFF
# THE
# RECORD

# ON
# AND
# OFF
# THE
# RECORD

*A Memoir of Walter Legge*

ELISABETH SCHWARZKOPF

With an Introduction by Herbert von Karajan

*faber and faber*

First published in Great Britain in 1982 by
Faber and Faber Limited, 3 Queen Square, London WC1.
First published in the United States by
Charles Scribner's Sons, 597 Fifth Avenue, New York.

Copyright © 1982 Musical Adviser Establishment
British Library Cataloguing in Publication Data
Schwarzkopf, Elisabeth.
  On and off the record: a memoir of Walter Legge
   1. Legge, Walter
   2. Music
   I. Title II. Legge, Walter
 780'.92'4  ML 429.L/
 ISBN 0 571 11928 X

Printed in the United States of America

ACKNOWLEDGMENTS: Certain portions of this book appeared in somewhat
different form in *Opera News* ("Walter Legge—An Appreciation"; "Lotte
Lehmann"; "Rosa—An Eightieth-Birthday Homage"; "Elisabeth Schwarz-
kopf"; "La Divina—Callas Remembered"); *The Times*, 27 Dec. 1975 ("The
Philharmonia"); *Gramophone* ("Otto Klemperer"; "Titta Ruffo"); *Opera*
("Sir Thomas"); and the *Manchester Guardian* (various reviews from the
1930's). *Meistersinger* excerpt, translated by John Gutman, © 1963 G.
Schirmer Inc. Used by permission. Introduction from Ernest Newman,
*Hugo Wolf* © 1966, by permission Dover Press. The author is extremely
grateful for permission to use this material.

PHOTO CREDITS: SECTION I: Schwarzkopf as the Marschallin, *Studio Lipnitski*;
as Elvira, *Erio Piccagliani*; Carlo Maria Giulini, *Godfrey MacDomnic*; Otto
Klemperer, *Godfrey MacDomnic*; Loren Maazel, *Godfrey MacDomnic*;
Thomas Schippers, *Eric Auerbach*; Schwarzkopf recording sessions, *Godfrey
MacDomnic*; Lucerne Festival, *Photo Paul Weber*; David Oistrakh, *Pathé
Marconi Press Service/Claude Poirier*; *The Merry Widow*, *Godfrey Mac-
Domnic*; Herbert von Karajan, *Godfrey MacDomnic*. SECTION II: George
Szell, *Reg Wilson*; Stockholm *Rosenkavalier*, *Enar Merkel Rydberg*; Joan
Sutherland, *Eric Auerbach*; Birgit Nilsson, *Erio Piccagliani*; Maria Callas,
*Erio Piccagliani*; Renata Scotto, *Eric Auerbach*; Maria Callas, with Walter
Legg and Tullio Serafin, *Erio Piccagliani*; Schwarzkopf, Parsons, Fischer-
Dieskau, *Reg Wilson*; *master* classes: New York, *Peter Schaaf*; Trieste,
*Foto Pozzar*.

"Well, what am I? I'm a midwife to music."

—Walter Legge
Radio Interview, 1974

# Contents

Was ohne deine Liebe,
was wär' ich ohne dich,
ob je auch Kind ich bliebe,
erwecktest du mich nicht?
Durch dich gewann ich,
was man preist,
durch dich ersann ich,
was ein Geist!
Durch dich erwacht,
durch dich nur dacht'
ich edel, frei und kühn,
du liessest mich erblühn!

But for your love's endeavor,
what could I ever be?
A childish girl forever,
till you awakened me!
'Twas you who taught me
what is right,
'twas you who brought me
mind's delight,
'twas you who bade,
'twas you who made
me noble, free and true!
I blossomed forth through you!

Die Meistersinger von Nürnberg, Act III

# Foreword

There seems to be a direct ratio between a singer's decrease in vocal resources and the increase in her friends' clamor for an autobiography. If you are lucky there might be a publisher among the clamorers. Both happened to me recently. But, although I do not totally disclaim the possibility of writing an autobiography at a distant date, I first looked around the house. Five filing cabinets, filled with my husband Walter's vast and always provocative correspondence; his articles, printed or still in manuscript; his translations of Strauss operas; his introduction to Ernest Newman's Wolf biography—they all were waiting there.

Of course Walter had been approached to write his autobiography; not only by friends but, as I found out from his files, by at least nine publishers in America, England, and Germany. His stalling and his excuses varied. Sometimes he would say, "I don't believe I'll ever have enough money to pay for all the lawsuits which will ensue." In one letter he said, "The very idea of being observed in print makes me feel like a eunuch in a nudist camp—the only difference being that he has nothing to hide whereas I have to conceal my ignorance." Then, later on, he would counter that he felt the few years still left him were better spent passing on his musical knowledge to pupils of our master classes. Whatever the reason: he is no longer here to write it. So I decided to do the best I could. Luck was with me: I found a short autobiograhy in Walter's files. He wrote it when he was given a special award from the Festival Musique Montreux, September 11 1969, "pour avoir contribué de façon éclatante au cours de sa carrière à faire progresser l'art du disque." It was, by the way, the only such award he ever received. To me this autobiography seemed the ideal structure on which to hang all those contributions, some by others but mostly by himself.

My role then is a new one: that of a narrator of sorts guiding the reader through that uplifting, exciting, infuriating, and sometimes frus-

*trating world, where Walter—as he used to say—served as "midwife to music." He would not have wished to live in any other world, and his midwifery, which delivered some of the most beautiful and lasting off-spring in the history of recording, made his life a happy one.*

*When I asked our friend Gustl Breuer to help me with this book, I knew that he had written several novels, that Walter liked his writing and looked forward eagerly to his letters, and that his Viennese background—maternal grandparents in whose home artists like Richard Strauss, Elisabeth Schumann, and Julia Culp were houseguests—would be right for a book of this kind. I had never been a writer and Walter had taken this burden from me to a degree where he dictated all my letters and wrote articles under my name, so that I really only had to sign autographs, contracts, and a succession of wills.*

*In a reply to a request from Yehudi Menuhin that I write a book on singing, Walter replied, "Elisabeth, when it comes to writing, is a cross between a Trappist and an unalphabetic. The only words she ever writes are her name on cheques."*

*I knew, although most of the book's writing is by Walter—two of the chapters are by Edward Greenfield and Dorle Soria—that Gustl would be able to help me express my narrative, a kind of guiding ribbon which winds its way through the book. Walter used to say, "When you grow older, mein Schatz, I hope your face will show only laugh lines, no lines of sadness." I looked at a snapshot from the time just after his death and thought, "Well, any further chance for laugh lines seems unlikely." What I did not know when I asked Gustl to come to Switzerland for five months' work was that after a year's in-activity the laugh lines would begin to be active once more and are now in the process of deepening. For the imagination to visualize this book and for bringing back laughter, I can't thank Gustl enough.*

*Marshall De Bruhl, the editor of this book—who, I pride myself, is now a friend of mine—was introduced to Walter by the late John Coveney of Angel Records, the most loyal and indispensable of artists relations men, beloved by every artist lucky to have been in his charge. Mr. De Bruhl's persuasive first letter to Walter asking for an autobiography elicited the response, "As Quickly sings to Falstaff, 'Siete un gran seduttore.'" And that was really the beginning of it all. . . .*

ELISABETH SCHWARZKOPF
*Zürich, 1981*

# Introduction  HERBERT von KARAJAN

My first meeting with Walter Legge was in Vienna in 1946 and took place under somewhat unusual circumstances. An exemption had been granted me by the American Occupation Forces to conduct a concert with the Vienna Philharmonic. For unexplained reasons, the concert was abruptly cancelled half an hour before it was scheduled to begin.

At 4 o'clock that afternoon, a Mr. Legge was announced at my home, asking if we could talk. I told him about my situation at the time and he assured me that all that sort of thing would soon pass. What was most important, he said, was that the two of us would be able to make recordings together. One thing became quite clear from this first long conversation: Our way of thinking about music was in complete harmony. This fact was proven again and again as the years went by.

Later on I helped Walter Legge with the development of the Philharmonia Orchestra of which he was the founder. I first conducted the orchestra in London in 1947. We enjoyed an exceedingly harmonious professional collaboration which consisted of many concerts, including tours with the Philharmonia to Europe and America, but which mostly involved the making of recordings.

Walter Legge demanded the utmost of himself and, in like manner, he asked a lot of those with whom he worked. This was a time when a whole new generation of singers grew up, many of whom were to command stages and concert halls for years to follow.

There is no doubt that Walter Legge was possessed by music. His raison d'être was to create ideal conditions, enlisting the best singers, instrumentalists, and conductors, to realize the interpretations he dreamed of.

Ours was a lifelong friendship. That all of us who worked with him felt an immense loss when Walter left us goes without saying.

HERBERT VON KARAJAN
Salzburg, 1981

xi

# ON
# AND
# OFF
# THE
# RECORD

# 1

# WALTER LEGGE
## *An Appreciation* DORLE SORIA

*Last summer, flying home from my San Francisco master classes, I stopped long enough in New York to see Dorle Soria. I had not seen her since her husband, Dario, had died. We talked mostly about how we were picking up our lives. She already had new and exciting editing and writing projects. I had my master classes and my work on this book. But we wouldn't be human if our talk had not turned backwards: when Dorle and Dario had founded Angel Records, when Walter made his fabulous records which they published, and when the three of them helped launch me as an international artist. We talked about the work that all of us had loved and what an incredibly happy life we both had with our men—Walter would have said with our "chumps."*

*I don't believe there is any better way to introduce Walter to the reader than by reprinting Dorle Soria's appreciation.*

THE NAME of Walter Legge, unknown to the general public, is a famous one in the recording industry and inner music circles. He was not only the producer of a legendary catalogue of classical recordings but he was responsible for the careers of many great conductors and artists of the concert and opera worlds. "A Diaghilev where music is concerned" is how Gerald Moore once described him. When he died, March 22, 1979, almost seventy-three years old, his death inspired a remarkable series of tributes.

*Opera:* "With the death of Walter Legge the world has lost one of the most important figures behind the music scene of the past fifty years . . . he was responsible for . . . some of the greatest musical achievement of his time, for the Philharmonia Orchestra, his unique recordings of music, to his talent-spotting and assisting of young musicians on their way towards world careers. Perhaps the greatest musical tribute I can pay to him is to put on the record that, on three different occasions, Wilhelm Furtwängler, Herbert von Karajan, and Dinu Lipatti once told me that they knew no man from whom they could learn more."

*Records and Recording:* "Possibly the greatest classical producer the industry has known."

*Gramophone:* "His achievement is huge, his contribution to twentieth-century music certain to survive for many decades."

*The Observer:* "The musical establishment regarded Walter Legge as a bold, bad baron; and as an old-style entrepreneur he did fit uncomfortably into the world of carefully balanced committees which increasingly determine most of our cultural activities. Legge was a loner. In a country that makes a fetish of the second rate Legge was a fanatic for quality, and therein lay the source of his achievements." In the same vein was this letter to the *Financial Times* signed by Lord Donaldson and Sir Isaiah Berlin, both long connected with the Covent Garden Board, and Sir Claus Moser, its chairman: "His founding of the Philharmonia Orchestra and Chorus, his prodigious knowledge of opera and singers and his ability to recognise talent, added very greatly to musical life in Britain. He trod on a great many toes, but in part this was due to his unswerving pursuit of the first rate, and undisguised contempt for anything that fell below it."

The French magazine *Lyrica:* "Through him masterpieces found a new audience. We found new ears. Legge made musicians of *discophiles.* Thank you, Walter. Most of them do not even know your name. May they bless you!"

*Die Presse,* Vienna: "If things were as they should be, and gratitude were still an esteemed virtue, the whole music world of today ought to stand at Walter Legge's graveside and mourn. What distinguished him cannot be learned: the instinct for music, the enthusiasm and total submersion in music, will surely not be found for many a day united in a single person."

After the Legge–Schwarzkopf Juilliard master classes in the autumn of 1976 Andrew Porter hailed the event and the participants: "When Legge married Schwarzkopf two perfectionists joined forces. Legge, although unmentioned in the 1975 *Grove's Dictionary of Music and Musicians,* has probably done more than anyone else alive to raise standards of musical performance—not just in Britain, where he founded and directed the Philharmonia Orchestra and engaged Karajan, Cantelli,

Klemperer, Giulini and, for two memorable Brahms concerts, Toscanini to conduct it, but internationally, through many, many recordings of performances executed to his exacting requirements—matching artists to repertory, casting, coaching, coaxing, and, at recording sessions, commending or criticizing until he was satisfied: as determined to put onto disc the best that artists could do under the best possible conditions. . . . Legge's genius was for recognizing and remembering in detail what constitutes greatness in musical execution, for perceiving potential greatness, and for inspiring new interpreters to learn from and emulate —not merely ape—the best achievements of their predecessors. The world owes him a debt for having sought out, sifted, promulgated and preserved for posterity the best in mid-twentieth-century musical performance."

Recently we heard Christa Ludwig talk of Walter Legge in the course of a telecast of a program of Brahms Lieder. "He taught me how to make the word *sun* shine and how to make the word *flower* bloom."

His patience with the great artists with whom he worked and his sensitivity to them were characteristic. Carlo Maria Giulini told us of this episode in their relationship. He was in New York a few days after Walter Legge had died and we talked of him. "He was musically incorruptible. And he founded a new school of recording—he was its leader, its *capo di scuola*. I think he would have liked to conduct. In fact, he said he once tried. But there was no accord between head and hand. But he knew everything there was to know about an orchestra and about voices. If he cast an opera you could sign without looking." Once, he said, Legge asked him to record the Tchaikovsky Fifth. He refused, saying he felt no sympathy for the work, but Legge persuaded him. The recording began. Fifteen minutes had gone by when Giulini put down his baton. "I can't go on." Legge said nothing. He dismissed the orchestra. "And you know what a loss that is to a company," Giulini said. "Then we took a long walk together in Hyde Park. We talked of other things."

Walter Legge was an Englishman by birth, a European by choice. He spoke German so well that many people thought of him as one and addressed him as "Herr Leg-geh." He was as much at home at La Scala as at Covent Garden, perhaps more so, and when he was producing Italian opera recordings there he might have been brought up on pasta instead of porridge. In Vienna his mother might have been a *Wienerin*; no Viennese could have created a more authentic or heady series of

Strauss and Lehár operettas which we were to successfully publicize as "Champagne" recordings. He was also comfortable in the United States, where during the past few years he and Elisabeth Schwarzkopf joined in master classes in California, the Middle West, and in New York. He had even talked of moving there. Perhaps the one place where he was not at home was France, the country where he lived after giving up a luxurious house on Lake Geneva with a private port and a garden which he had lovingly planted in the shape of the letter *E* for Elisabeth. Gardening, outside of books and music, was his greatest outside interest, along with a genuine feeling for good food and good wine.

He spent his last years at St.-Jean-Cap-Ferrat but he did not thrive on sun and sea and leisure. He longed for closed-in recording studios and libraries, concert halls and opera houses. After leaving EMI he was never a fulfilled person. In 1967, after a serious illness, he wrote us: "I wander from clinic to clinic, from doctor to doctor, quack to quack (and teach me the difference between doctor and quack and I'll give you an Oscar!). One thing is certain: three years' indolence were probably the cause of my illness. I must start doing what I and I only know how to do. If you have any ideas for a useful and profitable discharge of this dynamo, send them to your devoted old friend who still looks back with longing on Angelic days."

When Walter died they had finally sold their house and Elisabeth was busy packing. On March 25 there was a cremation service in Zürich at which a devoted friend, John Coveney of Angel Records, gave the eulogy and spoke of Legge's enduring monument, "the E.M.I. classical catalogue which even today is fifty percent composed of his productions." Among those present was Elisabeth Furtwängler, widow of the conductor. On the announcement card was printed the last lines from *Die Zauberflöte*: "*Es siegte die Stärke, und krönet zum Lohn/die Schönheit und Weisheit mit ewiger Kron'.*" It was in *Zauberflöte* that he first heard and saw a pretty young blonde soprano who one day was to become his wife. It was in Berlin, November 1937. He was recording the opera with Sir Thomas Beecham. Walter has recalled: "We had an admirable chorus of students and young professional singers, among them a Fräulein Schwarzkopf who had not yet made her debut."

On June 6 there was a "Service of Thanksgiving for the life of Walter Legge" in London at St. James's Church, the Wren-designed church which is an oasis of peace in the hurly-burly of Piccadilly. H.C. Robbins Landon, the Haydn scholar, gave the address. The Philharmonia Chorus sang Bruckner and Mozart. Manoug Parikian, former concertmaster of the Philharmonia, with Geoffrey Parsons at the piano, played Beethoven. Kevin Langan, Walter Legge's last protégé, sang Wolf's "Um Mitternacht." Elisabeth had told us that she had wanted someone to sing Wagner's "Träume." "Then my old teacher Maria Ivogün said, 'But you must be represented on the program. Isn't there an old recording?' And I said yes, there was." And so, at the end of the service, after the blessing, the voice of Elisabeth Schwarzkopf filled the church.

Family, friends, and members of Britain's musical "establishment" had gathered at the church to pay honor to Walter Legge. There were representatives of the Royal College of Music, the Royal Opera House and Royal Festival Hall, of the Philharmonia Orchestra, of EMI, Decca, and the BBC, and of the Arts Council of Great Britain; the University of Michigan, where Legge had participated in master classes, was also represented. And then there were music critics and artists and Antonino Tonini of La Scala, who had coached singers in many of the Italian opera recordings, and Lady Beecham. Walter Legge's last writings, a brilliant series of articles, had been devoted to a centenary tribute to Sir Thomas Beecham. After he died, Elisabeth arranged for a plot in Vienna's Central Cemetery near the graves of the composers Walter Legge lived for—Beethoven and Brahms, Schubert, the Johann Strausses, and particularly Hugo Wolf, for whose recognition he had fought almost single-handedly.

My husband, Dario, and I met Walter Legge in 1952. Dario, then president of Cetra-Soria Records, had been asked by EMI to start a new label, a North American outlet for the recordings of its subsidiary, the Columbia Gramophone Company—usually known as English Columbia—of which Walter Legge was artists-and-repertoire director. The company was launched in September 1953. We named it Angel Records, after an almost forgotten turn-of-the-century EMI trademark, "at the sign of the Recording Angel." Dario, who had sold Cetra-Soria to Capitol, became Angel's president. I was in charge of artists and repertoire and publicity.

Until January 1958, when Dario resigned, we worked with Walter Legge in closest connection and with a shared dedication. Brilliant, inventive, highly competitive, a man whose technical expertise matched his musical knowledge, Legge was indefatigable on behalf of Angel, persuading great artists, attracting young ones, developing a broad-based catalogue of extraordinary quality. He was a demon for work and had no patience with time-restricting unions or nine-to-five habits. Since we were equally absorbed, ideas flowed back and forth between us in almost daily letters. We had our own jokes and a private language like schoolchildren. If someone had a sudden inspiration it was called an F.O.G.—Flash of Genius. If it failed it was dismissed as just a mind-muddling FOG.

From our Angel years together I have chosen a few typical excerpts from a vast collection of letters and memoranda, each characteristic of some facet of Walter's erudite and entertaining personality.

*Sept. 11, 1953.* About the now legendary La Scala–de Sabata–Callas–Gobbi–di Stefano *Tosca*. "*Tosca* was a difficult birth. De Sabata reduced the whole staff to tears (literally) either of rage, exasperation, or nervous exhaustion. I alone remained dry-eyed and cool-headed, mainly owing to a daily consumption of six large bottles of mineral water per session. The results put all previous attempts to record Italian opera into cool shade—both artistically and technically. This is so far superior to both *Puritani* and *Lucia* that I beg you in your own interests to hold up the other Italian operas until *Tosca* is published. If we start with *Tosca* we shall probably sell the rest on the reputation we make with it."

*Nov. 16, 1953.* Until we started Angel all records had been left open for playing before purchase. We were the first to put out and advertise "factory-sealed records." Walter quipped: "Suggested slogan for your factory-sealed records: 'Every Angel a Virgin.' "

*Jan. 1, 1954.* "All the fears for Karajan's debut as a conductor of Italian opera in La Scala were groundless! *Lucia* was a triumph for him and Callas such as Milan has not seen for years."

*July 6, 1954.* During the McCarthy witch-hunting period in the States and concerning a possible recording of the Bach Double Concerto with the Oistrakhs. "What do you think the American reaction would be if we actually pulled off for Angel a recording expedition into Russia to record father and son Oistrakh and anything else we could pick up? Think this one over carefully. I don't want to read in *Time* magazine of a cross-examination of 2-D Soria before thrice-to-be-damned McCarthy!"

*May 4, 1954.* I was a Max Beerbohm fan and had asked Walter whether it would be possible to persuade him to read from his works. "I have spent one of the most enchanting afternoons of my life with

Beerbohm and the recording starts at 3 o'clock on 3rd June at the Hotel Moderne, Rapallo."

*June 7, 1954, 6 A.M.* The highs and lows of a producer's life. "Finis coronet opus! We have made the long doubted Max recordings. I am taking with me for you two exquisite cartoons, one of them hitherto unpublished (and also to be returned to their creator). Otherwise only chaos in Italy. Karajan telephoned at dawn that he cannot conduct *Pagliacci* because of his shoulder trouble. The night before, Callas suddenly decided she could not sing in the Verdi *Requiem*. De Sabata and I spent yesterday telephoning and telegraphing her. So far without avail. I am reminded of the occasion when Klemperer in a loud voice asked an orchestra: 'What is *merde* in English?' "

*Jan. 11, 1955.* After the publication of a deluxe edition of the Mozart Complete Works for Piano Solo played by Gieseking. "Unless you have already done so, do not protest against the *High Fidelity* review of Gieseking. We left out one or two small and such palpably inferior pieces in piety to Mozart's memory. Admittedly, he had sown all his musical wild oats before he was ten but there was no point in bringing up mistakes of his childhood. There is nothing worse than getting involved in controversies with musicologists."

*Sept. 13, 1955.* After recording sessions of *Rigoletto* beset with crises and prima donna problems. "I do not know whether the American Trade Unions have the same principle as the English of demanding danger money for those of their members who are engaged in particularly hazardous or possibly mortal work! If so, I am sending my bill to you for the *Rigoletto* recording."

*A handwritten memo, early 1956,* re Vladimir Ashkenazy. "Ash-Can-Azzy (spell it your way) is quite a boy. Diminutive, with a great shock of dark brown hair, he looks in profile like the Chopin portraits. In one session 6½ hours (!!!) we have completed more than one LP side. His hobby is football! If he kicks as hard as he can hit the piano, I should not like even to be referee! His nickname, like Horowitz's, is Volodya. The resemblance does not end there."

*Feb. 27, 1956.* For a year we had been talking of Weill-Brecht recordings and Legge was annoyed that Columbia Records had gotten ahead of him. "You probably think I have gone slightly mad on the subject of Weill-Brecht. I feel I owe you a word of explanation. When this extraordinary pair first came on the German musical scene at the end of the twenties, *The Threepenny Opera* (as it is called now), *Mahagonny*, and *Anna-Anna* made an impact on me as strong as *Carmina Burana* did in 1945, as Sibelius had done in 1926, and Wolf when I was fourteen and Bartok in the late twenties. These instinctive reactions of mine are almost invariably in conflict with the critics and are equally invariably proved right later on. I have been through the score of *Mahagonny* with Walter Goehr, who, like me, heard the first Berlin performance. It is even better than I had remembered." There had been a suggestion of Marlene Dietrich for the role of Jenny. "However, I doubt whether it would not be better to do the piece today with real singers. Jenny is a full-length soprano part getting up to high C: I am less convinced of Weill's purely symphonic works. His real genius lay in his ability (when working with Brecht) to capture the despair, irony, sordidness of life in Germany with seven million unemployed and the imminent danger of National Socialism. But I will ask Klemperer what he thinks of the Symphony."

*Apr. 11, 1956.* For the libretto of *Zigeunerbaron* we had no biographical material for a singer named Erich Paulik, who was listed for the small role of Pali. We asked for information. "Attached herewith a brief biography. 'Erich Paulik, illegitimate son of a Eunuch in the Cappella Sistina and the wife of an Admiral in the Swiss Navy. He studied singing at the famous Cruft's School in London where his teachers were Alsatians. His most famous role is the title part in *La Muette de Portici*.'" A postscript explained that Paulik was really a well-known singer whose name could not be used officially because he had recorded the same role for another company. "So we took this pseudonym which led you up the garden path. I do not see why you should not publish the biography. It is no more bogus than those that appear in *Who's Who*."

*Nov. 21, 1956.* Legge was deep into a series of Hindemith recordings. "To my inexpressible delight the recording with Hindemith is going like mumps at a prep school. The pieces are devilishly difficult, both for orchestra and conductor, but under Hindemith's happy smile and tireless energy we have gained one day in three on our schedule. Unless an unexpected snag arises we should get five or even six LP sides in the time we estimated as the irreducible maximum for four. I believe Hindemith will be the next living composer to be a good investment for recording."

*November 1956, undated.* A crisis before the recording of *The Barber of Seville* in London. England did not permit dogs to enter without going through a long period of quarantine. Callas would not come without her poodle. "If La Divina makes it a condition of her coming to London to bring her dog with her, then we are bitched. The trouble is that we have already engaged Gobbi, Alva, the orchestra, Zaccaria, Galliera, and the hall; and we cannot get out of these commitments. Nothing would be diplomatically more unpleasant and give us all years of misery than to record the opera without Maria but we simply cannot envisage that a dog should disturb the happy relations that you both, and I, have so carefully nurtured. Tell her I will give her a dog if she will come or she can borrow mine for the duration of her stay.

"I have already written to David Webster and told him that Callas would probably sing at Covent Garden if he could arrange to get her dog in without quarantine. I do not think there is much chance of raising the quarantine question in Parliament because Sir Anthony and others have quite enough on their plates, the fact that they have put it there themselves is beside the point. But frivolity apart, it is absolutely essential that you induce Maria to stick to her commitments in London. It is too ridiculous that a poodle should be the basis of a 'cause célèbre.' "
A few days later he sent us a copy of David Webster's reply: "I just do not think there is anything that anybody in the world could do about Callas' dog, short of smuggling, and I really do not know how that is done. Mrs. Patrick Campbell told me she introduced her dog once as her left breast and once as a diseased hip but that after that she was baffled."

*June 15, 1957.* There had been questions raised about cuts in *The Barber of Seville*, which Callas did record, and we referred them to Walter. "I am at home trying to recover from what English Doctors call angina, so I cannot refer to the tapes of *Barber* yet to give you the exact cuts. But I do think you must wean the American critics and the people who write silly letters out of the habit of believing that completeness is the essential virtue in recording an opera. There are certain cuts which are traditional. . . . With a gramophone record we have no means of showing the comic business and, therefore, we are doing the composers a real service in removing these longuers from the score. It is a curious thing that this bug of completeness afflicts so-called music lovers only; people who listen to music are far worse than those who listen to plays. Nobody ever attacks a producer if he cuts *Hamlet* or *Romeo and Juliet*. But cut four bars of the nonsensical incompetently written jingle that is called a libretto of an

11

early Italian opera and a few bars of the schoolboy nonsense that is called the recitativo and a crusader stands up on his hind legs in an excess of self-righteousness and wants to clip off the Angel's wings." A postscript. "No doubt you will get a hoard of letters, mainly inspired by a competitor, complaining about the cuts in *Rosenkavalier*. All the cuts are authorized by Strauss himself and as far as can be traced there has never yet been an un-cut performance of *Rosenkavalier* given in the Salzburg Festival."

*Nov. 1, 1957*. One critic has called the Klemperer concerts and recordings with the Philharmonia "Walter Legge's finest memorial." "The Klemperer concerts are going like wildfire. Eight sold-out houses to date! There has been nothing like this in London's musical life since Toscanini in the 1930's. Pray for me on November 12, the Philharmonia Chorus makes its debut with the Ninth Symphony. As long as Asian flu does not decimate the ranks, I am not worried. It is wonderful. Herbert, who had a spy at the rehearsals, actually asked to do the Verdi *Requiem* with it next season!"

*Nov. 9, 1957*. "Klemperer goes from strength to strength. When we have completed the Ninth I shall have given you a Beethoven cycle on record which will be prized as long as records are collected."

Shortly after, Walter answered a query we had sent him concerning a violinist who had been a soloist with Klemperer and about whom we had heard good things. "He played appallingly and afterwards suggested he should record the work with Klemperer. The following conversation may amuse you. Violinist: 'We must record the Beethoven Concerto together, Maestro. It would be a great monument.' Klemperer (aside to me): 'He means tomb-stone.' "

During the twenty years after our Angel period together we remained in touch, vastly enjoying each other's company when we had the chance to meet here or abroad. And Walter's letters continued. He gave us his schedules, told us his plans, asked for advice, begged for the news and gossip of that musical sea in which he swam most freely.

*Jan. 7, 1967*. Once again the old enthusiastic Walter. "FASTEN YOUR SEAT BELTS! I have accepted the Artistic Directorship of the Wexford Festival. Never heard of it? You will! The theatre is over a hundred years old, seats 480 people and specializes in unfamiliar opera. They have given people like Cossotto, Aragall, and Sciutti their first steps to international fame. The first thing I have to do is to collect funds to improve standards. How does one set about it? America has,

I believe, an enormous number of patriotic Irish, a small proportion of which has a lot of money. Have you any of them on your visiting list? Can you devise a way of approaching the Kennedys? No other news. We are sitting in the snow in Berlin and recording Wolf's *Spanisches Liederbuch* with Fischer-Dieskau and Gerald Moore for DGG. Strange sensation for both of us. It is Elisabeth's first recording for anyone but EMI in 20 years and my first 'outing.'"

*Feb. 1, 1967.* "Nemesis was waiting like a thug around the corner for me with a sack full of knuckle dusters and hardly was my Wexford letter on its way to you when I was rushed into hospital in Zürich with an illness which by name begins like a Mozart divertimento and ends with an 'itis' and has a 'tic'kle' in the middle! The doctors are threatening to keep me imprisoned here for six to eight weeks. A letter from you would do much to lighten the life of your reluctant invalid."

We will not forget those long evenings we would spend together when he came to New York. He would arrive about seven but dinner was a goal to be reached only after long hours of talk, stimulated by drink, soothed by a good cigar. We would bring him up-to-date on the news. When Dario told him that the Met was now over the hump and doing well, he was pleased but pessimistic about the state of opera in general. "Unless there is a radical change of heart and head the unions will kill opera within a decade or so. And from what I have seen lately I doubt if it deserves to live. Only an idiot would—and does—pay the high prices for tickets when they can get better singing and performances from records at less than half the price and undisturbed by the horrors of the senseless graffiti that 'producers' scribble on masterpieces." He referred to the scenery of a new *Siegfried* as "strips of *tagliatelle verdi* hung like the bead curtains of an Oriental bazaar."

We would always ask how his memoirs were progressing and he always said he was collecting material and making notes for them "but I am scared at the thought of wasting time on a job I may not live to finish." When he left—if Elisabeth were not with him—we sensed that he would not go directly to his hotel; he might stop by to see another night owl like himself. He did not welcome the dark hours of sleep. Once, on his fiftieth birthday, he had had a momentary but complete blindness. After that he always slept with the lights on in his bedroom.

In mid-June 1979, Elisabeth flew from Zürich, where she had moved to the small house she and Walter had owned for many years, to San Francisco, where she taught the Merola master classes by herself.

We spoke to her on the telephone. "I had to take the plunge," she said. "If I had waited I might never do it." She had just heard her first concert after Walter's death, conducted by Karajan. "It was shattering. Karajan said he had done the Beethoven Seventh for Walter." Would she go to Salzburg after California? "No. I will fly straight home, to Zürich. I must put my life in order." She spoke of her garden there. "Last December, after my birthday, Walter insisted on going to Zürich before returning to St.-Jean-Cap-Ferrat. He had brought with him a big satchel of tulip onions." (We call them bulbs.) "There were eight hundred. It was very late in the season but he insisted that they go in the ground before it froze. Just before I left they were all in full bloom."

# 2

# AN
# AUTOBIOGRAPHY

For years Walter had gathered material for his memoirs, and as he wrote to one publisher: "Frankly and with more than all due modesty I think I have a book or two in me but my muse is a costive wench and I am an almost incorrigible self-improver-cosmetician, if you like, of my own work. Wouldn't it be better for me to enjoy the sun or make a new garden?"

Walter, a quintessential Englishman, was often thought to be German; he spoke the language perfectly, with no trace of an accent.

Walter's parents had met when they were fourteen, but did not marry until they were thirty-four, in 1905, an aunt, Minnie Legge, recalls. Walter was born 1 June 1906 at Keith Grove, Shepherds Bush.

The elder Legge was a tailor, whose work was apparently perfection itself. He had chosen this profession because of a shortened leg caused by polio; it was necessary to have a job that did not require him to stand. Walter would inherit this desire for perfection, and also his father's love for music. The father had taught himself to play the piano and he took his young son to performances of the Carl Rosa Opera Company.

Walter's first school was a nearby "house school" run by a Miss D. A. Carlisle, the daughter of an army colonel. His sister, Mrs. John Tobin, who later attended the school, has told me that Miss Carlisle could have been a colonel herself. Maya Tobin caught just a glimpse of Miss Carlisle on a railway platform thirty years later and shook for half an hour afterward.

The stern headmistress took immediately to the precocious boy and he became her favorite. He won all the prizes. Walter later attended the Latymer School, where he studied Latin and French, in which he excelled. He left the Latymer School at age sixteen, and that was the *end of his formal schooling. He continued to live at home (he kept a room with his family until World War II), and one Sunday afternoon his father suggested that he attend the regular Sunday concert at the Albert Hall. He attended every one thereafter. In order to queue up early, he had to forgo church, which he gladly did. Music thus became a sort of religion.*

*He taught himself to read music, and after first hearing Wagner in German during the 1924 Covent Garden season his love affair with the German language began. He would teach himself German too.*

*The big problem was how to make a living with music without being a performer. Thus, in a sense, he had to invent his profession.*

I WAS the first of what are called "producers" of records. Before I established myself and my ideas, the attitude of recording managers of all companies was "we are in the studio to record as well as we can wax what the artists habitually do in the opera house or on the concert platform." My predecessor, Fred Gaisberg, told me: "We are out to make sound photographs of as many sides as we can get during each session." My ideas were different. It was my aim to make records that would set the standards by which public performances and the artists of the future would be judged—to leave behind a large series of examples of the best performances of my epoch.

As a small child a gramophone and records were my favorite toys and at ten I starved saving my pocket money to buy records for my own pleasure. It is even said that I learned to read first from record labels, then from European and American record catalogues, which I collected as other English boys collected postage stamps. I had first been to hear opera (in English) at the age of seven and the impression it made on me was so strong that I decided then and there that my future must be spent in music—preferably making gramophone records and directing an opera house! When I was twelve my father bought me what for those days was a large collection of records. It included examples of the work of the leading international opera singers of the period, some of the earliest orchestral records—mostly odd movements of symphonies, brutally cut opera overtures, and symphonic poems. There were also several records of great violinists. When I was sixty-two, I offered my collection to a venerable Swiss institution, which would accept it only on condition that an endowment for a curator and maintenance be provided also. In one of my better rages, I broke every record into bits and tossed the pieces into Lake Geneva.

The impact of certain of these records I must describe as comparable only to Keats's discovering Chapman's Homer. The manliness, power and dark resonance of the baritone Titta Ruffo's voice and the nobility and warmth of Fritz Kreisler's tone gave me a new and unimagined concept of sound—sounds which I became familiar with at firsthand. For me no male singer has matched Ruffo's golden splendour, and the only violinist I will compare with Kreisler is David Oistrakh. Soon after the first war, artists of international fame started visiting London again —conductors as well as instrumentalists and singers. I became the most avid concertgoer and soon found out how to slip in undetected to rehearsals. It was from listening to Weingartner and Beecham at work that I had my first insight into orchestral playing.

My parents were not more than averagely musical, and even if they had been the repertoire of music available on records would not have helped them much. The staple musical diet of my childhood was about the best that the record catalogues offered, popular overtures and operatic arias and ensembles sung by the famous singers of the period. To this day I do not know why I was never for long fascinated by the idea of becoming a performer. Perhaps it was the early realisation that I should never be a good pianist. Practice always seemed to me a waste of the time that could be better spent in listening to music or reading about it. Once I had learned to read music well enough at eight to strum out after my own fashion vocal scores of operas that I borrowed from the local public library, my interest in the piano was purely a matter of utility. A desire to become an operatic baritone died a similar death. Before my voice broke I learned to shout a few parts by heart but the desire to know operas I had heard about and never seen was keener than the wish to learn to sing a few songs beautifully. Even today I am sorry for my friends whose lives consist of playing the same few works year in and year out.

I began to be discriminating when I was twelve. I had saved up my pocket money to buy myself a record. There were four or five versions of the aria I wanted, and before I eventually made up my mind and parted with my seven and sixpence I had heard all the different versions in a dozen shops. I shall never forget that week of indecision, doubt, and the misery of eventually having to make up my mind. That process

17

was repeated at two-monthly and later at shorter intervals for some years. But it was wonderful training for which I can never be sufficiently grateful. From fifteen onwards I went through similar exquisite agonies deciding how to spend my money on concert tickets. Every day on my way home from school I went to the public library to read the musical criticisms. At that time Ernest Newman had become musical critic to the *Observer* and the freshness and vividness of his writing, so different from the rest of the phrase-making of other writings on music, sent me into the lending library to see if he had written any books. It was probably the best day of my life that I borrowed his monograph on Hugo Wolf. His magical prose writing in winged phrases of songs I had never heard or even heard of sent me searching for gramophone records of them. There was not one to be found anywhere. I wrote to the gramophone companies suggesting that records should be made of them and received polite replies thanking me for my suggestions but gently explaining that there was no demand for such records. From that moment I set my heart on getting into a gramophone company so that I could put such things right. In the meantime I set about learning the songs for myself, and guided by Newman's magical descriptions I found my way slowly into a world of wonder and sensibility that is my constant joy to this day.

In 1924 London had its first postwar international opera season at Covent Garden. For the first time I heard The Ring, *Tristan, Der Rosenkavalier, Ariadne auf Naxos, Salome* (as well as some of the standard Italian repertoire), many of them conducted by Bruno Walter and sung by such still-remembered singers as Lotte Lehmann, Elisabeth Schumann, Maria Ivogün, Frida Leider, Göta Ljungberg, Selma Kurz, Maria Olczewska, Alfred Piccaver, Jacques Urlus, Friedrich Schorr, Emil Schipper, and Paul Bender. From then on I missed hardly a performance in an international season in Covent Garden until the outbreak of the 1939 war.

*One of the many marvellous things in assembling this book was to come across the first criticism Walter wrote. I had never seen the pieces before; they cover the 1926 and 1927 Covent Garden seasons when he was twenty. Alas there is no record of his critiques of the 1924 and 1925 seasons, both of which he attended.*

*I am certain Walter's fondness for the human voice must have*

18

*broken through then and so much vocal splendour might, at times, have been almost too much for the young man. As I turned the pages of the hand-written booklet, I could not help smiling. Because here, at twenty, Walter's musical taste was already set. What he liked and disliked in a singer's voice is irrevocably stated in those pages. If he hated faulty intonation, this crime at times could still be forgiven. But what really caused an earthquake was: THE WOBBLE! Even at twenty! A wobble could be anything from a vocal flutter, to a wide vibrato, to—a wobble! Whatever its name, it was unpardonable, it was anathema, the enemy, a crime, the red flag! As with so many other things, Walter's view of the wobble never changed.*

*Later on, when he encountered a wobble, the earthquakes might give way to his flailing right arm, waving an imaginary scarf and moaning, "Und sieh' Isolde, wie sie winkt."*

*May 2, 1927. Der Rosenkavalier.* A feature of the performance was the marvellous singing of Schumann. For sheer beauty of tone and perfection of technique she towered above the rest of the cast. Lehmann was not up to her usual standard. In Act 1, her tone was rough but artistry remained supreme. Walter was just Walter. Whatever the fate of Strauss' other music the finale of this work is immortal.

*May 3. Tristan und Isolde.* A perfect performance! Laubenthal . . . was a superb Tristan. Leider was even better than in 1926. Olczewska is Brangäne even as she is Waltraute or Fricka—unequalled.

*May 5. Das Rheingold.* The first cycle of the *Ring* opened with a rather patchy *Rheingold*. Olczewska was as ever superb. The Freia (L. Markincy) was incredibly bad—an amazing wobble. The English trio of Rhinemaidens were as bad as only English sopranos can be.

*May 6. Die Walküre.* From the soprano point of view . . . last night can never be surpassed. Lehmann's Sieglinde . . . perfect, a finer performance is beyond imagination. Leider *sang* the Cry and although slightly lacking the heroic quality her B'hilde ranks second only to her Isolde. Melchior apart from xylophonic high notes and doubtful intonation ("Spring Song") was a good Siegmund.

*May 17. Parsifal.* This seems to be the logical ending of such a life work as Wagner's. It is the ultimate development of one who has immortalised all the human passions. For spiritual loveliness I know of nothing to compare with the choral parts of Act I. Mayr's Gurnemanz was dignified and perfectly interpreted tho' the voice is not steady. Melchior lacked conviction both vocally and dramatically.

Ljungberg looked well but her singing in Act II was bad—scoops–flat–sharp–screams—everything seemed wrong.

*May 19. Fidelio.* Beethoven, greatest of symphony composers, was right out of his element when writing for the voice. His songs are for the most part dull and his only opera is hopelessly so.

*May 25. Mefistofele.* What an opera!!! Surely *the* worst!!!

*May 30. Gli Ugonotti.* I have a premonition that last night's performance will stand for many years as the worst given in Covent Garden. Kipnis (debut) was the sole satisfactory member of the cast. It is sometimes pretty, fatuous, impressive dramatically, all in turn but this will suffice to shelve it for years.

*June 2. Die Walküre.* That Jeritza gave us a magnificent Tosca on the occasion of her debut (in 1925) is an accepted fact. That she sang Sieglinde in the Tosca style last night is also accepted as a fact, but it was not a success. Her interpretation (Sieglinde à la Grand Guignol) was not liked.

*June 8. Otello.* I am extremely fortunate in that—at the first hearing of this opera—I have at last heard a real tenor. He (Zenatello) has certainly the most lovely tenor voice and uses it with great artistry. His prime is undoubtedly past, and I can but wonder what he was like fifteen years ago. Lehmann surprised me by her exquisite art. I do not hope to hear a finer Desdemona. I cannot even imagine one. Stabile (debut) has a really nasty wobble. His voice (malgré the critics) is small and of fair quality but that wobble———. His conception (?) of the part left all to be desired.

*June 11. Don Giovanni.* It is not difficult as I should have imagined to find the reason for the lack of popularity of Mozart operas. However keen one is on Mozart the semi-spoken recitatives so cut it up that the interest is not maintained.

*June 29. Falstaff.* Stabile, wavering, wobbling, Stabile, whose Iago and Don were disappointing, gave us last night a remarkably fine reading of *Falstaff.* The opera itself is wonderful. The orchestration is in itself a revelation and yet it has Mozartean delicacy. A delightful evening.

## Musical Critic

*Walter would in less than five years' time become music critic for the* Manchester Guardian—*covering such disparate events as the 1933 season at Bayreuth (with Adolf Hitler in the audience) and the Russian ballet's visits to London. He was all the time sharpening his musical*

20

*skills and opinions. Changing some of them, of course, particularly his view of Beethoven's one opera and (need it be said?) of Mozart's recitatives.*

## August 1933. The Bayreuth Festival
## "Featuring Herr Hitler"

It would have been a pardonable error on the part of any casual visitor to Bayreuth to have mistaken this year's Wagner festival for a Hitler Festival. For previous festivals every shop, no matter what its wares, managed by hook or by crook to display a photograph of at least some reproduction of Wagner's face. From the windows of china shops dozens of ceramic Wagners used to gaze into space. Booksellers displayed Wagner's autobiography. This year the china shops are full of Hitler plaques, and *Mein Kampf* has displaced *Mein Leben*. From every flagstaff and nearly every window a swastika flag is flying. Brown shirts are almost de rigueur, and passing "Café Tannhäuser" and "Gasthof Rheingold" one hears nothing but the "Horst Wessel Lied."

Herr Hitler attended the first six performances of the festival, and the behaviour of the audience gave one the impression that for them "this is a Hitler festival, and, since Hitler likes Wagner's music, we are here, too." Thousands of people lined the streets from his house to the Festspielhaus, and, with the exception of the foreign visitors, the audience waited outside the theatre to cheer him as he arrived, and then rushed into their seats to gaze admiringly, almost reverently, at his box until the lights were lowered. At the end of each act the centre of attraction changed immediately from the stage to the Chancellor's box. And when business detained Herr Hitler in Berlin, two thousand people were made to wait an hour and a half for their opera until he should take his seat in the theatre.

It would be idle to pretend that this outward display of national politics increased the pleasure of the international music-lover whose only interests were artistic. But, unfortunately, Hitler's influence over Bayreuth was not confined to outward show. Through his policy we were deprived of the presence of Toscanini and consequently the performance of *Die Meistersinger* and *Parsifal* were considerably inferior to those that most of us expected when, five or six month ago, we bought our tickets. The fault is not on Toscanini's side—no one can blame him for his withdrawal.

21

## MUSICAL PROTECTIONISM

Toscanini's wire announcing his decision not to conduct at Bayreuth undoubtedly gave Hitler unpleasant food for thought. I am informed that the publication of that news practically stopped foreign bookings, and was followed by hundreds of cancellations from all parts of the world. The national pride that gave birth to the Nazi shibboleth "Only German art performed by German artists" must have been deeply wounded; but is it national pride? Conversations I have had with prominent German musicians of the Nazi persuasion have convinced me that the actuating motive is fear. The German performers have seen with dismay that in nearly every instance the finest interpretative artists are foreign and that the few of the first class who are German are also Jewish. They have noticed that of the great violinists of the world Elman, Menuhin, Heifetz, Huberman, and Zimbalist are all Russian or Polish and Jewish; of the pianists Schnabel is German but Jewish, Rachmaninoff and Horowitz are Russian, Paderewski and Rubinstein Polish, Cortot Swiss; of conductors Toscanini is Italian, Koussevitzky Russian and Jewish; their own Klemperer and Walter are both Jewish. Even the business of singing Wagner, their prewar stronghold, has passed out of their hands. Of the eminent Wagnerian sopranos, Lehmann is German, Leider is German (but, I believe I am right in stating, of Russian extraction), but Ljungberg is Swedish, so is Larsen-Todsen. Of the contraltos Olczewska's mother was Rumanian, Karin Branzell is Swedish. The finest dramatic tenor in the world, Melchior, is a Dane; his nearest rival, Graarud, is Norwegian. Among baritones Janssen and Bockelmann are pure Germans, but the most popular of all, Schorr, is a Hungarian Jew. And there are virtually no German basses. Kipnis is Russian and Jewish, List Austrian and Jewish, Andrésen is Norwegian. Musically at least, the fanatical nationalism of Germany is to a great extent a fear-induced protection of inferior home products against superior foreign competition.

## EXCELLENT ORCHESTRA AND CHORUS

Many of us expected that without Jewish string players the Bayreuth orchestra would be below its former level of excellence, but at no time during the festival has there been any evidence of deterioration. Both the orchestral playing and the choral singing have been of the highest quality, electrifying in their precision and unanimity and of the finest subtlety of detail. These, together with the staging of Emil Preetorius and the production of Heinz Tietjen, have been the great delights of the festival. We in England, accustomed to Covent Garden's badly painted cloths and inadequate stage machinery, and to the makeshift scenery of touring companies, have little idea of the advance in operatic staging that has taken place in Central Europe during the past twelve years. But even those of us who have watched with interest the development of Emil Preetorius as a scenic artist and of Heinz Tietjen as a producer have been astonished by the dramatic strength and stark realism of these Bayreuth productions. If a season of Wagnerian music dramas were given in an English theatre staged and produced as at Bayreuth, the purveyors of mammoth revues and musical comedies would have to find other outlets for their energies. For Preetorius and Tietjen give dramatic truth, and Wagnerian dramatic truth will outdo any other form of theatrical art.

Considering the nationalist views of Germany's ruling party, the choice of singers was surprising. The contraltos were both foreigners, Sigrid Onegin (Swedish), Enid Szantho (Irish-Hungarian); the tenors were German and with the exception of Franz Völker undistinguished. The best singing of the festival came from Maria Müller, Czech soprano: Rudolf Bockelmann (Wotan and Sachs), a German baritone, and two Jewish basses, Emanuel List (Hunding, Fafner, and Hagen) and Alexander Kipnis (Titurel and Pogner).

In a recent issue of the *Zeitschrift für Musik*, the journal founded by Schumann, I found this panegyric of Hitler's nationalistic policy: "Soon again German opera houses will give bread to German artists and become centres for the cultivation of German music. In our concert halls we shall see the return of German artists and German works . . . German homes, liberated from the alien pest, will rejoice again in works bequeathed to the German people by German composers . . . only German artists belong to the German home."

How small its writer must have felt when he realised that the absence of Toscanini has virtually ruined this year's Bayreuth Festival. Only the presence of Hitler and a special subsidy to provide free seats, accommodation, and travel for young Nazis has enabled the Wagner family to fill the Festspielhaus for every performance.

Bayreuth's substitutes for Toscanini were Richard Strauss to conduct *Parsifal* and Karl Elmendorff to add *Die Meistersinger* to his other duties. Twenty years ago Strauss might have drawn the public, but in 1933 his great days as a conductor are over. Elmendorff is an artist of but average talent.

Walter, Blech and Klemperer are out of the running on racial grounds, but I think Heger or Clemens Krauss or Knappertsbusch or Kleiber would have been preferable to Elmendorff. But perhaps that is only because Elmendorff's dull amble through *Die Meistersinger* is still fresh in my memory. Furtwängler was, of course, quite out of the question since he stipulated that if he were to conduct at Bayreuth the hood over the orchestra must be removed. If Elmendorff is the best Wagnerian conductor Germany can produce, we can only sympathise with the intelligent music-lovers who have to live in a land where only German conductors are allowed to appear. It looks as if "German music performed by German artists" were fit only for the German home.

Strauss's *Parsifal*. Although only Strauss's most fervent admirers could hope that he would prove a satisfactory substitute for Toscanini, those of us who are interested in his complex musical mind and unequal development have found plenty of food for thought in his performance of *Parsifal*. When Karl Muck conducted that work in 1930 his reading was generally condemned for its slowness. A year later, with Toscanini in charge, the official timing showed that his first act, acclaimed as perfect, was about twenty minutes slower than Muck's. According to the clock, Strauss took several minutes less than Muck, and is said to have told the orchestra that he was "twenty years too young for their sleepy tempi." And yet Strauss's first act was, with certain exceptions, dull. The music of Gurnemanz, Parsifal, of the Grail, of the Good Friday Spell seemed to mean nothing to him.

With Kundry's entrance he found music after his own heart, he knew just how to make the most of the wild phrases, but the rest of the first act inhabits a spirit world foreign to Strauss's own. The second act is more in his line; he understands the Klingsor-Kundry scene, he gave to the music of the Flower Maidens' scene sensuality that contrasted strangely with the absurdly modest dresses that covered the *Blumenmädchen* from shoulder to ankle. Later in the act his sympathies were obviously with Kundry; but his fast tempo ruined that

24

usually overwhelming dramatic passage in which Kundry tells Parsifal how she mocked Christ.

There is in the last works of nearly every great artist a strangely luminous quality, as if the creative mind had already seen the world beyond death and were conscious of things infinitely greater than the emotional experiences of this world. It is present in *The Tempest,* in *Die Zauberflöte,* in the last Beethoven quartets, in Brahms *Vier ernste Gesänge,* in Wolf's *Michelangelo Lieder,* in the last act of *Parsifal.* But the mysticism of this last act was lost on Strauss; he went through like an American tourist "doing" a picture gallery in record time, glancing at everything, seeing, but feeling nothing.

## October 1933. Maria Olczewska

If the art of Lieder singing were only a matter of producing ravishing tone, looking beautiful, and electrifying an audience by personal charm Maria Olczewska, who gave her first London recital at the Aeolian Hall this afternoon, would be the greatest of all Lieder singers. There is no singer of my experience whose tone is of such beauty as hers and no singer since Frieda Hempel who can so enthral an audience by her personal charm and intense but restrained vitality. There is so much of beauty in her tone and her appearance that the concert was enjoyable in spite of its artistic deficiencies.

For Olczewska is not a Lieder singer. She has faults both of execution and of musicianship which, although they have not passed unnoticed in her operatic work, stand out glaringly in the searching light of the concert hall. Her art, like that of so many operatic artists, is not fine-pointed enough for the delicate and subtle art of Lieder-singing. Much of the rare beauty of her tone comes from her dwelling so lovingly on vowels—she brushes lightly over consonants to pour out a flood of ravishing tone. In her determination to give generously of this tone she plays havoc with note values, and indulges in such exaggerated rubatos that in songs of slow tempo phrases are distorted; and she has no hesitation in breaking the back of a phrase regardless of its verbal meaning if by doing so her tone will profit. In "Ombra mai fu," for instance, she robbed the melody of its repose and its nobility of line by hanging on to the broader vowel sounds.

As an interpretative artist Olczewska is no better and no worse than

25

the majority of operatic singers who make occasional excursions on to the higher plane of Lieder. She has little ability to sink her personality in that of the song and the composer. She has two sharply defined moods, the serious and the pointedly arch, and songs which do not happen to coincide with either suffer.

## January 1934. Galli-Curci

The reappearance of the famous Italian coloratura soprano Amelita Galli-Curci at the Albert Hall this afternoon was an occasion of interest psychological rather than musical. Nearly 6,000 people had travelled across London through a fog that promised to develop into a "peasouper" and paid high prices for the privilege of hearing her sing a programme that contained not more than half a dozen songs of musical worth, a faded operatic aria, and an odd assortment of café songs and ballads. By way of relief from the sound of the human voice the accompanist and a flautist played groups of solos. And yet there have been several occasions during this musical season when programmes of great music have been performed in splendid fashion to rows of empty seats.

It is true that this audience contained none of the usual set of concertgoers—the people whose faces are familiar to those who make a habit of attending the Queen's Hall and Covent Garden whenever there is good music to be heard. But why should 6,000 people elect to go to this rather than to any other concert? By its behaviour this audience proved that its interests were other than purely musical. It received a group of old Italian songs politely but frigidly; it coughed and rustled its programmes through some Debussy pianoforte pieces. But it clapped its hands in naive delight when the singer sat down at the piano to play her own accompaniment, and it held its breath at the acrobatics of the Shadow song from *Dinorah*.

Nine years have passed since Galli-Curci first sang in London. Time has not changed her. Her voice has lost none of its suavity, it has still that oiled ease that delighted us when we first heard it through the medium of the gramophone. She can still fearlessly match herself with an able flautist and perform the vocal parallel of trapeze acts to which her uncertainty of intonation serves but to add a spice of excitement of the "will-she-do-it" variety. With the exception of a

26

lapse in Rossini's "Tarantella" (wherein she coyly transposed the final note down a tone without having previously warned her accompanist) her intonation was surer than of yore, but it still has that uncertainty that prevents the sensitive listener from enjoying to the full her lovely tone and otherwise accomplished vocalisation.

## May 1934. The Ring at Covent Garden

With Beecham at the prow and Beecham plus Toye at the helm a new era has dawned for Covent Garden. New scenery, new light plant, new dressing rooms, a new producer, even new paint on the foyer and façade have made the old theatre seem unfamiliar. People had become so accustomed to the old scenery that its faults and shortcomings were almost cherished. But new brooms sweep clean, and Beecham and Toye have seen to it that Covent Garden under their regime shall not be mistaken for the Covent Garden of yore.

Of the six familiar works given in this German season, five are having entirely new scenery, and the two new works, *Arabella* and *Schwanda*, are naturally having special settings, the former specially painted here, the latter bought from the Berlin State Opera because the Nazis object to Weinberger on racial grounds.

The new scenery for The Ring has been designed by Gabriel Wolkoff, and it is as good as it was overdue. On the other hand, it must be admitted that none of Wolkoff's settings for *Das Rheingold* or *Die Walküre* has the power, impressiveness, or dramatic quality of the Preetorius scenery which was seen for the first time at Bayreuth last year: neither are the special effects so convincingly realized. Valhalla is still suspiciously like a gigantic ice pudding: Alberich's invisibility is still achieved by the simple expedient of hiding behind a black curtain, and the Rhine Daughters, although they are nearer to the popular conception of mermaid, have an almost comical rigidity of form.

But these are mere details that can be improved in subsequent productions. The rainbow bridge looks like a rainbow, the lighting is appropriate and effective, the Valkyries' steeds look rather like horses in flight, and the dragon is far more impressive than anything Loch Ness has produced.

Orchestrally the performances have been vastly superior to all the post-war Wagner productions at Covent Garden. The brass is surer in attack, the chording is better, the tone is fuller, the string playing is silky where once it was ragged, and the woodwind and percussion could not possibly be bettered.

But there is not a correspondingly consistent improvement in singing. The performance of *Rheingold* was uneven; the familiar artists sang as well as ever, but the new-comers failed to come up to the standards of their predecessors. Bockelmann's Wotan was a magnificent piece of work; his voice is like finely polished mahogany, dark, rich, and smooth, and with his enormous reserve of power and his admirably controlled breathing he was both in wrath and in repose a superbly godlike being. Kipnis as Fasolt was rather hampered by the beauty of his voice; such tone as his ill befits even the gentler of the giants, and one could not help feeling that on vocal merits he should have been promoted to godhood. Gertrud Rünger, who sang Fricka for the first time here, failed both histrionically and vocally to eclipse memories of Olczewska in that part. Her voice is of lovely quality, but the occasions on which the end of a phrase weakened, seemingly through inadequate reserve of breath, were too frequent to give the sense of vocal dignity that the part demands. The new Loge, Martin Kremer, was no doubt handicapped by having been called in at the last minute. Loge, although he has to do so much of the dirty work for the gods, is himself a god, the most artful and clever of all the gods; and although interesting, Kremer's performance was more original than convincing.

Last night's performance of *Walküre* has been another triumph for established favourites. In the first act the delight one would normally have had from Lehmann's Sieglinde and Kipnis' sinister Hunding was frequently marred by the differences of opinion on the matter of tempo between the tenor, Franz Völker, and Beecham. This, however, was the only flaw, but a regrettable one, for otherwise Völker is the best Siegmund Covent Garden has had for many years. He is an intelligent, musical, and sensitive singer. For these differences of opinion neither singer nor conductor is to blame. Beecham rightly sees the symphonic nature of the work and gives the orchestra its head in a symphonic manner, and only when we have a permanent opera will it be possible for conductor and singer to get the unanimity that comes of frequent rehearsal.

The honours of the evening, however, went to Lotte Lehmann.

Magnificently as Leider and Bockelmann sang and acted, it is Lehmann's performances that haunts and will haunt the memory. Those of us who were privileged to hear her last night experienced what will one day be operatic history. As people now talk of De Reszke's Tristan and Ternina's Isolde, so in fifty years' time will our children reverence Lehmann's Sieglinde. And however highly they extol, they will not overpraise it.

## July 1934. Ballet at Covent Garden

Tonight at Covent Garden we have had the season's first performance of *Choreartium,* Massine's awkwardly titled but imaginative choreographic interpretation of Brahms's Fourth Symphony. This is pre-eminently a musician's ballet, in that only a man familiar with the score is in a position to appreciate the problems with which Massine was faced and to judge the measure of success with which he has solved them.

Massine has not, as in his other symphony ballet *Les Présages,* attempted to invent a story; his choreography is born of the melodic and rhythmic shapes of the musical design of Brahms's symphonic structure, and he has succeeded to a degree which one would have believed impossible. The beginning, indeed, the whole of the first movement, is a superb visual representation of the curve and shape of the music, and the movements of the six black-clad figures in the passacaglia seem to spring from the very core of the music's structure.

That is not to say that Massine has translated the Germanness of Brahms into stage action; he has not. What Brahms would think of this ballet is, in American parlance, "nobody's business"—an audience composed of honest, beer-drinking Teutonic Brahmsians would be aghast at what they would doubtless regard as a disgraceful denationalisation of German art. The scherzo, in particular, would wound their Teutonic pride, for it is as Russian as a novel by Dostoievsky or the traditional clowns of Russian opera. But regarded as an interpretation in terms of ballet of the music qua music *Choreartium* is one of Massine's most brilliant achievements.

*Cotillion* and *Le Beau Danube* are lighter fare. Balanchine's vivid, colourful choreography is the perfect counterpart of Chabrier's highly spiced music, and *Cotillion* whirled its breathless way in an almost uninterrupted crescendo of excitement. The evening ended with the graceful and delicately humorous *Le Beau Danube*. This is one of the best things of its type the Russians have ever given us. The pastel shades of the décor are exquisite; and the humour is always in perfect taste.

## November 1934. Stravinsky

The audience that almost filled the Queen's Hall last evening to hear the first performance in England of Stravinsky's *Perséphone* listened to the work with every semblance of real interest, and at the end of the sixty-five minutes it applauded as if it had enjoyed the experience of hearing a work of some musical significance. It would be interesting to know how the people who sat so quietly and applauded so enthusiastically would have behaved if they had been listening to *Perséphone* by wireless, ignorant of the name of its composer. The case of Stravinsky is one of the most pathetic in the history of music. Twenty years ago he was a vital and original composer. *Perséphone* shows him to be that no longer.

. . .

In an article first published in the Paris paper *Excelsior* on the eve of the premiere of *Perséphone*, Stravinsky told the world of his opinion of the work. His chief concern had been "to stress the syllabic values of the text." He warned us "not to expect to be dazzled by seductive sounds," and concluded, "I am following a path that is certainly the right one. Of this there can be no discussion or criticism. One does not criticise anyone or anything in the act of functioning. Noses are not manufactured; noses are. And so it is with my art." That, as far as Stravinsky is concerned, is undoubtedly that; and no doubt the people simple enough to have believed all the later Stravinsky productions are deluded by such a statement into taking the composer at his own valuation. It is as much as to say, "There is only one opinion, my own—other views are heresies."

It may be that in presenting the work in concert form the B.B.C. has been unfair to the original conception as a whole. But the music was there, and one does not hesitate to say that *Perséphone* is as empty as any work that has ever been produced under the name of a composer who at his best may truly be called great.

## December 1934. John McCormack

John McCormack, who sang at the Albert Hall today to an enormous and enthusiastic audience, is one of the most remarkable phenomena in contemporary musical life. His art and his singing command our deepest respect and admiration, but the uses to which they are often put are a depressing indication and reflection of the British public's taste in music.

In the course of a year we have had the best tenors of all types singing in London—the Wagnerian tenors with their huge baritoned voices, the Italians with their resplendent, sun-warmed voices, the delicate and engaging Austrian operetta tenors. They all sing the music that they believe shows them to the best advantage, and yet when it comes to the fine art of singing, they all have much to learn from McCormack's singing of songs that are unworthy of his art. Today, in a programme that offered poor comfort to the musician, McCormack again proved himself a singer of the finest kind and an artist of extraordinary subtlety and refinement. His moulding of phrases is reminiscent of Kreisler's in its natural grace and innate musicianship; his supple rhythm is a source of constant and unalloyed delight; his voice responds in colour to every shade of expression dictated by the words and his fine mind; and even in the most depressing ballads his style is impeccable. Curiously enough, it was in one of the few songs in the programme worthy of his art that there was any stylistic disparity; Schumann's "The Soldier," sung to an English translation, lost all of its essential Lieder style and took on the character of an Irish folk-ballad.

It is easy to reproach McCormack that a man of his genius should waste the sweetness of his art on the desert air of inferior ballads, but it is the public and not the artist who is to blame. Why on earth should a man sacrifice the fortune he can make by gratifying the public taste to the altar of an ideal that will bring him only the gratitude of the few? The public wants ballads—McCormack gives them what they want, and with the money he earns can afford to study and sing the music he loves for the delight of a few friends. And his art is such that those of us who deplore such ditties as "Fairy Story by the Fire" derive far more pleasure from McCormack's singing of them than we do from many another eminent singer maltreating the music we love.

## June 1935. Grace Moore

Not since the afternoon on which Galli-Curci made her first English appearance at the Albert Hall has there been such widespread interest in a musical event as there has been tonight for Grace Moore's first performance at Covent Garden. Galli-Curci had won her public in advance by a series of remarkable gramophone records; Grace Moore has won her fame through her excellent film *One Night of Love*.

We learn that for tonight's performance every seat in the house could have been sold ten times over, that some hundreds of people have waited over thirty hours for the privilege of paying for a seat in the remoteness of the "gods"—such is the power of the "talkies." Here, as every enterprising impresario will at once see, is the solution to the problem that has worried musicians for over a century—the problem of how to make opera pay.

Musically Grace Moore is one of the most pleasant surprises of the season. She was faced with the formidable task of living up to a great reputation, and she succeeded in delighting her admirers and confounding those who had come prepared to smile cynically at what they anticipated might be the pricking of the bubble of a film-made reputation.

The musical section of the audience found in her a singer with a voice of unusual warmth, richness, and colour, a personality of great charm, and a competent if rather too diligent actress. Her acting suggests that she is either comparatively inexperienced in opera or that she was on this occasion unduly nervous. Her film "fans," who were present in hundreds, were naturally delighted. What a surprise they must have had in finding opera such a pleasant entertainment! It would be idle to pretend that Miss Moore effaces memories, either vocal or histrionic, of the great Mimis Rethberg and Melba. She relies as yet too much on her charm of manner and her lovely face and figure and misses the poignancy of such phrases as "Addio, senza rancor," but film star or no film star, she shared with Pinza the honour of being the best singer of the whole cast.

## October 1935. Frieda Hempel

It has become the fashion to regard the prima donna recital with indulgent contempt as a relic of the deplorable taste of the unmusical

Victorian era. The real trouble is that prime donne are not what they were. The moment that Frieda Hempel walked on to the platform at the Queen's Hall tonight the glamour of the now legendary prima donna of the golden age of singing was reawakened as if by magic. Not since she last sang in London have we seen so radiant a personality on our concert platforms. And when she had sung her first group of songs we realised immediately the difference between perfect singing and what to-day passes for good singing. Hempel is above all things a mistress of the art of singing. She is of the school that worked hard for five or six years at exercises to acquire a perfect technique, and it remains with her still. In the last ten years three or four sopranos have "got away with it" in our concert rooms by giving us pretty, artless warbling. They will have to look to their laurels now that we have heard again from Hempel what real honest singing is. Time (Hempel made her Covent Garden debut twenty-eight years ago) has taken its toll of the high notes with which she amazed Drury Lane audiences in 1911 and 1912, but she still makes even the best of our English singers seem like talented amateurs. Apart from Rethberg there is no post-war soprano who can hold a candle to her in the use and management of a voice. The descending chromatic of Grieg's "Im Kahne" were sung with a skill comparable with Heifetz at his best, and there were innumerable touches of purely musical phrasing and colouring that evoked memories of Kreisler.

It is not, however, only as a vocalist that Hempel excels. She is also a very great artist. She has Gerhardt's flair for making the German language sound beautiful, and an uncanny genius for colouring words and conveying by purely musical means the inner life of the poems of the songs she sings. The truth and felicities of expression that she achieves with her voice and brain render superfluous the touches of acting with which she garnishes her performances. She can do all that one asks without moving a hand. No singer known to me can create the magical peace of shimmering waters as she did in "Auf dem Wasser zu singen," or so spin out the line of "Auf Flügeln des Gesanges." Tragedy and comedy come equally natural to her. The extraordinary pathos of the German folk-song "Schwesterlein" was in its way as vivid and moving as anything Chaliapin has ever done. Even where the passing of years told its tale—as in "Dich, teure Halle"—there was so much to admire, the inner joy that shone through it all, that one overlooked the inevitable in one's delight at lovely and masterly singing and rare and priceless qualities of heart and head.

### January 1937. *Barber of Seville* and *Hansel and Gretel* at Covent Garden

On Tuesday *The Barber of Seville* was sung in Italian by an entirely English cast. Only the conductor, Francesco Salo, was Italian. Superficially it seems anomalous to make English singers burden themselves with the additional difficulty of singing an opera in a foreign language when there is a good English translation in existence and when only 1 per cent of the audience understands the language in which the opera is sung. In practice the advantages of using the original text are manifold. No translation of Italian opera really preserves the character of the original libretto. This is particularly true of comic operas. The spirit of Italian comic opera dies when the text is translated into English.

. . .

With this experience fresh in our minds, last night's performance of *Hansel and Gretel* served to impress the advantages of opera in the original language and to show the further differences between opera in German and German opera.

### February 1936. Hugo Wolf

At the Grotrian Hall this evening Ria Ginster and Gerald Moore gave a programme of nineteen songs by Hugo Wolf.

In the choice of songs the singer showed herself to be a musician of rare discrimination and intelligence. Women singers as a class are given to making unwarranted raids on the songs that are properly male property, and it was refreshing to see that Ria Ginster had confined her misappropriations to three songs—"Der Genesende an die Hoffnung," "Der Gärtner," and "Anakreons Grab."

The nineteen songs covered an enormous range of types, characters, and emotions, as any tolerably well-selected Wolf programme is bound to do, and in embarking on them Ginster set herself a task no less formidable than that of an actress essaying, in a fortnight of Shakespeare, Portia, Desdemona, Ophelia, Juliet, Lady Macbeth, Cordelia, Olivia, Rosalind and Anne Page. The women Wolf pictured in

"Das verlassene Mägdelein" and "Geh', Geliebter" are not less dissimilar than Lady Macbeth and Rosalind. It would need a singer with Wolf's protean imagination, with Wolf's power of identifying himself completely with the new world that each poem presented, to do equal justice to each song. There is no such singer, there never has been such a singer; only an artist with a synthesis of the best qualities of Janssen, Gerhardt, Yvette Guilbert, and Chaliapin could convey to an audience all the beauty and magic of these songs.

For a programme so varied and exacting as this the best we can hope for is that a reasonable number of the songs will be within the singer's emotional range. Ginster's greatest assets are the exquisite purity of her voice and her quick and sensitive musicianship. Her technique is such that almost every note was admirably vocalised, but she lacks the temperamental fire that is necessary to bring to life the hot-blooded women of the Spanish and Italian songs and the darker shades of tone to convey the pain and the peace of such songs as "Neue Liebe" and "Anakreons Grab." The *Ewig-Weibliche*, the mothering instinct, is strong enough in nearly every woman to enable her to give credible and creditable performance of the *Frauenliebe und -leben* and of all the Wiegenlieds ever written, but it is given to few women to feel the longing, eagerness, and anxiety inherent in "Geh', Geliebter," making it one of the greatest conceptions and achievements in musical art.

Ginster was at her best in songs of untroubled charm, but her style is as yet too smooth to penetrate to the core of pain or to rise to the heights of ecstasy that are almost always present in Wolf.

In Gerald Moore she had a perfect collaborator; both imaginatively and technically he stands alone among Wolf players. With the mastery and insight he displayed tonight he might well give a Wolf recital and announce it as "Gerald Moore, pianist: Hugo Wolf recital," and then, in the small type usually reserved for accompanists, "At the voice——."

## February 1936. Toti dal Monte and the Coloratura Soprano

The scanty audience at the Queen's Hall this afternoon for the concert given by Toti dal Monte . . . was evidence of what Edwin Evans once called "the passing of the top E flat." A fashion is passing and soon the coloratura soprano will disappear from our concert halls.

She will be like the pianoforte virtuosi who improvised on themes provided by members of the audience, a mere legend.

At the moment it is impossible to determine whether this lack of interest in the coloratura soprano is the result of the decline in the standard of singing or whether the public has grown out of the infantilities of the style. Whatever the cause, one thing is certain; the passing of the coloratura soprano from the concert room will be followed by her disappearance from the opera house. And when she goes she takes with her Bellini, Donizetti, Rossini, and all that Verdi wrote before *Aïda*. The repertory and the attendances at Covent Garden during the past ten years—excepting the "boomlet" in Rossini—have already testified that the taste of the public is moving in that direction.

Dal Monte seems to be the last of the great line of Italian singers of her type. It is eleven years since she first appeared in London, and in that time no new Italian soprano has attempted to dispute her exalted position. How different from the pre-war days when Melba was surrounded by a host of rivals, Tetrazzini, Alda, Kurz, Hempel, Boninsegna, and half a dozen others. In style dal Monte is slightly reminiscent of Tetrazzini. She has plenty of by-play for the amusement of her audience; she lets you know that it is great fun to sing all these notes for such an enthusiastic audience; but she lacks the warm-hearted gaminerie of her prototype.

## June 1936. The Glyndebourne Festival

*Don Giovanni*. The third annual festival of Mozart's operas at the Glyndebourne Opera House began on Friday evening with a performance of *Don Giovanni*—the first production in that theatre of what E.T.A. Hoffmann called "the opera of all operas." Well-deserved prosperity has come quickly to Mr. John Christie's enterprise; in three years he has nearly doubled the length of his season and more than doubled the size of his repertoire.

To give *Don Giovanni* is the most thankless of all operatic tasks. The altruist who begins on the venture must be prepared from the outset for great expense, both in casting and in staging, abundant rehearsal, and, as a reward for all his labour, worry and money, for a mixed reception. He cannot hope for unanimous praise or even to avoid adverse criticism, because hardly any two men agree as to the meaning or the character of the opera, or indeed as to the natures and

36

characteristics of the protagonists. The producer has, however, one consolation; however wrong, or perverse, or inartistic, or even downright incompetent, his performance may be, there is no danger of complete failure. No amount of scenic or dramatic misconceptions can entirely nullify the effect of Mozart's music.

The failure factor does not enter into the discussion of this Glyndebourne production: The Hamish Wilson–Carl Ebert–Fritz Busch triumvirate has given us the most consistent, the most nearly ideal performance of the work that it has been our privilege to see and hear, even though one remembers better individual performances of many of the principal roles. The most arresting quality of this production is the unanimity. The scenist, producer, and conductor have decided together what the opera means, and they have set out as with one mind to present that meaning to us.

The biggest bone of contention where *Don Giovanni* is concerned is whether the opera is tragic or comic. Da Ponte called it a "dramma giocoso," a merry drama, and there the fun began. This Glyndebourne production takes the tragic line but makes a concession to Da Ponte's "giocoso" in Leporello, who is treated consistently as a "buffo" figure. The point of view is an interesting one, but it produces an effect of stylistic confusion, for Salvatore Baccaloni, who sang the part admirably, looked and sounded like a genial character from a Donizetti or Rossini comic opera who had wandered unwittingly and rather unwillingly into a strange world. I should like to see, and Ebert and Busch are the men to do it, a production of *Don Giovanni* in which the whole drama until the final sextet is treated naturally, oblivious of Da Ponte's "giocoso." No matter how the librettist may have thought of his play, it seems clear that Mozart had no time for the style conventions of tragic or comic opera; he saw the characters as human beings, each with his or her own personality, each reacting to the incidents according to his or her own point of view. In such a production the Leporello would be thin and cadaverous, willing, if the opportunity occurred, to betray his master for money, disapproving of his master's mode of life, yet ready and anxious to emulate it. The accepted manner of staging of the catalogue song, with Leporello pulling from a large satchel a tome that looks like a motorist's one-inch-to-the mile road map of the British Isles, is only inferior knock-about clowning. The scene would gain enormously in effect, and be more consistent with the rest of the opera, if Leporello furtively produced from his pocket a small book in which, partly with an eye to the future black-mail and partly with a servant's secret pride in his master's achievements, he has kept a record of the don's amours.

Ebert has made one admirable innovation in reducing the comic aspect of the work. In other productions Elvira's habit of popping up in the most unexpected places, and for Giovanni the most embarrassing, is treated comically. Ebert and Helletsgruber, who sang the part, seem to have taken the line that Don Giovanni is speaking the truth when he tells Anna and Ottavio that Elvira is mad. This new conception of Elvira as a crazed, jealous, spiteful woman, following her seducer about to prevent his being alone with other women and willing to lend herself to conspiracies to bring about his downfall solely because of her mad desire for him, is musically and dramatically a brilliant realization. Certain other points of the production were less happy. It was a mistake, I think, to make Ottavio address his aria "Dalla sua pace" to the audience, and still more of an error for the trio of masks to detach themselves from the action to pour out to the conductor their appeal for justice, which was obviously intended for Divine ears. Direct converse with the audience is justifiable only in the final sextet, where, the drama finished, the surviving participants may well point the moral.

*Die Zauberflöte.* The performance of *Die Zauberflöte* on Saturday was on much the same lines as that of last year. Certain changes in the cast have been made, one, the introduction of Alexander Kipnis as Sarastro, considerably for the better. The great artist scaled down the volume of his noble voice to the requirements of the theatre without robbing the music or the character of any dignity. Only those, perhaps, who have heard this superb voice fill Covent Garden and the vast Continental opera houses could appreciate the skill and mastery of technique by which the singer adapted his vast resources to the acoustics of Glyndebourne. The new Papageno and Papagena were Roy Henderson and Lili Heinimann. Aulikki Rautawaara, whose sensitive and girlish Pamina was so admired last year, has made considerable improvement as a singer, at the expense, however, of the enchanting unsophistication of her acting. In Hans Oppenheim, who conducted this performance, Glyndebourne seems to have found a worthy colleague for Fritz Busch.

*Die Entführung aus dem Serail.* The world has been informed by an eminent English writer upon matters musical that *Die Entführung aus dem Serail* "is not much more than a concert of charming music against a background of theatrical scenery, enlivened with occasional comic scenes of a rather puerile nature," and that "it survives on account of merits which are not its own . . . because it is sufficiently similar in style to *Figaro* and *Don Giovanni* to make the average listener think it must be an equally good opera." Those of us who have studied the work have long known how wide of the mark is this judgment, and last night's performance at Glyndebourne was a magnificent and conclusive refutation of these reflections on Mozart and the average listener.

It would be absurd to claim for *Die Entführung* that it is consistent in quality or style, but then none of Mozart's operas are. An excellent case could be made to prove that in neither *Figaro* nor *Don Giovanni* was Mozart invariably working at white heat of inspiration. The arias of Marcellina and Bartolo in the last act of *Figaro* are inferior to the dullest pages of *Die Entführung* and Don Ottavio has even less character and individuality than Belmonte. For the student of Mozart *Die Entführung* will always be one of the most interesting works. Interspersed between much that is musically immature are passages of dramatic force that Mozart never surpassed, and the naiver parts themselves are infected with a sparkling freshness rarely excelled even in Mozart.

In spite of some singing that was rather below Glyndebourne's usual standard and some excessive exuberance of movement on the part of certain of the principals, the performance went splendidly. Fritz Busch was in his element. This opera provides him with a concertante aria that is akin in texture to the Brandenburg Concertos, with nimble ensembles, with exquisite, heart-easing tunes, and with some dramatic music that needs such driving power as his. He has done nothing better than this.

On the stage the honours went to the interpreters of the smaller parts. Carl Ebert as Pasha Selim gave the whole company a valuable lesson in stage deportment. His immobile silences are more eloquent than the all too vocal cavortings and semaphorings of most opera singers; and as a dumb slave endeavouring to call attention to escaping captives Joseph Childs gave us two minutes of brilliant miming. The real burdens of the opera fell on the Osmin (one of the most perfect of Mozart's characterizations) and the Constanza. These roles were sung by Salvatore Baccaloni and Julia Moore, respectively. Baccaloni, who is probably the best basso comico of our time, made Osmin a conventional buffo, thereby depriving the old rascal of the malice and sadism that is the most essential part of his character. This Osmin was a lovable, jovial knockabout, Mozart's a dangerous rogue. The singer was also obviously handicapped by his unfamiliarity with the German language.

Frl. Moore threw herself with admirable courage at the appalling difficulties of "Martern aller Arten," but she has not yet the technical control successfully to sing the more intricate passages. The part was written for a singer with a voice large both in compass and volume and with extraordinary skill in coloratura. The Blondchen, Irma Beilke, is a valuable acquisition to the company; she has charm, a fresh, clear voice, and assurance both in singing and acting. Koloman von Pataky sang Belmonte's part with what Oscar Wilde once called Wagnerian vehemence; and it was left to Heddle Nash (Pedrillo) to give us in his serenade the best singing of the evening.

*Così fan tutte.* As the thermometer passes the seventy-in-the-shade mark there is a sharp decrease in the Englishman's desire and capacity for intellectual activity and in his critical perception. To have listened to *Götterdämmerung* or even to *Don Giovanni* would have been a physical impossibility yesterday; but by a rare and happy coincidence it happened that the weather, the geographical position of Glyndebourne, and the opera given there were in perfect harmony. When the temperature is nearly ninety in the shade time ceases to matter. There are many who normally resent the amount of time that one has to devote to visiting Glyndebourne—leaving London shortly after midday and returning shortly after midnight—but yesterday the trip ceased to be opera-going—it became a perfect outing. One left by car after lunch, idled through the unfrequented Surrey roads, and, passing into Sussex, came to the richest of all the South of England countryside—long, winding, undulating lanes shaded with fine old trees, rose-covered cottages, and peace. It seemed for a while sacrilegious to contemplate frittering away the cool glory of such a heaven-sent evening in the sticky darkness of a theatre; but the temptation to "cut" Glyndebourne passed with the sight of Mr. Christie's shaded lawns, his long beds of pinks, his sheltered stream, and the prospect of an opera that makes light of opera, that is a perfect work of art and yet no more than a charade.

The lights went down, but the theatre doors were left open—a concession to human comfort possible only in Glyndebourne where music is, as it should always be, surrounded by silence. *Così fan tutte* has never been and never will be a popular opera in the sense that Wagner's music-dramas and the operas of Verdi and Puccini are popular, but for civilized men and women gifted with a delicate sense of humour it is an exquisite entertainment, and for this Saturday night it was the ideal entertainment. It is, and was, particularly in Mr. Christie's theatre, the perfect fulfillment of George Meredith's definition of comedy: "A game dealing with human nature in the drawing room of civilized men and women, where we have no dust of the struggling outer world, no mire, no violent crashes to make the correctness of the presentation convincing. Credulity is not wooed—the comic spirit conceives a definite situation for a number of characters and rejects all accessories in the exclusive pursuit of them and their speech."

One sat in the theatre oblivious of temperature and heard and watched the delicate filigree of Mozart's and Da Ponte's comic detail, the delightful permutations and combinations of figures no more human in their action than six marionettes moved here and there by ingenious whim of Da Ponte's imagination, and yet made by Mozart into graceful parodies of human fallibility. The first act lasted an hour and a half. One strolled through the garden to dinner, regaled oneself with cold—delightfully cold—ambrosia and nectar, then sauntered beside the stream, idly chatting—far too happy to debate or seriously to discuss the performance. And when the sun had already set we returned to the cooler theatre to let Mozart and Da Ponte unravel the tangle they had made before dinner.

It was not yet quite dark when the opera was over. Walking to the car through cool, scented gardens, one forgot momentary irritation at Busch's occasional square, thick-fingered handling of delicate passages, and that the new Despina was not, as Eisinger was in previous years, the finely adjusted mainspring of the action. One was content to reflect on the enchanting beauty of the terzetto "Soave sia il vento," the delicate fun of the finale of the first act and the love scenes of the second, the parodies of tragic operatic heroines, and the charming unresolved end. A church clock struck two, the fresh night air stimulated us to a chorus of praise for Roy Henderson's unforced comedy acting as Guglielmo, the admirable style of Souez's singing and acting as Fiordiligi, Hamish Wilson's scenery, and, above all, the taste and foresight of John Christie which had made possible this enchanting evening.

41

October 1936. *Das Lied von der Erde*

Tonight's concert of the Royal Philharmonic Society at the Queen's Hall calls for some plain speaking. . . . On Friday Sir Hamilton Harty, on account of ill-health, had to inform the Philharmonic Society that he could not conduct the concert . . . and on Monday Mr. Julius Harrison was induced to conduct. In the circumstances it was little short of marvellous that most of the notes of the Mahler work were played at the right time and in the right place. There is, however, no avoiding the fact that the performance was a travesty of Mahler and should not have taken place.

It does not greatly matter at this time in the world's history if a poor performance is given of any one of Beethoven's or Brahms's symphonies; their greatness is universally accepted, and the audience, from previous experience of excellent performances of these works, can draw upon memory and imagination to supply the deficiencies in a bad performance. With *Das Lied von der Erde* the position is entirely different. It has been played in London only two or three times in twenty-five years. . . . Thus the large audience in the hall and of listeners had no means of knowing whether what the Philharmonic Society presented to them was a just and proper representation of Mahler's intentions.

*Das Lied von der Erde*, like all Mahler's works, is in performance a matter half of notes and balance, half of faith and feeling. Much of its melody is, on the face of things, commonplace; much of the work is so naive and simple that insensitiveness of handling will push pathos over the line to bathos and make of its simplicity vulgar commonplace. Only those who have carefully studied the score or heard the work conducted by Bruno Walter or Otto Klemperer know how profoundly moving is this long-drawn farewell. There is but one way in which the Philharmonic Society can atone for this fiasco—by giving at the earliest possible moment a properly rehearsed performance of this work. Bruno Walter should be engaged; Kerstin Thorborg and Charles Kullman too. It would not be amiss either if Julius Harrison were given a proper opportunity of showing his qualities in a program of his own choice.

November 1936. Stravinsky and Hindemith

A large audience assembled at the London Contemporary Music Centre (the British section of the International Society for Contemporary

Music) on Tuesday evening for an exhibition of some recent and some up-to-the-moment fashions in chamber music. The designers represented were Igor Stravinsky and Paul Hindemith. It is significant that the really "modern" composers have given up the use of opus numbers. The opus number carries with it—as far as the listener is concerned—some expectation of progress as the numbers advance. One looks to a composer's opus 90 to be materially and stylistically better than his opus 1. The composer of today who lets himself be labelled "contemporary" does not, it seems, altogether relish the idea of being expected to mature as the years pass, so instead of opus numbers he affixes to his productions the date of composition. In future, then, if we talk of the composers of the fourth decade of the twentieth century, our manner of reference will savour of the jargon hitherto used for women's fashions or will borrow from the vocabulary of the wine list.

The vintages (so to speak) displayed by Antonio Brosa, Adolph Hallis, and Franz Reizenstein were a Duo Concertant for Violin and Piano (1932) and the new Concerto for Two Pianos (1935) by Stravinsky; and by Hindemith one of a new set of pianoforte sonatas (1936) and a Sonata in E for Violin and Piano (1935).

It is difficult to write with restraint of these four works. There is nothing in them to offend the ear. One resents them only because they bear evidence to the poverty of ideas that has fallen on two men who were once promising composers. The nine movements by Stravinsky show him looking in vain for a style that suits him. He is like a well-equipped factory, with no plan of production, turning out a strange medley of queer objects neither useful nor decorative. The Hindemith works exhibit the facility he has always had. His latest fashions are "Back to Czerny, Raff and Reger" and the affirmation of belief in the major chord. If these sonatas did not bear the characteristic stamp of his highly efficient technique, one would be tempted to believe they had been written and published under Hindemith's name by a couple of malicious professors from an English academy of music.

## November 1936. Bruckner

Since the publication in August in the *Manchester Guardian* of the articles concerning the alterations made in Bruckner's symphonies by Franz Schalk and Ferdinand Loewe there has been much discussion on the rights and wrongs of the case. Last night, at the Queen's Hall,

Karl Böhm and the Dresden State Opera Orchestra gave the first public performance in England of Bruckner's Fourth (*Romantic*) Symphony in its original form.

It is as well here briefly to review the relation between the scores by which Bruckner's symphonies have hitherto been known and upon which the existing estimate of him has been based, and the recently published scores, which are held to be authentic Bruckner. The old scores are the result of editings made by at least three hands—those of Franz Schalk, his brother Josef, and Ferdinand Loewe. Bruckner's simplicity and servility are proverbial—in his naive gratitude he tipped Hans Richter a thaler after the first performance of the Fourth Symphony. Bruckner was not well treated by his Viennese contemporaries. Brahms despised him, and Hanslick, as the avowed anti-Wagnerian and loud-speaker of the Brahms party, saw to it that Bruckner was well and thoroughly damned in the Austrian press.

Bruckner had a small but gifted group of admirers who regarded him as the symphonic counterpart of Wagner. The leading lights of this group were Hugo Wolf and the aforementioned editors of his works. To the end of his life he lacked complete confidence in his powers, and he craved performances of his works. His childlike reverence for men of any eminence made him wax in the hands of such cultivated young men as the Schalks and Loewe. They were above all things Wagnerians. Their idea of instrumentation was that music should sound like Wagner's, and to their ears Bruckner's scores were not Wagnerian enough, so they altered them until they came near to their ideal specification. It is not known to any degree of certainty to what extent Bruckner himself acquiesced in these emendations. There is, however, evidence which leads one to believe that he regarded his editor's alterations as a temporary measure. Only in the last two years have some of Bruckner's own scores been published.

The alterations are in few works more drastic or extensive than in the Fourth Symphony. In the first movement the edited score indicates seventeen changes of tempo, none of which is in Bruckner's manuscript. The edited score has two large cuts. One of sixty-six bars in the repeat of the scherzo and one of forty-nine bars in the finale, and the scoring throughout has been so changed—usually thickened—as to alter the whole character of the music.

Karl Böhm's performance was a model of clarity and in the main of obedience to Bruckner's score. He took only a couple of minor liberties, which, if music were left to the hands of accountants, would cancel each other—one accelerando and one rallentando. These did nothing to obscure the noble proportions and manifold beauty of the symphony, which fully merits a regular place in the repertory. There are few works in the whole of symphonic literature which begin as nobly as this. The mood is of Scheffel's *Wächterlied auf der Wartburg*—a call from the mountain tops announcing the dawn of a new century. The second subject is one of the most haunting of all symphonic themes, and the whole movement is built in the true symphonic style. Thematically the second movement wavers between the characteristics of Roman Church music and the *Ländler* of the village green, but it is packed with ideas that come only to a genius and flawlessly realised. The hunting-call scherzo is in many ways the best quick movement that Bruckner wrote. By comparison the finale is a failure. The Brahmsians may continue to dub Bruckner as a clumsy workman, but until Bruckner's symphonies at least share the place in the repertory with Schumann's swollen piano suites which masquerade as symphonies and Mendelssohn's, Tchaikovsky's, Franck's and Dvořák's symphonies, the English concert repertory will still present an Alice-thro'-the-looking-glass appearance to the initiated.

## November 1936. Strauss

The *Ariadne* Performance. It is well over twenty years since Richard Strauss last conducted opera in London and twelve years since his *Ariadne auf Naxos* was given here, so Covent Garden was sold out some weeks ago for last night's performance of that work under Strauss's direction.

It was clear from the attitude of the audience at the end of the prelude that the evening had fallen below expectations. *Ariadne* is not a work for the general public. From its first days as a pendant to Hofmannsthal's adaptation of Molière's *Le Bourgeois Gentilhomme* through the vicissitudes of alteration and rearrangement which led to its present form of an opera consisting of a prelude and one act it has never been a reliable box-office attraction. It is what the Germans aptly call a *Kabinettstück*, a collector's piece. The opera is really a highly organised charade, a delicate joke arranged with great care by two men of great intelligence. The joke rather misses fire because it is too cleverly and sophisticatedly poised. The idea was a delightful one: the bourgeois gentleman insists on a classical opera being played simultaneously with a commedia dell'arte—an anticipation of the present-day film magnates. The prelude is what the film industry calls "backstage stuff"—on one hand a temperamental pair of opera singers, on the other the harlequin troupe, with the balance held by a composer and the bourgeois staff. Strauss handles this with dazzling skill, a wonderful mosaic of exquisite scraps of melody and with subtle sense of style and styles. The simultaneous performance is not so successful. He begins well enough with an enchanting trio for female voices and a noble aria for his prima donna, then caps it with brilliantly witty music for the clowns. A dazzling tour de force in the form of the most difficult and intricate coloratura aria ever written seems to have convinced him that his classical pair are dull and for the rest of the work he writes mechanically for them.

Orchestrally and scenically the performance was flawless. Strauss's prim, precise, steel-knitting-needle beat works wonders in getting clarity and fineness of texture from an orchestra, but it was not conspicuously successful in procuring good singing. The much-praised Zerbinetta, Erna Sack, produced a few brilliant notes high up in the ledger lines, but the middle of her voice is colourless and not particularly well managed. Marta Fuchs sang much of Ariadne's music impressively, but her management of the upper registers occasionally makes one wonder if she was well-advised to change from mezzo-soprano to dramatic soprano roles.

London's Richard Strauss week came to an end this afternoon when the great composer conducted the Dresden State Opera Orchestra in a programme consisting of Mozart's G-minor Symphony and his own *Don Quixote* and *Till Eulenspiegel*. Admiring Strauss the composer, the world has of recent years somewhat overlooked Strauss the conductor. In the long run it is all to the good that Strauss should have given the greater part of his life to the activity that produces enduring results, and future generations will resent the time that he has given to conducting that might have been spent in writing music. If he had not been the creative artist he is, his interpretative gifts would still have made him world famous. The performances he gave to-day will be talked of for years to come by those who were so fortunate as to hear them.

Strauss is the least demonstrative conductor we have ever seen. He seems to the uninitiated to be perfunctory, laconic. His right hand beats time with little visible arm movement, his left hand hangs limply

46

at his side and is rarely used for any more important function than that of turning over the page in the score. It would be impossible to make less show or fuss than he does. His methods are the antithesis of those of such men as Toscanini, Beecham, and Koussevitzky, all of whom in conducting become an integral part of the music in hand. These men seem to enact within their beings the performance they wish to conjure from the orchestra, they live and feel each work as they play it within themselves and communicate that playing to the orchestra. Strauss remains aloof, calmly, coldly watchful. He leaves it to the orchestra to play and to feel the music; he is at the conductor's desk to watch points, so to speak. His conducting is a perfect example of his own famous dictum about *Tristan*—"The brain which conceived that score must have been as cold as ice."

There have been more dramatic readings of Mozart's G-minor Symphony than his—especially of the first movement—but none in which the beauty of the work was more evident. He made, incidentally, an unusual repeat in the third movement, by playing first the minuet and trio, both with repeats, then repeating both the minuet and the trio. In his own works the clarity of the texture was a refutation of the charge which has so often been brought against him of over-filling his scores with detail. While those who heard this concert still live, there will be testimony against any conductor who makes a Strauss work sound thick or fuzzy that, properly played, these works are as clear and transparent in texture as Mozart's.

## March 1937. Busoni's *Doktor Faust*

The music of Busoni's last opera, *Doktor Faust,* was given its first performance in England at the Queen's Hall last night by a large array of British singers with the BBC Chorus and Orchestra, under the direction of Sir Adrian Boult. Divorced from its stage setting and action, the music could not make its full effect, but even the somewhat shortened concert version gave opportunity enough of appreciating the nature and quality of this much-discussed work. Its most enthusiastic champion, Professor E. J. Dent, has claimed for it that "it moves on a plane of spiritual experience far beyond that of even the greatest of musical works for the stage." Tonight's performance was complete enough to allow a reasonable estimate of that pronouncement as well as of the work itself.

Busoni was a devout and admiring student of Goethe, but he rejected the idea of basing his opera on Goethe because it was, as he noted in his diary, "from a literary point of view too difficult, owing to comparison with Goethe"—because the problem of respectful condensation into the libretto of a one-night opera was a superhuman task. It is more than likely, too, that Busoni wanted to get away from the influence of his predecessors' romantic attitude to *Faust*: the nineteenth-century outlook, culminating artistically in Wagner's music-dramas, was antithetic and antipathetic to his theories on opera. Accordingly he turned to the puppet-play forms of *Faust* which had been popular in German for three hundred years.

There his troubles began. Busoni was not a man of the theatre in the sense that Weber, Wagner, Verdi, Puccini, and Strauss were. He had little or no practical participation in operatic production. He talked and thought of opera with the keen intellectual interest that he had for most forms of human activity, but the theatre was not in his blood. His adaptation of the puppet-play lacks, both for theatrical and concert-hall purposes, the cohesion, drive, and sustained interest essential to opera. Half the evening is given up to preludes. His so-called "first scene" does not begin until half-way through the work. Its one really moving moment is that in which Faust, bargaining with Mephistopheles, asks: "Obtain for me, so long on earth I live, the unconditional fulfillment of all my desires" and the rest. That cry was wrung, not from Faust, but from the heart and soul of Busoni himself. "Give me genius, give me, too, its agony"—*Doktor Faust* shows that creative genius was the one quality Busoni lacked.

It has already been suggested here that Busoni chose to adapt the puppet play in order to escape from the romantic musical associations of the Goethe drama. Like all the post-Wagnerian operatic composers, except Strauss, he was driven to seek new and un-Wagnerian methods of expression, to try to be different. Yet paradoxically, his *Doktor Faust* is musically reminiscent at one time or another of most of the previous musical settings of *Faust,* and of Richard Wagner. These echoes are so clearly the products of influence and association of ideas that it is impossible to avoid the conclusion that consciously or unconsciously, *Doktor Faust* is to a great extent a derivative work. It was more than coincidence that caused much of the music of the first scenes to resemble *Parsifal* in melodic shape, harmony, and orchestral texture; that made most of Busoni's tavern scene a pale shadow of Berlioz's cellar scene; and that induced the Duchess of Parma to sing of the ecstasy of love in phrases almost identical with some of Salome's. These innumerable echoes are interspersed with music more original but less distinguished.

The one thing Busoni did not learn from his predecessors was the art of writing for the voice. The cruel musical texture of Mephistopheles' part could only have been the work of a man with little knowledge of the limitations of the singing voice and little feeling for a singable line. Most of the many singers battled bravely last night with the difficulties, and Mr. Dennis Noble emerged their master, throwing out a magnificent high G after three hours of ungrateful toil.

### April 1937. Yvette Guilbert

Mme. Yvette Guilbert occupied the platform of the Grotrian Hall for nearly two and a half hours this afternoon. It cannot be said that she sang or acted or talked, or even that she performed. Hers is an art that defies classification. To describe her as an actress would be to reduce her, to dub her singer would be to pay her a compliment which she would be the first to reject and to ignore nine-tenths of her art. In her strange and irresistible way she transcends the regular forms of interpretative art. Her voice is not a musical instrument—and I believe it is as musical now as ever it was. Yet there is no singer of our time who would not double his present artistic stature if he could borrow half of Guilbert's genius.

The glorious, expansive, outrageous, subtle septuagenarian chose "La femme dans la chanson" as the theme of her recital this afternoon. She discoursed mostly in French, but occasionally in excellent English, on various aspects of the relations between women and men, and brought to teeming life a dozen songs. She is the great mistress of the art of modulation. She will carry an audience laughing through four or five sentences, then pause imperceptibly on a word and modulate her hearers suddenly and enharmonically, so to speak, into an entirely different emotional key. She will gossip outrageously about women's intimate artifices for attracting men, with her audience chuckling at every word, then leave their laughter suspended through every gesture or sound, gentle and touching in its kindly pity for such human folly.

Her songs are either of the folk or of the café chanson variety, and the manner in which she interprets them could not be applied to more highly organised music. As she works, the timing of pauses and the weight of inflections are adjusted to suit the quickness of her audiences: such freedom may safely be exercised only where the musical content is so slender that the organic life of the song is subservient to the text. Her greatness lies not so much in this quick judgment of her hearers' receptivity as in the intense vividness of the imaginative life which actuates her interpretations. To her, interpretation is not a veneer applied to the surface of an object, but an instinctive creative act born of wide sympathy, pity, humour, and understanding.

The success of this recital was such that Mme. Guilbert announced that she would give another matinee on Thursday at the Wigmore Hall.

## May 1937. Toscanini

No conductor but Toscanini would have drawn a hundred pounds into the Queen's Hall with the programme which he conducted this evening for the second concert of the London Music Festival. There were two virtually unknown works, two pieces for specialists, and the *Meistersinger* overture, but the house was packed and the audience was impelled by a series of magnificent performances to frenzied enthusiasm.

History, and particularly artistic history, proves that no man is completely versatile. Even the greatest artists have lacked one quality or another. Goethe was wanting in warm humour, Michelangelo in the hard tissue of male strength. In the smaller world of the art of interpreting music, limitations are too obvious to call for mention. Except Toscanini's and they elude us. It stands to reason that this man has his limitations, but they have not yet revealed themselves to us. We have heard him conduct works as different in style as *Tristan* and *Falstaff*, the *Eroica* and Rossini overtures, but there seems to be nowhere a chink in the man's artistic armour. He is cosmic in his understanding, clairvoyant in his sympathies.

Early in this evening's performance of Elgar's Introduction and Allegro for Strings it seemed that Toscanini was not fully imbued with the expansive warmth of Elgar's Englishness. He appeared to be softening the imperious arch of Elgar's Imperial Roman nose. Two minutes later we were lifted out of our seats by the noble surge of Elgar's melody made real as we had never heard it before.

In this work and indeed throughout the whole concert we were treated to playing the like of which we have never before heard from an English orchestra, or any orchestra except under Toscanini's command. From the strings alone he secures more variety of tone and colour than other conductors with a Straussian array. In all that he does one is supremely conscious of his masterful vitality or clarity that must be heard to be believed, as remarkable in details and balance of orchestral colours as in cross rhythms where each impulse has intense and independent life. He does not fit two rhythms together, but gives each its own life and urge and like the planets moving in their own time and orbits around the sun arriving at certain points of coincidence only by Divine law.

The symphony in this programme was Cherubini's in B Flat, which was being given for the first time in London since 1815. Delight with Toscanini's exquisite sense of style got one through the first two poor movements to the fine minuet as original and witty as a Goldoni comedy. After the interval there was the first performance in England of Tommasini's incredible *Il Carnevali di Venezia*, the rowdiest joke, intentional or by default, that we have ever heard in a concert-room. This set of thirteen variations in the style of Paganini makes Walton's *Façade* seem sober-sided. If Toscanini takes this piece seriously, his deficiency is a sense of music-hall fun.

There followed a miraculous performance of Berlioz's "Queen Mab" Scherzo, more lovely, more transparent, more entrancing than any we have even imagined, and to close the concert the *Meistersinger*. It was with the emotion of personal loss that we heard the piece drawn into the concert ending when we had been so prepared for the wondrous hush of the church scene. Toscanini should never play an operatic overture at his concerts.

## May 1937. *Turandot* at Covent Garden

*Turandot*, Puccini's last opera, was given tonight at Covent Garden under the direction of John Barbirolli, with Eva Turner, Mafalda Favero, and Giovanni Martinelli in the principal roles.

If Puccini had lived to complete the work it would undoubtedly have been his masterpiece. Even as it stands, with the final love scene provided by another hand, it surpasses his earlier and more popular operas in originality and in direction of dramatic utterance. The deficiency of

*Turandot* from the popular point of view is that the sacrifice for love is made by Liu, who is a secondary figure, and not by Turandot, who is the cause of all the fuss.

## August 1937. *Manon Lescaut* and *Fledermaus* at Covent Garden

There have been two new productions at Covent Garden this week. On Monday Puccini's *Manon Lescaut* was sung in Italian, and on Wednesday Johann Strauss's *Die Fledermaus* was given in English. Neither performance endorsed the contention of those who insist that England has a host of first-class opera singers who would prove themselves every bit as good as the foreigners if only they were given the chances. In both performances the presence of foreign artists showed up the stylelessness of the English members of the casts. *Manon Lescaut* is not to be numbered among Puccini's most masterly works. It was written only four years before *La Bohème,* but in those intervening years the qualities which are sometimes present and often implied in *Manon* quickly came to ripeness, and the crudities which make certain passages in the earlier opera almost embarrassing to hear were shed in the maturing of the composer's style and mind. The trouble is that the tunes are undistinguished. By far the best music in the opera is that of the embarkation scene at Le Havre. The two Italian singers, Augusta Oltrabella and Piero Manescardi, who filled the principal roles, did a familiar job in the manner which hard work and experience have made second nature to them. Dennis Noble sang, as Constant Lambert conducted, with considerable skill and power.

*Die Fledermaus* was treated unashamedly as a Ruritanian musical comedy. The libretto has been brightened in several places to make it more palatable to audiences fed on the broadcast humour of 1936. Only two members of this case, Irene Eisinger and Percy Heming, helped to keep alive the happy memories of the ravishing performances of *Fledermaus* that Bruno Walter gave at Covent Garden in 1930 with Lehmann, Schumann, Hüsch, Wörle, Habich, and Stagemann. Neither her colleagues nor the pedestrian playing of Strauss's melodies could take the sparkle and the essentially Viennese charm from Eisinger's singing and acting. Her piquant sense of fun and the delicacy and quickness of her by-play had no relation to anything that was going on around her, except Percy Heming's ripe and subtle character study of the prison governor.

## October 1937. Stravinsky

The newest product of Stravinsky's industry was given for the first time in England this evening at the Queen's Hall under the direction of the composer. The piece is called *Jeu de Cartes* ("A Game of Cards") and is described as "A ballet in three deals." In June 1936, Stravinsky was commissioned by Edward Warburg, director of the newly founded American Ballet, to provide that company with a ballet, the subject of which was left to the composer's choice. *Jeu de Cartes* is the result of that invitation, and the score is prefaced with a précis of the action. "The characters in the ballet are the chief cards in a game of poker disputed between several players on the green cloth of the card-room. At each deal the situation is complicated by the guiles of the perfidious joker, who believes himself invincible because of his ability to become any destined card." At the end of the ballet the joker is beaten by a "royal flush" in hearts.

From internal evidence of the music it seems that the composer intends this work, if not to be autobiographical, at least to depict its author in its chief character. Stravinsky, like his own joker, "complicates the situation because of his ability to become any destined card." He writes in the manner of an array of popular composers, the Strausses—Richard and Johann—Auber, Delibes, and Rossini, but like the joker who may for the purposes of the game be called king, queen, or knave, Stravinsky is all the time and all too obviously himself.

It may be that to perform this orchestral part in the concert-room is unjust to the work as a whole. The plot and the stage action are as much a part of the whole conception as is this music, and it may conceivably happen that these jingles may assume a very different aspect when played as the accompaniment to stage action. There is not much musical stimulation to be had out of listening to a rehearsal of the orchestral part of *Il Barbiere,* but whereas Rossini would not have countenanced the performance of his orchestral accompaniment as concert pieces, Stravinsky not only consented to this concert performance of *Jeu de Cartes* but conducted it, and so put it onto the plane of concert music.

The music of his earlier ballets, *The Firebird, Petrouchka,* and *The Rite of Spring,* stands on its own feet and makes its effect as concert music. This new piece has two positive qualities, clarity of texture and restless rhythmic energy; for the rest of it is but a gawky pastiche which marks the nadir to which Stravinsky has straggled from the apogee of *The Rite of Spring.*

## December 1937. Sibelius

Sibelius had the programme to himself at the Queen's Hall last evening. His three austere symphonies, the Sixth, the Seventh, and the Fourth, were played in that order. By the time the Fourth Symphony had finished, the scowling, misanthropic bust of Beethoven which stands before the platform at the Philharmonic Society's concerts had several times cocked a quizzical eye up at Sir Thomas Beecham's back as much as to say, "A gloomy sort of entertainment, this." The few who left the hall at the end of that work must have been surprised to see that there is still active life on this planet. Sir Thomas wisely rounded off the programme with the *Karelia* Suite as evidence that the Finnish Nestor is really a Janus with one jolly Bacchic face— a fact not to be discerned from the three symphonies.

These works make no concessions to the listener. They seem to have been written without any thought or care for an audience. Together they represent the sum total of Sibelius' thoughts on the problems of symphonic concision and economy. There are only two other works in the whole of his 112 opus numbers which show him working directly upon the same lines. The tone-poem *The Bard* and the eerie song for soprano and orchestra *Luonnotar.* But even in the Fourth Symphony, which was written ten years before the Seventh and is the limit even he has reached in sparseness, he employs the devices and exhibits the mannerisms of his most popular works. These symphonies are tough nuts to crack. One may study them for years and know them as one knows one's own handwriting, but they fascinatingly retain their mystery. To a man unacquainted with the simpler and more expansive Sibelius they are almost unintelligible. Those who have surveyed the composer's output delight in seeing the familiar mannerisms put to new and strange uses.

There is no music so uninhabited as these three symphonies, and no music so uninfluenced by other composers. Sentimental writers have attributed these characteristics to Finland's geographical position, to the country's flat wastes, lakes and brief summer. The solution lies deeper than that. The inner consciousness, or unconscious awareness, from which this music springs is primeval. As a young man Sibelius wrote in the manner of Tchaikovsky; throughout his life he has poured out facile drawing-room music in the manner of salon composers of all nations, only occasionally betraying his own hand by a personal turn of phrase. But beneath this facade there has always been this elemental, laconic Adam of the art who broke out in these strange compelling works, uttering eternal yet prophetic verities in the simplest but most forceful language—an idiom that is neither archaic nor advanced. There is no other music of the last century of which one can say with such certainty that Bach would have understood and admired it. And it will still be modern a century hence.

Such uncivilised and uncomfortable music as this is the very antithesis of Sir Thomas Beecham's personality and outlook. Sibelius' basic English, so to speak, is as the poles apart from his exquisite choice of the finely mounded phrase of apt polysyllables. He cast his innate grace and polish aside as if it were a mere top dressing of soil and came to grips with Sibelian granite in a way which must have surprised and shocked his most devout admirers. His performance of the Sixth Symphony showed more of its unyielding core than any we have heard, and he hammered his way through it without so much as a glance at the opportunities it offers for effective polishing. London has heard no performance of the work to compare with this. Of the Fourth Symphony, too, Sir Thomas gave the best performance that London has ever heard.

## December 1937. Two British Composers—Walton and Ireland

A concert of music by William Walton and John Ireland made a proud and loud show this evening at the Queen's Hall in the presence of the Queen. Four works were played, all of them written in the last six years: *A London Overture* and *These Things Shall Be*, by John Ireland; and *In Honour of the City of London* and *Belshazzar's Feast*, by William Walton.

It was an occasion for every musician proudly to hold up his head, even if he sometimes defensively put his hands to his ears. Putting aside the gingering-up of harmony and Walton's rhythmical intricacy, the concert was in effect a triumph of the Elgarian spirit in British music. Ten years ago the younger generation of English musicians scoffed at Elgar for his honest, patriotic, yeoman spirit. Tonight's concert was a vociferous affirmation of the Elgarian manner.

The clubs and cliques of English music never really liked Elgar. He was too "professional" for them. They preferred to rally round Parry and Stanford who were socially "gentlemen" and musically amateurs. Delius was never of the English musical world: his antecedents were German, and he lived in Paris among painters and writers, creating music in an idiom too personal and too exhausted to found a school or tradition. The other main branch of British music is a legacy from Cecil Sharp's curious passion for folk-song. This has produced a set of pastoral, or rather, agricultural, composers who can never see farther than the nearest folk-song.

Walton and Ireland are gloriously free from the gentlemanliness of Parry and Stanford, the Delian dreaming, and the market-day modalism of the folk-songists. Musically speaking they are neither gentlemen nor gentlemen-farmers; they are professional musicians who speak the international language of music, albeit personally, when they extol the glories of London. Their music springs, like Elgar's, from the soil and soul of England. They speak the language not of the Mus.Bac.s or farm-hands but of the nation.

Ireland, who was born in Bowden and whose father was editor of *The Manchester Examiner and Times,* represents the bulldoggish aspect of the national make-up. Walton, an Oldham man, is more than twenty years his junior, and his more nervous temperament shows clearly enough the difference between the generations. He conducted the first London performance of *In Honour of the City of London,* which was first given at the Leeds Festival in October, and at once showed up the shortcomings of the first performance and the intrinsic worth which that first performance partly obscured. The rest of the programme was conducted by Sir Adrian Boult.

## HMV

I joined His Master's Voice when I was twenty, as lecturer and on six months' trial. After three months I was dismissed as "unsuitable"; I afterwards discovered that I had been too outspoken in expressing my views in the policies and activities of the Recording Department. Within less than a year I was back in HMV as head (and only member) of the staff of a newly created "Literary Department." I had to write all album and analytical notes and sales copy for each bimonthly new issue of records. A new responsibility was added a little while later, when I was made editor of *The Voice*, HMV's monthly magazine for record retailers. These years of work brought me into almost daily contact with printers from whom I got a solid grounding in such matters as typefaces, printing processes, and layout. Twenty years later this experience enabled me to make the programmes and printed material of my own Philharmonia Concert Society unique in the world for taste and elegance of presentation. The advantage of editing *The Voice* was that I had a free run of the studios. By this time I was on good terms with the Recording Department, but while I wanted to expand the recording repertoire, my suggestions were turned down as sure ways of losing HMV money.

In early summer 1931, I devised a plan which the company could not very well reject: to collect subscriptions in advance for great recordings of unrecorded works and make the records only when the requested number of subscribers had been enlisted, not only to cover the costs but to yield the company a reasonable profit. My rapid development of this idea is admirably told in Roland Gelatt's book *The Fabulous Phonograph* (rev. ed. New York, 1966, pp. 259–261):

> Legge's idea was to form different societies for the purpose of recording the more recondite works of various composers and to obtain enough subscriptions in advance to defray the cost of the undertakings. Attention was first directed, in the autumn of 1931, to the songs of Hugo Wolf. An album of six HMV records to be sung by Elena Gerhardt was proposed as the first of a series; texts of the songs in German and English together with annotations by Ernest Newman were also to be furnished. For this project the Gramophone Company required subscriptions of thirty shillings each from five hundred people. If the Hugo Wolf Society were to prove successful, it was hinted that a similar society devoted to Beethoven's complete piano works would also be formed. The Wolf quota was filled by December, thanks in part to 111 subscriptions emanating from Japan, and in April 1932 the Gerhardt album was issued. . . . Once the healthiness of this scheme had been demonstrated, Walter Legge was given a free hand to set up other Society projects; his second venture, The Beethoven Sonata Society, which was to record every major Beethoven piano work in performances by Artur Schnabel, met with an extraordinary response. The first volume of seven records, contain-

ing the Opus 78, 90 and 111 sonatas, appeared in June 1932. Three years and three volumes later, HMV reported that £80,000 had been spent on these records by customers throughout the world (of which England alone had accounted for £24,000). Schnabel completed the fifteen-volume series in 1939, and it stands as an enduring memorial to his compelling and penetrating musicianship. . . . Society sets were added to the regular catalogues, and today many of them . . . have been reissued in long-playing form. In 1933, the Society idea spread to France, where it yielded such valuables as Bach's Goldberg Variations played on the harpsichord by Wanda Landowska, and subsequent issues by this same artist devoted to harpsichord works of Couperin and Domenico Scarlatti; they contributed measurably to a reawakening of interest in the instrument throughout the world. Before World War II brought the Society program to a halt, the recorded literature had been expanded by it to include Albert Schweitzer's performances of Bach's organ music, the Forty-Eight Preludes and Fugues performed on the piano by Edwin Fischer, Bach's unaccompanied cello suites in the seminal interpretations of Pablo Casals, twenty-nine Haydn quartets played by the Pro Arte String Quartet of Belgium, Beethoven's ten violin sonatas in performances by Fritz Kreisler and Franz Rupp, Sir Thomas Beecham's authoritative readings of the large orchestral works of Frederick Delius, several Sibelius symphonies and tone poems, and—most ambitious of all—the incomparable Glyndebourne Opera performances of Mozart's *Nozze di Figaro, Così fan tutte* and *Don Giovanni* conducted by Fritz Busch, together with an equally finished recording of *Die Zauberflöte* made in Berlin under Beecham's direction.

A pity that Gelatt overlooked the first recording of Mahler's *Das Lied von der Erde* by Bruno Walter and a Society devoted to the songs of Yrjö Kilpinen!

With the Hugo Wolf Society safely launched, I decided to try my hand as an impresario to increase the public interest in Lieder and the art of Lieder singing. With the help of a rich patroness who guaranteed any losses, I formed the London Lieder Club. The first concert was given by Elena Gerhardt and during the four years of its existence Herbert Janssen, Alexander Kipnis, Gerhard Hüsch, and several other distinguished artists gave recitals which covered a wide range of the voice and piano repertoire. Naturally Wolf songs were well represented, Schubert, Schumann, and Brahms, too, and the programmes also included Mussorgsky, Sibelius, Grieg, and Kilpinen.

The launching and success of the Hugo Wolf Society brought me much credit and suddenly the circle of my friends grew. The most important of these was Ernest Newman, the greatest of all musical critics and musical historians and a man of deep and wide knowledge on an infinite variety of subjects. Newman was sixty-three when we met, I twenty-four. Every thing I know I owe to Ernest Newman. He educated me, gave me his fearless integrity in artistic matters, and as much of his worldly wisdom as I was capable of absorbing. He fed me with books but in such a way that I did not at the time realize I was being educated. We remained close friends to the end of his life. Even today I never do any musical work or writing without asking myself: Would E.N. approve?

One of the first subscribers of the Hugo Wolf Society was John McCormack, the Irish tenor. I invited him to make a record for the second volume of the Hugo Wolf Society and out of that meeting came another enriching friendship. McCormack was not only a great singer but a highly intelligent musician who had sung with all the best singers and conductors of the first thirty years of this century. For more than ten years McCormack and I spent countless long evenings together discussing the art and technique of singing: another invaluable teacher for me.

A third friend was Albert Schweitzer, with whom I recorded three volumes of Bach's organ music. The first set was made on the organ of All-Hallow's-by-the-Tower, one of the few instruments in England which Schweitzer considered suitable for the purpose. The later volumes were made on the Silbermann organ in the church of Ste. Aurelie in Strasbourg—a marvellous instrument of which Schweitzer had supervised the renovation. The friendship which developed between us lasted until Schweitzer's death. It is worth mentioning that on the eve of the Philharmonia Orchestra's first American tour, Schweitzer went to hear my orchestra conducted by Karajan. I introduced the two great men and Schweitzer was induced to try the Festival Hall organ. Karajan watched, fascinated. When we had taken Schweitzer to his home, Karajan said: "Watching Schweitzer play with that mane of grey hair over his concentrated brow revealed to me how right the old Italian painters were to paint angels and saints with haloes."

A fourth friend was Sir Thomas Beecham, and although I at the time was almost exclusively concerned with HMV, Beecham insisted that all his recordings should be made with me. The first major fruit of our collaboration was the famous and as yet unequalled *Zauberflöte*. This was made in Berlin in 1937 with the Berlin Philharmonic Orchestra and a cast of my selection. This was my first complete opera recording and I prepared it with particular care for every detail imaginable. I selected the members of the orchestra and even rehearsed the singers in Berlin so that when Beecham arrived the company was ready for him. The work went so happily and smoothly that a few weeks after this recording was finished, Beecham insisted I should be—as a part-time job—Assistant Artistic Director of Covent Garden Opera. At the age of thirty-two! With this enviable appointment I gladly gave up my other part-time job as musical critic of the *Manchester Guardian*, which I had been doing since 1931.

Beecham told me: "We will agree on the repertoire for the season. I will tell you which operas I shall conduct and it is entirely in your hands to engage all the singers as well as the conductors." Beecham kept his word, and I gave London an array of great conductors such as Covent Garden had never experienced in one season: in addition to Beecham the conductors were Furtwängler, and for the first time Erich Kleiber, Vittorio Gui, and Felix Weingartner. I also engaged the following great singers to make their Covent Garden debuts: Richard Tauber, Jussi Björling, Maria Reining, Hilde Konetzni, Julius Patzak, and Helge Roswänge. The outbreak of war in 1939 stopped musical life in Britain for some time.

## The 1939–1945 War

The war years were hard on the record industry. Within less than a year Britain was cut off from the European continent, so no new recordings came from that source. Britain was in desperate need of aid from America and more important objects than record matrices and stampers, which were either taken entirely for war work or were in short supply. In England records were rationed and to buy a new one the customer had to pay not only the price but give two old records as well. These were broken up and used as "filler."

I continued to work for EMI throughout the war, keeping the catalogue refreshed with local talents, but I also accepted the invitation to take over ENSA, the organization that supplied concerts of serious music for the British army, navy, and air forces—in all theatres of war where there were British troops—as well as for workers in war factories. I kept three orchestras, the Liverpool Philharmonic, the City of Birmingham, and the Hallé, busily occupied with these concerts as well as dividing up the work nearer London between the London orchestras. The range of the programmes was as extraordinary as the willingness of soloists to travel in great discomfort and often danger. Solomon, the best of British pianists, travelled the Mediterranean and Near East warfronts giving recitals to huge audiences on pianos ranging from concert grands to bar pianos and even mini-upright pianos.

I arranged a seven-day Beethoven Festival near some large camps, and took the BBC Orchestra under Sir Adrian Boult to the Royal Naval Barracks in Portsmouth for a week of six concerts in which the audience totalled 20,000. There were similar festivals at other large troop concentrations. I also organized circulating libraries of records to supply small and isolated units.

When the British Army landed in France, they too had to be supplied with music, partly from England, later with the help of French artists. I was in Paris a couple of days after the city was liberated and took over the Marigny Theatre and other buildings in the Champs Élysées for troop entertainment. I was greatly helped to find good French artists by my old friend Jacques Thibaud, who produced the wonderful violinist Ginette Neveu for an audition. She played not only for troops but immediately made an exclusive contract with EMI. Samson François was also brought to me by Thibaud and within a few days he had been flown to Britain for a long tour of camps and factories. And so it went on—as soon as important areas were liberated I had to supply music. Just before Christmas 1944, John Barbirolli and the Hallé Orchestra went for a long tour to Belgium. Brussels and Antwerp were under the fire of V1's and V2's and it was forbidden as well as dangerous to have any large number of servicemen and women under one roof in the towns. Barbirolli at once asked that he be sent up close to the firing areas, and day after day he and his orchestra played to refresh troops who were on a few hours' leave from the fighting. Some days the orchestra played for twelve hours with only short breaks for meals. And at night Barbirolli would not go to his billet until he had seen all his orchestra safely in their quarters.

I also had some other pleasant surprises. Auditioning a string quartet in Brussels I was impressed by the beautiful style and tone of the very young violinist. It was the now famous Arthur Grumiaux, who did wonderful work in playing as soloist for the troops. One night outside

Hannover, I dropped in at a performance being given for troops of *Die verkaufte Braut* and heard a young tenor whom I immediately engaged exclusively for EMI—Rudolf Schock. In the summer of 1945, I resigned from my troop concert-giving and returned with all my energy to engaging for EMI all the best young talents that had come along.

*It was Beecham apparently who got Walter his ENSA assignment. Walter's deplorably bad eyes had automatically eliminated him for any Army or Navy duty. His idea of the music British troops should be served was typical. Never mind that one was fighting the Germans, the armed forces had to get a diet of Wagner, Strauss, Beethoven, Brahms, and Mozart. To keep things balanced: one Elgar. No wonder he never got an order from the British Empire!*

*Walter's duty had sometimes gratifying sidelines. When Elisabeth Schumann wrote from New York, where she had spent the war singing and teaching, asking Walter whether there were any chance he could help her to see her son in Germany, Walter immediately assigned her to ENSA (although she was an American citizen) and scheduled her concerts near her son, Gerd Puritz, who had fought in the war as a German pilot and had lost a leg. He had not, as yet, been united with his English wife and two sons, who were not allowed to leave Hamburg. Later, when publishers urged Schumann to write her memoirs, she always declined. "The only thing really interesting," she said, "would be how I re-met my son after the war and how I 'smuggled' him into my ENSA Quarters. At that time not even mothers and sons were allowed to fraternize!"*

## Postwar Recording
### 1945–1963

I had set my heart on renewing the contracts which had lapsed with artists who had been with EMI before the war, and I was determined to collect for my company the best of the new generation of artists who had come into prominence in the war years. I had already been in Germany providing music for the British troops and made new contracts with Tiana Lemnitz and Margarete Klose. But most good German artists had found their way to Vienna, where the Staatsoper—profiting by the destruction and difficulties in Germany—had built up an array of singers in the Theater an der Wien which today reads almost like the dream casts of the Metropolitan Opera in the days of Toscanini, Mahler, and Gatti-Casazza.

It was not an easy matter for a British civilian to get into Vienna and it was at that time illegal for every British subject to "trade with the enemy." To avoid this I went to Switzerland to my old friend and colleague J. P. Jones, who had been watching EMI's interests in Europe from his house in Ascona. He arranged that I should be seconded to Turicaphon, a Swiss company in which EMI had substantial minority holdings, and get to Vienna as quickly as possible, making contacts in Turicaphon's name. In Zürich I renewed contracts with Edwin Fischer and Wilhelm Backhaus and arranged to make a few records with the Lucerne Festival Orchestra. In Geneva, I signed an exclusive contract with the now legendary pianist Dinu Lipatti, a young Rumanian who, alas, was already in the early stages of leukemia which killed him within a few years. Our work together produced a small but perfect collection of records which are a permanent monument to this supreme artist.

Waiting in Zürich for some way, legal or illegal, to get into Vienna, I met in the bar of my hotel a chatty American officer whom I asked if he could help me to get the essential papers and travel permit. The mellow American, delighted to be helpful, pulled from a pocket a bunch of papers—visas, travel permits, and even a first-class sleeper ticket for that same evening. This was in January 1946.

My first day in Vienna was adventurous. I telephoned a few old friends—the first of whom invited me to go with her to a party the Russian Commander of Vienna was giving that evening in the Hofburg. I had tried and failed to get in touch with Furtwängler in Switzerland, but on my way to the Hofburg I got lost in the dark Vienna streets and asked a group of three people coming towards me to direct me. To my delighted astonishment I recognized the tall man in the group as Dr. Furtwängler, who gave me a telephone number to call the next day. That contract took several months to negotiate and was eventually finalized in the restaurant of the Luzern Hauptbahnhof.

The Vienna trip had started well. At the Russian party I met several old friends and acquaintances, among them Dr. Egon Hilbert, whom I had known in 1937 as Austrian Cultural Attaché in Prague. Hilbert was now in charge of all Austrian State Theatres and gave me the free run of the Opera. In less than a fortnight I had made exclusive recording contracts with the Vienna Philharmonic, Josef Krips, Irmgard Seefried, Ljuba Welitsch, Maria Cebotari, Hilde Konetzni, Walter Ludwig, Max Lorenz, Hans Hotter, Ludwig Weber, and Wolfgang Schneiderhan.

I had already heard Schwarzkopf at a private concert in a friend's house and as Rosina in *Il Barbiere* in the Theater an der Wien, but when I met her to discuss a contract, she insisted that I must give her a proper audition because she did not want me "to buy a cat in a sack." Several weeks passed until I had time to hold an audition but she had her wish: I kept her working on one Wolf song for two hours to see whether I could make out of her the Wolf singer I had been searching for for nearly twenty years. I told her that she would soon outgrow her coloratura *Fach* and was potentially one of the world's best Lieder singers. She was a lyrical soprano who should concentrate on such parts as Pamina, the *Figaro* Contessa, Donna Elvira, Eva, and, in time, the Marschallin. That afternoon she signed her contract!

*Much has been made—in interviews and articles—of the first time I met Walter. Actually it was the second time. The place was grey postwar Vienna, the year 1946. Walter had come to shop around for new talent. He had heard me as Rosina, which I studied in its entirety with Maria Ivogün, and, a second time, at a house concert at the home of Baron Otto Mayr, a famous lawyer and key figure in Vienna's music life. It is true that Walter offered me a recording contract and it is also true that I refused to sign it until he listened to me at a proper audition. Such an audition was set up and at the appointed time Walter appeared, accompanied by Herbert von Karajan. What is also true is that this strange Englishman who spoke accent-free German asked me to sing Wolf's "Wer rief Dich denn? Wer hat dich herbestellt?" ("Who called for you? Who asked you to come?"). It is further true that this stranger had me sing the last phrase in untold different ways, colors, and expressions until—after an hour—Karajan fled, mumbling, "This is pure sadism." Walter kept on polishing the phrase for almost another hour. I did not know Walter's eminence when it came to singers. I did not know of Walter's search for the ideal Wolf singer. I did not know anything else about him, but I must have sung for dear life. It would make a nice romantic story if—via Hugo Wolf—we had fallen*

64

*in love, and Walter had proposed. But it isn't so. That came much
later. Still, I was offered a contract.*

In January I had started negotiations with Herbert von Karajan. Although I had known Karajan's work from his Aachen period and on the strength of that had recommended him to the director of the Berlin State Opera, the two of us had never met. The day the Russians banned what would have been Karajan's second concert in Vienna, it looked as if his musical activities were finished for an unspecified period, perhaps years. That afternoon I, having discovered Karajan's secret telephone number, called him to make an appointment for that evening. Here Karajan's description of our first meeting quoted from Haeusserman's book: "I did not know him at all. At our first meeting we talked together for four hours and discovered, which seems hardly credible, that he too had been present at all the important musical occasions which had been vital to me." Soon we became close friends, and after months of discussion Karajan signed an exclusive contract. One of my most prized possessions is a score of Bruckner's Eighth Symphony with the dedication:

"Meinem zweiten musikalischen Ich und lieben Freund zur Erinnerung an einen lang ersehnten Tag.

Herbert von Karajan 26.X.47

("To my musical alter-ego and dear friend in remembrance of a long wished-for day.")

On that day Karajan had given his first concert since the Russian ban.

The first international recordings with the new array of artists I had collected began in September 1946. Not auspiciously. In the afternoon of the day before the first session, the Vienna Philharmonic office telephoned to say the session could not take place. "Would Legge go to their office at once?" Karajan was already there with the management of the orchestra. The Americans had refused permission for Karajan to record. I telephoned the British Military Command to check that the ban on Karajan applied only to public performance, then called the American officer who had tried to ban the recording to tell him that the sessions would take place. They did. Working conditions were appalling. The Viennese electrical supply was haywire. To get sufficient and stable current to operate the machines and heat the waxes, I had to hire a petrol-driven, dynamo-like contraption. That was a lesser difficulty. The problem was how to get the petrol to make the thing work. The only help the military would give me was empty petrol cans; they too were short of petrol. So each evening my Viennese secretary and I took a taxi, loaded it with empty petrol cans and did the rounds of the taxi stands bartering with cabbies for their petrol which often had to be syphoned from the vehicles' tanks.

Very few, if any, of the records made in those years have survived into today's catalogues. That is one of the tragedies of recording: each important technical development in recording means that in a short time all recordings made by the older process will become out of date. When Karajan decided that he preferred the Philharmonia to the Vienna Philharmonic, London again became the centre of my recording activities. At about this time I bought a house in Hampstead with a large garden and the only relaxation in these years was the planning, improving, and supervising of my garden.

EMI was later than its rivals in producing its first LP records, and although it had plenty of 78 recordings which could be transferred to LP the need to build a new catalogue was a challenge made for me. I threw myself into it with all my energy and enthusiasm. Unfortunately EMI's American outlets were not publishing European recordings as quickly as both the artists and I wanted. As I said at the time: "I am making a Mississippi of splendid recordings by great artists and they are dripped out in America through a pipette." Eventually—at long last—EMI decided to establish its own selling organization in the United States. It was called Angel Records and Dario Soria, who had already made a name for himself through his own Cetra-Soria company, was the managing director; his wife, Dorle, a genius for tasteful and exciting publicity, ran public relations and advertising. The first Angel list was published in November 1953, only a year after EMI had made its belated entry into long-playing records. Angel Records quickly became the most admired label in the U.S.A. All the records were imported from England with surfaces far superior to anything on the American market, presented in albums and with notes and illustrations better than either Europe or America had yet seen. In the Sorias I had at last found my ideal collaborators—people who believed that only the best was good enough. With the same thought in mind,

I married Elisabeth Schwarzkopf shortly before she made her American debut.

Angel had an imposing list of artists to offer—the cream of European talent—headed by Karajan, Gieseking, Callas, Schwarzkopf, di Stefano, Gobbi, Serafin, Giulini, and a host of other celebrities. I had heard Callas in *Norma* in Rome and I had been negotiating a contract for a long time, but her husband, Meneghini, was the toughest of nuts to crack. She had already made some 78 records for Cetra, which did not make the impact they deserved. She had also recorded *La Gioconda* for Cetra-Soria. Eventually the contract was signed and she made her first records with me in 1953 in Florence—*Lucia di Lammermoor*, with di Stefano, Gobbi, and Serafin.

On December 27, 1951, Karajan began rehearsals for *Der Rosenkavalier* at La Scala. The cast was star-studded: Schwarzkopf, Jurinac, della Casa, Edelmann, and Kunz. Karajan conducted and produced. The whole company rehearsed ten to twelve hours a day for more than a month. I came to an arrangement with the director of La Scala to record all the performances to publish the complete opera. The recording gear was sent from London and installed but at the last moment the orchestra asked such unreasonable terms that the project had to be dropped. However, the good relations established with La Scala soon led to an exclusive contract for EMI to record in that theatre. Each year, until Callas ceased to sing at La Scala, several weeks of July and August were devoted to recording Italian opera in the theatre. The series was launched with *Tosca* conducted by de Sabata with Callas, di Stefano, and Gobbi, all at the peak of their powers. It was the most successful recording of an Italian opera that had ever been made and remains one of the great recordings of all time. Unfortunately de Sabata suffered a severe heart attack soon after this recording, which brought to an abrupt end what would have been a unique series of recordings. He came out of his self-imposed retirement to make only one more recording—the Verdi *Requiem*. He never appeared in public again except to conduct the Funeral March from the *Eroica* at the funerals of Cantelli and Toscanini.

Five years after the foundation of Angel in America, EMI decided to transfer the Angel label to the management of Capitol, a large American company which it had recently bought. The Sorias resigned. In the meantime I realized that Karajan would inevitably be Furt-wängler's successor as director of the Berlin Philharmonic and decided to engage Klemperer—at that time written off by the musical profession as an ill man—so that in the event of Karajan having to record with Deutsche Grammophon Gesellschaft, EMI would still have a great conductor for the classical symphonic repertoire. Foresight was well rewarded: Furtwängler died in 1954, Karajan signed an exclusive contract with DGG, and EMI had in Klemperer an artist whose conception of the classics from Bach through Beethoven to Richard Strauss and Mahler was entirely different from Toscanini's, Furtwängler's, or Karajan's but was welcomed by the public both in Europe and America. Klemperer soon became the undisputed idol of the London public. Even the critics still praise him.

Seen in retrospect, the departure of the Sorias from Angel and, soon after, Karajan's decision not to renew his exclusive contract with EMI were the beginnings of my dissatisfaction which eventually led me to retire from EMI. A widespread reorganization of the recording activities of EMI took the authority and the power to make decisions from the individual, and the company became in my view "committee ridden." It was only the advent of stereophonic recording which restored my enthusiasm.

*Reading the memos and letters from Walter to officials of EMI, I am astonished—and grateful—how little of those daily struggles and annoyances he brought back home. His best relations were of course with his recording technicians, transfer crew, factory workers, and his staff—a mutual admiration society.*

*His relations with EMI's top echelon were at best love-hate. However, what was quite clear to everyone—and sometimes Walter suffered for it—was his complete loyalty to the company and his unswerving pride in working for EMI. When one realizes that his salary in 1953 was only £4,000 per annum, it is quite astonishing that Walter didn't pack up, take along some of the artists he had brought to EMI (and he brought many important and loyal ones), and move on. But although this was frequently suggested by artists as well as by other record companies, his loyalty won out. Also, I would guess, his belief that no other company could match EMI played a large part.*

*It must have been infuriating to watch every record company go ahead with their LP records, while stolid, slow EMI watched for years whether this new invention would really catch on. And it must have been as difficult to swallow that EMI was about to enter the all-*

*important stereophonic era without one Karajan, Callas, Klemperer or, for that matter, Schwarzkopf issue.*

*When, in 1958, Walter joined the Board of the Royal Opera house, Covent Garden, things were also far from his liking, as may be seen in the following extracts from his letters to its chairman, Lord Drogheda, and to Sir Isaiah Berlin, a fellow member of the Board.*

TO THE EARL OF DROGHEDA: 15th September 1958

I am extremely surprised that, having been on the Board for five months, no official of the theatre has told me what operas we are doing next season, what casts have been engaged or what casts it is proposed to engage. It seems to me quite ridiculous to have me on the Board at all if I am not to be consulted on these things, in which I have an acknowledged expertise.

I am also much disturbed to hear that Glyndebourne has engaged the best team of scenic designer and producer (Rennert/Maximova) for their *Fidelio*. For the past two years it has been evident that these two people for certain works are without equal and yet we let Glyndebourne get away with it.

TO SIR ISAIAH BERLIN: 11th December 1958

It is evident that nothing concrete has been done by the General Administrator [David Webster] to get *Don Giovanni* on its feet. I feel that one of us has to say, in no uncertain terms, that we, as a committee of reputedly responsible men, are spending money to provide the public with first-class opera. The pious hopes of individuals that it is possible to give first-class opera with local talent has no foundation. In fact, although I was to a great extent guilty of letting my fancy play with the idea of a *de luxe* Offenbach production, I do feel that that sort of thing is dodging the major issue. Covent Garden will not be what it should be until we have first-class productions of two or three great Verdi operas, two Puccini, two Mozart, three Wagner and *Fidelio* as the mainstay of our programme.

And I feel that before you retire for your sabbatical year we must ram this down the throats of our colleagues.

TO THE EARL OF DROGHEDA: 23rd January 1960

I am not prone to asking for free tickets but I feel that the Administration of Covent Garden is being a little extortionate in insisting that I should pay for the two tickets for Dr. Klemperer for last Friday's performance of *Traviata*.

I paid without murmuring for Dr. Klemperer's daughter and nurse to come to *Salome* but since there is every likelihood that Dr. Klemperer will now do *Fidelio* for Covent Garden, it seems unfair that I should be expected to pay for his tickets to attend Covent Garden performances simply because I prefer not to reveal to him that Covent Garden is not prepared to extend to him the courtesy of free tickets, which any other theatre in the world would be proud to give him.

4th February 1963

The purpose of this letter is to tell you that I met Callas and Zeffirelli in Milan. Zeffirelli arrived while Callas and I were discussing Donna Anna. He immediately suggested that what he would most like would be for Callas and Schwarzkopf to sing Donna Anna and Donna Elvira in his Covent Garden production. He would also like Wächter for the Don, Panerai as Masetto, Freni as Zerlina and Gedda as Ottavio. He would naturally come to Covent Garden to rehearse them. Since Callas's acceptance of the idea was so quick and enthusiastic I propose that Covent Garden should follow it up at once finding out when all the singers named would be simultaneously available.

*One of the finest of all of Walter's many productions was this historic recording of* Tristan und Isolde. *Flagstad had agreed to sing Isolde only if Walter produced the set and on the condition that I would supply a few high notes for her. She still had those top notes but was afraid of having to sing those phrases more than once or twice. Furtwängler had refused ever to work with Walter again and objected to his being the producer of the recording. Walter, of course, had been a buffer between Furtwängler and Karajan for years.*

*I have often encountered antagonism between conductors and am always astonished. Perhaps at the core of the problem is the certain knowledge of the other man's ability. Furtwängler's resentment toward Herbert von Karajan was quite irrational, to the degree that he was unable to pronounce his name! ("This man K!") And this antagonism was transferred to Walter, who had invited Herbert to be permanent conductor of the Philharmonia Orchestra and who produced all of Karajan's recordings for EMI. There surely has been enough written about the special Karajan-Furtwängler feud. As far as it concerned Walter, he always maintained that his white hair was the direct result of being in the eye of the storm. He was at times, as in this memorandum to Bernard Mittell, a senior executive at EMI, desperate, and this outburst should be seen in this light. Furtwängler had attempted to have Walter removed as producer of the* Tristan *recording. Ironically, when the recording was completed, Furtwängler told Walter that his name should also be on the label since it was truly a joint effort. It was, ac-*

*cording to Walter, the only praise he ever received from the great conductor.*

Dear Mr. Mittell,

> *Furtwängler—your two notes of April 21st.*

Thank you for your two memoranda of April 21st. They put me in a position which must inevitably be construed as an adverse criticism of my work on the part of the Company, and result in a loss of my personal prestige throughout the profession: as you yourself say, "There are only too many people ready to put a wrong interpretation on words which are not entirely favourable."

The best course would seem for me to write a personal letter to the singers engaged for *Tristan and Isolde* explaining that Furtwängler in his resentment and fear of Karajan has forced the Company to this change.

The position is particularly difficult with Flagstad, who has asked me that she should never have to see Mr. [David] Bicknell, and with Fischer-Dieskau, who was advised by Furtwängler not (to) sign a contract with our company.

You tell me that this change of managership must not alter my former enthusiasm for Dr. Furtwängler. My greatest moral asset is that neither love, friendship, money, ambition, enmity nor hate can influence my artistic judgments. In that field of musical activity where I have a completely free hand, I have, in spite of knowing that Furtwängler has been intriguing against me . . . consistently engaged him for concerts. That he fears my critical judgment of him as a performer of music is understandable. . . .

To save the Company from unpleasantness, I have been extremely guarded in any comments I have made upon him. But that you should yield to this pressure from him makes me feel that the time is very near when Schwarzkopf, Karajan, and the whole circle of the great artists of the future who work harmoniously with us should move in a block to some other company.

*Within EMI there apparently was almost ceaseless criticism of Walter's long absences on the Continent and in America. Then too there was the issue of so-called questionable political associations. Both these issues reached a peak in 1953 and led to Walter's finally answering the charges in a blistering memorandum to Mr. Mittell.*

I was considerably disturbed by a note from [John] Macleod which was delivered to me when I went to pick up Christoff half an hour before the first *Faust* session in Paris—virtually forbidding me to attend any of the *Faust* recording sessions, which placed me in a most invidious position with both Christoff and Gedda. The last sentence— "I thought you had come over for Elisabeth's concert."—I took to be a joke or an attempt to ease the awkward situation. Only when I saw Soria in Rome over the weekend did I realize this had a deeper significance. In Rome, Soria opened my eyes to things of which I had not been aware.

The Company was dissatisfied with me because I neglected its work to go, at the Company's expense, to keep Elisabeth company wherever she might be singing and that I was a close friend and associate of Nazis but that there was nobody else to do the job.

If you knew how Elisabeth arranged her work and neglected the offers with which she is inundated so that she could be in the same place as I, you would be able to repudiate this dirty little piece of Jesuitical insinuation. If you turn your mind back, you will remember that when I went to Rome, at my expense, to make a film with Karajan, I secured for the Company a contract with Christoff. My visit to Stockholm in the spring of 1952, to see Dobrowen, which I timed to coincide with Elisabeth's concerts, resulted in my finding Gedda. In Milan, in January of this year, I was able, first of all to take the steps which have led to the Scala contract and landed the best baritone in Europe—Panerai—who had been sitting under the noses of our Italian company for the last five years without anyone tumbling to the fact that here was one of the best voices in Europe.

I do not think the people who try to decry me realize what an asset the Company has in Elisabeth's goodwill and judgment. Whether they like it or not—and they don't—she enjoys the goodwill of every able person professionally concerned with music. It seems that her worst enemies are inside our organization. If it were necessary for me to justify the times my presence in any city coincides with Elisabeth's performances there, it would be the simplest matter to prove, by dates, that in her present eminence her performances are usually with artists under contract to us who regard it as essential that I should be present at *their* most important performances, and not Elisabeth's. It is the nature of distinguished artists to believe the company for whom they make records is sufficiently interested in their careers for the senior person with whom they deal to be present at their most important performances. In my case it is particularly acute because several artists of the front rank value my criticisms of their rehearsals.

If Macleod imagines he is justified in trying to prevent me from going to America for Elisabeth's debut, he has an eye-opener coming to him. When Karajan goes to the U.S.A., I shall certainly be with him. These attentions to a limited number of distinguished artists may appear to you unnecessary but I assure you that they are the stuff of which an association of an artist with a recording company is woven. For what other reason do you suppose Karajan chooses to stay in the comparative discomfort of our spare room whenever he is recording in England?

It seems to me ridiculous that a person who has been entrusted by the Board to develop the international interests of our company should expose the company, or artists under contract to the company, by raising this question—that I am a close friend and associate of Nazis. The function of our company is to sell records. To dub an artist or member of the staff as a Nazi sympathiser is sabotage. These best-selling artists had no choice as to which side of the fence they should temporarily sit.

*Like the other storms, this one too blew over. Walter went on to record the legendary series of operas with Callas, for example, and he was constantly on the lookout for important new artists for EMI and the new Angel label. As late as 1958, he could say in a prophetic memo to the Angel office in America concerning a new album entitled "Renata Scotto—Operatic Arias":*

Renata Scotto is the young Italian soprano, only 23, who made a great impression when she last sang in London two years ago and last year stepped in for Callas at the last performance of *Sonnambula* in Edinburgh. She made her debut about a week ago in Vienna. She is in the world-beating class.

My declared principle in recording was: "I want to make records which will sound in the public's home exactly like what they would hear in the best seat in an acoustically perfect hall." The increased ambiance of stereo recording gave me the opportunity more completely to realize this aim than ever before. I soon came into conflict with the technical and sales departments over this. They believed that the public wanted the "gimmick" of stereo—would like to listen to the left and right extremes which in these days left a hole (I called it a "frozen nose" or "ping pong listening"!) in the space between the loudspeakers. It took a long time for me to induce these people that their ideas of stereo were the very opposite of what musicians and the musical public wanted. In the early sixties EMI began to reduce the number of artists under exclusive contract as well as the number of records they made. In June 1963, I had decided, after much heart-searching that nearly forty years in one company—the only full-time job of my life—were enough. I resigned, giving the Company a year's notice, declining even to discuss why I had come to that decision.

27th June, 1963.

R. Dawes, Esq.,
Electric & Musical Industries Ltd.,
E.M.I. House,
Manchester Square, W. 1.

Dear Dick,

When we last met, you agreed that I should have six months paid leave within the following twelve months. Circumstances have prevented me taking more than five days in the mud of Ischia to help cure my broken arm: nevertheless I intend to take the six months leave in periods which do not conflict with the Company's interests.

My contract with the Company stipulates that it may be terminated by twelve months notice in writing. I hereby give you that notice. I shall consider myself free from my obligations to the Company twelve months from to-day's date.

With kindest regards,

Yours sincerely,

WALTER LEGGE.

My last important recording for EMI was the Verdi *Requiem* with Giulini, Schwarzkopf, Ludwig, Gedda, and Ghiaurov. Nine months after my resignation, in March 1964, with a sad heart I suspended the Philharmonia Orchestra and Chorus. I had decided that England was no longer a country in which I could work in the way I believed right. The only records I have made since then are the concert I arranged in homage to Gerald Moore—which was simply a recording of a public event which I had devised and supervised—and all Elisabeth Schwarzkopf's own records.

*We settled in Switzerland, first in Ascona, then in Geneva. Later we moved to the South of France, to Cap-Ferrat. The now-historic*

*Farewell Concert for Gerald Moore in 1967 was invented, programmed, and masterminded by Walter. It brought together Victoria de los Angeles, Dietrich Fischer-Dieskau, and myself; and the three of us accompanied Gerald Moore "on voice." Four weeks before the concert Walter had his first heart attack. We had come to Zürich from Ascona for a recital there the next day. On the morning of the concert the heart attack happened. Walter was taken to intensive care while I sang the recital, about which I remember nothing. He continued to supervise all the arrangements, programme, printing of the memorial booklet, and all the other details not from an office but from his hospital room in Zürich, which was soon turned into a veritable music library. Three and a half weeks later, against doctor's orders, he travelled by train to London, to supervise our praise of Gerald. At 7:00 A.M. the morning after the concert, we left the Savoy by ambulance for the hospital. In spite of severe chest pains, Walter was clutching the rave reviews.*

## Correspondence 1965–1979

*In his "self-imposed exile," as Walter called the years of his life after London, he accompanied me on most of my concert tours. His correspondence, which had always been vast, became even vaster. The lion's share of this letter exchange was directed to musical writers or music critics on both sides of the Atlantic.*

*His chief correspondents were Peter Heyworth, Desmond Shawe-Taylor, George Szell, Andrew Porter, Irving Kolodin, Paul Hume, Robert Jacobson, and Dr. Alfred Frankenstein, an Israeli critic. In the world of recordings there were Gustl Breuer of RCA Red Seal and John Coveney of Angel Records. And, of course, he was always willing to help young artists, such as mezzo-soprano Joanna Simon.*

*Topics could be anything from the sorry state of opera to the sorry state of the world, from opera producers who surely would ruin this beloved hybrid once and for all, to politicians and heads of state who were doing the same to civilization.*

*Walter and I began to work rather late in my career with Maestro Szell—a concert with the incomparable Cleveland Orchestra and three records. But they were some of the most rewarding music-making experiences we had.*

Notes made during last night's work [recording session of *Des Knaben Wunderhorn*]:

1. *Antonius.* I think it would be both prudent and economical to repeat the *Fischpredigt*. The edit at bar 50 does not work as it should and I am not happy with bars 85 to 90. Kingsway Hall's resonance is such that to put in the last bar, as we wanted, there is a too perceptible gap between piatti, horn and pizzicato.

2. *Trost im Unglück.* Elisabeth wants to do her bits again, which means starting with bar 49 until 85.

3. *Wer hat dies Liedlein erdacht:* perfect.

1. *Verlor'ne Müh* must be repeated. The voices, particularly the soprano, are too backwards.

2. *Das irdische Leben:* if we have got time, this must be repeated because we discovered, after it had been recorded, that Fidi's [Dietrich Fischer-Dieskau's] microphone was more sensitive, so there is a lack of focus.

3. *Rheinlegendchen* is absolutely in order.

4. *Lob des hohen Verstandes* in order.

5. *Revelge:* three bars after 3 took an hour and a half of my expert time and another patient expert to hush up the deficiencies of the trumpets (perhaps the "s" should be at the beginning of the word!). If you are not satisfied with what you hear tonight, we shall have to repeat it from about six bars before 3 to figure 4. We have only one take of section 11 and in the tenth bar after this fugue the oboe interprets "grell schreiend" by quacking an octave on a semi-quaver, an effect more hilarious than dramatic. To cover this, we shall need to rerecord from figure 11, and I would like to do it to the end, because the piano crescendo to fortissimo in the fifth bar from the end does not come through nearly as well as in the concert hall.

6. *Tamboursg'sell:* it does not appear to me too slow. But unfortunately, *die kleine Trommel* marked *p* diminuendo *pp* seven bars before the end is appreciably slower than the first dozen bars marked *pp*. I would like to repeat this from five bars before 11 to the end.

When I have found a fortress or Sputnik safe from revenge I shall write and publish my memoirs. Those who read them will be astonished to see that you and de Sabata, for both of whom I have done so little, have remained friends while others who have every reason to be grateful have never forgiven me for helping them.

I shall die furious if I have not had the opportunity of showing a few of the operas I love and how they can be presented. Is there nowhere in America?

How do you feel about the big Elvira aria, not as Mozart wrote it but as he transposed it down for the first performance, preceded of

course by the recitative? Then the two Dorabella arias and finally
"Deh vieni non tardar" with recitative. Elisabeth protests that she
feels ridiculous imitating a teenager, but she sings it well.

TO ROBERT JACOBSON:

The modern, or rather contemporary, mania for disinterring well-
forgotten operas even by the greatest composers is an awful waste of
time and money. Do you consider that on its musical merits *Corinthe*
was worthy of mouth-to-mouth resuscitation even though one of them
was Verrett's?

Victoria de los Angeles is begging us to do a tour of duet evenings
with her. I'm a bit nervous, between ourselves, if it would be wise:
it leaves the door open for ill-mannered comments on two middle-aged
singers squeezing the last drop out of the orange and worse still the
repertoire of songs for two sopranos is not musically exciting.

Vickers' cancellation—on religious grounds!—of Tannhäuser has
put Covent Garden in a nasty spot. Considering that his religious con-
victions allow him, in other rôles, to screw his sister and his aunt and
murder his white wife, the Tannhäuser cancellation story is a bit thin.

I've spent two long evenings comparing scores of records of Rossini
overtures. Fascinating! Take Beecham's *Gazza Ladra*. It has the sort of
charm and smile-compelling way that made Rossini the idol of his era
and of the cultivated world of his time.

May the Met stay afloat. Being Bliss is no blissful existence.

His [Brahms's] trouble was that he did not get syphilis—all the
good *Lieder* composers did. I propose to start a "Society for the Syphi-
lization of Brahms."

I wish Verrett would listen to plain common sense. She is by
achievement the best mezzo in the world. She should be forbidden
to sing Norma. Adalgisa won't harm her, but Norma will. It's the
last act that really kills. I adore her as an artist, her application,
natural acting ability, lovely velvety timbre, agility and brilliance.
These particular qualities are so rare in one beautiful young woman
that someone should lay down the law and see that it is kept. She can
earn as much glory (more indeed) and as much money by concen-
trating on the repertoire for which she is predestined and is at the
moment—perhaps for ten years to come—unique.

I have never seen anyone fail in that part [Herod]; it is the last
and safest harbour for any German tenor.

Escamillo is impossible for every normal baritone or bass. I've heard
only two good ones in 65 years—Journet and van Damm.

I was merely amused, but my wife was so furious at and with the letters you sent from the gallery girls of both sexes, protesting my Callas piece, that it has taken me a good deal of time to induce her to set foot on American soil again.

The joy of the evening is Frederica von Stade, an actress of seemingly unlimited resources: I've never seen or heard a better Cherubino. I'd gladly retire to a luxurious island with her to rehearse and perfect all the Kama Sutra. If she can learn to darken her voice a little, she will be the Oktavian and Komponist for the next 15 years. Breasts and buttocks are essential to give the essential spice, the *haut goût*, to trouser roles.

You may not know it, but in matters of vocal technique my wife is La Gazza Ladra in person. At Olivero's second *Tosca* she studied every physical device with a pair of eagle eyes. Back home she started working for herself trying out all she had filched and she is now starting *ppp* with her own famous softly perched notes and swelling them to *ff* and back to *ppp*. A's are already mastered. This afternoon it will be the coaxing of the B flats.

The packed hall [Berlin] cheered the toughest Wolf and Strauss songs like Leontyne's audiences in the South when she gives them spirituals.

A new sequel to the Callas saga. Meneghini telephoned me in hospital in Zürich. He must see me and will go anywhere to suit me. I stipulated Geneva last Tuesday at 10:00 A.M.: he arrived with Italian and French lawyers, and chauffeur, and a middle-aged nurse housekeeper at 6:30 P.M. It was all about Maria's will. He claims to be the only beneficiary of a will made in April 1954. At his advanced age he is as sprightly as a cricket on an LSD diet, his eyes glinting at every mention of royalties, preparations for assaults on La Scala, and Cetra, every recording company, every pirate—Battista Meneghini is out for blood to go in his various banking accounts. I suggested to him that since he is eleven years my senior I know who should be his sole heir—and gave him my visiting card. Even he laughed. He is curiously honest about her defects of character although he evidently loved her deeply.

Rudolf Bockelmann, who couldn't read a word of English, conned the columns of London criticisms seeking the word *but*. If he found it, he grunted in German, "It's all shit anyway."

TO DESMOND SHAWE-TAYLOR:

I was delighted to read your appreciation of *Rosenkavalier* (the most recently composed opera to take a secure place in the world repertoire; *Turandot* depends on the availability of a soprano who can really sing the part). I had despaired of reading in English a wise, civilized discussion of the piece—from which observation you, no doubt, deduce that I loathe Bill Mann's book on Strauss, particularly the *Rosenkavalier, Ariadne, Arabella,* and "Frosch" [Strauss's term for *Die Frau ohne Schatten*] chapters.

I left the applause in the Schwarzkopf/Furtwängler Wolf record for two reasons:

1. to leave in the sense of the occasion.
2. to protect my own reputation as a stickler for accuracy, as well as beauty, sensibility, and atmosphere.

There are rumbles from Furtwängler and some poor ensemble which is acceptable only because of this occasion. As a reminder that many a great concert experience is not, in that hideous German expression, *Plattenreif.*

Decca's *Rosenkavalier.* I am not as enthusiastic as you. Solti too often reminds me of a remark of Wieland Wagner's: "Walter, if you don't soon find me a good *Tannhäuser* conductor, I shall be reduced to Solti and his orgasms in every second bar."

TO JOANNA SIMON:

Where can one live without being crippled by inflation, buggered by Arabs, or bored to death?

Never attempt Eboli; it is and always has been the grave of mezzo-sopranos.

When I tell you that I went to hear *Götterdämmerung* at the Nice Opera last night, you will appreciate how lonely this place is.

You can't be serious with that programme . . . start with Gloomy Joe [Brahms] and work backwards to Monteverdi? That is what in English slang is called "arse-backwards." Experience proves that chronological order is wisest and most acceptable. To finish the French group Debussy's "Mandoline" is ideal—lasts only a minute and as P. G. Wodehouse says, "Knocks them in the aisles." Transpose if necessary to vocal comfort. *Damnation of Faust* ought not to give you any difficulties. Elisabeth did it with Furtwängler but pleased as he was, we found it essentially a mezzo part. The arching phrases of the "Chanson Gothique" need slow, careful practice. Look also at Duparc's "Phidylé," perhaps the most perfect of all French songs. Do think seriously on Stephen Foster—that man wrote himself, and alone, the real folk-songs of America—Negro dialect and all.

TO ANDREW PORTER:

I told him [Ceccato] that only a madman would venture to do such works as *Otello* and *Ariadne* in Covent Garden and Glyndebourne without having first tried them out on the dogs of minor provincial theatres. I wish you could have heard and seen Furtwängler's rage and disgust when he heard that Solti was doing the first *Tristan* of his life in München!

I regret having put myself on the shelf. My only pleasures are rehearsing with Elisabeth, traveling with her, and helping young artists like Ceccato. And all the time I am sitting in Death's waiting room, waiting to realize that now it is my turn.

I greatly enjoy your *New Yorker* pieces, my only fear is that they are too good for the American public because they are still a way behind the best European standards of judgment and appreciation.

With its new management the Met will be having a roughish passage. Chapin is extremely agreeable but I shall be surprised if, with his scant experience of opera, he can manage the artistic side successfully and much as I like Kubelik, I doubt if he knows his way about the repertoire, knows a good singer from a dud, or has a firm enough will to get the desired and necessary results. I would gladly go there as artistic director if they would have me, but since I left London no one seems to have thought of making use of my talents.

TO IRVING KOLODIN:

I wonder how sound was the judgment of your predecessors? Certainly better than that of the homosexual chauvinist gossip writers who have much too much space for the display of their ignorance in today's British press—except for one pretty young witty-bitch.

Ann Arbor went very well. Nearly all the best voices were black—skin not timbres! Although we were forced to concentrate on Schubert I'm wondering if *Lieder* are really what will most help in such master classes. It seems evident to me that when Fischer-Dieskau and Elisabeth stop singing there will be neither supreme performers nor interested audiences for that particular branch of music. The emotions of the poems (leaving out Chamisso and hundreds of Schubert songs of no real distinction musically or poetically) are almost certainly strange and old fashioned to the mores and morals of the under forties. The *Lied* was born with Mozart's "Abendempfindung" and died with Strauss's *Four Last Songs*—he did not realize how prophetic his title was to be!

If we are invited again would it not be better to work on Mozart's Da Ponte operas, two or three Strauss, and, if the voices are there, *Rigoletto*, *Otello*, and *Falstaff*? Even La Price sugar-coated the pill of her Salzburg recital with Puccini, Verdi, and Gershwin encores.

The tasteless production soaked in anachronisms and unnecessary extravagance is fuel for a polemic against the whole tribe of sodomite regisseurs, which one of us will have to pour like Vesuvius on Pompeii.

There would be no point in my visiting Bayreuth: as (probably) Wieland's only male friend I have been persona non grata since his funeral. The book by Nike Wagner, his second daughter, will almost certainly spill a Niagara of poisonous beans on the whole quarrelsome Wagner-Liszt progeny. I once told Wieland, having frequently stayed in Wahnfried, that his household maintained the tradition of *Tristan* and The Ring—whenever drink or food was proffered treachery and dastardly deeds inevitably accompanied or followed them.

But I suppose the Met audiences are for the greater part "canary fanciers."

I wish New York were not so far from here: I ache for the stimulation of sitting and conversing with you. One of the major snags of advancing age is the lack of wise men from whom one can learn.

May I suggest that you take out your fleuret, rapier, sabre, scimitar, cutlass, broadsword, and any other weapons you have in your armoury from stiletto to pen (even typewriter) to eviscerate the recording companies for deleting records which by artistic right should be *permanently* available. New generations grow into the class of people with money which they would gladly spend on records of performances vastly superior to anything most of the companies are producing today. It is bad with books but the record companies have less conscience and savoir faire than the Knopfs of their world.

Heard Levine at work and performing, and later spent an evening with him. He is enormously skilled, clear thinking, and very able— or have I lost my sense of values? Found the Nibblet [Carol Neblett] much improved but that voice is by many sizes too large for Mozart's corsets. The Met ought to let her loose on big early Verdi.

Troyanos has a sumptuous voice, a very sharp intelligence, enormous ambition, and do-or-die determination to be a great artist. Whether her strenuous schedule as an opera singer will give her time and wisdom enough to paint with the fine brush that the *Lied* demands instead of swashing it on with a scene-painter's brush remains to be seen. I am not happy that in the provinces she is being forced to temper the quality of her programmes to what your impresarios believe to be the prescribed diet for what they call Community Concerts. It would be sad if, as is happening in Europe, the *Lieder* recital deteriorates into the old mixture of songs and operatic arias with which my youth was plagued.

A pity that no intendant has learned that the only way to maintain standards is not to say, "Wouldn't it be fun to put on Rossini's *Otello*?" unless he has half a dozen able tenors in case there is an epidemic of influenza. When you have a Melchior and a Flagstad or Nilsson then and only then do you or should you risk *Tristan* and . . . The Ring.

A Happy New Year! You *made* Christmas for me with the Mengelberg *Heldenleben*—first your cover note then the incredible restoration —revivication. How the devil is it done? Has RCA done much publicity on the technique or . . . what devices they have used. And what else are they publishing in this astonishing guise? If only the recording companies can so improve the riches they have in their archives with like skill they have the artistic capital to cut down on their spending on recording for years to come, except, of course, on the few contemporary public favorites whose admirers buy whatever they produce.

Musically speaking Strauss's own recordings are the greater enrichment. We listen to them evening after evening and come up rich in new ideas about music-making and admiration of the man's genius, not only as a composer. I've compared his performances of his own works with those of other conductors from Toscanini to Karajan: none of them gets near to Strauss's natural, essential music-making; for me Szell and Richter come nearest but even they for all their clarity, understanding, and affection often lack his basic pulse, the magical ease and naturalness of transition from one tempo to another, the human warmth, the humour, restrained pathos, the aristocratic and refined taste in final ritardandos, and the incredible energy of the man, and this in the weeks or even days around his 80th birthday.

Until I studied these records I have felt that Strauss habitually overpraised the Wiener Philharmoniker, probably because they were useful to him both in the opera house and in their own programmes and would repay him by encouraging frequent performances of his own works, which was an obsession with him. I know better now. I worked with that unsympathetic gang of rapscallions for several years with Furtwängler, Karajan, Böhm, *et al.*, all of whom were important to their (the orchestra's) earnings but no conductor known to me— not even Toscanini in the Salzburg Festivals—got out of them the extraordinary warmth of sound and, considering the miserable conditions of life in Vienna in 1944, the glow, intonation, and accuracy.

For me the Strauss portrait in the Met with the *Così* score is a profoundly moving and revealing document and piece of iconography.

TO PETER HEYWORTH:

Re Klemperer: I ponder a good deal on what his posthumous status and influence will be five, ten, and twenty years after his death. Perhaps he has me and Hitler to thank for his glorious late years in London? Hitler provided the audience, I the orchestra.

You will, I am sure, live long enough to see that Shostakovich and Prokofiev are and have been the best composers of our time.

I am working my way slowly through O.K.'s [Klemperer's] *Così*. It is extraordinarily clear in texture, so painstakingly concerned with every note in every part that a good copyist could take the score down as dictation from the records, but the spirit of comedy and the humanity of what is for me Mozart's supreme masterpiece are drowned in Teutonic earnestness. No sun shines through it; the laughs and heartaches and tenderness and jealousies are swamped under Schopenhauer.

I have just looked at your *Conversations with Klemperer*: What surprises me, knowing me as well as you do, is that you did not ask me whether what Klemperer said was true before putting damning mis-statements about me in print.

You will understand that whenever we meet and dine together—which I hope will be frequently—the subject of Klemperer shall not be raised. "Immer war Undank Legges Lohn."

TO JOHN COVENEY:

Although Elisabeth had to cancel the New Zealand part of her tour—my fault!—she did Australia and had spectacular successes.

Her March 1972 visit is not planned to be her Farewell to U.S.A. She is still in wonderful voice and I am in favour of her withdrawing gradually from concert life. If she stopped suddenly, the shock might well take toll of her nerves and health. I am sure my heart-trouble was the delayed result of cutting off suddenly all my active musical life.

I am delighted that Victoria's and Maria's sales are keeping up. Both they and Elisabeth are suffering from EMI's late entry into stereo. Decca were wise: they recorded in stereo for years before the system became a commercial fact. EMI failed to learn from the lesson they had already had by their long wait before going into LP.

No doubt I owe it to you that Maria telephoned here to ask kindly after my health. I was in Salzburg but I telephoned her next day and had a marvellously stimulating conversation with her. She is a wonderful person to talk with! You, lucky dog, now have the pleasure and privilege of being in the same city with her. I envy you! Give her my love and hug her for me if she'll let you.

I am convinced that in the arts committees are useless. What is necessary are people like Karajan, Culshaw, and me; we know not only how to achieve the best artistic results but how to attract the public and carry out the whole operation with carefully chosen collaborators. Democracy is fatal for the arts; it leads only to chaos or the achievement of new and lower common denominators of quality.

Your absence from Salzburg left a nasty hole. The new productions were disastrous. The only good thing about *Don Pasquale* (apart from the music) was the conductor, a greatly talented young Italian called Riccardo Muti—potentially much the best since de Sabata and Serafin.

I had as you know, a friendlyish letter from M.C. [Callas] and wrote offering her dates when I could go to Paris to give her lunch or dinner: so far no answer. She did a marvellous two hours and fifty-five minutes programme on Paris TV. She looked lovely, her speaking voice has mellowed almost beyond recognition, she comported herself with exceptional grace, charm, naturalness and dignity, and she spoke admirable sense. The effect on the ordinary public here is extraordinary: those who formerly thought of her as an unsympathetic tigress and prima donna in the pejorative sense, are now enchanted by the gracious, relaxed grande dame. An abridged version in English for American TV with equally sympathetic collaborators would be invaluable to the presentation of an entirely new image of her. She revealed that she had just finished half a record! Dallas seems to be off for this year. Her reappearance will be at the Paris Opera in a new *Traviata* with Visconti. We shall see.

I will do everything in my power to fit in with your wishes and time schedules, provided that the artistic results do not lower the standard that Elisabeth and I have maintained in our 23 years of recording together.

I am all in favour of re-working, re-titling, and re-covering this record ["The Elisabeth Schwarzkopf Christmas Album"]. I am unhappy about the re-mastering because almost every word I have read in American and English journals and newspapers opposed this bogus-stereo conversion. The only people who have got away with it with some dignity and without loss of face are DGG.

I shall be in London in June and I intend to spend as much time as necessary getting a decent bogus-stereo sound. I have just talked to Alan Stagg on the telephone: he is not very optimistic about the results although the Abbey Road people have, like all important studios, done some hard thinking about the problem of making four wheelers out of bicycles.

I gladly acknowledge the receipt of three copies of the E.S. Christmas songs in pseudo-stereo which arrived a few days ago.

These transfers sound excellent—the first bogus stereo to please me. Two criticisms:

(1) the untidy lettering of the title on the cover; can't you induce your Hollywood colleagues to set titles in the most legible type, to be legible at a distance like a sign-post. This one is meaningless squiggle at one and a half to two yards distance—the distance from the window-gazer's eyes from the cover in the normal shop display.

(2) your hideous coloured new label—in colours which Geoffrey Parsons calls "baby's mess."

Olympia is the one rôle properly suited to the coloratura soprano since it calls for the very negation of human intelligence.

TO PAUL HUME:

I need your advice. I was Wieland Wagner's closest friend—as far as he had friends. Since his death his widow has referred her many difficulties to me. Three days ago she asked my help in the toughest of problems: Siegfried Wagner's heirs are seriously considering selling the Festspielhaus and the invaluable archives of the Festspielhaus! This includes the manuscript scores of *Parsifal* and *Tristan und Isolde* and maybe of other operas, as well as masses of still unsorted correspondence. I have advised them to sell the theatre as one object and the manuscripts and archives as another.

To whom can I make approaches in America? Who would be interested? Library of Congress? Ford Foundation?

Wieland and I discussed the eventual destination of these treasures in the last months of his life and he was much against the idea that they would eventually repose in a German library. He hated postwar Germany as much as he loathed Hitler's Germany.

TO GUSTL BREUER:

Give my warmest regards to Jimmy Levine, who is in every way exactly my musical intellectual cup of Dom Perignon.

I had seventeen enchanting days in Salzburg. The standards of singing have fallen badly but there were compensations. An incredibly splendid *Otello* from Karajan with Freni, a near perfect Desdemona. Vickers and Glossop behaving rather surprisingly for two nice blue-eyed Anglo-Saxons as two black-hearted villains coerced into conviction by H.K. *Così* was beautifully set and produced by Ponelle except for Miss Stratas's Despina—the sort of Neapolitan slut I have chucked out two or three times in my life. The whiz-kid wonder conductors Mehta and Ozawa are simply not yet ripe to conduct Mozart, least of all in Salzburg.

You make New York sound much more attractive than it ever is when I am around. Perhaps I have a depressing effect on the place. But parties at Dorle's and night taxi trips with La Baker sound like High Life to me. In spite of the glorious weather Ascona is dead as last Saturday's roast mutton. Even the dog complains. He can't find a trace of another dog on any single tree or lamppost in the neighborhood.

85

TO ANTHONY DEAN:

Hope you have matched my diminution of sheer bulk from kg. 85 to kg. 80. "Il faut souffrir d'être Béla Bartók."

TO DR. ALFRED FRANKENSTEIN:

I begin to fear that since the majority of people living have been born since the end of the last World War, the generation born since then, knowing nothing of war's horrors, subconsciously craves the excitements and dangers of war.

I have cancelled the invitation we extended to a highly gifted young Korean student to stay and study with us. I discovered that she is singing with a N.Y. jazz-pop group and I see no point in spending three months teaching a girl surgeon's skills when she may have the secret urge to be a butcher.

If producers and scenic designers are allowed to continue their writing of graffiti and vulgarity and stupidity on masterpieces as you experienced in *Fidelio* and *Così*—not to mention Chéreau at Bayreuth—we shall be forced to insist that they write the libretti and music to match the rubbish they put on the stage!

I have done a biggish piece on Callas for the U.S. *Opera News* —not a conventional obituary, rather an autopsy.

I have sat through most of Schönberg's output without being convinced that he is a major composer—and sitting patiently study-ing his scores has done more to convince me that he does not deserve that epithet. . . . Schönberg's eccentricities were the fruit of his own realization that he was incapable of writing a natural melodic and original line. Don't be furious with me!

Is Mehta a great conductor? My faith in him shrinks. He has become too extrovert. At rehearsal he lacks the intensity or preoc-cupation with the music and at concerts he puts on a show for the public rather than concerning himself with communicating his in-tentions to the orchestra. Scuola di Bernstein?

The Israeli distaste for Bartók astonishes me. The Quartets are, to my conviction, the greatest creations in the form since Beethoven Op. 59 to Op. 135. I am less convinced about the Piano concertos and the stage works but I have an instinctive—as different from a considered—aversion to folk-song of any nationality or source.

Orff until the last two stage works still impresses me—in spite of the *Wiederholungen*. After the *Hauptprobe* of *Trionfo di Aphrodite* I gently suggested that he cut some of his repeated verses. He replied, "I know the effect of my rubber stamp music."

I've heard some good singing from the younger generation: a superb Russian mezzo, Obraztsova; Margaret Price, an English soprano who discarded her love and discovered her potentials; Troyanos, who has shed her vulgarity and done *Titus* superbly, I thought, in Salzburg: Janowitz and Popp in *Arabella* in Wien— but I find it a deplorable piece. Strauss, after *Frau,* went through a very bad period.

The lady in the *Meistersinger* photo is Lisa della Casa. Kna [Knappertsbusch], during a rehearsal, asked where she was born. She answered: "Bern, Herr Professor." Kna: "I thought so."

On the few occasions I have anything to say about the choice of works for conductors' competitions I habitually insist on the slow introductions to Haydn symphonies: that is where one sees and hears if a young man has the makings of a real conductor.

New York is musically below its reputation. I heard a Ring deplorably sung except by Nilsson and even she is now variable, often having intonation troubles and sometimes lacking the heroic brilliance and size which were uniquely hers. The one great asset of the Met is its orchestra—consistently the best playing despite bad conductors—that I've heard in any opera house since Karajan left Vienna.

Hofmannsthal's exquisite preoccupation with symbolism bores me. Why can't the fellow sometimes say what he means? Simply!

I doubt if any great conductor of his epoch was more widely disliked in the profession, yet I who knew him [Szell] from about 1931, got through without a cross word. We talked the same musical language—"der Komponist hat immer recht."

My wife is going to the U.S.A. on Sunday and I follow twelve days later to try to extract from an American accompanist some of the sensitivity I squeezed out of Gerald Moore and more recently Geoffrey Parsons. Accompanists are made, not born.

At a greater distance of time I doubt if I shall so carefully conceal some of his [Klemperer's] darker side or so conceal my conviction that when I decided to give up the Philharmonia Orchestra, his—to me—evident falling off as a conductor was a contributing factor.

Fischer-Dieskau's unenthusiastic reception [conducting] in Israel saddens me but it confirms the general impression he made in England. I have known him since the start of his professional career, made his first records with him, and we have worked together many times since, but we have never become friends. I don't know why because he is a great artist and I admire most of his work. Perhaps it is his *Aussprache beim singen*, the Prussian exaggeration of consonants, particularly in Schubert, Strauss, and Wolf, that slightly irritates me.

Marriner is an admirable artist who used to be 2nd *Konzertmeister* of my orchestra. A pity you had to miss Brendel: I consider him the nearest approach to Schnabel, than whom he is much more accomplished technically. And he is developing steadily.

*Suor Angelica* is the only Puccini opera I actively dislike; to me it is an over-sweet cocktail of *Weihrauch* and Eros.

She [Leider] remains for me—despite Flagstad and Nilsson—the supreme Isolde and Brünnhilde.

It is only people of our generation who know how good Ivogün, Schorr, Reinhardt, Leider, Melchior, and scores of others were and understand the reason why, after the last war, when I had the power to record a complete Ring, I could not bring myself to do it.

I think it's unfair for Israel that my wife's and Karajan's records are banned from your radio transmitters. They were both about as Nazi as you or I are, and it seems grossly unjust to a generation too young to have heard either of them live that they should be deprived of the testament of two of the greatest artists that Austria in the case of Karajan and Germany in the case of Schwarzkopf have produced. And to ban Wagner or Strauss is robbing [Israelis] of two of the most important factors in their artistic heritage. I hope you will live long enough to rectify this monstrous deprivation of all Germans in Israel of one of the factors of which they have every right and reason to be most proud.

*As for me and my letter writing, I really don't know what would have happened to me if I had not been born into the age of the telephone. I certainly would not have made a singing career if I had also had to answer letters by hand. The reason there are so few letters between Walter and me is not coy reticence. It is that we were either together or, when we were apart, we telephoned each other daily, no matter where we were. And when Walter proposed to me, he picked— telephonically speaking—the most expensive place. He was in London . . . I in Australia. Still, it was such a momentous phone call that I sat down and wrote the following note:*

—and I totally accept your suggestions for the year. Only, I, on my part, am also adding some "iron" goals!

1. To make you happier than you have ever been.
2. To make you so proud of me, so that you will love me even more—
3. To make you *completely* healthy and young.
4. I leave the financial suggestions entirely to you and shall try to collaborate with all my strength.
5. I, too, long for a "not-bohemian" life. But that we shall manage.

> With haste, with love, with yearning,
> with joy in our forthcoming reunion—
>
> Your E.

# 3

# THE
# PHILHARMONIA
# ORCHESTRA

*In 1952, a reporter asked me in an interview, "Mme. Schwarzkopf, you never seem to wear any jewels in your concerts. Don't you like them or does it mean that a prima donna like you doesn't have them?" To which I replied, "I might not have any jewels, but I do have an orchestra."*

*There are many stories about the founding and subsequent history of this jewel of an orchestra, and particularly so about its demise. Indeed, there are as many stories as there are musicians in an orchestra. I am, naturally, not an objective bystander. I do know, as a personal witness, that the version in Peter Heyworth's Klemperer book is incorrect; although this is certainly not his fault. I do wish he had asked Walter his side of the affair, which follows.*

AFTER THE outbreak of war, I was soon cut off from the Continent and the two English friends from whom I had learned so much: Ernest Newman was working on his Wagner biography in the depths of Surrey, and Beecham had gone to Australia, explaining his presence there by saying, "The Government declared a state of emergency, so I obediently emerged." I was left to my own devices.

To keep my hand in I suggested to four members of the Salon Orchestra, which the BBC had tucked away in Evesham, that we should spend our weekends rehearsing to make a good string quartet: if we succeeded, I would record it. We worked on a Mozart quartet, Schubert's *Death and the Maiden*, and Beethoven's first *Rasumovsky*. Within a year the Mozart was ripe for recording, which we did in Cheltenham Town Hall. Columbia published it under the name Philharmonia Quartet, taken from the miniature score with which I worked. The reception was enthusiastic enough to justify recording the Schubert and Beethoven and to make the first step of Philharmonia's growth, Mozart's Clarinet Quintet with Reginald Kell. Soon we had blossomed into a Septet—Ravel's. The Philharmonia Concert Society was formed to present the eponymous quartet's first concerts, given in the Wigmore Hall.

I had become preoccupied with the state and structure of public and recorded music when the war was finished. Fondly confident that Beecham and I would be in control of opera at Covent Garden, as we had been in 1938 and 1939, I decided that the only practical steps I could take were to prepare the creation of a first-class orchestra for the opera, concerts, and recordings. It should be on the lines of the Vienna Philharmonic, which was and is in fact the Vienna State Opera Orchestra, but without the insidious snag of nearly all opera orchestras that, after the premiere, the players themselves decide which of them shall play which performance. After establishing such an orchestra I should be able to provide regular well-paid employment for the best young musicians as soon as they were demobilized.

The Philharmonia Orchestra was not, as the Arts Council report states, formed specifically for a "very special purpose" of recording. Neither did EMI encourage its formation. EMI appeared to ignore my connection with it and at no stage did I negotiate with EMI for any contract for the orchestra. That was done by Jane Withers, the Managing Director, who had been on my staff at ENSA during the war and who was the most able, loyal collaborator imaginable and also had the advantage that she was completely unmusical. Even when she was a schoolgirl, her headmistress invariably prefaced her upbeat to the singing of the National Anthem on Empire Day with "Withers, don't sing!"

Wing-Commander O'Donnell had made an astute picking of many of the best young players for his RAF band stationed at Uxbridge, and a dozen or so rather older artists were in the BBC Salon Orchestra. When this group was disbanded I induced David Webster, then Chairman of the Liverpool Philharmonic, to take the majority of these players to lead and strengthen his very provincial orchestra.

My duties at ENSA—providing serious concerts for the forces—gave me frequent opportunities to hear all the British orchestras as well as the military and marine bands. I was in the unique position to find out who and where the best players were. One icy day in winter 1943–44, a bandmaster gave me an invaluable lesson. The best bands had been summoned to Drury Lane Theatre to audition for long tours overseas. The intonation of all these bands even in the near-Arctic conditions of the unheated theatre was flawless. At the lunch-break I congratulated the assembled conductors on this extraordinary feat, which I had never been able to achieve with Europe's best orchestras under better conditions. One of them opened my eyes—"You would have no intonation troubles if you had our authority to put any man who played out of tune on seven days latrine duty." This is a luxury no great conductor has yet enjoyed.

By 1944 full mobilization had reduced orchestral playing in Britain to its nadir but with peace in sight the time had come for me to canvass the players I had earmarked for my postwar orchestra. Apart from those I had placed on ice in the Liverpool Philharmonic, the next people I approached were Marie Wilson, then of the BBC Orchestra and still fortunately a pillar of strength in the profession, and Jack Thurston, one of the most distinguished wind players of the age. Both promised me their enthusiastic cooperation.

I had already formulated certain basic principles in my mind:

There are enough first-class musicians in Britain to make *one* orchestra at least equal and in certain sections, superior, to the best European orchestras. All these players must be in one orchestra—the Philharmonia.

I would make an orchestra of such quality that the best instrumentalists would compete for the privilege of playing in it.

No "passengers." One inferior player can mar an orchestra's ensemble and intonation.

An orchestra consisting only of artists distinguished in their own right can give its best only with the best conductors.

No permanent conductor. An orchestra working with only one conductor, no matter how gifted he may be, inevitably bears the mark of its permanent conductor's personality, his own particular sonority and his approach to music. The Philharmonia Orchestra must have style, not a style.

No contracts for players. I changed this rule later and gave guaranteed minimum annual fees to key players for first call on their services up to seven days before every duty. Human nature being what it is, security sometimes breeds casualness. Every player must give all he has from the first note of every rehearsal until the last note of every concert (a wise conductor knows from experience how to spare players in rehearsal). I must retain the inalienable right "to hire and fire."

A few days before the plans for the reopening of Covent Garden as an opera house were announced I was invited to lunch by Ernest Makower (founder of the prewar London Museum Concerts) at his country house, and literally taken down a garden path. Leslie Boosey, at that time, I believe, chairman of Boosey and Hawkes, was with us and he had made arrangements to put Covent Garden on its feet again. Boosey told me that although I had all the necessary knowledge and experience to run Covent Garden my standards were notoriously higher than those they aimed at—how right he proved to be—and that I was too intransigent. David Webster had been appointed General Administrator, Karl Rankl would be virtually Musical Director, and they would form their own orchestra. They would not have Beecham in the place.

Intransigence has certain advantages. I invited Sir Thomas Beecham to conduct the first concert of the Philharmonia Orchestra at the Kingsway Hall on October 25, 1945. He conducted an all-Mozart programme. More than 60 percent of the players were still, officially, in the services. In the excitement of launching the Philharmonia's first concert I had forgotten to discuss a fee with Beecham. After the concert I tried to amend the oversight. "The privilege of directing this magnificent consort of artists is such that my pleasure would be diminished if I accepted a fee," said Beecham. "I would, however, gladly accept a decent cigar."

Two days after the concert Sir Victor (Bob) Schuster, an old friend and passionate amateur musician, invited Beecham and me to lunch at Boodle's to discuss plans for the future. I do not remember what the moon's phase was but a changed Beecham fired his first broadside. "Before my departure from America I announced that I was returning to England to form a new orchestra. I cannot break my word. I shall employ most of this admirable nucleus you have assembled, enlarge it to full symphonic strength—in which I am sure you will assist me, my dear Walter. I have access to all the money this venture will need. I am already well advanced in negotiations with the Royal Philharmonic Society to employ the name Royal Philharmonic Orchestra for which I shall remunerate that august body with a certain participation in the royalties earned by the recordings we, my dear boy, shall make together. The name Philharmonia is ridiculous anyway: no one will ever remember it."

I told him that I had no intention of handing over my orchestra lock, stock, and barrel to him, nor of changing its name. I expressed the opinion—which I still hold—that London had no need of two new orchestras, and that there were neither the players nor the work to employ them. However, if he insisted in fulfilling his American boast the best solution would be for us to employ exactly the same players: under his direction the orchestra would be called the Royal Philharmonic and for my concerts and any other work I could get with conductors of my choice the orchestra would continue as the Philharmonia. In this way we should together be able to offer more and better work to the best musicians. Beecham left angrily: Schuster and I drank our sherry in pensive silence.

Neither Beecham nor I had enough work to keep a large orchestra adequately employed but the Philharmonia had a useful start in film studios where they were already well liked and kept fairly busy by Ernest Irving and Muir Matheson—enough work to ensure the players' loyalty and faith.

For the first season, I engaged Artur Schnabel to give six concerts at the Albert Hall in the course of which he played all the Beethoven piano concertos and the Triple Concerto with Arthur Grumiaux and Pierre Fournier: three of the concertos were subsequently recorded. The conductors were Issay Dobrowen and two newcomers, Alceo Galliera and Paul Kletzki—all three of them brilliant orchestral trainers. These concerts yielded a substantial financial profit soon depleted, alas, by Ginette Neveu having to cancel a concert at short notice.

By 1947, the Philharmonia Orchestra had gained for itself fame enough for Richard Strauss to choose it for his triumphant post-war concert in London in October 1947. To my lasting regret, I could not hear the rehearsals or the concert because I was recording in Vienna. (Less than three years later I had the consolation and honour of presenting the first performance of Strauss's *Vier letzte Lieder*, sung by Flagstad and conducted by Furtwängler at a Philharmonia concert.)

But neither isolated events of this importance and the growing number of recording sessions were yet sufficient to coalesce the orchestra into the sound body I was aiming for. Something of the standard

94

of the concerts I was determined consistently to give London was shown when von Karajan made his London debut with Dinu Lipatti as soloist in 1947. At the inquest Karajan and I held after the concert, we agreed that the woodwind, horns, brass, and percussion were better than any other European orchestra but that the strings, violins in particular, were too light and anaemic for the sound we had in mind: the old, old story.

Since 1946 I had been producing the most important symphonic recordings in Vienna with Karajan, Furtwängler, Böhm and the Vienna Philharmonic. I employed the Philharmonia mainly for concertos, accompanying singers, and a limited orchestral repertoire—engaging able and promising conductors capable of educating the orchestra.

The Philharmonia's future was still precarious when suddenly the whole financial outlook changed. I had exchanged a few letters with the Maharajah of Mysore, a man interested in Russian and contemporary music, particularly Nicolai Medtner's, whose works he would have liked to be recorded. I had told him that EMI would not face the certain financial loss of recording any of Medtner's music, for which there was little public interest in England, America, or anywhere else. In his next letter the Maharajah asked me to telegraph when I could travel to Mysore to discuss these problems—the air-ticket was ready for me at Air India and £300 "for incidental expenses" would be transferred to my bank.

The visit to Mysore was a fantastic experience. The Maharajah was a young man, not yet thirty. In one of his palaces he had a record library containing every imaginable recording of serious music, a large range of loudspeakers, and several concert grand pianos. He had intended to be a concert pianist and had been accepted by Rachmaninoff as a pupil when both his father and uncle died and he succeeded to the throne—which meant giving up all ideas of a musical career and returning home at once. In the weeks I stayed there, the Maharajah had not only agreed to paying for the recordings of the Medtner piano concertos, an album of his songs, and some of his chamber music; he also agreed to give me a subvention of £10,000 a year for three years to enable me to put both the Philharmonia Orchestra and the Philharmonia Concert Society on a firm basis. The only condition was that there should be a committee of distinguished personalities in British musical life—excluding performers. I returned to London happy about everything except the prospect of a committee to advise on programmes. As things turned out, it was only in the first year that the generous subvention would be paid in full.

The malign interference of the late Krishna Menon reduced the annual subvention to £5,000 after the first year and stopped it completely after two more years.

But the Maharajah's generosity bridged the period until the royalties from the Philharmonia's record sales were sufficient to maintain the orchestra without subvention. This sudden increase in royalties was the result of EMI's decision to establish its own selling organization in the United States. When EMI established its own American sales company, Angel Records, under Dario Soria and his wife, Dorle, our European production of highest-class English pressings rocketed to a leading place in the favour of discriminating American record buyers.

Already in 1951 Karajan had decided that in future he would record only with the Philharmonia in London and in 1952 we agreed that Europe must hear the Philharmonia. Neither the British Council nor any private person I approached would contribute to the costs, but Jane Withers and I had built up sufficient reserves to take the risk—concerts in Paris, Zürich, Basel, Geneva, Turin, Milan, Vienna, Munich, and Berlin. An hour before the Turin concert, which was being broadcast, the Contessa Castelbarco, Toscanini's daughter Wally, telephoned me to tell Karajan and the orchestra to play for all their worth: her father intended to listen but he would not be at either of the Milan concerts; he was having one of his habitual rows with the directors of La Scala. She knew that Cantelli and I, through mutual friends, had been lobbying to induce Toscanini to conduct the Philharmonia in London. The next day we had our first concert in La Scala—a fantastic triumph followed by a sumptuous supper given to the orchestra by Victor de Sabata who took me aside and said: "Your orchestra is the most wonderful English virgin. All she needs to achieve the ultimate perfection is to be raped by a hot-blooded Italian. I will do that for you." (Unfortunately his ill-health deprived the orchestra of that enriching experience.)

The next day, Elisabeth Schwarzkopf, now my wife, and I were invited to tea with Toscanini, who knew of my designs on him. We sat with his daughter over tea, then cocktails, for nearly three hours before the Maestro appeared. He immediately explained that he was too old to start work with an orchestra new to him, then suddenly asked me my opinion of certain of his records. Since Wally and Elisabeth were sitting beside me I could not see their faces but I could almost hear them drop: they knew I mince no words in musical matters. No words were minced. The Maestro fixed me with his hypnotic half-blind eyes, cross-questioned me on details of my opinions and grounds for my criticisms then to my relieved astonishment put his hands gently on my shoulders and said: "Figlio mio, you are right. I'll lend you some tests of my latest records. Come here tomorrow and tell me what you think of them."

That evening after the second La Scala concert we were changing and packing when Wally Toscanini telephoned that her father wanted to see me immediately. In the large drawing-room were Toscanini and about ten very old men. In a fortunate flash I sensed who they were—old and trusted colleagues of Toscanini's days in La Scala's orchestra who had been to the concert that evening and reported in detail on Philharmonia's playing. Toscanini came to the point: "I am not too old to conduct your orchestra. I will give six concerts in July and August. Now we make the programmes." We planned together a conspectus of works, many of which he had not conducted in London during his prewar concerts with the BBC Orchestra: Sibelius's Fourth Symphony, the *Symphony Fantastique*, among others in a cornucopia of masterpieces. Dennis Brain and Gareth Morris were patiently waiting for us to drive over the Gotthard Pass to Zürich. In our joy we overlooked the warning "Pass closed to traffic," but Dennis, with his matchless skill at the wheel, drove, slithered and skidded through deep snow and ice in our big old Hudson. From Zürich I telephoned Jane Withers, in London, to book the Royal Festival Hall for six dates, at least three, if possible four, days apart for six Toscanini concerts in July-August, 1952.

There was soon and evidently dirty work at the crossroads! The Royal Festival Hall was not available to me at all, not even for Toscanini during the period he wanted to come to London. The management of the Festival Hall had a private arrangement with the BBC not to let their hall for orchestral concerts which would be in competition with the BBC's Promenade Concerts in the Albert Hall. I flew back to London, but the musical Establishment in England, was doing all it knew to prevent my having the kudos of taking Toscanini to London, even though it meant depriving England of hearing the great

97

man. Eventually a compromise was reached. On his way to America, Toscanini gave two concerts (September 28 and October 1) with the Philharmonia, all Brahms—the four symphonies, the two overtures, and the *Haydn Variations*.

The concerts were announced as being jointly presented by the LCC, a well-known concert agent, and the Philharmonia Concert Society. Like the honours, the profits, as I remember, were also carved up, since the PCS appeared to receive only a third of them. I was too proud and happy to protest. After the second concert Toscanini embraced me, saying that if he were ten years younger he would have all his published records withdrawn and devote the rest of his life to recording his whole repertoire with me: I was the only man who had ever told him the truth about his work.

I am not an orchestral player, but I had an extraordinary experience almost the last time I saw him. Elisabeth and I were driving up from Milan to Zürich and passed by Palanza, where he lived on an island about sixty or seventy yards from the coast. He was very sensitive and I said that we had better just telephone because if he finds out that we have passed by and not saluted him he will either be hurt or very angry, probably both. There is a hotel opposite the island and Elisabeth went in to call and just say "hello" for both of us. She came back almost immediately. "His butler is coming over in a boat; the Maestro insists on seeing us." He seemed to love being completely alone, but if he had company he liked a lot of people around him. It was a big house and we looked in and saw one room with several people we knew—singers of the past and one or two singers of the present, who were at the moment engaged in Milan. We went into a smaller sitting room: there were two sofas, one either side of a low table, and he started, with a glowering brow, complaining, virtually cursing German and Austrian conductors who took Mozart two/fours, particularly the slow two/fours, beat four, instead of beating two, and he said, "Now I will show you the difference," and he would hum a Mozart two/four tune. "Now you sing it and follow my beat," and with his terribly penetrating eyes and this old slightly bent first finger, he conducted, first in four, then a slow two. And we had to sing. I understood in that moment why he had this power over orchestras. We compared notes afterward, and my wife and I both felt as if we had had steel belts around our waists, slightly elastic steel belts, which were held on to the point of that finger and that finger made it impossible to move more than the tiny liberty that he would allow you.

On his eighty-fifth birthday Toscanini gave a lunch party, with again a rather large gathering, and he asked us to stay and talk to him when the others had gone, and he said, "During the night I thought back over my career and my musical experiences. The happiest event was the rehearsal of Brahms's Second Symphony with your orchestra. Do you remember? I stopped only once, and that was to tell the oboe to play with exactly the same *espressivo—ma in tempo!* For the only time in my life I was simply a musician making music with other musicians."

The impact of these Toscanini concerts (there had been over 60,000 applications for the 6,000 seats) gave the musicians and the orchestra's fame an enormous boost. In 1953 the Philharmonia was in the Edinburgh Festival, this time with Karajan and Boult: with Karajan we played the concert inaugurating the new Casino at Ostende.

The year 1954 was a festival year: two concerts in the Aix Festival (at the second in Les Baux the mistral suddenly whisked the parts from the desks, leaving the orchestra to play the last pages of *La Mer* from memory!), then the whole of the Lucerne Festival (with Karajan, Furtwängler, Edwin Fischer, Kubelik, Fricsay and Cluytens), followed by six concerts in Edinburgh with Karajan and Cantelli and another European tour with Karajan—Belgium, Switzerland, and Italy (even down to Palermo). In 1955 there was the first United States tour, twenty-four concerts in twenty-eight days! This was our only subventioned tour; Angel records paid the fares and transport costs.

That year Wieland Wagner fought an unfortunately unsuccessful battle with the German Musicians' Union to have the Philharmonia Orchestra for the Bayreuth Festival, but we were in some measure compensated by opening the celebrations of Mozart's bicentenary in Salzburg followed by a tour in Germany, Switzerland, and France. Each year involved participation in continental festivals—Lucerne almost every year; Vienna with Klemperer, Giulini, and Krips; and in 1963 the opening concerts of the 150th anniversary of Verdi's birth at Parma, where the frenzied enthusiasm for both the orchestra and the Philharmonia Chorus was such that Giulini had to repeat the Sanctus of the Verdi *Requiem* as an encore. As a farewell the chorus of the Parma Opera serenaded my orchestra and chorus as they assembled in their buses with "Va pensiero." An emotional tribute and occasion for British musicians, professional and amateur, on Verdi's homeground.

From the early days of our friendship I had sensed that Karajan's ambition and intention were to succeed Furtwängler as director of the Berlin Philharmonic, a life appointment, the most desirable and eminent position for a conductor in European musical life. It was evident long before Furtwängler's death that Karajan would be Berlin's inevitable choice even though Furtwängler had obsessively prevented Karajan from conducting his orchestra. I knew, too, that from the moment of his appointment to Berlin, Karajan would concentrate on the Berlin Philharmonic for his concerts, tours, and recordings. In short, I had to build up in the ears and eyes of the London public other conductors to work with me maintaining the sound and virtuosity as well as the purely musical standards we had established. I had already tried several distinguished conductors without finding what I wanted.

For the Philharmonia's two concerts in the Festival of Britain, Schnabel had been engaged: the Festival's promoters however declined Karajan. I asked Szell, who was not free, but in discussion with him and Schnabel the latter suggested Klemperer. I followed their advice. Schnabel became too ill to play the concerts; Solomon and Myra Hess deputized for him. I heard only the last movement of the *Jupiter* Symphony from the wings. At the end of the concert Marie Wilson came off the platform in tears. "I feel like a tart taking money from you for making music with that man." A severe fracture from a fall at a Canadian airport delayed the accident-prone Titan's return to London and left me more than ever preoccupied with covering the orchestra in depth with suitable conductors. I wanted Guido Cantelli, but his London impresario insisted on having the Philharmonia and presenting Cantelli's concerts himself; the main thing was that Cantelli was a great conductor and good for the Philharmonia, the only British orchestra he would work with.

I had great hopes for Sawallisch when he first went to Aachen: a beat as clear and uncomplicated as Knappertsbusch's, a quick learner, a better pianist than any greatly gifted conductor had the right to be, and exceptionally sensitive ears for balance and texture. Unfortunately London did not take to him, but he inherited Knappertsbusch's musical directorship of the Munich Opera, where he displayed a unique sense

100

of his proper duties by engaging the best of his colleagues to conduct the works in which they specialize.

De Sabata was already ailing when he appointed the then unknown Giulini as his assistant at La Scala. I went to his first rehearsal. The tall, distinguished, youngish man was getting a much better than usual sound from the orchestra and holding the player's attention. His spacious beat suggested de Sabata's influence. I telephoned Karajan to come at once; I had found a conductor! In a few minutes he was sitting beside me in the stage-box watching like a lynx. At the end of the rehearsal we went to make Giulini's acquaintance, congratulate him, and promise him any help he might need. What he most needed, as I later discovered, was a repertoire: he learned slowly, even reluctantly.

From the Ghedini-Pizzetti desiccating school, he was shy of even Verdi except *Falstaff* and the *Requiem*; he was shocked by Puccini and had conducted little Mozart, Haydn, or Beethoven. By shuffling his specialities his useful attractive concert repertoire was sufficient for only three or four concerts a season. The Verdi *Requiem* he conducted superbly, and it became an annual event on the Philharmonia Concert Society's programmes and a guarantee of a full house. One season, four very celebrated conductors each tried to make it a condition of accepting engagements that they should conduct the Verdi *Requiem*: I was impelled to tell them that I would put on that work in all Philharmonia's 30 RFH concerts with the same soloists and thirty different conductors starting the series with Giulini! But he almost succeeded in popularizing the *Quatro Pezzi Sacri*. He invariably made the Philharmonia play very well: his recording of Ravel's *Alborada del Gracioso* is a *locus classicus* of orchestral virtuosity and distinguished taste.

When Lorin Maazel rehearsed concerts for the Gulbenkian Festival in Portugal I was much taken with his musicianship, style, penetrating intelligence, technical mastery, and repertoire. After long ponderings I decided to offer him a contract as second string to Klemperer with succession to the senior position when the time came. I even consulted de Sabata, whose judgment was reliable and who, unlike other great conductors, feared no rival and always gave honest and considered counsel. He rated Maazel very highly. Unfortunately Maazel wanted more money and authority than I was prepared to give him, and we reluctantly agreed to disagree.

Klemperer had suffered many lean years when he was finally able to work seriously and regularly with the Philharmonia. Manic-depressive by nature, his successful career had been interrupted in Germany by the political situation there: within months of being awarded the Goethe Medal he became the Wandering Jew, although like Bruno Walter before him, he had long been converted to Catholicism. His years in America had won him much respect but meagre reward, much suffering and near poverty. After the war, Aladár Todt (husband of Annie Fischer and one of Bartók's earlier champions) became director of the Budapest Opera. Todt, a remarkably sensitive musician and a gentle, wise man, appointed Klemperer Generalmusikdirektor. Those who experienced those years, storm-racked by Klemperer's malady, speak with awe of that Klemperer era. But his illness drove him out and again luck was against him.

After a poorly attended concert in Milan, he explained that the renewal of his American passport (he had taken American citizenship in the 1930s) depended on his returning there that winter. Did I think he should return or could he make a living in Europe? He was in a trough of depression, maimed, but very clear-thinking. I advised him to stay in Europe, promised him enough concerts with the Philharmonia to ensure him £2,000 a year and slowly increasing royalties if his records were liked. He decided to stay in Europe, making his home in Zürich. Years later he told a friend: "If it had not been for Legge no dog would have given me bread."

He was not an easy man to know or approach and I was warned that I was asking for trouble. Having been the buffer between Karajan's ambitions and Furtwängler's insensate jealousy I felt able to cope. From the first concerts and recordings in October 1954 we worked harmoniously together. His stern authority and magisterial command, his extraordinary power of communication of his musical intentions despite his physical handicaps were respected and much liked by the musicians, who also treasured his cruel, mordant wit.

His best work was invariably done when he was in the depression stage of his malady when for me at least he was open to discussion, suggestion, even criticism of tempi, texture, and sonority; ready to argue and, if convinced, cooperate. At the other extreme he was stubborn, irresponsible, and euphorically delighted with whatever he had done, completely lacking in self-criticism.

His powerful sense of musical form left little place for elegant phrasing, sensuous beauty of sound, or charm in either line or texture. He was the musician of the Ten Commandments carved in granite.

Even in the years of his greatest triumphs, which were with the Philharmonia, he suffered physical setbacks which would have killed any man of less will. In retrospect I sometimes regret that in an unguarded moment of sympathy I appointed him principal conductor for life when he had recovered after his long fight back from accidental self-immolation. But for this, I might have retained his friendship after I had to suspend the Philharmonia.

By 1961, I began to be seriously concerned about the future not only of the Philharmonia but of musical life in London. I had been invited to join the board of directors of Covent Garden in 1959 not, I believe, because they knew they needed my expertise and experience but because Lord Drogheda had been led to believe that I was advising Klemperer and my wife (Elisabeth Schwarzkopf) not to appear at Covent Garden. This was not true. When I accepted the invitation and before attending any meeting I explained that the basis of a first-class opera house today is a first-class orchestra. Covent Garden's was not. The healthy solution would be to engage the Philharmonia and the Royal Philharmonic or the London Symphony Orchestra to share the work equally. With those excellent orchestras in the pit they would immediately raise Covent Garden's standards.

The only important contribution I was allowed to make was at, I believe, the first meeting I attended. Lord Harewood announced that Joan Sutherland was to sing *Lucia di Lammermoor* at Covent Garden in English. I urged that since Lord Astor was willing to give £5,000 a year to be spent at the board's discretion Sutherland should learn the part in Italian (in which language she would be able to sing the opera in any important theatre in the world), go to Italy to study it with Tullio Serafin and engage him to conduct the performances. The suggestion was accepted and Sutherland was most successfully launched on her great career. I cannot recall that any other suggestion of mine was accepted.

The experience of an Establishment board at work, an assembly of men distinguished and justly famous in their particular fields of activity but innocent amateurs on musical matters, filled me with horror, a sensation they no doubt experienced at my every utterance.

The cuckoo in the nest of that acoustic miscarriage, the Royal

Festival Hall, was the general manager, T. E. Bean. Obsessed with "organization" he began what he called "rationalizing" programmes. His aim was apparently to determine each conductor's programmes. The bait for submitting to this unwarrantable intrusion was an annual subvention of—as far as I remember—£10,000 a year, the acceptance of which also obliged the recipient to engage three British conductors each season. Bean was capable of devising the kind of programmes that any conductor worth his salt or fee rejected or audiences would have dwindled and the subvention gone down the drain of empty seats taking some Philharmonia capital with it. He had evidently not heard the story of the Scot, the Irishman and the Jew who decided to build a large acoustically perfect concert hall—no ferro concrete—each participating equally in costs and profits. When the hall was finished except for the seat-coverings there was the first dispute: the Scot insisted on Black Watch tartan, the Irishman on Kerrygreen linen. The Jew had the last and wisest word: "Those seats will all be covered with bottoms."

I did not at the time need the subvention nor Bean's programme building but when warning came that the hall might not be available to the Philharmonia Concert Society unless I accepted their conditions I had to give way. The woodworms of official interference had begun to bore into Philharmonia's fabric. Soon other difficulties loomed. EMI decided to curtail its classical recording programme; the Beatles were more immediately profitable than Bach, Beethoven, and Brahms. The BBC had successfully raided the Philharmonia of a few vital players by inducements of higher fees for less work. And worst of all the Philharmonia playing was not what it had been.

Karajan had rejuvenated and polished the Berlin Philharmonic to superior virtuosity, beauty of sound, and depth of sonority. He had a marvellous group of double-basses all with five-stringed instruments: if I had raided all the orchestras of Britain taking their first-desk basses they would not have made a foundation comparable with the Berliners'. The only way I could see of stopping the rot was to go to America and try to collect from the leading recording companies sufficient work to keep the Philharmonia fully employed and refreshed with the infusion of new conducting blood. I could not do this with clean conscience without resigning from EMI, which I did at the end of June 1963—giving them the contractual twelve months' notice which they seemed to regard merely as a ploy. The American companies were not interested, and I returned empty handed.

For four months I sought other solutions and found none. Ted Greenfield, then a political correspondent on *The Guardian*, lobbied Harold Wilson and Edward Heath without avail. Jane Withers and I found sufficient work to keep the players profitably employed until September 1964. I had no reason to worry about the Philharmonia players' finding other engagements; for sixteen years it had been legendary in the orchestral profession, "If you have survived three months working for Legge you can get a first-class job in any orchestra." At one time ex-rank-and-file Philharmonia violinists were leading six other orchestras.

Having agreed with Klemperer and his daughter the text of the press announcement of the indefinite suspension of the orchestra I called a meeting of its committee and broke the grim news to them. Copies of the press statement had been posted to the members of the orchestra but unfortunately not all the letters arrived before they read their morning papers. Klemperer later denied that he knew anything about my decision or the announcement.

There was still work to be done—particularly *Messiah* with Klemperer and *Die Zauberflöte*, which was the first complete opera I had produced for HMV and planned to be the last opera I should produce for EMI. The cast was as perfect as the world's vocal resources could yield: Janowitz, Popp, Schwarzkopf, Ludwig, Gedda, Berry, Crass, Unger, and the rest to match. The day before the cast assembled Klemperer sent word that he would not allow me to be present at the piano rehearsals. Consoling myself with a paraphrase of Loge's plaint "Immer war Undank Legges Lohn," I wired Klemperer that I would never set foot inside a building where he was conducting. I kept my promise.

In the years since then I have not ceased to regret the accumulation of circumstances that made inevitable the end of the best orchestra Britain ever had. I deplore the fact that in the years of Philharmonia's greatest glory (1951–1962) the English critics had poisoned the public taste for Richard Strauss, Sibelius, and Elgar, three composers I much admire and which the orchestra could have played supremely well. The programmes may have been considered conservative by composers I left unplayed, but a great performance of a masterpiece has always been more important to me than the world premiere of a "novelty." Besides the *Uraufführung* of Strauss's *Vier letzte Lieder* by Flagstad (with the music in her hands) and Furtwängler, we gave the first

British performances of the closing scene of *Capriccio* and Anne True-love's arias from Stravinsky's *The Rake's Progress*. These works will last.

I must not close this account of Philharmonia's history without paying tribute to some of the great artists who contributed to its glories: Dennis Brain, who raised the horn to his lips and, by example, the standard of horn-playing throughout the world, and his successor Alan Civil; Jim Bradshaw, the tympanist with perfect intonation, rhythm, and variety of tone who insisted that tympani are melodic instruments and accurately forecast changes in the weather "because ah can feel it in me timps"; Clem Lawton, the tuba player who played Strauss's First Horn Concerto at his audition and the trill in the *Meistersinger* overture with a nightingale's beauty, smoothness, speed, and ease. The remarkable woodwind known in the profession as "Legge's royal flush"— Arthur Gleghorn on piccolo, Gareth Morris as first flute, Jock Sutcliffe, the incredibly sensitive oboist phrasing with profoundly musical line and inflection; the succession of clarinetists—Reg Kell, Jack Thurston, and Bernard Walton; and the bassoonist Gwydian Brooke, who arrived looking like a man from Mars and played like an emissary from Heaven. And two concertmasters, Manoug Parikian and Hugh Bean. Philharmonia was also a nursery for some now-famous conductors—Raymond Leppard, Neville Marriner, and Norman Del Mar.

Looking through the programmes of those years, I am proud that I gave London a golden age of musical performance which may never be surpassed. I ran the Philharmonia as a benevolent dictatorship. Democracy has no place in the arts; the word *democracy*, as it is presently misused, is a euphemism for deterioration.

Walter's parents on holiday early in their marriage (*right*). Young Walter with his mother (*below*) and fifty years later at a La Scala premier.

EMI produced a legendary series of recordings with Edwin Fischer (*right*) and Albert Schweitzer (*below*). Walter became life-long friends with both of these giants.

"I am going to marry the most beautiful woman in Europe," Walter wrote to an American friend, and Ernest Newman (*opposite, bottom*) gave us our wedding. Perhaps Walter was thinking of me as the Marschallin (*left*) or Elvira (*below, with* Walter at La Scala). What he got (*bottom*) was very different!

Many famous conductors were to conduct Philharmonia: Furtwängler (*opposite, top*), Giulini (*opposite, middle*), and Klemperer (*opposite, bottom*), to mention only three. Walter also engaged promising younger men: Maazel (*left*) and Schippers (*bottom*). The Maharajah of Mysore (*below*), a young Indian nobleman, put the orchestra on a firm financial footing.

One of Walter's closest friends was the great conductor Wolfgang Sawallisch (shown here greeting Walter at the Sawallisch home outside Munich). A virtuoso pianist, Sawallisch made his London debut accompanying me in my first recital there. As *Generalmusikdirektor,* the Bavarian State Opera, he is one of the strongest supporters of young talent in the musical world.

All of my own recordings were supervised by Walter. The *William Tell* aria we are discussing (*opposite, top left*) was dropped from the final recording. Not good enough! Walter, Gerald Moore, and I spent many happy hours striving for, and sometimes attaining, perfection in recording the songs of Hugo Wolf.

With Lucerne Festival director Dr. Strebi, we listen to pianist Dinu Lipatti rehearse with Philharmonia. I often photographed such events myself. Walter recorded the Beethoven Violin Concerto with David Oistrakh and Maestro André Cluytens (*center*). The Champagne Recordings were a brilliant series of operetta on disc. *The Merry Widow* was recorded twice, this time with Gedda, Steffek, and myself, with Matačić.

Musical alter egos: Walter Legge and Herbert von Karajan.

# 4

# THE
# AUTOCRAT
# OF THE TURNTABLE
Legge in the Studio  EDWARD GREENFIELD

*The distinguished British critic and musicologist Edward Green-field often observed Walter in the recording studio. At my request, Ted supplied the following recollections of some of those "events," which those of us who took part in them certainly felt they always were.*

"I WAS the Pope of recording," said Walter Legge to me in a candid but frustrated moment. The time was the mid-1960's, during his early years of exile not just from London musical life but from the world of recording. He continued to act as recording producer for Elisabeth Schwarzkopf's records, but the enormous range of record-making that marked his years with EMI was gone forever. In my meeting with him on that occasion he went on to lament that no one in the industry wanted to employ him any longer. I felt compelled—though it hardly made him any happier—to point out an obvious moral: no one employs the Pope.

For Pope of recording he was, a figure who brought together qualities in a unique combination: part impresario and musical dictator, part musicologist, part inspirer, part socialiser and bon viveur, part technician but above all enthusiastic music-lover and the possessor of acute ears, the ideal appreciator and listener. Others may have excelled him in certain aspects of the craft of making records, but his peculiar combination of qualities turned that craft into an art. As he says himself in his own autobiographical note he was the first real producer of records, the first who treated the record as more than a "sound photograph." In his aim of making records that would set standards for the future he used every weapon in his armoury, created the role of record producer and has so far defied any successor to match him.

As I know myself from the sessions I attended, a recording supervised by Walter Legge was invariably an occasion. It was partly his presence that created the atmosphere of expectancy and tension (of the right kind). In the control room—it was usually Kingsway Hall where I saw him at work in the semi-basement vestry behind the stage—he would sit on a podium surveying the room in front of him, a presiding genius, as often as not puffing on a large cigar. The effect of his presence—and his arrival in a rehearsal of his Philharmonia Orchestra could be electrically felt—was a challenge which went along with the natural musical challenge between artists carefully chosen. When great artists work together, whether in the concert hall, opera house, or recording studio, greatness adds to greatness, and the assemblage of the right people was for Legge a first essential involving long preparation and hard work. It was Legge who first insisted in major opera recordings on giving even the small roles to major artists, and the expense of that policy was one of the causes of friction which led in 1963 to his resignation from EMI. He did not repent. In the late sixties when Schwarzkopf was recording Mozart concert arias with George Szell and the London Symphony Orchestra, I remember congratulating him on getting Alfred Brendel to play the piano solo in "Ch'io mi scordi di te?" Pleased, he noted "the touch of luxury" it gave.

In his preparations, lining up the casts of major projects such as opera recordings, the factors affecting Walter Legge were no different from those which always beset producers, then and now: what was distinctive was that as an impresario, founder of a great orchestra, husband of a great singer, he approached even the most celebrated artists on very different terms from those which limit most recording producers. The very fact that Legge was known as a king-maker in the recording world—even Karajan's rise owes much to his Philharmonia period, and Klemperer might well have remained undeservedly neglected had it not been for Legge—made it easier for him to persuade the artists he wanted to take part in his projects. His experience signing up artists for EMI on his first postwar trip to Vienna in 1946 was a prime example of his flair, and gave him a hunter's guile when the artist in question did not immediately capitulate. The celebrated story of Schwarzkopf's refusal to sign a contract immediately on the grounds that she did not want him to buy "a cat in a sack," insisting on an audition, was a very special case. So was that of Maria Callas, who, at a crucial and difficult period in both her artistic and her private life, hesitated over signing a contract with EMI, but was persuaded finally by Legge. From then on until his resignation from EMI, he was the producer for Callas, one who guarded her and guided her in the studio at a time when technical problems came to beset her, and who helped to draw from her a uniquely vibrant series of opera recordings. Attending the editing sessions for the second of the Callas à Paris recital records, I remember a series of unsuccessful takes on a Massenet item, resolved finally in a single superb take which at Legge's suggestion had been taken at a fractionally faster tempo. It would not have married with any of the earlier takes, had editing been needed, but Legge's finesse succeeded triumphantly at a moment in the session when the diva was growing tired and frustrated.

Preparations nearer the time of sessions on a big project were just as thorough as the initial planning stage. Being occupied in so many fields, not just as a recording producer, Legge insisted on having an assistant of the highest calibre on his sessions. With his assistant— for many years Walter Jellinek, later Suvi Raj Grubb, who at the end of the Legge era graduated to the role of recording producer himself—he would draw up in good time a schedule of sessions. In that, his long experience of organising big projects was an enormous help. He may have acquired the reputation for being a dictator and taskmaster, but as a lover of singing and the voice he knew very well the limits to which any individual singer could be driven in the taxing work which recording involves.

As one who had his clear image of perfection, and sought to achieve it without compromise, he still took the greatest care to draw up a schedule which would allow each artist consistently to sing full out. It meant—as it should for recording producers today—that schedules had to take into account not only the other commitments of individual singers but their need to spread the load over a series of sessions. Thoughtfully he would try to put ensembles after a solo session, so that a particular soloist would still be available to do a retake of a major solo item if necessary. But schedules once worked out would then be followed with an exactness which latter-day recording producers might very well envy. Like all producers he knew that if the temptation to vary the schedule was indulged too freely, then problems tended to escalate. It was an enormous help in the studio that—as Suvi Raj Grubb has put it—his supreme confidence in controlling any crisis radiated itself to those around him, including above all the artists. If Legge was counted by EMI as an expensive producer, it was rather because he chose artists of the highest calibre, not because he often required extra sessions, and many in the industry will now tell you that the difference in overall fees against the total cost for a big project is relatively small, whether it is the best possible cast or a penny-pinching one.

The stage of preparation immediately before a major recording project generally took place at Legge's North London house in Oakhill Avenue, Hampstead. There, in the music room, he would supervise piano rehearsals. It was at his house too that he would entertain all the major artists, and a conductor like Karajan would frequently be staying as the guest of the Legges. That factor alone put Legge on a different footing when he talked to artists. He himself, with long experience of the major areas of repertory, caring passionately, often had very positive ideas on interpretation. It made an important difference being in a position to state them without giving offence, if necessary to argue them from personal strength as a friend. A positive artist like Karajan or Dietrich Fischer-Dieskau might very well counter what Legge suggested, but Legge's word, particularly if it had a bearing on the presentation of an interpretation on record as such, was not easily ignored.

Paradoxically the very fact that he had not completed a formal musical training seemed to make him the more acute as a commentator on interpretation and performance. He worked as a music critic himself early in his career. William Mann, chief music critic of the *Times* in London, wrote in his obituary of Legge in the May 1979 edition of *Gramophone* magazine: "As a musical coach, he was nonpareil, able to realise the potential and artistic viewpoints of other musicians by his deep understanding of scores, and his feeling for the particular quality of each artist's musical personality. That, he was eventually to realise, represented his particular creative musicianship amid the musical life of his time." The culminating example of that achievement must be in the guidance he gave to his wife, Elisabeth Schwarzkopf.

110

Both of them perfectionists, they actually delighted in the tough-talking of preparation and rehearsed to a degree that made others marvel.

One of the first recording sessions of Walter Legge that I myself attended was when Carlo Maria Giulini conducted the Philharmonia Orchestra in Dvorak's *New World* Symphony. In a work which the conductor had not in fact directed in the concert hall, Legge's long experience of getting that music recorded spiced the detailed discussion after each take. Without hectoring an artist for whom he had the highest regard—indeed he did more than anyone to get Giulini appreciated on record, well before his worldwide acclaim—Legge talked in terms which would have been impossible for any other producer.

The relationship was, of course, different with each artist. A few months later when I went to sessions in which Klemperer was conducting Schubert symphonies, the crucial coffee-break and play-back saw me being ushered out of the sanctum of the control room and Legge having a private tête-à-tête with the maestro. Legge later, during further takes, noted points which he himself had suggested, but Klemperer was less easily swayed than younger colleagues, and there is the celebrated story, well authenticated, of when he was recording Beethoven's *Pastoral* Symphony with the Philharmonia Orchestra. Klemperer rehearsed the third movement scherzo of the peasants' merrymaking, adopting a tempo far slower than usual. After a while Legge came through on the phone from the control room, suggesting to the old man that it might be too slow. Klemperer wryly gave the answer direct: "Walter, you will get used to it!" and continued on his deliberately merry way. After a few more minutes it was Klemperer who picked up the phone, asking: "Walter, have you got used to it yet?"

Not many artists could tease Walter Legge like that, but with him Legge relished it, and even more he relished retaining anecdotes from and about Klemperer, whom he could impersonate to perfection, exactly imitating the old man's creaky voice. In this instance of the *Pastoral* Symphony, Legge was in principle quite right about the movement being dangerously slow, but it was his doing as well as Klemperer's that the distinctive reading was caught at full tension. To this day it remains one of the supreme versions of this much-recorded work, while an earlier less idiosyncratic version which Klemperer recorded for Vox is understandably forgotten. Klemperer could not resist the temptation to tease in that instance, but invariably what Legge said and the

111

way he said it immediately commanded respect, a point which came out
when Arturo Toscanini asked Legge direct what he thought of his New
York recording of Verdi's *La Traviata*. The honesty of Legge's reply
on the excessively fast speeds was one of the factors which led to the
Toscanini's tribute to him—that if he were younger he would withdraw all his recordings and re-record the entire repertory with Legge.

It was during actual sessions in the studio that the role of the
assistant recording producer proved most valuable of all, and in this
both Walter Jellinek and Suvi Raj Grubb worked with complete harmony. On one level they undertook a number of time-consuming
chores that beset a recording manager. As well as following the score
at a table in front of Legge, they would keep the detailed record of
takes. That meant that during the crucial editing process they would
regularly be able to present a series of clear-cut decisions on questionable point which had already been clearly defined. Legge's pinpoint
memory ensured that each decision was sharply related to context, was
never arbitrary.

It was a consistent help having a second pair of highly perceptive
musical ears on hand during the takes. Very frequently the engineer
can be of musical as well as technical help, but Legge's way helped
him to achieve what most recording producers would recognise as an
ideal middle way, for there are almost invariably two opposite dangers
during recording takes. On the one hand the producer can become
so engrossed in following detail, and making sure, nose in score, that
every note is correct, that he will fail to appreciate whether the performance has "taken off" in terms of musical communication. On the
other hand during a project, often undertaken against the clock with
musical excitement built up, it is very easy for the producer to get
swept away and to fail to notice detailed errors which would be dis-
turbing on repeated hearings. In Suvi Raj Grubb's view it was Legge's
long experience of recording particular works coupled with his care
over preparing himself beforehand that gave him the ability while
registering the communicative quality of a performance as a general
listener acutely to register detailed flaws simultaneously. So during a
take he might suddenly sit up with some such instruction as "Check
five after B," preferring not to stop and analyse until later, the flow
of the music always important.

On certain technical matters too his long experience was of enormous help, particularly with works he had recorded many times before. He would anticipate what lines in a score could easily be ob-

scured, and what effects might give the engineer trouble. For example if two women are singing in thirds, the vibrato often catches the microphones oddly, but Legge had worked out that separating the soloists avoids that problem. In all this the EMI engineers played a vital part, as Legge himself would agree when talking of such former colleagues as Chick Fowler, W. S. Barrell, and Bob Beckett, not to mention Christopher Parker, who is still with EMI, the senior engineer. With such helpers Legge was able to achieve standards of an excellence recognisable to this day, when niceties of balance are often less important than extended frequency range. As Legge wrote to me in a letter in 1977, "I maintained that I was making tapes which would sell as records for twenty or thirty years or more and sound better when the originals were subjected to better transferring and played on the reproducing apparatus of the future." The current flow of reissues from Legge's EMI days in the 1950's and early 1960's certainly confirms his success in that, and will continue to do so. One might cite for example Karajan's 1958 recording with the Philharmonia Orchestra of an orchestral showpiece which one normally expects to require the ultimate in high fidelity, Respighi's *The Pines of Rome*. In many ways it outshines even the most recent versions.

Legge, with his acute ears, took a keen interest in technical development. At Bayreuth in the early 1950's he noted that the Decca engineers in the next control room—with whom he did not personally fraternise, be it said—were getting better results than he was, and shrewdly he deduced that the reason lay in the microphones they were using. In the face of opposition from his head office in Hayes, he went out and with his own money bought similar microphones himself, with great success. Nonetheless he always kept in mind that high fidelity is only the servant of music and not an end in itself. He was not an innovator in this field for innovation's sake, and remained curiously suspicious of the benefits of stereo. He would often cite his mono recording of Humperdinck's *Hänsel und Gretel*, conducted by Karajan, as an example of mono sound matching anything stereo can offer. In Act 2, scene 1, when the children are lost in the forest, Legge was able magically to capture the distant echoes by clever placing in the studio. In that instance the atmospheric quality of his mono sound still matches that of modern stereo, but it is sad that during the transition period before stereo was fully accepted, Legge would often not pay sufficient attention to the stereo takes, which were recorded in another control room. Thus the classic recording of Strauss's last

113

opera, *Capriccio,* with Sawallisch conducting and Schwarzkopf as the
Countess, made as late as 1958, had to remain in mono only.

Legge was not in fact infallible. When he learnt from a Decca
colleague that that company was attempting the first recording of
Wagner's *Rheingold* in Vienna with Solti conducting, he predicted
that it "would not sell." In fact it was a runaway classical best-seller.
Some might criticise him for encouraging British artists too little, tending to prefer among singers stars from abroad. But he gave Joan
Sutherland her first major operatic role on record as Donna Anna in
the Giulini recording of Mozart's *Don Giovanni,* and it was not for his
want of trying that she signed a contract with Decca rather than EMI,
even if there was an obvious problem of a repertory clash with Callas.
One might note too that he gave the emergent Janet Baker a solo
role in Klemperer's recording of Mendelssohn's *Midsummer Night's
Dream* music alongside Heather Harper, both of them making their
first records for a big company. One might also point out that he
succeeded in creating an orchestra of world class, arguably the finest in
the world, in a country which had no long orchestral tradition.

Undeniably he could be arrogant, whether in the studio or outside, but Suvi Raj Grubb as his closest colleague for many years had
nothing but admiration for his supreme confidence in himself and the
sureness with which he sought, and usually achieved, his dream of
perfection. Here is a typical Legge memo to Grubb after listening to
the lacquers of a Schwarzkopf recital album. Legge was no longer with
EMI and had to supervise the final product from Switzerland.

S. R. Grubb, Esq.
EMI Ltd.
20 Manchester Square
London, W.1.                                         5th April 1965

Dear Suvi,
    Attached our comments which I would like you to observe as if I
were sitting beside you and would sit on your head if you did not
do what I want.
    Please send pressings for E.S.'s approval.
    Kindest regards to you both.
                                    Yours.

P.S. *Urgent:* Please send lacquers of unapproved "Wiegenlied"
("Schlafe, schlafe") and "Die Forelle." Also two copies of the
Schwarzkopf/Moore recital record.

## ELISABETH SCHWARZKOPF HUGO WOLF LACQUER
### 1109 ICS Side 1 & 2

**SIDE I**

Band a) o.k.
    b) o.k.
    c) Reduce 2 DB vol. and 2 DB top.
    d) sounds hard, ease top in transferring; *particularly first verse.*
    e) Heavyish tape noise, try to reduce. Reduce aggressive top.
    f) as (e)
    g) This sounds constricted and thin: consult E.F. about warming the sound. Certainly ease the top. Here it is *shrill.*
    h) o.k.
    i) o.k. All songs should match *this.* Please transfer this song to side 2.

**SIDE II**

Band a) o.k.
    b) perfect.
    Increase gap by 4 seconds. This is the end of the opus.
    c) o.k.
    d) If this can be transferred 2 DBs up without distortion do it.
    e) Open up: this is constricted. And 2 DB louder.
    f) Change of tape noise at edit. Add bass to warm up the whole thing.
    g) 2 DB less volume.
    h) *Nachtzauber.* Leave this song out from the record. The diction is not clear enough.
    i) *Die Zigeunerin.* This sounds *horrid.* Hard and bathroomy. Leave this out of the record.

As an exacting taskmaster he regularly—as with Grubb—attracted deep and lasting loyalties, and with those he trusted and respected there was no doubting the kindness behind the aggressive façade. Without the positive, thrustful side of his character he would certainly not have been able to achieve the results he did in whatever musical field, but above all in the legacy of recordings which, for all the diversity of repertory and musical approach from many great performers, have a stamp that is Legge's own. He rejected the idea of the record as a "sound photograph" partly because that implies something inanimate. With Legge more than any previous producer it became impossible to dismiss the record as a mere substitute for music. The trademark of his records is that almost invariably they convey musical life and vigour, the fulfilment of an artist's work, and that is a quality unlikely to fade, however sound reproduction develops in the future.

# 5

# TITTA RUFFO

*Walter's studios in "exile" from where he either wrote or dictated, were—I am happy to say—always lovely. In Geneva at our "Petit Port" alongside the lake, it was a little pavilion right in the middle of Walter's rose garden, which he had planted with so much care. In Cap-Ferrat, it was a lovely room on the second story, overlooking the Mediterranean. There he would write, for eight hours at a clip. Walter's piece on Titta Ruffo, dated 1928, must have been his first published article. He was twenty-two then. Three years later came his Society Series and his annotations to the three Da Ponte operas, Giovanni, Figaro, and Così, as performed at the brand new Glyndebourne Festival. From this early piece it is already clear what Walter felt recordings could accomplish.*

TITTA RUFFO, the world-famous operatic baritone, was born at Pisa on June 9th, 1877. He was the fifth of the six children of Oreste Titta, owner of a small iron foundry. When Ruffo was three, his family moved to a larger foundry in Rome. In this city Ruffo was educated. Owing to his aptitude for modeling and drawing, Oreste Titta intended that his gifted son should enter his business as a designer, so Ruffo entered Rome University to study metalwork designing. At fifteen, however, he conceived a passion for music, and spent much leisure at concerts and the opera. A performance of *La Favorita* at the Quirino deeply impressed him, after which his brother, Ettore, a Conservatoire student, hearing him sing "Spirto gentil," and struck by the beauty of his voice, casually told Ruffo that he ought to have it trained. Later Stagno and Bellicioni in *Cavalleria Rusticana* so stirred Ruffo's imagination that he asked paternal sanction to enter the Conservatoire. This being withheld, he secretly went to a friend in Albano, but he was soon traced and persuaded to return home. He completed his metal-designing course the

117

same year, taking highest honours. He won an open competition for designing the wrought ironwork for the mausoleum of President Carnot.

Still determined to be a singer, he persuaded his father to let him apply for admission to the Conservatoire de Santa Cecilia. He was accepted, and studied singing with Persichini, teacher of Battistini, and declamation with Virginia Marini. Contemporary with him were his sister, Fosca, a dramatic soprano who made her début as Leonora in *Il Trovatore*, with Ruffo as Di Luna, and Giuseppe De Luca. From the outset there was a dispute as to the timbre of Ruffo's voice, the master insisting it was bass, whilst the pupil maintained it was baritone. Dissatisfied with his tuition, Ruffo went to Milan, where he applied to Mingardi, artistic director of La Scala, who obtained for him a hearing at the Costanzi, Rome. An engagement resulting, Ruffo made a successful début as The Herald in *Lohengrin* shortly before his twenty-first birthday. Soon afterwards he sang his first big part, Di Luna in *Il Trovatore*, at Livorno. A tour of Southern Italy and Sicily followed, and he scored his first great success as Nelusko in *L'Africana* at Salerno in 1899. Between 1900 and 1905 he sang at the principal South American opera-houses and in nearly all European capitals, becoming an especial favourite with the hypercritical audiences of St. Petersburg, Odessa, and Warsaw.

Ruffo's London début was made at Covent Garden on June 5th, 1903, as Enrico in *Lucia di Lammermoor* with Bonci and Erika Wedekind. His next appearance was on July 1st as Figaro in *Il Barbiere*, on which occasion Maria Barrientos, then only nineteen, made her début. Bonci, Journet, and Gilibert were also in the cast; but on neither occasion did Ruffo's performance attract much attention. He was first heard at La Scala in 1905 as Rigoletto, with Anselmi as the Duke. His success was complete, as he sang the part frequently that season. He was engaged as principal baritone and sang in the first Italian production of *Le Jongleur de Notre Dame*. Paris (1907–08) was the scene of some striking early triumphs. In the Sarah Bernhardt Theatre, with Caruso, Selma Kurz, Chaliapin, and other operatic stars, he sang—in addition to his usual Italian repertoire—Giordano's *Fedora* and *Siberia*.

Idolised by South America, Ruffo was chosen to appear at the inception of the Colon Opera House, Buenos Aires, in 1909. *Hamlet*—one of his most successful roles—was the opera, as it also was when he opened the Municipale, São Paulo, and the Real, Havana. The majority of his operatic appearances are now at the Chicago and Metropolitan Opera Houses. At the latter he made his North American début as Rigoletto on November 4th, 1912. Never has a more enthusiastic reception been accorded any artist, and in America his popularity is comparable only to Caruso's. Throughout the war he served in the Italian forces as an aviator.

Ruffo is remembered by English music-lovers almost entirely by the three concerts he gave in the summer of 1922. At his first concert at Queen's Hall on May 5th he was assisted by Yvonne D'Arle. From his first phrase the audience was vanquished by the overwhelming beauty of his voice—manly, broad, sympathetic, of unsurpassed richness. Such ease of production, such an abundance of ringing high Gs! But more: Ruffo's infinite subtlety, varied tone-colour, interpretative insight and sincerity, his magnificent control, stupendous breathing powers, and impeccable phrasing stamped him as a genius.

His greatest successes have been in roles which, for their ideal presentation, make the utmost demands on both vocal and histrionic powers. Rigoletto, Iago, and Figaro are considered his finest parts, and in less familiar works Nelusko, Renato, Hamlet, and Gerard. In America he is inseparably bound up with *Andrea Chénier,* for his electrifying realism as Gerard has given that work a permanent place in the Metropolitan repertoire. There is little doubt that the popularity Giordano's works enjoy is largely due to the vividness with which Ruffo has portrayed his villains. *Siberia,* now almost forgotten, was a definite success when Ruffo sang in it at Paris. Giordano's latest opera, *La Cena della Beffe,* founded on Sem Benelli's play, was in Italy a comparative failure; yet, thanks to Ruffo's artistry, the American première in January 1926 was decidedly successful. The intensity of his acting in the final scene, in which, finding that he has murdered his brother, Chiaramantesi goes insane, has earned for the work numerous Metropolitan presentations.

A recital of Ruffo's histrionic and artistic abilities may seem beside the point where gramophone records are concerned, but actually it is not so. From people who are merely *singers* come those uninspiring discs which, though technically perfect, impress the hearer only with their dullness. Ruffo's artistic qualities go far to make his records what they are—and, of course, that wonderful voice of pure baritone timbre, gloriously warm and sympathetic, of gigantic proportions, and of even quality throughout. He can produce a greater volume of tone than any other living singer without sign of physical effort, and his phrasing and colouring are unequalled.

Ruffo's career as a recording "star" began with the Pathé Company. Of the records he made in 1904 four still remain in the catalouge. These are "Largo al Factotum" (*Il Barbiere*) coupled with "O Vin Discaccia la Tristezza" (*Amleto*) and "Zazà, Piccolo Zingara" coupled with "Buona Zazà" (*Zazà*). Some of the subtlety and much of the warmth and colour of the HMV records of the same titles are missing from these early discs, but the voice is surprisingly well recorded, and its timbre has not been altered by the Pathé phono-cut system of recording. Since the autumn of 1907 Ruffo has made over one hundred records for the Gramophone Company. These may be divided into three groups; The Italian recordings, 1907–12; the pre-war American recordings; and the post-war (also American) recordings.

# 6

# LOTTE LEHMANN

*Walter first heard Lehmann in the 1924 Covent Garden international season, when he was eighteen. In 1926 he heard Verdi's Otello for the first time and Lehmann remained for him the supreme interpreter of Desdemona. I don't believe it was a role she sang much outside her artistic home, the Vienna Staatsoper, and Walter felt privileged to have heard her in it. Fifty years later he wrote his appreciation.*

IF SHE had been born in Texas they would have called her a gusher, so impulsively did she pour out her voice in an exuberant, generous flood. Reference books says she was born in Perleberg, a small North German town. I doubt it. Shelley had hymned her coming:

> Hail to thee, blithe spirit!
> Bird thou never wert,
> That from Heaven or near it
> Pourest thy full heart
> In profuse strains of unpre-
> meditated art.

Lotte Lehmann will be as enduring a part of vocal history as Malibran and Patti. Her impact was, is, and, through her best records, will remain irresistible and engulfing. Lotte sang and acted as if she were inviting, urging every member of her audiences to enjoy her generous heart and her very self.

She came of modest stock. Her father was a minor civil servant who had to restrict her spending even ten pfennigs for a postage stamp. As a schoolgirl she had a promising voice and loved play-acting, but she set her heart on being an oratorio singer: to her family, opera and the theater were "cloache d'ignominia," sinks of iniquity. Her father's ambitions for his only daughter went no higher than schoolteacher or secretary, almost any job as long as it was proper, safe, and had a pension

121

at the end of it. At sixteen she did not know a note of classical music, but she learned Siebel's aria and a solo from Mendelssohn's *St. Paul* for auditions. Since there was no money for singing lessons, she wrote to voice teachers begging for auditions and free tuition. Etelka Gerster, once Patti's bitterest rival, accepted her but gave her up after a year. Mathilde Mallinger, Wagner's first Eva, put her on the right road. It was Mallinger who, at a *Meistersinger* rehearsal, for the devil of it, sang a trill on "werben" in the phrase "Keiner wie Du so hold zu werben weiss"; Wagner laughed and insisted that it stay in.

Lehmann started at the Hamburg Opera in 1909 with a salary of 150 marks a month, nearly twice as much as Herbert von Karajan started with twenty years later as conductor in Ulm. Out of this she had to buy her own stage footwear, tights, and makeup. She had heard only two performances of opera (*Lohengrin* and *Mignon* with Destinn), knew nothing of theatrical routine or stage technique, and rattled conductors by her incurable carelessness with note values. She made her terrified debut as the Third Boy in *Die Zauberflöte* and followed it with Gerhilde, various Flowermaidens, and the usual diet of pages and esquires that young women are given to cut their teeth on in German opera houses. Gutrune and Freia, with the luxury of Nikisch conducting and enveloping her in his legendary charm, came her way.

Criticisms of "her touching helplessness, both in singing and acting" from reviewers who noted that "among the gods of Valhalla she looked and sounded like a pretty chambermaid" got under her skin, as she thought she had been very good. But she was already tough: you have to be to make a career like hers. She sang Euridice in Gluck's *Orfeo*, a slow upbeat to the attraction of the evening, Caruso in *Pagliacci*. He heard her from the wings and congratulated her—"Che bella, magnifica voce! Una voce italiana!"—and wanted her to sing Micaëla to his Don José a couple of nights later. She was willing, but the director refused, because she did not know the part.

In 1911 she was promised Sophie in the Hamburg premiere of Strauss's new opera *Der Rosenkavalier*, but Elisabeth Schumann, already a firm local favorite, was given that honor, which aroused Lotte's fury and hatred. Later that season she too sang Sophie, and the two young singers became lifelong friends.

Otto Klemperer, who had recently joined the Hamburg musical staff, asked if she would trust herself to sing Elsa with him in a week's time. She was sure she could, but at the first rehearsal Klemperer, "sitting like an evil demon at the piano," told her she had no idea of the part, and at the orchestra rehearsal he screamed up at her, "What's the matter? Has the big role gone to your head so that you forget everything?" The performance, however, was her first great personal success and the real beginning of her career. Nearly fifty years later, the two met in the hall of London's Hyde Park Hotel:

"What are you doing here, Frau Lehmann?"
"I'm giving master classes. They're a great success."
"So? I had hoped that since you stopped singing you'd have been learning the parts you used to try to sing. You were always a famous swimmer." ("Swimmer" is German opera-house slang for an inaccurate singer.)
"And you always had a wicked tongue! You may laugh, but the audiences love my master classes. They even made me sing!"
"Sing? Ha, ha! What did you sing?"
"The *Fidelio* aria. Of course, I sang most of it an octave lower."
"Oh, an octave lower? In E or in E-flat?" (A gleeful reference to the fact that Toscanini had let the aria be transposed down a semitone for her at the Salzburg Festival.)

Klemperer had admired her highly enough to name his daughter Lotte.

Lotte had already accepted an invitation from the Vienna Court Opera to sing a guest performance on trial for an engagement there when in June 1914 she sang Sophie twice in three days with Beecham at the Drury Lane Theatre in London. There was a different Marschallin at each performance—first Margarete Siems, who had created the part in Dresden, then Frieda Hempel, the first Marschallin in Berlin and at the Metropolitan. Ochs was twenty-seven-year-old Michael Bohnen. With such colleagues it is no surprise that Lotte's London debut passed almost unnoticed and was quickly forgotten, particularly because she had the misfortune to follow Claire Dux, who had endeared herself to the London public in all the previous London performances of the opera and had sung still legendary Paminas and Evas. I doubt if Lehmann was ever in the Elisabeth Schumann class as Sophie. I have found no evidence that she had the light, floating C-sharp for the second act, or that in timbre or mien she would convincingly suggest a slip of a girl just out of a convent. Ten years were to pass before London would hear Lehmann or *Die Rosenkavalier* again.

That November she made her Viennese debut as Eva, and her engagement was confirmed at a starting salary of 1,000 marks a month. The Vienna company was rich in celebrities when she joined it. Selma Kurz, Gutheil-Schoder (who excelled from Pamina through Carmen to Strauss's Elektra), Leo Slezak, Alfred Piccaver, Richard Mayr—and Maria Jeritza, the beautiful Czech soprano who had been Strauss's choice for his first Ariadne in Stuttgart and was already the idol of Vienna. She had a flamboyant flair for the stage, and her repertory overlapped many of Lehmann's favorite parts—Elsa, Elisabeth, Sieglinde, Octavian (to which Lehmann had already changed in Hamburg), and Tosca.

Lehmann's brisk, down-to-earth manner, which had served her well in a North German provincial theater, isolated her from her new colleagues in the courtly atmosphere of the Vienna Court Opera, and she had to wait nearly two years for whole-hearted acceptance. It came with the first performance of the revised *Ariadne auf Naxos*. Gutheil-Schoder was to have sung the Composer while Lehmann had been coached only for the second cast. But when Gutheil-Schoder failed to appear at two rehearsals, Lehmann deputized for her and so impressed Strauss that he insisted she sing the premiere. It was her first triumph in Vienna, and next morning she read in the leading Viennese paper, "At 8:30 last night all Vienna knew who Lotte Lehmann is." That evening Jeritza was the Ariadne, and three years later they were cast together again in the world premiere of "Frosch," as Strauss familiarly called his *Frau ohne Schatten*. For years to come Lehmann and Jeritza were bitter rivals, particularly when they sang together in *Die Walküre* (Lehmann as Sieglinde, Jeritza as Brünnhilde), *Ariadne* and *Die Frau* (Jeritza as the Empress, Lehmann as the Dyer's Wife). This casting of the two divas in the same opera was manna for the box office and the claque, but it often led to street fights between fan clubs of the two ladies, who buried the hatchet only decades later at a reconciliation staged in New York and widely publicized by the American media.

Lehmann's repertory in her golden Vienna years makes fascinating reading, as it included many works that contributed little to her later fame. In addition to her Wagner and Strauss roles and of course Fidelio, she sang—all in German—Marguerite in *Faust,* Massenet's Manon and Charlotte, Mimi, Tosca, Butterfly and the first Vienna performances of *Suor Angelica* and *Turandot* (with Slezak, the alternating cast being Nemeth and Kiepura—Lotte said she preferred listening to Nemeth to singing the part herself), *Andrea Chénier, La Juive,* Desdemona, Tatyana and a few ephemeral local contemporary operas like Korngold's *Die tote Stadt* and d'Albert's *Die toten Augen,* each of which gave her a hit tune. No "modern" music: Alban Berg wanted her for Marie in *Wozzeck,* but this, like *Schwanda,* Wellesz's *Bakchantinnen,* and even *Pique Dame* she declined. On the composer's insistence she created in Dresden the heroine in Strauss's *Intermezzo,* adding both this and Arabella to her Vienna repertory. She also sang Pamina, Donna Elvira, and the *Figaro* Countess.

*Fidelio,* which she first sang in 1927 for the centenary of Beethoven's death, became a pillar of her fame. She was the only Leonore in the Salzburg Festivals from 1927 until 1937, first with Franz Schalk, then with Clemens Krauss, and the last ten with Toscanini conducting. Leonore was her most profoundly moving achievement; there has been no one since who can justly be compared with her. She maintained incredible tension, from her first spoken word to the last chord of the opera, encompassing every facet of the character—its nobility and tenderness, pity and force, humanity, anxiety and courage and, in the closing scene, "nameless joy." Scores of phrases, sung and spoken, echo down the corridors of memory after forty years as vividly as her acting of the part. That five cruel bars in the great aria have sometimes been more exactly vocalized by others is beside the point: Lehmann *was* Leonore.

In the early thirties, the idea of adding Isolde to her repertory was uppermost in her mind. Both Schalk and Bruno Walter urged her to sing it, with unfulfillable promises to keep the orchestra down and only accompany (many a singer has paid dearly for believing this favorite perjury to which conductors are prone). Even dates were agreed with Clemens Krauss for performances in Vienna. Wiser counsel came from Slezak and Melchior, who both warned her that Isolde would be vocal suicide. Her record of the "Liebestod," made in 1930, supports their argument.

Lehmann's great international career began in London in May 1924 as a member of that extraordinary group of new singers (World War I having obliterated memories of her prewar Sophies) Maria Ivogün, Frida Leider, Göta Ljungberg, Richard Mayr, Lauritz Melchior, Maria Olczewska, Delia Reinhardt, Friedrich Schorr, and Schumann, all of whom revealed the vocal and dramatic splendors developed in Central Europe since 1914.

Lehmann made her Covent Garden debut as the Marschallin in

*Der Rosenkavalier* in a cast that has never been equaled—Schumann, Reinhardt, and Mayr, with Walter conducting. She accepted the invitation to sing the Marschallin, her first, only for fear that the whole London engagement might otherwise fall through. The honors on the first evening went to Mayr, the only perfect Ochs in the opera's history, the artist Strauss had in mind when he composed it. In subsequent performances Lehmann found her way into the role most closely associated with her. The success was such that two extra performances had to be given that season; it was her first and was to be her last role in Covent Garden.

Her schedule in 1924 was cruel; in fourteen days, May 21 to June 3, she sang five Marschallins, two Ariadnes and a Sieglinde, with not a day's rest between the third Marschallin and first Ariadne or between the last two Marschallins. Between 1924 and 1936 she was the most constantly admired soprano in London and sang twelve parts at Covent Garden—the Marschallin, Ariadne, Sieglinde, Eva, Elsa, Elisabeth, Gutrune, Countess Almaviva, Leonore, Donna Elvira, Rosalinde in *Die Fledermaus*, and Desdemona. Elvira and Desdemona were sung in Italian. She had every reason to be happy at Covent Garden, the majority of her performances being conducted by either Walter or Beecham. The other principals were mostly colleagues from Vienna, Paris, and later New York; there were few rehearsals, no nonsense from stage directors. There was no scrim, and the stage was well lit, because the Styx had not yet overflowed into Covent Garden. It would be idle to pretend that her Mozart performances added to her laurels. She was lucky that they coincided with the 1926 General Strike, which reduced attendance and stopped the newspapers. "There are very few singers," she said, "who have the ideal combination of flawless technique and passionate feeling [for Mozart], and I am not one of them."

The year 1938, her last season at Covent Garden, began and ended sadly for her. Erich Kleiber had thoroughly rehearsed *Der Rosenkavalier*, a work he conducted supremely well. During the levée in the first act, Lehmann was evidently uneasy. I had invited Hilde Konetzni, who was due to make her London debut as Chrysothemis the next evening, to sit in my box for the first act, because she had never heard Lehmann's Marschallin. As Ochs left the scene, the assistant stage manager suddenly came to say that Lehmann wanted me immediately. I whispered to Konetzni that if the worst should happen she must take over to save the performance.

126

As I reached the pass door, the curtain was being lowered. Instead of the words "Als müsst's so sein," she moved towards the wings whispering, "I can't . . . finish." I made an announcement that Mme. Lehmann could not continue but that Mme. Konetzni had agreed to take over as soon as she was dressed. Easier said than done! While Richard Tauber comforted Lehmann (he too had been in the audience), Konetzni, whose measurements exceeded our wardrobe's resources, was pinned into black velvet cloaks—they were *en vogue* that season—hastily borrowed from astonished members of the audience. The performance started again after twenty minutes, and Konetzni was a new celebrity overnight. Next day Lotte, in good spirits, gave a small lunch party. She said she needed a rest and explained privately (not the usually published, politically colored version of the incident) that a few minutes before the performance she had been told that relations of hers who were trying to smuggle valuables out of Austria had been held up at the customs, but now she knew they were safely through. Unfortunately she flatly refused to sing the two contracted *Fidelio* performances, but she did agree to do two more *Rosenkavaliers*, her last in London.

No Marschallin enjoys the end of the trio, and kind young Sophies have often helped nervous or older Marchallins by singing the long "Männer" on a top B for them. Schumann, who had not sung in Covent Garden since 1931, did more: unasked, she stood behind the scenery throughout Lotte's last two performances, ready to sing the Marschallin's part with, or if necessary for, her friend. It was not the first time she had helped Lotte: in the 1933 recording of excerpts from *Rosenkavalier* Schumann sang the Marschallin's famous last words "Ja, ja," because Lotte had already left. The deception went unnoticed for years.

For all the adoration of the public and all her popularity among musicians, her professional life behind the scenes in Vienna was not all milk and honey. Not only was Jeritza a glamorous rival but she was much better paid. Shortly before Jeritza to all intents and purposes left the Court Opera, a new headache entered the Vienna theater in the form of Clemens Krauss as director. He was a first-class man of the theater, civilized, highly intelligent, an elegant diplomat, and an excellent conductor, particularly of all the Strausses from Johann the First to Richard himself, who was mainly responsible for Krauss's appointment. But he brought with him, among other singers who had worked with him in Frankfurt, Viorica Ursuleac, who was later to become his wife and whose repertory was almost identical to that of Lehmann, to whom she was much inferior as singer and actress.

Both Lehmann and Schumann soon felt that the newcomers were being favored. Hugo von Hofmannsthal, whom Strauss believed— wrongly, I am convinced—to be essential to him as a librettist, evidently took a dislike to Lehmann, whom he repeatedly referred to as "middle-class." From what has so far been published of the Strauss-Krauss correspondence, the latter was also gently poisoning the well. It is clear that these two adverse influences worked against Lotte, because after *Intermezzo* she was never again asked to create a Strauss heroine. She left the Vienna Opera in 1938.

Considering her European popularity and fame, America was slow to invite her. Starting at the Chicago Civic Opera for a few weeks in 1930, she had what she called "a decent average success," even though she started as Sieglinde. She hated the overheated hotels and dressing rooms, the icy draughts and the blizzards outside, but returned there until 1934. New York first heard her in a recital at Town Hall in 1932, which at last convinced the Metropolitan, and she was engaged for the 1933-34 season—a piece of timing perhaps belatedly triggered by Jeritza's decision to leave the Met in 1932. Sieglinde was her first role there, on January 11 with Melchior, Schorr and List, which gave her a comfortable feeling, "like being at Covert Garden." Her first act was praised as "not having been matched in years," but her appearances that season were few and far between. In *Tannhäuser* and *Die Meistersinger* "she made vibrant drama of what had recently been dull make-believe," but in *Der Rosenkavalier*, revived for her in 1935, she was described as "singularly cool and dispassionate," a phrase appropriate to Eames, Melba, or even Flagstad on occasion, but miles wide of everything I heard Lehmann do.

It took her two or three Met seasons to establish her supremacy in this role. Possibly she used too fine a brush for both her vocal and histrionic nuances to make their full effects in a theater twice the size of those she was accustomed to. A few weeks later, imprudently singing Tosca—Jeritza's personal vehicle for a decade—Lotte scored her one resounding failure. As Irving Kolodin, one of the shrewdest judges and evidently an admirer, ruefully remarked, "Felinity and suppleness were not in Lehmann's movements."

Lehmann always resented the fact that the Met made her wait until she was forty-six before her debut there. She reasonably thought that if she was good enough for Vienna, London, Paris, and Berlin she was good enough for the Met. I doubt if she was ever happy there. The established Elisabeth Rethberg, who sang the same German repertory and had all the vocal and musical assets if modest personality and acting ability, was competition enough. But the arrival only a year after her own debut of an almost completely unknown Norwegian soprano, also specializing in Lehmann's roles, was a cruel and unexpected blow. When *Fidelio* was revived, it was given to Kirsten Flagstad. Lehmann, as senior member of the company, was piqued and refused ever to sing the part at the Met, even after Flagstad had departed for Norway. Lehmann's last appearance in that theater was in *Der Rosenkavalier* on February 21, 1945, for which she had the luxury of George Szell's conducting. She sang the Marschallin three times after that in San Francisco, in 1945 and 1946.

More than thirty years after she last sang opera, and a quarter-century after her farewell Lieder recital, Lotte Lehmann is the most vividly and affectionately remembered of all sopranos of her generation. Why?

First of all, hers was an unmistakable voice: two revolutions of an LP and you immediately recognize her, and no singer has made a great career without that. If she were active today, with the qualities she had in the habitual form of her mid-thirties to her mid-forties, most of the presently esteemed ladies in her line of operatic business would and should shut up shop.

As for her style, she tended to begin phrases with breathless enthusiasm and spent her breath extravagantly, as if there were plently more where that came from. She replenished her lungs as and when she needed, not always where the composer indicated, but her conviction in the reality and importance of what she was expressing enabled her to do this without relaxing the back of a musical phrase or seeming to interrupt it. She projected words like the best Tuscan baritones, so that every syllable had its own life and carried its meaning as a personal message to every member of the audience, irrespective of their knowledge or ignorance of German. She meant what she sang and experienced every phrase anew as she sang it. The more elemental and direct the sentiment she had to express, the more convincing she was. That is why I have always ranked Sieglinde and Fidelio as her supreme achievements, both "profuse strains of unpremeditated art."

For the purpose of this article I put on her *Ariadne* record. Where I expected visionary exaltation I heard only rather unenthusiastic, honest vocalization. Neither in life nor on record have I heard her make a virginal sound—the nearest she came was on a now lost record of the Eva-Sachs second-act duet, on the phrase "Könnt's einen Witwer nicht gelingen," but even there a not inexperienced minx makes a knowing pass at the older man. The intensity of her first phrase as Elsa, "Mein armer Bruder," was delivered as if she had just been reading Thomas Mann's "Wälsungenblut." Even when she sang settings of religious poems in her recitals she veered towards Teresa D'Avila's tightrope teeter between eroticism and religious ecstasy.

She never did set a firm foot on the oratorio field, despite her childhood aspirations, but during World War I, Lehmann had already started to give Lieder recitals, which later enabled her to prolong her career, particularly in the U.S., where she sang not only in the great cities but in places that had never heard opera. Lehmann, even more than her distinguished predecessors Julia Culp and Elena Gerhardt, paved the way in America for widespread appreciation and acceptance of the art song. Though she habitually reiterated, "My great weakness was the lack of a perfect technique," she had the recitalist's rarest and most valuable quality, a great power of communication. Lehmann's was not a big voice, but it was a double-bedded voice of the most inviting, promising, endearing, all-embracing warmth.

Music was not her only passion. As a juvenile rhymester she earned her first ten marks for a published poem, and she poured words onto paper in books and letters with the same prodigal enthusiasm that informed her singing. She painted too, and the clarity of her observation of scenes and people is reflected as a valuable element in her musical art. As you can hear from her records—the first *Freischütz* aria, for example—her description of a starlit night sounds (I almost wrote "smells") of the German woods at night. The world and humanity, which she loved with all her heart, were the breath and source of her art.

The opening night of the rebuilt Vienna State Opera in 1955 was attended by celebrities invited from the four corners of the earth. The seated audience studied each newcomer through binoculars. As Lotte at last entered, the whole audience quite instinctively stood.

# 7

## ROSA
### An Eightieth-Birthday Homage

*". . . I am tired of corpse-washing; I only write about the dead,"*
*Walter wrote to Robert Jacobson of* Opera News. *But how happy he*
*was to write a tribute to Rosa Ponselle, on her eightieth birthday*
*in 1977.*

ROSA PONSELLE celebrated her eightieth birthday on January 22,
nearly sixty years after her astonishing debut at the Met and nearly forty
after her quiet retirement from it. She is, at the time of writing, as
mentally alert and energetic as a woman half her age, runs the Baltimore
Opera, and still for her own self-discipline sings "to keep the voice flexible." The unforgettable timbre is still there. Paul Hume, music critic of
the *Washington Post*, told me he recently dropped in unannounced at
her house and heard the most lovely sounds. His immediate reaction
was, "Rosa's found a wonderful new pupil." It wasn't; it was Rosa accompanying herself. Whenever some aggressive socialist says to me, "All men
are born equal," my instinctive reaction is to answer, "Bring me another
Ponselle or Caruso or Melchior, or for that matter another Marshal Tito
or Brezhnev; then we can start talking." Rosa was the daughter of im-
migrant parents (the Ponzillos) from Caserta in southern Italy. The
basic quality of her vocal material, her head resonances, the texture and
tension of her vocal chords and the muscles surrounding and controlling
them were most unsocialistically completely unlike yours, mine or any
other singer's. They were created for unique singing. She also had
exceptional musicality and the intelligence and ability to develop a rare
sense of style and line.

The last time I saw Tullio Serafin, a few weeks before his death, he
was playing the slow movement of a Beethoven sonata. Also on his
piano was the score of *Parsifal*—strange but so apt musical com-

131

panions for a great and wise Italian conductor who had earned his living as a practicing musician for eighty years. As always the conversation turned to singers. "In my long lifetime there have been three miracles—Caruso, Ponselle, and Ruffo. Apart from these have been several wonderful singers."

As Rosa Ponselle, she made her opera debut on November 15, 1918 —a few days after the end of World War I—as Leonora in *La Forza del Destino,* with Caruso, De Luca, and Mardones. She was only twenty-one, suffering terribly from the nervousness that plagued her throughout her career, singing opera for the first time in her life to a vast audience in what then ranked as the world's greatest opera house. She had not been through the opera mill, starting with small parts; "O Sole Mio" and "Carry Me Back to Old Virginny" to your own mandolin accompaniment are unorthodox training for "Madre, pietosa Vergine." She began and ended *prima donna assoluta.* She overwhelmed the audience, and the critics acclaimed hers as "one of the most voluptuous voices ever heard," as "vocal gold, dark, rich and ductile," though one dispenser of acid drops soured his praise by adding, "Doubtless some day Rosa Ponselle will learn how to sing." The stupidity and injustice of this bitchiness and the magnitude of her triumph are proved by the records Rosa made a few weeks later. The American Columbia recording company snapped her up with an exclusive contract that ran for four years. This had one major incidental disadvantage: Caruso was equally bound to Victor (now RCA), and he died before her contract had elapsed. Furiously though I resent pirate recordings made without artists' permission and exploited without sanction or remuneration, I shall never cease to regret that no recording exists to show how the voices and art of the mature Caruso and his young discovery (nicknamed "Caruso in gonnella"—Caruso in petticoats) matched, contrasted, and blended. The only example we have of two of Serafin's miracles singing together is the finale of *Otello,* Act II, by Caruso and Titta Ruffo. Listen to that and imagine if you can how Verdi could sound sung by Serafin's *three* miracles!

In those days men's voices recorded more faithfully and substantially than women's, and child as I was at the time, I had been unable to reconcile the thin sounds of famous sopranos which came out of the gramophone horn with the physical amplitude of the buxom-balconied ladies whose photographs were used to advertise their vocal charms. For me the revelation of first hearing Ponselle's 1919 records was akin to Paul's adventure on the road to Damascus. At last, here was a woman with a recognizably woman-sized voice not showing off how fast or how high she could sing but communicating emotion in velvet magic. Her voice was, in retrospect, extraordinarily gramophonogenic.

Those early Ponselle records have unique qualities. She was at the age of the characters she was portraying, in her impulsiveness (incredibly controlled by technique and taste) singing every note and emotion with the freshness of youth in life's spring. This with the most glorious voice that ever came from any woman's throat in the Italian repertory, with a precocious sense of line, style, and emotional honesty. In "Voi lo sapete" she is an anxious, shamed girl confiding in her surrogate mother; "Mi chiamano Mimì" is simply an unaffected account of herself. Sometimes the conductor takes breakneck tempos that defy the laws of vocal nature, as in the *Vespri Siciliani* bolero, where she takes up the challenge to her virtuosity and agility with joyous insolence and dazzles one into not believing one's own ears. And this with a Norma-Aida-Gioconda voice.

She had retired long before the days of tape recording and editing, so all her records are uncooked in terms of intonation and breathing. The Italians, at any rate from Corno di Basetto [*Bernard Shaw*] to the 1930s, were more careful about singing in tune than their German contemporaries, and the acute ear will have to spend a long time trying to fault her on a note even slightly off pitch—her own ears and her coach, Romano Romani, saw to that. The best of her records—and in her case they are well in the majority—are such models of style, expression and technique and give such delight that they should be compulsory listening for students, audiences and critics. Both CBS and RCA, who I understand have all her matrices intact, should be compelled (by law if necessary) to refurbish but not doctor their supreme examples of this incredible locus classicus, this distillation of the art of bel canto.

It was an ample voice, amazingly rich in overtones (Romani's teaching? Compare the same characteristic in Ruffo's "All'erta, marinar" and the *Zazà* arias). Her legato was perfect—utterly seamless, sinuous, exquisitely modulated and with a control of breath that leaves the listener breathless in wonder. She had the reserves of power, when the role or dramatic situation called for it, of a big dramatic soprano, but her habitual range was that of a lyric spinto with dazzling exactitude in agility. Ernest Newman extolled her for taking coloratura out of the aviary and using her phenomenal mastery for psychological penetration. citing particularly the revelation of Violetta's changing states of mind in the repeated "E strano" in the *Traviata* first-act aria. After her first *Amore dei Tre Re* he remarked that "If as a divorce-court judge I had heard her one 'Ritorniam' breathed to her lover I would have given her husband a divorce without hearing further evidence."

She never ventured into high-voice trapeze parts, being too intelligent to echo tootling flutes. Levity was not her forte, but her coloratura surpassed belief. Each of a succession of notes marked *staccato* was genuinely separated, not by a *coup de glotte* or instrusive "H"; they were like rows of equally matched pearls with a glimpse of light separating each one, without a trace of attack on any of them. Legato scales and chromatics up or downward ran like golden ball-bearings, smoothly as through invisible oil. The voice was in one piece, so even from top to bottom that changes of register—if she made them—were inaudible; there was only a slight and gradual darkening of color as she moved down to its lowest notes. Imagine Rostropovich playing with a circular bow on one string covering Ponselle's full compass, and there you have Rosa's legato. On top of this she had words and specific emotions to express, which she did without ever producing a sound that was not in itself musical, beautiful and meaningful.

Ponselle's was a strange career. She was at the Met for nearly twenty years, but her only appearances abroad were at Covent Garden in 1929–31 and two *Vestales* at the Maggio Musicale Fiorentino in 1933. Mussolini for all his faults was an intelligent man, and the fact that in his last ignominious flight he spent his leisure translating into Italian the poems of Mörike, Germany's greatest lyric poet after Goethe, awakens our sympathies. But the fact that he did not succeed in inducing Ponselle *at any price* to sing six months a year in Milan and Rome proves he was no patriot. If he had managed to link Italy to Ponselle instead of to Hitler, he would have saved everybody, himself included, a lot of trouble.

Rosa's excursions to Covent Garden were overshadowed by the financial anxieties of the period. She made her debut there on May 28, 1929, as Norma. She was svelte, statuesque in bearing and notably handsome. Her records, particularly those made by the new electrical process, had aroused great expectation, but the reality far surpassed all anticipations. The calm, noble beauty of her "Casta Diva," the melodic line shaped as if in marble by a Greek master sculptor, the pianissimos gently projected into the remotest corners of the theater on a firm column of breath, were experiences new to the whole audience. Her radiant authority completely took the laugh out of the ridiculous cabaletta. Covent Garden seemed to have considered her luxury enough for each performance of *Norma;* the surrounding cast was undistinguished, with Bellezza conducting. Her second opera that season was *La Gioconda*—again a personal triumph, this time aided by a powerful baritone, Giovanni Inghilleri. Curiously enough, Meta Seinemeyer, five years Rosa's junior and the only soprano of the period who might have developed to comparable historical quality, made her only Covent Garden appearances later that season, after Rosa had left. Tragically, she died a few months later.

In retrospect it seems it was Ponselle's impact on the London public that spurred Covent Garden to raise its Italian standards: Gigli and Pinza made their London debuts in 1930. Pinza, already an established colleague of Rosa's at the Met, was a tower of strength as Oroveso, and London has not since heard his equal.

Lauri-Volpi considers that Rosa's excursion into *La Traviata* was the cause of a deterioration that led to her premature retirement from the stage eight years later. She sang Violetta for the first time in her life (June 13, 1930) and both sang and acted Gigli into the wings. There were no signs in any of her sovereign performances that the part put any strain on her vocal resources, and Francis Toye, a distinguished Verdian and connoisseur of singing, wrote, "I do not think I have heard anything to surpass or perhaps even to equal it." I know that I, nearly fifty years later, have not. Its only fault, as I recall it, was that though she moved lightly onstage, her deportment before the first-act aria was too well-bred for a lady of Violetta's profession, though it cast anticipatory shadows on her marvelously sung and acted later acts. The elder Germont ought to have been delighted that his son had found a girl of such superior class. *La Traviata* remained, however, in her repertory. Perhaps it is significant that she never made a commercial recording of the aria, though this may be due to the slump in the record trade that followed the 1929 Wall Street crash, causing the leading American recording companies to shed their stars like ripe apples in a hurricane. The choice of *L'Amore dei Tre Re* as her third opera that season was probably her own. It was a marvelous vehicle for her, though she had nothing to sing in the third act.

For her third and last year at Covent Garden, Ponselle opened the Italian season with *La Forza del Destino*. Leonora was the role most closely associated with her; her large house near Baltimore, called Villa Pace, commemorates the affinity. Strange though it now seems, *Forza* was being given for the first time at Covent Garden. No doubt it was Serafin who insisted that the opera should be cast from strength— Pertile (who had every quality except a beautiful voice), the stentorian Franci, and Tancredi Pasero, one of the best Italian basses of the time. By now the slump had badly hit London and the attendance at Covent Garden, according to Harold Rosenthal, shrunk to 58 percent. The astonishment of the audience at hearing decent orchestral playing, ensemble between pit and stage, Serafin's intensity and masterly style focused the audience's attention on the whole performance rather than on individual excellences on the stage. She repeated *Traviata* three times —without vocal deterioration—but her characteristic stubborn generosity led her to insist on singing an opera composed by her vocal coach, Romano Romani. His *Fedra* was given as part of a double bill, pathetically following *Gianni Schicchi*. As a vehicle for her many-faceted art it was made to measure, but it lacked any vestige of melodic, musical or dramatic distinction. Interestingly, *Fedra* was her only role outside her entire repertory she did not sing at the Metropolitan Opera.

A curious lack of self-knowledge tempted Ponselle to risk her neck on Carmen, and despite or perhaps because of much preliminary publicity, it nearly cost her her head. The *ordinaire* was never her strong suit, and to all accounts (I didn't see it) she chose to play it "tough." I have heard a recording of a performance (April 28, 1936) and can only endorse the disappointment that seems to have been unanimous even among the most devoted of Ponselle's admirers.

Her break with the Met and with it the end of her career as an opera singer after little less than twenty years came unexpectedly. She had set her heart on *Adriana Lecouvreur*, a part that seems as if made for her. Edward Johnson refused on the grounds that even with Caruso at the crest of his powers and popularity it had failed to attract more than three or four audiences. Rosa uttered an impudent "Either . . . or" and she, who had recently married, broke off relations with the Met, to which she never returned. She had no Constance Hope, the incomparable publicist to whom Lotte Lehmann attributed much of her own American success. Kolodin's account of her departure reads sadly: "It came to an end with no other public emotion than uncertainty whether there would be an eventual *da capo*. . . . The *Carmen*, on Febuary 15 ended Ponselle's Metropolitan career, although stories continued to be heard for the following decade and a half that she sang nearly as well as ever but only for her own pleasure and that of friends." She was the supreme alchemist who turned to the purest gold everything—except Carmen—that she touched. We shall never hear her like again.

# 8

# ELISABETH SCHWARZKOPF

*For years I have called myself and been called by others (sometimes not so kindly!) "Her Master's Voice." Actually, of course, I owe my career to my parents; to my teacher, Maria Ivogün, and her husband, Michael Raucheisen; and last but not least to Walter. As Irving Kolodin has said, "Legge turned Schwarzkopf, an uncommonly good soprano, into a great singer." Or as Andrew Porter remarked, "When Legge married Schwarzkopf, two perfectionists joined forces." Walter planned my concert programmes and coached both me and the pianist, and it was he who early on decided on the best operatic repertoire for my career.*

I DID not even notice her when Sir Thomas Beecham and I were recording *Die Zauberflöte* in Berlin in 1937. She was in the chorus— Favre's *Solistenvereinigung*, the German equivalent of the Robert Shaw Chorale. I must have been blind!

In the later war years her name—Elisabeth Schwarzkopf, as an exceptional young soprano—seeped through to me in letters from young friends serving in the Mediterranean and North Africa who had heard her on German Services broadcasts. She went on my list of artists to be heard and perhaps engaged for EMI when the war was over. By January 1946, when I first reached postwar Vienna, the State Opera had collected the cream of Austrian and European singers into their company. The Theater an der Wien, where both *Leonore/Fidelio* and *The Merry Widow* had had their premieres, was then and for years to come the State Opera's temporary home, and it was there that I heard her, as Rosina in *Il Barbiere di Siviglia*—a brilliant, fresh voice shot with laughter, not large but admirably projected, with enchanting high *pianissimi*. She was a lively, winning actress and evidently very musical. I listened to her in two or three other roles, and once at a party at a friend's house (despite near-starvation, the Viennese still maintained their traditions of *Hausmusik*), before inviting her to discuss an exclusive recording contract. Some singers internationally famous from prewar years, others yet to win renown, pursued me with uncapped fountain-pens ready to sign anything. Schwartzkopf was made of sterner stuff and insisted on "a proper audition—two or three hours. I don't want you to buy a cat in a sack and regret it, and I don't want you to offer me less than you think I am worth." I ought to have recognised in this frank tenacity, which invited detailed criticism and even possible rejection, the firm will and guts necessary to make an exceptional career in what Toscanini described as "the primeval jungle we call the world of music." Sir Terence Rattigan wrote, "What makes magic is genius, and what makes genius is the infinite capacity for taking pains."

Her stubbornness rattled me, and the audition was severe. After she had shown what she could do in her own choice of a variety of arias from both opera and oratorio, I started to work with her on a very difficult little Hugo Wolf song, "Wer rief dich denn?," bar by bar, word by word, inflection by inflection, a song demanding changing emotions often on one syllable, one note: it was the beginning of the way we were to work together for the next twenty-nine years. I soon realized that in this unflinching perfectionalism I had found my match. After an hour-and-a-half, Herbert von Karajan, who was sitting with me, said, "I'm going. You are a sadist. Don't crucify the girl. I told you weeks ago she is potentially the best singer in Central Europe." Half-an-hour later she demonstrated her diverse musical skills by accompanying, either at sight or from memory, other singers who had been waiting for auditions. That evening she signed her first recording contract, and so began the longest and happiest musical association of my life.

Schwarzkopf was evidently too intelligent to waste her natural endowments—which also included patrician bearing and rare beauty—as a high soprano. As you can hear from her 1946 recording of Handel's "Sweet Bird" from *Il Penseroso,* high D's gave her no difficulties. Blondchen and its top E had led Karl Böhm to engage her for Vienna, and Zerbinetta had been her first triumph in a major role. She demonstrated hair-raising agility as Constanze in *Die Entführung,* but the voice was by nature a lyric soprano. At my urging she was soon singing Agathe in *Der Freischütz* and the Countess in *Le nozze di Figaro;* the younger Rosina was a girl of the past.

She had been rescued from a series of so-called singing teachers by Maria Ivogün and Michael Raucheisen, who tenderly laid the foundations of her technique and sense of style. She was born with a fine, analytical ear and that rare gift—the *sine qua non* for international fame as a singer—an immediately recognizable and unforgettable personal timbre. At that time she had not hoped to be more than a principal soprano in Vienna or Berlin, perhaps to be engaged for Salzburg and Bayreuth. She was soon to be surprised.

Her first records for EMI were made in the autumn of 1946—Bach, Handel, Mozart, and a few Arne songs. Some of these have never been issued, but in late 1981 EMI will begin to publish the best of her recordings, starting with the period 1946–1954. We selected the contents and were ourselves astonished at the consistent quality, artistically and technically, achieved even before the days of tape and splicing. In 1947, Karajan recorded the Brahms *Requiem* with Schwarzkopf and Hans Hotter. Recovering from a recent operation, she came to the sessions white and wan. Noticing that Karajan and I were desperate because the chorus sopranos could not keep in tune, she volunteered to stand in their midst to keep them up to pitch. Back to the chorus! That was only her first anonymous rescue operation in important recordings. There would be no Furtwängler-Flagstad *Tristan,* for my taste still the supreme *Tristan* recording, unless Schwarzkopf had promised to sing the top B-flats, B's and C's for her friend, as she had done in earlier Flagstad duets with Svanholm. She also spoke Marzelline's dialogue in Christa Ludwig's *Fidelio* recording and sang some words for a colleague in Karajan's *Falstaff,* which have not yet been detected. There is also a pirated "Marten aller Arten," circulated as by Cebotari.

Schwarzkopf's breakthrough to her international career came quickly and on a broad front. It began at the 1947 Lucerne Festival, the Brahms *Requiem* with Furtwängler. A few weeks later came her London debut at Covent Garden as a member of the visiting Vienna State Opera —Donna Elvira in *Don Giovanni*, then Marzelline, which became one of her best roles.

On the strength of her London success and the spreading fame of her records, Covent Garden engaged her as guest member of its resident company. It was not a generous contract—£60 a week, if I remember rightly—and everything was to be sung in English, which she had learned at school and as a teenage League of Nations student in the English provinces. Between 1948 and 1951 she sang Pamina, Sophie, Mimi, Violetta, Susanna, Marzelline, Eva, and—much against my will, but at management's insistence—Manon and Butterfly, neither of them her cup of tea. All these roles except Eva were soon to be dropped from her repertory, but she accepted the Covent Garden offer because it enabled us to work together. This caused a break with Vienna. The music director, Josef Krips, and general manager, Egon Hilbert, told her that if she left their theatre even for three months a year she would lose her voice and be useless to them. But she and her voice survived it, in exile from the Vienna opera stage until Karajan took over the State Opera and welcomed her back.

Now her international career raced apace: Countess Almaviva at the 1948 Salzburg Festival with Karajan; her La Scala debut with the same company five months later; and from then until 1963 two or three roles every season at La Scala, probably the longest and most distinguished career of any German singer in that Italian theatre.

At that time the *stagione* system worked perfectly, and there in 1952 she first assumed the Marschallin, a part we had been preparing for years. This music and text are honey for a fine Lieder singer's subtle art. After a month's intensive rehearsal, often ten or twelve hours a day, Karajan conducted a series of performances still unforgotten in La Scala's history.

There she sang her only staged Mélisandes, under Victor de Sabata; her only Elsas; the *Tannhäuser* Elisabeth; the premiere of Carl Orff's *Trionfo di Afrodite*; even Marguerite in *Faust*, in which she, like Goethe, sank without trace. To her usual Mozart-Da Ponte parts she added Fiordiligi for Mozart's bicentenary at the newly inaugurated Piccola Scala. Giorgio Strehler was to have directed it, but at the sight of Eugene Berman's murky decor he stormed out of the theatre belching clouds of quadrilingual obscenities, leaving poor Guido Cantelli to conduct (and produce!) an opera for the first and last time in his life with a cast nearly all new to the subtlest and most difficult Mozart opera. It turned out to be an exquisite, unaffected performance.

Schwarzkopf had already fulfilled her Bayreuth ambitions when she took part in the postwar reopening with Beethoven's Ninth Symphony under Furtwängler. She sang Eva there with Karajan, then Knappertsbusch; Woglinde (as an example to her generation by reverting to the old Bayreuth tradition wherein leading singers lent their lustre to small parts); and a recital in the beautiful old Margraves' Theatre, designed by Galli Bibiena, to aid the Foundation of the Friends of Bayreuth. Between performances she learned the words and music of Stravinsky's *Rake's Progress*, whose premiere lay close ahead. That year the Venice

Festival opened with the Verdi *Requiem,* conducted by de Sabata, with Schwarzkopf, di Stefano, Stignani, and Siepi. A few days later Stravinsky, his head buried in the score, conducted the first performance of his new opera.

She bided her time to make her U.S. debut, but in 1953, after we had rehearsed for nearly a week with the pianist Arpád Sándor, she gave her first New York recital, in Town Hall—and returned the same evening to Switzerland. On the flight home she studied Leonore in *Fidelio,* which she had promised Karajan to sing in a series of concert performances. The effect of young, impulsive voices in the two leading parts had moving overtones, but Leonore demands more vocal weight than she ever carried.

We had been warned that it was impossible to make a successful concert career in America without having first established oneself at the Metropolitan. That fallacy had to be disproved. Concert engagements came in plenty after the Town Hall recital, and the perceptive Kurt Herbert Adler immediately engaged her for his San Francisco Opera, where she sang for ten years before the Met condescended to engage her. In the meantime, we had proved that without a Met background it is possible to give Lieder recitals entirely in German and pack large halls even with all-Hugo Wolf programmes, events beyond the comprehension of New York impresarios but much to the taste of the intelligent American musical public. Her subsequent American concert career, having finished its last lap, is already history.

In the 1930s Titta Ruffo had told me that though he had sung something like a hundred operas, if he could start his career again he would restrict himself to five or six parts, study and polish them in every vocal and dramatic detail, and sleep happily without fear of competition. He was a wise man.

For the stage, Schwarzkopf whittled down her repertory to three Mozart parts—Fiordiligi, Donna Elvira, the Countess Almaviva; two Richard Strauss parts, the Marschallin and the Countess in *Capriccio;* and because she delights in playing comedy, Alice in *Falstaff.* All are intensely human characters, with wide emotional ranges, expressing themselves in distinguished texts and free from conventional operatic fustian. She hankered after Desdemona and Strauss's Ariadne, but no theatre could give her both the three weeks' rehearsal and the conductor we wanted at the times she was free.

There are interesting disparities between Schwarzkopf's recorded

142

opera repertory and the works she sang in public. She recorded but never publicly sang *Hänsel und Gretel* (our nearly twenty-five-year-old recording is still unequalled); *Ariadne auf Naxos; Der Barbier von Bagdad,* an exquisite score and diverting text but box-office poison; *Les Contes d'Hoffmann,* which I had planned to record with Callas, Schwarzkopf and De los Angeles, a project that lost much of its sparkle after I resigned from EMI; Carl Orff's *Die Kluge; Arabella,* of which only highlights were recorded, but which Lotte Lehmann, Viorica Ursuleac, and Clemens Krauss repeatedly urged her to put into her public repertory; *Troilus and Cressida,* which our friend William Walton wrote for her, but which she regretfully declined because the text was Ivor Novello-ish and in English. And the operettas.

I had set my heart on recording the best Johann Strauss and Lehár operettas since the 1930s, when Bruno Walter conducted *Die Fledermaus* at Covent Garden with Lehmann, Elisabeth Schumann, Maria Olczewska, and Gerhard Hüsch. To launch the recording project and attract the widest possible public, I intended to start with *The Merry Widow.* I had the cast, but Karajan declined to conduct, and a year passed before it struck me that Otto Ackermann was the man I had been searching for, a conductor of near-genius with marvellously flexible rhythm, a light hand, vast experience, and sound theatrical instinct. Everything we had all learned from lives dedicated to the greatest music was gaily devoted to restoring the elegance, tenderness, and infectious high spirits needed to make real the unreal world these masterpieces inhabit. Their launching as Angel's Champagne Operettas was carried out with the usual unparalleled flair of the promoters of the series, Dario and Dorle Soria. The nearest Schwarzkopf came to public performance of operetta was a few concerts at American summer festivals and at London's Royal Festival Hall.

Since Schwarzkopf has so often spoken of herself as "Her Master's Voice," casting me as Svengali, let me give some indication of how we worked together. My predecessor in the recording world was Fred Gaisberg. He believed that his job was to get the best artists into the studio and get onto wax the best sound pictures of what those artists habitually did in public, intermittently using his persuasive diplomatic skill as nurse-maid and tranquilizer to temperaments. Having watched him at work, I decided that recording must be a collaboration between artists and what are now called "producers." I wanted better results than are normally possible in public performance: I was determined to put onto disc the best that artists could do under the best possible conditions. From the start of the Hugo Wolf Society, when I began to exercise my craft (with Elena Gerhardt, Alexander Kipnis, Herbert Janssen, and others), the new approach was a success. After the war I found in Schwarzkopf, Karajan, and Lipatti (to mention but three) ideal and incurable perfectionists—self-critical, hungry for informed criticism, untiring, and acutely aware that their recorded performances were the true proof of their qualities and the cornerstones and keystone of their careers.

When Schwarzkopf came to London in 1947, she had never owned a gramophone. My first and favourite toy had been an ancient cylinder model: I had learned to read from record labels and catalogues, saved my pocket money to buy records, and over the years built up a mammoth collection. Her father's profession, teaching the classics, meant that he and she changed schools every two or three years through the German provinces. She was nineteen before she heard decent singing. She had started with piano at seven, viola and organ at ten, and taken part in school opera performances, including Kurt Weill's *Der Jasager*.

First I set out to widen by recorded examples her imaginative concept of the possibilities of vocal sound. Rosa Ponselle's vintage port and thick cream timbre and noble line; the Slavic brilliance of Nina Koshetz; a few phrases from Farrar's Carmen, whose insinuations were later reflected in Schwarzkopf's "Im Chambre séparée"; one word only from Melba, "Bada" in "Donde lieta"; some Rethberg; and large doses of Meta Seinemeyer to show how essentially Teutonic voices can produce brilliant Italianate sound. Then Lehmann's all-embracing generosity, Schumann's charm and lightness, McCormack's incredible octave leap in "Care selve," Frida Leider's dramatic tension—all these were nectar and ambrosia for Schwarzkopf's musical appetite. Instrumentalists, too: Fritz Kreisler for the dark beauty of his tone, his nobility and elegance, his vitality in upbeats, his rubato and cavalier nonchalance; Schnabel for concentrated thinking over long musical periods, firmly rhythmical, seemingly oblivious to bar lines. From the analysis of what we found most admirable in these diverse models we made our own synthesis, most adaptable to what we believed would best develop her voice for the repertory we were to concentrate on.

We made it our aim to recreate to the best of our abilities the intensity and emotions that music and words had in their author's minds in the moment of creation. Therefore utmost obedience to every composers' markings—he knew best. This has involved and still does involve hours of merciless rehearsal, domestically known as "Walter crucifying the pianist." She has had rare luxury in pianists as partners—Furtwängler and Karajan, Sawallisch, Ackermann and Rosbaud, Edwin Fischer, Gieseking and Ciccolini, and, for over twenty years as a steady diet, the incomparable London-based pair, Gerald Moore and now Geoffrey Parsons. And in the summer of 1975, Sviatoslav Richter, for three recitals after twenty days' rehearsal.

From the outset I sat in with a secretary in opera rehearsals and performances, quickly dictating detailed notes on musical and acting nuances, sometimes having these passed to her in the wings. At performances I sat whenever possible in a stage box to watch both what she was doing and how the audience reacted—the exact moment when women fumbled in their handbags for handkerchiefs and men tugged them from their breast pockets. This is *not* calculation; it is in my view obedience to composers' intentions, to involve the audience in the action. We tried for years and once or twice succeeded in achieving Pamina's "Ach, ich fühl's" so heart-breakingly that there was no applause. The length of the silence after Strauss's "Morgen" is more eloquent than clapping.

We have tried to communicate and stir emotions like painters, by beauty and truth of line and colours in the voice. From what we have heard, most of her best younger colleagues have different aims. In two consecutive evenings at the Paris Opéra we listened to galaxies of stars singing beautifully, obeying every dynamic marking and conveying nothing but the glory of their voices and their technical skill—no trace of emotion or the meaning and overtones of the words for which composers had so tenaciously wrestled with their librettists. For this the producers and conductors are most to blame.

More farewell concerts in Europe—finally, in 1976, three in London, the city where she has sung more than any other; some new recordings and then . . . ? She will play tennis, ski, and walk in her beloved Austrian mountains. Then, perhaps, we shall teach. But where shall we find pupils like her? What we would *really* like is to run an opera house with the musical and artistic standards Elisabeth and I have maintained in all the records we have made together.

# 9

# SIR THOMAS

*The last piece Walter wrote was an essay on Sir Thomas Beecham. He gave difficult birth to all his essays and profiles. He rewrote and polished them until they gleamed, just as he would re-record and re-record a phrase in a Wolf Lied of mine until he was satisfied with it. But his letters he dictated without the slightest change or hesitation. I always marvelled at his letter-writing skill and loved taking them down and typing them for him.*

*My farewell concerts were slowly coming to an end. When we travelled to Zürich for my farewell there, he said, "The deadline for this piece is going to kill me." But he finished it and sent it off on time. The Zürich concert, 19 March 1979, turned out to be my last. When it was over, Walter—with a huge grin—said, "You know, you're a bloody miracle." Three days later he died.*

T.B. would be vastly amused if I marked the centenary of his birth with pious platitude. In my mind's eye, I can see him reclining in his armchair dressed in his habitual white silk pyjamas under a floral dressing gown slowly exhaling Havana cigar-smoke ceilingwards and smiling, perhaps even laughing at the very idea of it. No biographer will ever be able to publish an "All about all of Sir Thomas Beecham, Bart., O.M.": there were simply too many Thomas Beechams. Neither his colleagues, nor his collaborators, nor his staff, nor his three wives, nor his long-and-short-term girls knew all that was going on in that subtle brain.

He was lavishly generous, had a fine palate for wines and a nose for cigars, and he was a gourmet—apart from occasional lapses at home to Lancashire hotpot and Irish stew. One night over supper in an Edinburgh hotel, T.B. complained to the promoter of his Scottish concerts that in all first-class hotels throughout Europe and America the menus and food itself were identical. "Is there no Scottish food?" The guest invited us to dine at his house where he would give us only Scottish specialities. We started with superb smoked salmon while our host expatiated on the methods of smoking this fish which he had caught in the River Tay for our benefit. As he finished this saga, Scotch broth was served. T.B. passed his spoon through it: "And this, my dear Jock, you presumably bailed straight out of the Clyde?"

Beecham had devoted three years to unravelling the tangled skeins of his father's will, the involvement in selling the estate, not to mention the chaotic state of his own finances, when I first heard him at the Royal Albert Hall on April 8, 1923. After a preliminary canter with the Hallé, he celebrated his return to London's musical life by conducting the combined London Symphony and Royal Albert Hall Orchestra, with Dame Clara Butt as makeweight soloist. It was a typical Beecham occasion: *Oberon* Overture; *The Walk to the Paradise Garden*; Berlioz's *Royal Hunt and Storm*; then Dame Clara. After the interval, *Ride of the Valkyries* and *Ein Heldenleben*. The whole concert was played with a vitality and panache new to me. No wonder that with his musical batteries recharged in the three-year rest from music he nearly blew the roof off with the loud bits of the Berlioz, the Wagner, and the Battlefield section of the Strauss.

In everything but physical build this spruce, strutting little man was a giant and probably the last of the great British eccentrics. He was elusive, myriad-faceted—a complex of ever-changing personalities—too generously endowed by nature with too great a variety of talents for him to organise himself into an integrated personality. His intelligence was as penetrating as it was versatile, and his memory almost photographic in its accuracy for both music and words. In public speeches and private chats that memory unhesitatingly presented him with an apt quotation or allusion, however recondite.

In the sixty years when he was involved in British musical life there was hardly a musical pie in which Beecham did not have a finger or two. Beecham had only one aim: to build and firmly establish under his own absolute control new, higher standards of musical performance, both operative and orchestral, in Britain. He aimed at collecting perceptive paying audiences who would appreciate him and what he was doing for music and for them. As long as he could afford it he did not care about differences between profit and loss, but he expected due praise for what he was doing. He rarely got all he deserved. In 1927 he launched the Imperial League of Opera, on which he spent much enthusiasm, time, and oratory in an attempt to form cells of opera lovers in every city in the country which had a suitable theater. For a small annual subscription, members would be able to enjoy opera near home at modest prices. Unfortunately the initial public response lost impetus and the project petered out.

The only enduring proof of his musical qualities are his records. In the repertoire he loved he was the most prominent, stimulating, and deeply musical conductor Britain had yet produced and one of the few to win international recognition.

To the musical Establishment, Thomas Beecham was an outsider. The fellow had attended none of the academies, conservatories, or schools of music (a source of resentment because none of them could claim him and bait new pupils with his achievement). He did not rise in the estimation of the heads of the music-teaching institutions when he publicly advocated that Dante's immortal warning on the portals of Hades, *Lasciate ogni speranza voi ch'entrate* ("Give up every hope ye who enter"), should be emblazoned on their doors.

His conducting technique was unorthodox, and he was extremely rich—*ergo*, the man was a damned amateur! Worse, his money came from trade. His chemist-grandfather had laid the foundations of the family fortunes by selling his own patent-medicines from a stall in St. Helens market and was credited with becoming a millionaire by the enormous sales of a vastly popular laxative—Beecham's Pills. T.B. maintained that the sales slogan "Worth a guinea a box" was all his own work. At the turn of the century a guinea was the price of a back-street abortion and word-of-mouth propaganda whispered that swallowing as one dose the contents of a whole box of Beecham's Pills made surgical interference unnecessary.

Beecham was hardly twenty (1899) when he set about forming an orchestra of local amateurs with which, strengthened by some Manchester professionals, he gave a concert or two. His father, that year mayor of St. Helens, had engaged the Hallé Orchestra for a concert in his hometown. Hans Richter, amanuensis of Richard Wagner and only recently established as the permanent conductor of the Hallé, who was to have conducted the concert, called off a day before the event: the brash but inexperienced young Beecham induced his father to let him deputize for the revered Richter, which he did much to the distaste of the orchestra, some of whom had conducting ambitions. It is said that conductor and orchestra started and finished together.

Already T.B. had acquired a firsthand knowledge of several orchestral instruments without completely mastering any of them. He took an as yet unmastered trombone with him on a visit to Lucerne, where he stayed at a lakeside hotel. Fellow-guests complained to the management about the agonised noises he was making. Not to be beaten or muted T.B. hired a boat and rowed his trombone and himself to the middle of the Vierwaldstättersee to practice in peace, overlooking the fact that the surrounding mountains would echo and re-echo his efforts to all the hotels and houses around the lake. He never became a virtuoso on the trombone.

He learned the essence of his art from the great interpreters he heard in his youth. His father had taken him to America on a business trip and to hear the best music the U.S.A. could offer. In his teens, for school and university holidays, he was given ample funds, in golden sovereigns to go wherever in Europe his fancy took him. I am convinced that he learned much about conducting from Artur Nikisch and Richard Strauss, about the only two great conductors on whom I never heard T.B. vent a disparaging remark. His own flamboyant style, the beard which over the years dwindled from a chest-protector to a goatee, the cuff-shooting as well as the extempore freedom of his interpretations were probably Nikisch-inspired. From Strauss he learned the importance of clarity and transparency.

Let us first look at the means by which he achieved his exceptional results. At their first rehearsal with a conductor new to them, all orchestras play up—or down—to the man's reputation. Richard Strauss's father—the Dennis Brain of his time—said that from a conductor's walk to the podium the players knew who was master, he or they. T.B.'s leisurely, self-assured strut to his podium settled that question.

What is conducting technique? It is the means by which any man gifted with authority and strong powers of communication conveys his musical intentions unmistakeably to a body of musical executants by movements of a baton, his fingers, hands, arms, facial expressions, and glances. Mutual understanding and detailed preparation must be achieved in rehearsals. Beecham was not an ostentatious time-beater but he got what he wanted. His technical mastery of orchestras began with his unfailing courtesy to his players. He often said: "Get the best players, pay them well, then conducting is not *so* difficult." He had a clear down-beat, usually slashed (from the audience's view) from northeast to southwest. He trusted, encouraged, and helped his wind principals and string players—when they had soli—to play freely and with more expression than they had imagined themselves capable of, and smiled to them his own delight at each beautifully shaped phrase.

For his first *Heldenleben* with the Hallé he had brass-band players as necessary reinforcements. Brass-band players are usually at sea with orchestral parts and this Strauss was for them mid-Atlantic. After an hour's patient rehearsal trying to get the bandsmen to play the right notes at the right time, he put down his baton: "Gentlemen. Unfortunately I have no more time now but we shall meet again this evening at the concert. You will then keep in touch with me, won't you?"

Beecham had a soft spot for what orchestral players call "the Kitchen." One of the most typical gestures was a violent lunge as if he were chucking a cricket ball overarm at the noisiest section of the orchestra. He beamed at every loud cymbal-crash and at the tintinabulations of high percussion which gave extra sparkle to the general din. In later years his technique was extended to include his own noisy vocal urgings to orchestra to play louder. He loved what he called "grand tunes" and in his extravagantly generous heart he wanted the orchestra, the audience, and, last but not least, Thomas Beecham, to enjoy themselves. A good time must be had by all! After devoting the best part of his life to popularizing opera and concerts in Britain he ruefully remarked: "The British don't like music—only the noise it makes."

The busiest man in the Beecham entourage was the copyist whose job it was, often with two or three assistants working as long as they could keep their eyes open, to pencil into each orchestral part all the meticulously marked inflections T.B. had so exactly put into his scores. They were myriad, often reconsidered and even radically altered between rehearsals. Much of the charm of Beecham's music-making was the fruit of this patient labour, particularly the infinitesimal rubati, minuscule crescendi and diminuendi, changes of accents, all of which contributed to the shape and eloquence of the phrases as he felt them. This is probably the reason why he ignored the researches of musicologists. His attitude was "Mozart and Haydn were composers: my duty is to present their works to the public in the most engaging light."

The first meeting with Delius' music in 1907 changed the course of Beecham's life. He became its most energetic proselytizer and soon

150

its only true exponent, as well as the composer's best and most generous friend. Beecham was then twenty-eight. Delius was seventeen years older and although he had champions in Germany, his music was little known in Britain. Beecham said, "The printed scores were vilely edited and annotated and if played in exact accordance with their directions of tempo, phrasing, and dynamics could not help being comparatively ineffective and unconvincing." Beecham took them in hand and made of them a magic, nostalgic sound-world to which he alone had the key. I believe Delius was the composer with whose works Beecham could most completely identify himself, even more than Handel, Mozart, Haydn, or Wagner.

The healing of the nine-year breach with his father gave Beecham access not only to great riches but the cooperation of that parent who was also an opera enthusiast. The first manifestation was Beecham's first Covent Garden season (February-March 1910), not in the fashionable months which were the Grand Opera Syndicate's preserve. He was an off-season tenant. It was an odd repertoire: Strauss's *Elektra* (the first British performances, conducted first by Beecham and later by Strauss himself); *Tristan und Isolde; Carmen; Hänsel und Gretel* and *L'Enfant Prodigue* as a double-bill; and as English works, Delius' *A Village Romeo and Juliet,* Ethel Smyth's *The Wreckers,* and Sullivan's *Ivanhoe.* The first performances of *Elektra* were more sensational events than any in the history of opera in Britain: two extra performances had to be given to meet the demand for tickets.

Beecham's oft-repeated dictum that clear, meaningful diction was the very essence of opera-singing sometimes escaped his memory. Before the dress rehearsal of his first *Elektra* he exhorted his hundred-and-eleven-man orchestra: "Those singers up there on the stage think they are going to be heard: it's up to you and me to take damned good care that they are not." George Bernard Shaw wrote: "It was interesting to compare our conductor, the gallant Beecham, bringing out the points of Strauss's orchestration until sometimes the music sounded like a concerto for six drums, with Strauss himself bringing out the meaning and achieving the purpose of his score so that we forget there was an orchestra at all, and could hear nothing but the conflict and storm of passion."

During this season Bruno Walter made his London debut conducting *Tristan* and shared with Percy Pitt the other operas. Beecham rightly reserved the Delius for himself. According to T.B., audiences were only "fairly good." To other accounts, Walter's *Tristan* was a triumph; it must have been, because an extra performance was added. This season made Beecham the musical hero of Britain. The critics hailed him as a visionary and an idealist, and gave a dinner in his honour.

T.B. followed this first Covent Garden adventure with a three-month season of opéra comique in English at His Majesty's Theatre. The choice of repertoire was little more conventional or, to be frank, the work of a man who knew what the public wanted or even should want. *Hoffmann* was an indisputable success but ticket sales dictated that *Werther* have only one performance. A piece by the recently deceased Edmont de Missa followed its creator to his grave, although Beecham both liked and conducted it. Works by Stanford and Clutsam mollified the critics. *Fledermaus* was a success—it always is, no matter what vulgarities scenic designers and producers impose on it or what conductors do to it. Mozart was given (also in English)— *Figaro*, *Entführung*, *Der Schauspieldirektor*, and *Così fan Tutte*, the last two virtually unknown to Britain. Even when he was sixty-five, T.B. described *Così* as "a long summer's day spent in a cloudless land by a southern sea"; this pretty phrase reveals how little he understood that opera. Bernard Shaw's essay "Mozart with Mozart Left Out" (1917) is most illuminating. In Beecham's first two seasons only *Elektra*, *Hoffmann*, *Tristan*, and *Fledermaus* were popular successes.

His second Covent Garden season opened with d'Albert's *Tiefland*. T.B. again stuck his neck out with French operas: the first nights of *Hamlet* and *Pelléas* were also their last nights. By then he realised that *Carmen*, *Contes d'Hoffmann*, *Faust*, *Louise*, and perhaps *Samson et Dalila* were the only French operas for which there was a loyal London public. Again the sensation of this season was a Strauss masterpiece —this time *Salome* with the Finnish soprano Aïno Akté, a slim and ravishingly beautiful woman whose understanding of the role was highly praised.

Félia Litvinne and the Dutch tenor Urlus, who sang what was considered the best *Tristan* since Jean de Reszke, were also much admired and feted. *Fidelio* and *Der fliegende Holländer* are reputed to have been inadequately cast. Frieda Hempel and Beecham seem soon to have taken a dislike to each other. I have been told that one *Zauberflöte* evening Hempel sent her German cavalier to T.B.'s dressing room to explain—in almost unintelligible English—that Madame was indisposed and would be grateful if Sir Thomas would transpose her aria. Beecham agreed, but since Hempel's friend had not specified whether up or down, T.B. asked the orchestra to transpose it up.

Although Beecham had in that one year (1910) presented 200 performances of 50 operas, 20 of them new to London, it was evident to him that he must radically change his concept of what the London public wanted. Then he had an idea of genius: he would present, for the first time in Britain, Diaghilev's Russian ballet in the summer of 1911. The shock of the preliminary announcements galvanized the Grand Opera Syndicate, who controlled Covent Garden, into action. They had already put out feelers about Beecham joining forces for the summer of 1911: he let it be known that he had taken an option on Drury Lane to coincide with Covent Garden's Grand Summer Season. When the Syndicate realized the nature and force of his challenge, they made a proposition which he bent into acceptability: the Syndicate would take over the contract with the Russians and he would provide his own orchestra for the large repertoire of music new to the Royal Opera's orchestra and for which they had no time to rehearse. Beecham would put his own orchestra at the disposal of the ballet.

Diaghilev was a perfectionist and a martinet, and the impact of what was an entirely new art form in which every constituent was of the highest imaginable quality was a revelation to British audiences. It was easier to understand than symphonic concerts or opera and above all it was a new kind of feast for the eyes—beautiful bodies moving poetically or dramatically with a new vocabulary of expressive gestures. Scenery and costumes—particularly Bakst's—using hitherto unimagined contrasts and combinations of colours brought new vitality, excitement, and splendour to staged spectacles. Beecham brought the Russian ballet back and in 1912, on Diaghilev's insistence, took his orchestra to Berlin to accompany the ballet as it had in London.

Feodor Chaliapin was known only to the comparatively few record buyers and the fewer much-travelled operagoers. When Beecham, as a director of the Covent Garden Opera Syndicate, proposed bringing Chaliapin and the cream of the Imperial Theatre of St. Petersburg, together with their decor and costumes, to London, they coldly rejected

153

the idea. Beecham resigned from the board and took a lease on Drury Lane as the temporary scene of the activities of his Russian Opera Company. His megalomania took wing at that time.

Dramatic development was less of a feature of Russian opera than Russian legends and historical personages or novels on which they were based. In short, Russian opera was like a gorgeously illustrated picture book of subjects every Russian knew. The London public soon fell under the new exotic spell and even though the works were so new to them the public response was soon as wildly enthusiastic as it had been for the ballet. Chaliapin became an idol: the spendor of his voice, the expressiveness with which he coloured it, and the complete newness of his acting—indeed of the whole company's—overcame the limitations of communication between two peoples neither of whom knew a word of each other's language.

It was at this period that Beecham surpassed himself as a Nietzschean peacock, announcing first in a prospectus, and a year or so later when he launched an ill-founded rumour, that he was bringing to London the stars of the New York Metropolitan Opera. In both cases it was "Signor Toscanini will assist Mr. Thomas Beecham as conductor." No wonder then when T.B. conducted *Falstaff* at Covent Garden in 1937 Toscanini left the theatre after the first act saying, "That is not *Falstaff* but he [meaning Beecham] is a *Pagliaccio*."

I first met Beecham early in 1934 in the Midland Hotel, Manchester. Late in 1933, I had planned a new venture, the International Music Society, and took my exposé to Ernest Newman, with whom I was spending Christmas. E.N. was impressed by the scheme but warned me that the only chance of its acceptance was the support and advocacy of Thomas Beecham, who had easy access to all the right people. Hence my trip to Manchester.

Invoking Newman's name, I rang Beecham asking for an appointment. He said he was very busy but I could have fifteen minutes of his time at 10:15. In his apartment he read and re-read my project and at length gave me his assurance that he would back it to the hilt. I left him late that evening completely under the spell of the most irresistible charmer I had yet met. Discussion of these plans kept us in almost daily contact. Its first fruit was that Sir Thomas, although under contract to Columbia, insisted that I should supervise all his recordings although I was in the HMV stable (the personnel of the two companies was then still kept separate in the lower echelons despite the

merger to form EMI). Beecham's unpunctuality at rehearsals and recording sessions was almost as proverbial as his penchant for asking
for a large orchestra, and after a short while, changing his mind about
what he would record, dismissing half the players, to concentrate
happily on a movement or two of a Mozart symphony. With patience
and raillery, I got him to be punctual and to keep to agreed working
programmes. In retrospect I surmise that these last-minute changes of
repertory were a ruse to get the company to shoulder some of the wages
he had to pay the young London Philharmonic Orchestra. For his
first concert with that orchestra in October 1932, Beecham had had
seven sectional and six full rehearsals. The programme was *Carnaval
Romain*, Mozart's *Prague* Symphony, *Brigg Fair*, and *Ein Heldenleben*.

He was as helpfully cooperative in the studios as any man at that
time and when it came to approving pressings for publication, more
self-critical than most conductors, even to the point of insisting on his
own choice of recording engineer. For a long time, his favourite was
Bob Beckett, later appointed senior recorder in Berlin. Formerly a
violinist and one of my most able colleagues, Beckett was the technical
engineer for both Beecham's *Zauberflöte* and de Sabata's *Tosca*.

Soon I was able to induce T.B. to let me make experimental recordings of his concerts at the Leeds Festival, of which he was artistic director. Some of these turned out well enough for Columbia to publish
excerpts from Sibelius' Incidental Music to Shakespeare's *Tempest*,
some rousing Handel choruses magnificently sung by the Leeds Festival Chorus, excerpts from Mozart's C minor Mass, and the Polovtsian
Dances from *Prince Igor*. These results encouraged us to record much
of the Covent Garden Coronation season. The crop of saleable records
was small—excerpts from *Götterdämmerung* with Janssen and Ludwig
Weber—great Wagnerians both and unequalled today—and four sides
of *Meistersinger*.

For me, the best of all Beecham recordings is *Die Zauberflöte*. I
kicked over a lot of traces organizing the whole undertaking. The
Glyndebourne Mozart-Da Ponte opera recordings had been organized
and nursed through by Fred Gaisberg who wished them on to me to
be exploited as a Mozart Opera Society. The Glyndebourne contract
was a clever deal on Gaisberg's part: HMV got admirably rehearsed
performances which they could record in few sessions, therefore quite
cheaply, and Glyndebourne was in those days very much *en vogue*.
Carl Ebert, the brilliant regisseur, had drilled his polyglot casts into

clear conceptions of at least what each singer had to contribute dramatically to their roles. The mixture of accents in not-so-near Italian drove me to remark that there was a fortune to be made out of a Glyndebourne-Italian dictionary, and Busch's ban on *appogiature* in Mozart's Italian operas wrung from me the rumour that there was a notice inside the artists' entrance at Glyndebourne, "Ladies must remove their *appogiature* before entering."

There are splendid accounts of the ritual mating dances between Beecham and John Christie in Spike Hughes's entertaining book on Glyndebourne. They met rarely and no two men were more clearly predestined by nature to disagree. Beecham could be pompous when it suited him; Christie was always pompous and believed that if only he could beguile Beecham into collaboration between Covent Garden and Glyndebourne, he, as one-time master at Eton, could outsmart Beecham and be enthroned as king of both opera castles, wearing the *Lederhosen* he long affected. The two men achieved only two minuscule collaborations. In 1949 Beecham did four concerts at Glyndebourne and in the 1950 Edinburgh Festival he conducted the first (Stuttgart) version of Strauss's *Ariadne auf Naxos*, which he wrongly preferred to the superior and more practical Vienna version. For the Scots they were billed as Glyndebourne productions.

Christie was furious that I had succeeded in inducing Tauber to sing Tamino and Belmonte at Covent Garden that summer, and the more enraged because Gigli had rejected his pathetic attempts at revenge; Christie had offered him peanuts for singing a series of Don Ottavios in Sussex. The great Italian tenor had already signed a contract with us for *Bohème, Rigoletto*, and *Tosca*. At a dinner of the now defunct London Opera Club, Christie ended a long and tedious speech by confiding to the guests that "Sir Thomas' recurrent malady was due not, as he let it be known, to his foot, but to his Legge." Beecham's reply was brief: "My Lords, Ladies and Gentlemen, I will not detain you long—only long enough to remind you and the last speaker that Mozart, like good wine, needs no Busch."

I had long set my heart on recording Mozart's best German opera with an all-German cast with the Berlin Philharmonic conducted by Beecham. First I asked him if he would record *Die Zauberflöte* in Berlin. He agreed like a shot. I took into my confidence James Gray, then EMI's financial wizard and a man in whom both T.B. and I had implicit trust. He gave us his wholehearted support. Having made sure that the Beethovensaal, the Berlin Philharmonic, and most of the singers I wanted were free, I dropped my bomb at a weekly meeting in which such matters were discussed. I knew I would win because nobody would risk offending Beecham, but there was the danger that I might be sabotaged by a shoestring budget. I was allowed, if I remember rightly, £3,000 for the whole undertaking including Beecham's and my fares and living expenses, soloists, and orchestral and chorus fees. This was no incurable headache because I knew where I could change British currency into German marks at a most advantageous rate. The last vestige of concern about money disappeared when Jimmy Gray explained that if need be we could evade Germany's strict currency controls by exporting to London for worldwide distribution some of Electrola's accumulated profits in the form of waxes or matrices.

I was not quite so lucky with the singers: three of those I wanted were not available, and Ludwig Weber, the last of the great black basses and a close friend, explained that two notes in the part—the repeated "Doch"—were too low for him and that he would not waste our time and money on the caprices of his vocal cords. (He did record the part for me with Karajan after the war, quite admirably.) We have only Hitler to thank for the other changes: Kipnis, my first choice for Sarastro, and Richard Tauber, for Tamino, were both Jewish and could not be expected to expose themselves to the evident dangers. Herbert Janssen, envisaged as Sprecher, had become a political refugee. I had tests made of all the other possible Sarastros to whom Austrian or German was their mother tongue, but they all had wide wobbles or poor intonation so we took Strienz—a good singer, his voice of fine quality, smallish for the role, but with a sensitive feeling for the shape of phrases. I was much criticized at the time over this choice but there was simply no better German-speaking bass available. The use of Roswänge also got me black marks in some quarters but since he had been Toscanini's choice for the part in Salzburg those criticisms cost me no sleep.

Before we started the recording I had gone ahead to coach and rehearse the singers. We had an admirable chorus of student and young professional singers (among them a Fräulein Schwarzkopf who had not yet made her debut) and I spent untold hours finding the right singers for the three ladies and the three boys:—voices individual enough to be immediately recognisable as characters, pure and steady enough to blend without causing distortion which was then and still is a major headache when recording trios of women's voices. In seven days in November 1937, usually two sessions a day, we had the whole of what is still generally acknowledged as musically the best performance of Mozart's penultimate opera on disc. We had two more sessions for necessary repeats in the first week of March 1938. Now, more than forty years later, it can be told that one side of this set was *not* conducted by Beecham and *not* played by the Berlin Philharmonic; neither was free when the hall was available and I desperately needed all three. It was Bruno Seidler-Winkler, Electrola's house accompanist, who conducted the Berlin State Opera Orchestra and followed Beecham's tempi and nuances through headphones. No prizes are offered for identification of which 78 r.p.m. side!

It was Beecham's first complete opera recording abroad, my first ever. I had the extra responsibility of interpreting for him: he spoke few words of German, and the cast and orchestra spoke no English, while T.B. repeatedly twigged me, "Why d'you waste your time acquiring foreign languages? Any damned foreigner will understand an Englishman if he speaks slowly and loudly enough!"

An incidental gain was that through careful housekeeping—black-market marks or Jones's genial benevolence—T.B. and I found ourselves sufficiently underspent to buy from the Staatsoper beautiful scenery and costumes by Araventinos for *Elektra* and *Die Entführung* for Covent Garden in the coming year. If I remember rightly that deal cost about £300. We also managed to hire the famous Schinkel scenery for *Die Zauberflöte*, which, like our two purchases, helped to improve some optical aspects of Covent Garden's stage in 1938.

One day over the Christmas holidays that year I lunched in his apartment. T.B. suddenly became earnest. "There will be no international opera season at Covent Garden unless you join me as my assistant artistic director." I was deeply moved by his proposal but had to explain that I did not think EMI would even consider giving me leave or permission to accept the honour and undertake an appointment which would occupy most of my time for much of each year. Additionally I could not afford to risk my future in that company. Beecham put my mind at rest: "I shall invite the Chairman of EMI to lunch, tell him that a summer season at Covent Garden is dependent entirely on his personal understanding and that if the way is not made clear for me to enjoy your collaboration I shall not renew my contract with EMI." As usual T.B. won.

Since I had been given a free hand I went out first for conductors. Furtwängler, who was already idolized at Covent Garden, was immediately cooperative—we had had preliminary discussions during the *Zauberflöte* recording without my realising how soon I was to be involved. Weingartner, who had a great following as a concert conductor but had never conducted opera in London, immediately agreed. Vittorio Gui, who was new to London, did all the Italian operas. I was particularly delighted that Erich Kleiber would conduct *Rosenkavalier* and *Der fliegende Holländer*.

Since the first part of the season was to be devoted to the German repertoire I tried to get that into shape first. One morning there was the following exchange:

T.B.: "How's *Rosenkavalier* shaping?"
W.L.: "Well. Lehmann will do all the Marschallins. Lemnitz Octavians. I've found an excellent new Ochs, Fritz Krenn. He's a dyed-in-the-wool Viennese with a splendid voice, oozes charm, and Kleiber's delighted with him."
T.B.: "Kleiber? Good God! You must reconsider it. He can't be any good! Why—what's the name of that little Italian chap in New York—?"
W.L.: "Tosca. . . ."
T.B.: "Yes, that's the fellow. Well, this T—ninny invited your precious Kleiber to conduct his own orchestra for six weeks, so he can't be any good!"

These last two prewar International Seasons at Covent Garden were a baptism of fire for me. The seething political anxieties in Central Europe, Britain, and France made negotiations of all kinds extremely difficult and we had started late engaging artists—less than five months before the season began. Kleiber, Weingartner, and Gui were unfailingly cooperative despite the paucity of orchestral rehearsals such as no man of comparable eminence would tolerate today.

T.B. would sometimes wound a friend rather than waste a witticism. Jokes at the expense of singers were a favourite form of mischief for him. I had engaged Lina Pagliughi for Gilda in 1938. She was almost as broad as she was short but musically and vocally the best interpreter of the part at that time. At his first glimpse of her on the stage,

Beecham said: "My dear boy, we can't let her be seen. She looks like a tea-cosy."

At the dress rehearsal of *Elektra* in 1938 I sat, as usual, immediately behind him to his left. The marvellous Chrysothemis was Hilde Konetzni, who was in those days a broth of a girl. So that she could follow T.B.'s beat as he flailed with both arms at his hundred-and-eleven-man orchestra, she edged down to the footlights to make sure of her entry at the phrase "Kinder will ich haben bevor mein Leib verwelkt" ("I want children before my body withers"). T.B., still flailing, asked me over his left shoulder: "What's that woman saying to me?" I paraphrased: "She's asking you to be the father of her next child." T.B., still flailing, looked up at her and said: "Send word to her that I'll reconsider her offer on some very cold winter's night."

In the years from June 1940 to May 1945, Beecham was in Australia and the Americas, although he spent the last three months of 1944 conducting a few concerts in England. He started his Australian visit on the wrong foot. To the journalist who, on his arrival, asked why he had left England when his country was at war, his reply has become the most often and correctly relayed of his *bon mots*: "The government declared a state of emergency so I obediently emerged." Less well-known is his remark to a reporter who asked when he was returning to Australia? T.B. froze him with, "Does anybody ever return to Australia?"

His long stay in the United States, during which he finally severed his association with Lady Cunard after some thirty years, was divorced from his first wife, and married the English pianist Betty Humby, were probably the most unsettled of his mature life. He was an itinerant musician conducting what the Metropolitan's director, Edward Johnson, knew he loved, French opera—both in the Met and on that company's spring tours—plus *Tristan, Falstaff*, three Mozart operas, and *Coq d'Or* coupled with *Phoebus and Pan*. He was a highly praised guest conductor with most of the leading American orchestras but often for only isolated pairs of concerts except with the Philadelphia Orchestra with which he had particularly good rapport. T.B.'s Seattle seasons must have been the very nadir of his artistic experiences.

An American diplomat and political counsellor who spent much time in Beecham's company in those American years has told me he was much concerned that T.B.'s capricious behaviour might be harm-

ful to his well-being. However, Beecham was in good shape when he
returned to England. By then he must have known that the control
of Covent Garden Opera House had fallen into the hands of people
who feared and disliked him as much as he rightly despised them. It
seems that with this banishment from Covent Garden an iron entered
his soul. It was not mentioned between us for many years, not until
1951 when for some unfathomable reason he accepted the near insult
of Covent Garden's invitation to conduct eighteen performances of
*The Bohemian Girl*—he who nearly forty years before that had introduced in that very theatre *Elektra, Salome,* and *Rosenkavalier.* Eventually they gave him six performances of *Meistersinger.*

*Sir Thomas' role in the early years of the Philharmonia is recounted
in that chapter. The break between him and Walter was repaired,
however; and Beecham would invariably turn to him for advice about
casting for opera or recordings.*

Apart from a prodigy like Karajan, the repertoires of most eminent
conductors have curious lacunae and excrescences. For example, from
Harvey Sachs's book on Toscanini, there emerge such strange facts
as that "Il Maestro" conducted the *Symphonie Fantastique* (fourth
and fifth movements only). Even odder, the great Italian fairly frequently conducted *Die Walküre, Siegfried,* and *Götterdämmerung,*
but never *Das Rheingold*—he, who often seems to have extolled
Wagner even above Verdi.

In Beecham's case the repertoire was odd. His instinctive, almost
archaeological interest in French eighteenth-century music and painting
was a lifelong obsession. *Grove* reports that he presented a hundred
and twenty operas. He admitted "putting on some outmoded operas
just for the fun of hearing them"—a foolish extravagance for a man
who could hear in his mind's ear whatever his eyes read. Why did
he, in whose musical heaven Berlioz was almost a deity, not spend
the money he threw down the drain on *Hamlet, Ivanhoe,* and Messrs.
Clutsam and Stanford—to mention but four of his deserved failures—
on a handsome production of *Les Troyens* in French or English or for
that matter Trojan?

He had a soft spot for the mixed odours of Patchouli and incense—
sex and saintliness—that permeate the operas of Massenet and Gounod.

161

He rated *Manon* so highly that he said he would gladly exchange all six *Brandenburg* Concertos for it and feel he had done well on the deal.

Beecham was the most widely admired British Wagner conductor and Britain has certainly produced no champion who has so energetically sponsored that composer's cause when it was most needed. Even during the 1914–1918 war he stoutly kept Wagner in the public ear and eye. He was not, I feel, a dyed-in-the-wool Wagnerian. All four nights of the Ring went on too long for him and the *leitmotivs* were repeated much too often. He habitually took great care in the preparation of Wagner operas in terms of beauty of orchestral sound but his cultural preferences were such that he felt Schumann to be the quintessence of the Teutonic spirit in music. Strange! Long stretches of the first two acts of *Tristan* he played marvellously. I believe that although he admired *Meistersinger,* he would have preferred it shorter with less "Protestant counterpoint." He was better at soaring lyricism than the comfortable *bürgerliche* world of *Die Meistersinger.*

In my time, he administered plentiful doses of Tchaikovsky the public gladly swallowed but did surprisingly little Verdi whose "grand tunes" and elemental vigour would seem to have been right up his street. It may have been that early and mid-period Verdi was too earthy and proletarian for him. The quickmindedness of *Falstaff* would seem to have been made to measure for him, but neither of the 1937 performances I heard had the wit or brilliance one expected from him.

With his nearly contemporary composers, T.B.'s relations were erratic. He gave the first British performances of *Elektra, Salome,* and *Rosenkavalier* with success unprecedented in London's operatic history. But after the production of *Josephslegende* in 1914, Beecham seems to have lost interest in Strauss as a composer. He conducted *Rosenkavalier* again in 1933 and there were two superb *Elektras* in 1938. Apart from a performance of the *Vier letzte Lieder* in Amsterdam, I have found no trace of him conducting any of the masterpieces of Strauss's long golden sunset. But he seemed rather pleased when I announced the probably first British performances of *Friedenstag* and *Dafne* for the 1939 season. They did not materialise. He entirely overlooked *Frau ohne Schatten* and *Capriccio,* two of Strauss's later masterpieces. He certainly could not unravel Hoffmansthal's involved symbolism in the former and he probably did not want every vital word of the *Capriccio* text to be heard over Strauss's magical instrumentation.

Beecham attributed much of the credit for the excellence of his American *Bohème* recording to close study with the composer, but there is little evidence that they were on personally friendly terms. It is unlikely that the morose Puccini would have much in common with the effervescent Beecham and there were acrimonious disputes about the staging (and later dropping) of *Suor Angelica* at Covent Garden.

*Later, when it appeared that Beecham might return to Covent Garden to conduct* Bohème *he wrote to Walter:*

> If it were possible to obtain most of those singers who took part in my recording of *La Bohème*, it would save me a good deal of pre-liminary labour. I am not of course including Victoria de los Angeles in the above selection, as I did not find her fulfilling most of the requirements Puccini himself had in mind for his ideal Mimi.

*I was much surprised to find this comment from Sir Thomas. Victoria's Mimi is considered the finest on records—an opinion I most definitely share. I also remember her first appearance at Covent Garden in the rôle and the great emotions her performance stirred in me, moving me to tears, some of them of envy. I realized that here was the ideal interpreter and that I could never match her overwhelming impersonation.*

It was almost certainly Beecham's lifelong attachment to French music that gave his *Carmen* its particular lustre. One morning in the fifties T.B. telephoned me and began rather pompously: "I am informed that you are the only person on whose musical judgment a certain Madame Callas relies implicitly. I am recording Carmen in Paris next year for EMI. Do you believe the lady could sing the title role to my satisfaction? And if so, will she place at my disposal the time I require for rehearsals and recording?" I told him that if she agreed to do it he would have every reason to be satisfied. I talked over the project with her, stressing that even for her there was an added nimbus of recording with Beecham. She declined with more than habitual grace: "I don't think my French is good enough yet and I won't take the risk of some damn' fool critic saying that I've lost my top—which I haven't—and that now I'm only a mezzo." All the same *Carmen* [*with de los Angeles in the title role!*] ranks among Beecham's

best operatic recordings, surpassed only by *Zauberflöte* and *Bohème*.
Alas not among Callas'!

*Years earlier Walter had also asked Callas to sing a mezzo part—in
the Verdi Requiem—and had sent her the following telegram:*

7th June 1954
MARIA MENEGHINI CALLAS        GRAND HOTEL        MILAN

ADORED MARIA VERONESE THE DAY AFTER I FIRST INVITED YOU TO
GRACE OUR REQUIEM RECORDS BY SINGING MEZZO SOPRANO PART I
DISCUSSED EVERY PHRASE WITH DE SABATA AND WE ARE BOTH CON-
VINCED THAT NO ONE COULD SING IT AS BEAUTIFULLY AS YOU STOP
LAST NIGHT AND TODAY HAVE READ IT THROUGH AGAIN WITH THE
SOUND OF YOUR INCOMPARABLE VOICE AND ART IN MY EARS AND
AM MORE THAN EVER CONVINCED YOU SHOULD FOR YOUR OWN
INTERESTS MAKE THE WORLD DE SABATA AND YOUR DEVOTED WALTER
HAPPY.

*She declined. Seconda donna!*

In the mid-1930's I tried to interest Beecham in several works I prized
highly but usually found him either suspicious or supercilious about
adding to his repertoire composers he did not know. I lent him pressings and a score of Mahler's *Lied von der Erde* only to be asked two
days later why I had inflicted on him "this monstrous afterbirth of the
illicit amours of Tristan and Isolde." Of Bruckner's Fourth and Seventh
Symphonies he said, "You'll never succeed in foisting that stuff on the
British public. The only thing that interests me in either of them is to
know who falls asleep first—the audience or I." I fared little better
with Bartók. T.B. took up Sibelius willingly, partly because the great
Finn had become a box-office magnet and because he knew that I
wanted to record several works for the Sibelius Society—and at that
time he seemed the best choice. (More sessions for T.B.'s orchestra!)
The incidents surrounding the recording of the Fourth Symphony
now seem more amusing than they were at the time. I sent test pressings of Beecham's first recordings to "Old Sib," as T.B. referred to
Sibelius, who replied in a long hand-written letter to me his detailed
criticisms, four pages of them—tempi wrong, expression wrong, and
so on. I telephoned Beecham that he would have to repeat certain
sides in view of the letter Sibelius had written me but that would

overspend my budget. The same afternoon Beecham's secretary insisted on having Sibelius' private number but that I must not know about it. No doubt Beecham talked the composer into sending him a congratulatory telegram.

Next morning, T.B. telephoned that he had received an important telegram from Old Sib; I must go to his apartment at once. With the composer's letter in my pocket, I went straight into attack and asked why he had not told me he wanted Sibelius' telephone number instead of slinking through secretaries. Unabashed he showed me a telegram from Sibelius expressing his complete satisfaction with the tests. Then I read him Sibelius' letter. With the blandest smile he said: "You win this round, my boy! We'll do the whole damned piece all over again and I'll pay the orchestra. I'll take the symphony on a provincial tour and you will be at every rehearsal with the score and the old cove's letter in front of you." When I said that Sibelius Four was a tough nut for provincial audiences to crack he merely said, "Leave that to me." Each morning he rehearsed Sibelius Four and in the evening substituted it for whatever popular work was on the programme, prefacing the announcement of the change by congratulating the audience on its perspicacity in asking him "to let them hear what is undoubtedly the greatest symphony written in the twentieth century—Sibelius' Fourth Symphony." Some twenty years later, I took the proofs of Karajan's recordings of the Fourth and Seventh Symphonies and *Tapiola* to Sibelius. A couple of days later he said, "Karajan is the only man who really understands my music: our old friend Beecham always makes it sound as if he had learned it and conducted it from a first fiddle part."

Many of us feel that T.B. was right in saying that performances of Handel exactly as they were done in the composer's time would be unacceptable to today's audiences—cranks, of course, apart. Beecham popularized some Handel works from various sources by dressing them in eighteenth- or even twentieth-century orchestral attire and made them popular as concert pieces. I have heard it said that in some recess of Beecham's brain there lurked an expert musical cosmetician.

In my youth, kind, and I believed musically trustworthy, seniors said they were sorry for me because I had not heard Beecham's exquisite performances of Mozart's operas between 1910 and 1918. I believed them. My friend Harold Rosenthal, whose library and filing system are stored with everything about opera from Monteverdi and his contemporaries to next year's as yet unconceived opera and are infinitely more reliable than any airport computer, produced evidence of strange Beecham monkeyings with Mozart. He had proof from the diary of a friend that Beecham had performed a version of *The Magic Flute* with the dialogue as orchestrally accompanied recitative. I knew that T.B. had inserted a chunk of translated Beaumarchais into the third act of *Figaro*. Did he flatter himself he knew better than Mozart? After reading Shaw's 1917 essay on the subject, I am glad that I did not experience those legendary "exquisite performances."

T.B.'s enthusiasm for Dame Ethel Smyth warms a couple of pages of his autobiography. He obviously had great admiration for that tweedy old battle-axe but whether it was as a composer or his near equal as a great British eccentric is less evident.

In the Diaghilev London years, and for a brief while afterwards, Beecham was infected with a passing interest in Stravinsky. He conducted *The Firebird* and *Petrouchka* on occasions. He took permanently into his repertoire *Scheherazade*, some excellent Russian overtures and pieces like *Thamar*. The collaboration first with Diaghilev in 1913 and 1914 and an ill-starred and almost forgotten season in the vast Lyceum Theatre in 1931 show that Beecham understood and had a good nose for Russian opera, from Dargomyzhsky to Rimsky-Korsakov. Chaliapin's preference for roles in which he could display his unique vocal and histrionic genius no doubt influenced T.B.'s choice, but Beecham's performances of *Prince Igor* in 1931 are among my happiest experiences of his art. But not the admirably cast though otherwise disastrous 1935 *Prince Igor*. The soundness of T.B.'s judgment is evident in the choice of works he mounted in 1931, many of which have not since been heard in London and certainly deserve revival rather than the minor works of Donizetti and their likes.

I have asked musical friends and concert-going acquaintances which piece in Beecham's repertoire they thought he did best in public. I was not in the least surprised that the National Anthem won, hands down. He did not admire Elgar, but no other conductor suggested the Edwardian pride and assurance, and the sheer panache and proud patriotism, that T.B. brought to make pomp and circumstance out of "God Save the Queen." (American friends assure me that he habitually made the stars in "The Star-Spangled Banner" sparkle more brightly than they have ever done before or since.) Close competitors in favour were Berlioz's *Royal Hunt and Storm* and *Carnaval Romain*; his suite of four pieces from the *Damnation of Faust*; Chabrier's *España*; a couple of Rossini overtures—particularly *La Gazza Ladra* and *La Scala di Seta*, of which we have recorded evidence that he made rings around all competition; *L'Arlésienne* Suite; works as diverse as *Thamar*, the slow movement of Mozart's Sinfonia Concertante for Violin and Viola, Borodin's *Prince Igor* Overture and Polovtsian Dances, "The Walk to the Paradise Garden," "Summer Night on the River" and "On Hearing the First Cuckoo in Spring," "The Entrance of the Queen of Sheba," *Messiah* (in the late twenties and early thirties), and the Trojan March. Not one classical symphony among this feast of "lollipops."

I do not know whether these answers are a criticism of the tastes of the company I keep or a key to the understanding of Beecham's unique qualities: the latter I believe. Apart from the Mozart and Delius pieces, there is virtually no slow music and no lengthy works. There is no Wagner, but he last publicly conducted a Wagner opera in London, *Meistersinger*, in 1951. As for other considerable operatic works, the last forty years of his life he conducted them only in New York and of course for the BBC. But it is surprising that the only Symphony that got even three votes was Bizet in C—a work of the teenaged Bizet.

T.B. occasionally remarked to me in the thirties: "I don't give a damn for the necessities of life: all I'm interested in are the luxuries of life." This phrase was always uttered seriously and seems to have been a basic part of his artistic philosophy. For me it links up revealingly with the frequent early morning telephone calls which so often began with: "My dear Walter. What are we going to do to rescue British musical life from the hegemony of the three bloodiest bores in the history of music? I am referring, of course, to Bach, Beethoven and Brahms." Those three B's were in his view the necessities of life to British musical taste and for which he did not give a damn.

Bach was for T.B. a particular bugbear: "Too much counterpoint and Protestant counterpoint at that." He was not alone among great conductors of his epoch in steering clear of Bach. Toscanini did hardly any and Richard Strauss laconically remarked, "St. Matthew's Passion perhaps, but not mine." The only Bach I heard T.B. conduct was a rehearsal of the *St. Matthew Passion* at a Leeds Festival which raised my hackles so that I took the next train to London. I missed *Phoebus and Pan*—an arrangement of a Bach cantata which Beecham coupled with *Coq d'Or*. The only Beethoven I heard him do as if with complete conviction on his part were the slow movements of the Second and Fourth Symphonies and the introduction to the canon in the first act of *Fidelio*—but I have yet to hear the conductor who can ruin that.

No attempt to show Beecham in the round could omit his eloquence. Public speaking gave him a chance of saying what he could not express in music, and pretty scurrilous it often was. Fortunately for his detractors, he occasionally lacked continuity of purpose and frequently changed his targets. Facts, even simple truths, had to take back seats when his words took wing. His verbal fireworks often made him enemies in the corridors of power but his audiences enjoyed them and that was what he was playing for. Audiences often seemed to favour his speech-making as much, or alas, even more than they understood the qualities of his music-making. And what I believe was dearest to his heart: he created and hypnotized two or three generations of a loyal public for the music of Delius, whom he regarded as an English composer, even the best composer of his era, if not of all time—a view to which he seduced many. Much as T.B. loved and helped popularize Mozart and Haydn, the Delius cause was his fondest preoccupation. He must have known subconsciously that his own death would be the death blow to the proper performance of Delius' music.

In Lord Drogheda's memoirs, I read to my complete astonishment that "the suggestion was mooted by Jack Donaldson [now Lord Donaldson, Minister for Arts and Education] and one or two other colleagues that Walter should be offered the post of Artistic Director [at Covent Garden] and I fancy that he would have welcomed the opportunity of moving in, with Sir Thomas Beecham following close behind." This episode was in 1958. Lord Drogheda's concern that T.B. "would follow close behind" me is engagingly and deceptively naive, coming as it does from the then managing director of the *Financial Times*. Covent Garden had missed the bus twelve or so years earlier when they appointed David Webster and Karl Rankl—two blunders which had rankled both T.B. and me. In 1951 Beecham had conducted his eighteen *Bohemian Girls* and the six *Meistersingers* and had since been neglected by Covent Garden. In 1958 he was nearly eighty. If Beecham had felt up to it, I would have invited him to fulfill his dream of conducting *Les Troyens* and to rehearse and conduct a few performances of whichever popular Italian operas we could cast supremely well for him—to crown his operatic life in the theatre where he really belonged.

# 10

## OTTO KLEMPERER

*Klemperer was the forgotten man of music when Walter enagaged him to be principal conductor for the Philharmonia Orchestra. He soon became the idol of the British musical public, and the concerts and recordings are part of musical history. That Walter and Klemperer eventually broke with one another is also part, a sad part, of the story.*

DEATH, WHO had so often unsuccessfully wrestled with Otto Klemperer, finally overcame him while he slept: only in sleep could Klemperer's adamant will have been broken. Misfortune, accidents, severe illnesses, major operations and often extreme poverty assailed him for a great part of his life but he faced them all inflexibly. No one who saw him interviewed on BBC Television after he had recovered from one of his worst accidents will forget his answer to John Freeman's question, "Did you ever think during the months you were in hospital that you might never conduct again?"—a grim, laconic "No." And throughout all these batterings of fate he was, as both Schnabel and later his daughter told me, handicapped by cyclothymia, the uncontrollable alternation of euphoric and depressive states, an illness "most frequently found among worthy persons of the upper social and intellectual classes." This incurable cyclic fluctuation of his nature was partly responsible for the erratic course of his career.

Klemperer was born in Breslau. Both parents were Jewish; his father, according to him, was a good amateur singer and an incompetent businessman, his mother a professional piano-teacher. When he was four the family moved to Hamburg where he had his first piano lessons from his mother. He left school at sixteen and went for a year to the Frankfurt Conservatoire, then to Berlin, where he studied conducting and composition with Hans Pfitzner. In 1905 he entered for the Rubinstein competition for pianists: the prize-winner was Wilhelm Backhaus.

In 1905 Max Reinhardt, the great Austrian regisseur and, with

170

Richard Strauss and Hugo von Hofmannsthal, co-founder of the Salzburg Festivals, gave Klemperer his first engagement as chorus-master and
deputy-conductor of Offenbach's *Orpheus in the Underworld* in Berlin
at what is now the Theater am Schiffbauerdamm. Fortunately for Klemperer the principal conductor quarrelled with a singer on the first
night and from the second performance Klemperer was in charge.

He had met Mahler two or three times and having been told that the
best way to win that composer's sympathies was to show interest in his
music, Klemperer had made a piano reduction of his Second Symphony,
the Scherzo of which he played to the composer by heart. Mahler was
so impressed and flattered that he gave Klemperer a recommendation on
his own visiting card, a souvenir Klemperer prized all his life and always carried with him. Mahler's introduction was enough to secure
Klemperer his first job in an opera-house, a five-year contract as chorus-
master and conductor at the German opera-house in Prague, a theatre
which until 1938 had a great tradition and which was the spring-board
for several illustrious careers. Muck and Nikisch had started there and
it was an important rung in Szell's ladder. So good was this theatre's
reputation that many Central European singers chose to take their
first engagements there rather than in other opera-houses which paid
better. Like Furtwängler starting in Zürich, Klemperer had to conduct
*The Merry Widow* in Prague where he stayed for three years until he
was dismissed on suspicion of having influenced a music-critic to dis-
parage the Director. Again Mahler came to his aid and induced the
Hamburg Opera to enagage him.

To all accounts he was happy there for a while. He conducted
*Rigoletto*, *Carmen* and *Martha* for Caruso and he frequently spoke of
his *Lohengrin* there as one of the greatest successes of his life. The first
and second "pages" were two young sopranos making their débuts in
Hamburg—Elisabeth Schumann and Lotte Lehmann. In spite of some
disagreements, even ruptures, these three remained friends. Klemperer's
daughter, Lotte, was named after Lehmann.

His involvement with Elisabeth Schumann led to an unpleasant
incident when, during a performance of *Lohengrin*, Klemperer was
assaulted by her offended husband. Again he had to leave an engagement before his contract had expired.

171

## Cologne and Marriage

The next stages of his career were Barmen (1912), some steps down from Hamburg, then Strassburg (1914), where he stayed until 1916 when he was appointed to Cologne. In the time I knew him he never spoke of the Barmen and Strassburg years. In Cologne he married Johanna Geissler, a soprano in the Cologne company by whom he had two children, Werner—now a well-known American film and television actor—and Lotte, who for thirty years smoothed her father's way, cared for him and tended him with superhuman patience and devotion to the end.

In Cologne Klemperer started building his reputation as a champion of contemporary music and his fame began to spread beyond the German frontiers. The Berlin Opera offered him a contract as a conductor which he rejected in favour of the musical directorship of Wiesbaden. It was there I first heard him in 1926 on my first visit to Germany and to a German opera-house. His performances of *Fidelio* and *Don Giovanni* were revelations even though the singing was not comparable with much that I had heard at Covent Garden in the 1924/25/26 seasons. Twenty years later I mentioned these Wiesbaden performances to Josef Krips, who at that time had been engaged in Dortmund. He confirmed my impressions and told me that Klemperer's work at Wiesbaden was so revealing that whenever he was free he habitually made the 120 mile journey to hear and study Klemperer's interpretations.

Klemperer's Wiesbaden contract is said to have allowed him six months leave each year—a rather unusual arrangement in those days and it seems strange that he, who had been such a strong advocate of the ensemble opera company and opponent of the repertory opera system, accepted it. It gave him the opportunity annually to conduct for six weeks in Russia and to accept other guest engagements abroad. From 1924 to 1936 each year he went to Russia as guest conductor and even conducted *Carmen* at the Bolshoi Theatre. In the latter part of his Berlin period Klemperer, like many of his Jewish intellectual friends, was freely spoken of as a "Salon-Communist," a term much used at the time for affluent or eminent extreme left-wingers.

## Berlin—1927

In 1927 Klemperer moved to Berlin to take over a new opera-house, the Staatsoper am Platz der Republik, the Kroll-Oper as it was usually called. At that time Berlin had an incredibly rich musical life. Three opera-houses, the Berlin Philharmonic Orchestra with Furtwängler as its chief conductor, concerts by the orchestras of the opera-houses and innumerable recitals by the greatest instrumentalists and best concert-singers of the period. The most able singers of the time who could sing in German were engaged at one or the other of the opera-houses and great conductors were in abundance: Furtwängler, Bruno Walter, Erich Kleiber, Leo Blech, Georg Szell, Klemperer (and occasionally even Richard Strauss)—all conducting opera—not for occasional visits but, except Strauss, living and working in Berlin. It was paradise for young musicians avid to learn but torture for them to decide which opera or concert to hear each day.

The administrative director of all the Berlin state opera-houses was Heinz Tietjen, a highly intelligent, unscrupulous operator. His skill at playing artists off each against the others was proverbial and hated, but he achieved the diplomatic miracle of holding his position first under the Weimar Republic, then under the Nazi régime, and finally played a leading role in Germany's musical life after World War II. He was also a brilliant producer and an able conductor who was virtually dictator of Berlin's operatic life and director of the Bayreuth Festivals from 1931 until they ceased late in the War. He was the Talleyrand of German musical life.

The theatre Klemperer took over with a ten-year contract was a new venture. It was large, rather uncomfortable and acoustically harsh. The declared policy was to provide opera for a large public at low prices. Klemperer chose operas which, with few exceptions, were not in the repertoires of the other theatres and he put into practice his ideas on modernization of production. I saw the much discussed *Der fliegende Holländer* in modern dress with Moje Forbach as Senta wearing a coarse woolen blue pullover and a rough tweed skirt. The *Fidelio* scenery, probably influenced by Appia or early Bauhaus ideas, was cold and rectilinear. To my eyes the revolutionary sets were anachronisms, ugly and contradictory to the music. Fritz Krenn (Ochs at Covent Garden in 1938) sang Rocco. Rose Pauly, at that time an untidy but intense singer, sang Leonore. The repertoire was not really suited to the public it was supposed to attract and apart from the few standard favourites which were mostly produced against the music and subject, little of the novel repertoire Klemperer introduced has stood the test of time. The era of the producers who blight the world's opera-houses today seems to have been Klemperer's innovation. At his concerts with his opera-house orchestra he did much Stravinsky, less Hindemith.

After three years the Kroll-Oper venture closed and Klemperer, unwillingly, was transferred to the Theater Unter den Linden, then Berlin's principal opera-house. I went to the dress-rehearsal of a new *Der Rosenkavalier* production: a charmless, insensitive performance from Klemperer. Lotte Lehmann was the Marschallin. That glorious artist who instinctively poured out warm radiance and impulsive femininity was not the most accurate of singers. Having been stopped and corrected by Klemperer two or three times, she lost patience, walked down to the foot-lights and said to him: "Don't keep on interrupting me! I'm only singing a few performances here, then I'm off to sing it at Covent Garden, then at the Chicago Opera." Klemperer's reply was a typically laconic question: "Strauss or the Lehmann version?"

On February 12, 1933, Klemperer conducted his last performance for many years of opera in Germany, a few weeks after he had been awarded the Goethe Medal for his "services to German art" and less than a fortnight after Hitler had taken power. Klemperer was not to conduct opera again until fourteen years later.

Already in the twenties Klemperer had begun to give concerts outside Germany. He went to New York for the first time in 1926. In 1927 the Royal Philharmonic Society invited him to conduct a concert in London on January 26, 1928, but broke off negotiations because he inflexibly insisted "that his programme should consist of Beethoven's Third and Fifth Symphonies and nothing else." However his London début was not to be long delayed. On Schnabel's recommendation Mrs. Courtauld invited him to London and he made his début at the Queen's Hall in 1929. He was well over forty. The programme was what Heifetz many years later described as "poison to the box-office"—Schoenberg's orchestration of Bach's E-flat Prelude and Fugue and Bruckner's Eighth Symphony (its first performance in Britain, I believe) but the Courtauld-Sargent concerts were fully subscribed, even over-subscribed. The press reception was cool—as far as I remember the only critic who sensed Klemperer's qualities was W. J. Turner—and there was mutual dislike between orchestra and conductor. But Klemperer returned in 1930 and with the same orchestra gave a revealing performance of Beethoven's Ninth with an incredibly exuberant finale which brought the audience shouting to its feet. London did not hear him again until after the War.

174

## Early 78s

It was during his Berlin period that Klemperer made his first recordings, mostly for Polydor, but there were three works for Electrola published here on the HMV black label which I treasured for years: Brahm's *Academic Festival Overture,* the *Tristan* Prelude with Wagner's own concert ending (on four 10-inch sides!) and above all a glowing, sensual performance of Salome's Dance. Strauss and Klemperer collectors please note!

Within two weeks of Hitler's accession to power Klemperer left for Zürich. At first things did not go too badly for him. His wife, who followed him with the children, had smuggled out some money in a cake (Jews were not allowed to take money out of Germany) and he conducted some concerts. Through a chance acquaintance in Italy he was invited to take over the Los Angeles Philharmonic Orchestra, which was looking for a resident conductor. This also involved open-air concerts in the Hollywood Bowl, which he must have hated. However, he accepted and in 1935 he moved his family to California and eventually became an American citizen. He must have felt quite at home there because the cream of Berlin's Jewish left-wing intellectuals—philosophers, historians, doctors, lawyers—had found their ways to California. From 1934 to 1936 he conducted the Philadelphia Orchestra for a few weeks and in 1936 he took over the New York Philharmonic-Symphony Orchestra from Toscanini for three months. At about this time he was invited to choose the musicians for the foundation of the Pittsburgh Orchestra.

It seems that he was in poor health and worrying financial circumstances in the years immediately before the War. He was habitually reticent about this period. In 1939 he had a major operation for a brain-tumour believed to have been the result of falling from the podium during a rehearsal in Leipzig several years earlier. The operation left him partially paralysed and for many years he was unable to conduct standing. This operation and the long convalescence had drained his financial reserves and for the greater part of the War he had very little work. He was a discounted, if not forgotten, man and his daughter worked in a factory to bring in some money.

# Return to Europe

In desperation he returned to Europe in 1946 and found himself not only well-remembered but in demand, particularly because the Americans, French, British and Russians had decided that every distinguished Central European musician who had performed in German-occupied Europe during the War was *ipso facto* a Nazi whose rehabilitation must be delayed until they had been cleared by de-Nazification boards.

In Stockholm, Klemperer had the good fortune to meet Aladár Todt, the husband of Annie Fischer. They were living there as refugees from Hungary. Todt was one of the wisest and most cultivated of men and certainly the gentlest I have known. He was, so Hungarians tell me, one of their best writers. He had been a vigorous proselytiser of Bartók, a friend of Dohnányi and Kodály and a distinguished critic in Budapest. Soon Todt was invited back to Budapest as Director of the Opera there and on taking up this appointment he invited Klemperer to become his principal conductor. It was a stormy period; part of the time Klemperer was in his euphoric state. Disputes and temperamental outbursts were frequent but to all accounts he made wonderful music. He conducted the three Mozart-Da Ponte operas, *Entführung* and *Zauberflöte, Fidelio, Tannhäuser, Lohengrin* and *Die Meistersinger* as well as some Italian operas, and many concerts. But yet again the engagement ended in disputes although Klemperer remained friendly with the Todts.

Klemperer was still an itinerant musician. He conducted, in Vienna, one performance of *Figaro* and an orchestral concert in Salzburg in 1947 and should have conducted the world première of von Einem's opera *Dantons Tod* but after one or two rehearsals Ferenc Fricsay, then unknown outside Budapest, was suddenly called in to take over. These performances launched Fricsay on his brilliant but short international career.

In 1948 Klemperer conducted in Buenos Aires and *Carmen* at the Komische Oper in East Berlin. Felsenstein was the producer and spent so much time in preparing the first three acts that Klemperer had to remind him that his own contract was expiring in a couple of weeks. The last act was quickly put together and Klemperer conducted a few performances. In the summer of 1949 he toured Australia.

It was Richard Austin who first brought Klemperer back to London at the end of the 1940s. Austin was trying to resurrect the spirit and organization of the pre-War Courtauld-Sargent concerts under the name of "The New Era Concert Society" at the Albert Hall, for which he engaged my Philharmonia Orchestra and several distinguished European conductors, among them Klemperer. I went with William Walton to hear him conduct a programme which, if I remember rightly, was a Bach suite, a Stravinsky symphony and the *Eroica*. It was an unhappy occasion. My orchestra seemed unable to understand Klemperer's beat, and the Stravinsky was new to them. Walton and I left at the interval.

In 1951 the Philharmonia Orchestra was invited to give two concerts as part of the Festival of Britain. I had engaged Schnabel as soloist for both of them and wanted Szell to conduct but he was not free, so in Schnabel's suite at the Hyde Park Hotel the three of us discussed possible alternatives. Both Schnabel and Szell urged me to invite Klemperer because "he is still capable of marvellous performances and it would help him." So I engaged Klemperer.

As it turned out, Schnabel was too ill to play. Solomon was engaged as soloist for one concert, Myra Hess for the other. I was not in London at the time of the rehearsals of the first concert but a crisis occurred before the second when Klemperer, without warning, refused to conduct the *Enigma* Variations and threatened to cancel the concert unless he could substitute Mozart's *Jupiter* Symphony for the Elgar. My incomparable and imperturbable assistant Jane Withers telephoned me and I agreed to let him have his own way; I would fly back as quickly as possible. It was not until well after the interval of the second concert that I reached the Festival Hall in time to hear the last movement of the *Jupiter*—powerful, incredibly transparent and the structure marvellously revealed. This time the public and critics understood what they had heard and on those two evenings Klemperer laid the foundation stone of what was to be the longest, the most successful, the last, and I hope, the happiest epoch of his career.

But there were still many hurdles to be overcome. A day or two after the second concert he and his wife came to dinner at my house. Conversation was easy and I had ordered a car to take them home at 10:30 P.M. The car arrived but in spite of his wife's prompting he refused to leave: "Now I've found someone to talk with, you want to drag me away. Lie down on that sofa and go to sleep." His wife obeyed. The car waited and we talked until half past four in the morning. I had to tell him that I must start work at nine-thirty that morning. He woke his wife and they trundled off to the car. Four hours later the telephone beside my bed woke me. It was Klemperer. "Since you turned me out of your house while I was in the middle of a sentence I want to finish now what I was saying." He talked for five minutes and finished with, "And now it's time you went to your work."

Klemperer's reported recollections of the conversation of that evening differ from mine. I did suggest, as I have said earlier in this article, that the untimely collapse of the Kroll-Oper was probably in part due to a misjudgement of what that type of public would like. But the fascinating and revealing part of the conversation came when I asked him why he had stopped including so much contemporary music in his programmes. Klemperer, who was then sixty-five, said he had decided that he had so much to think about and clarify in the great German classics from Bach to Bruckner that he intended henceforth to concentrate on them. Except for very minor differences of opinion he and his daughter turned to me for advice and help for the next thirteen years and I soon put him on the road to a very substantial annual income for the rest of his life.

The public and critical reaction to the two Festival Hall concerts made it clear to me that Klemperer had begun to establish himself with the London public and that his approach to the classical repertoire was to the taste of the time. He represented for the refugees which then made up a substantial part of London audiences a father figure and a nostalgic symbol of happier days in Berlin. I urged EMI to let me make an exclusive recording contract with Klemperer and told them that whether they agreed or not I intended to engage him for several Philharmonia concerts. They agreed—reluctantly.

## A Contract with EMI

I met Klemperer in Salzburg that summer; he was shabby, depressed and reluctant to sign a contract with the British Columbia Gramophone Company because he felt a moral obligation to George H. de Mendelssohn-Bartholdy of the Vox company for whom he had made several records in Vienna, including the grave and powerful performance of the *Missa Solemnis*. That autumn Klemperer slipped on ice at Montreal airport, broke a hip and was in hospital for the best part of a year. I find a slip inserted in the programme of the Philharmonia Concert Society concert of October 21, 1951, regretting that "owing to his unfortunate accident Dr. Klemperer will be unable to conduct the Society's concerts in January and February 1952." However, he signed his first contract with Columbia on May 10, 1952. We were soon in further trouble. As a naturalized American subject Klemperer had to return to the U.S. at specified intervals; otherwise, his American citizenship would be revoked. In August 1952 he wrote me saying that James Petrillo, the Caesar of the American Federation of Musicians, of which Klemperer had to be a member, had refused permission for him or any other American member of that union to record in Europe. A reply drafted by EMI's legal department but which I had to sign threatened him with "an actionable breach of contract." The storm slowly abated and in July 1953 at his wish signed another letter terminating his contract.

In the spring of 1954 I went to Milan to see him, his wife and daughter. He conducted a late afternoon concert with a poor orchestra (apart from a wonderful first oboe) in the Teatro Nuovo, a low-roofed, depressing hall. Although Klemperer had conducted a Beethoven cycle at La Scala in 1935, given concerts there in 1946 and 1947 and conducted *Zauberflöte* four times with an all Italian cast (except Lipp as Astrafiammante), the audience was small and apathetic. But the performance of Mozart's A-major Symphony No. 29 was so enchanting that this and the *Jupiter* were the first Mozart symphonies he recorded for me.

That evening the Klemperers had dinner with me. Sensing that there were serious matters to be discussed I took them to a quiet restaurant which specialized in chicken roasted on the spit. Klemperer ordered two boiled eggs in a glass, and a glass of milk. They put their problems to me. To retain his American passport he had, according to the McCarren Act, to return frequently (I believe it was once a year) to the U.S. In America he could not earn enough to live on. If he gave up his American passport he could re-claim his German nationality and probably get the pension due to him for his years as a conductor in Germany. What did I think would be best for them? I told them frankly I could not myself, nor did I believe EMI would, guarantee him a minimum annual income but I felt confident that from concerts with my orchestra and royalties from recordings he could soon count on £2,000 a year. I considered they would be wise to stay in Europe. I would do all I could to help him. Next morning his daughter telephoned me that they had decided to follow my advice. Soon they settled in Zürich, which was his home until he died.

In the meantime we had made a new exclusive contract for recording for Columbia. The first sessions in the Kingsway Hall on October 5 and 6, 1952, went splendidly. I had supervised and produced Beecham's recordings since the early 1930's, Weingartner's since 1938, von Karajan's, Kubelik's and Krips's since 1946, Böhm's and even Furtwängler's since 1947 and found them all not only amenable but grateful for suggestions, open to discussion and criticisms; I felt no reason to change my technique for Klemperer in spite of his physical size, his grim silences and Old Testamental severity. It worked.

On the morning of the third day, October 7, black clouds loomed. To set Klemperer's mind at rest that Columbia was not basically against good contemporary music and incidentally to please Dennis Brain, who had begged to record the Hindemith Horn Concerto with Klemperer, we started on that work. Within an hour I sensed on the horizon another of the storms that had plagued Klemperer's career. At the interval Dennis came to me and said: "Guv-nor, I can't risk it with that old man; he's got no rhythm and he can't or won't accompany me." (Dennis sometimes enjoyed the sport of hurrying.) Lotte Klemperer, fearing yet another crisis in her beloved father's embattled career, was deathly pale although she had not heard Brain's plaint. Tension grew. At the end of the session Dennis, the gentlest of men, refused even to come to the evening session—he was not going to blow his lips to shreds for something that could never be published. I told him I would phone him in the afternoon. I could feel that the orchestra was on Dennis's side. I went home, drank a strong Martini and refused lunch.

That afternoon at about three o'clock Lotte Klemperer arrived unannounced at my office still paler, not yet knowing that Brain had refused to go on but all too aware of the impending danger and fearful that yet another break might put us all back to square one. To save everybody's face I changed the programme for that evening to another Hindemith work which I know Klemperer admired—*Nobilissima Visione*. Lotte telephoned her father who agreed and when she had left, I called Dennis that he must come to the evening session and behave as if nothing had happened. Faces and honour were saved that afternoon.

*Nobilissima Visione* was new to the orchestra but we completed it in two gratefully relaxed sessions and as a coupling we recorded the *St. Antony Variations*. From the moment I asked Klemperer to insist that in the statement of the theme the contrabassoon should play much louder a musical rapport was established between us which was to last for many years. We then recorded the *Jupiter* Symphony and the Mozart A-major Symphony No. 29, two works which we both particularly loved and which he did incomparably. That batch of work was completed with his recording of the four Bach Suites—today's pedants prefer to find his performance "old fashioned", but their clarity and integrity will command respect, probably reverence, in years to come. Klemperer mistrusted musicologists. "They know nothing about music but all about 'ology.'" Fashions of style in musical performance are variable and as much a matter of vogue as the length of women's skirts, the location of their waists or—today—men's hair-dos. We finished that year's recording with all the four overtures Beethoven wrote for *Fidelio*.

Before the end of this batch of work Klemperer and the orchestra had, so to speak, fused. He was always at the hall early and sat on his rostrum watching each player's arrival with a baleful eye. He worked carefully, stopped rarely and used few but explicit words. He usually played a whole movement through then rehearsed all his wants in detail. Slowly he thawed a little and over the years we made a good collection of his caustic witticisms. The first, I think, was when the sub-principal first violin looked repeatedly and pointedly at his wrist-watch because Klemperer was rehearsing a minute or two over time. Klemperer at first feigned to ignore this, then stopped the orchestra, leaned over to the player and asked mock-solicitously: "Is it still going?" and continued rehearsing.

## Karajan's Visit

Klemperer's recording history from then on is history if not yet legend. In October 1955 we recorded Beethoven's *Eroica*, Seventh, and Fifth Symphonies in that order. The slow movement of the *Eroica* was so profoundly moving, so different from anything I had ever heard that I telephoned Karajan and tried to explain to him the miracle Klemperer had achieved in this movement. Karajan said: "Put it on next season and I'll come over specially to hear it." He came and, deeply moved, went down to the artists' room to thank the old man.

Klemperer: "Herr von Karajan, what are you doing here?"
Karajan: "I have come only to thank you and to say that I hope I shall live to conduct the Funeral March as well as you have done it. Good night."

By now Klemperer had passed his seventieth birthday but for a man who had suffered major illnesses he was working with extraordinary vigour, and although the hearing of one ear was impaired I do not believe orchestral players noticed it. We were in the middle of recording the Brahms symphonies when he quietly telephoned me one morning to say that his wife, to whom he was devoted, had died in Munich during the night. He was sorry to have to cancel some sessions but he would fly back immediately after the funeral.

One year in the fifties his daughter telephoned me to say that he had been rushed into hospital with a perforated appendix and undergone an emergency operation. When he had recovered from that he had to undergo another major operation but this too went well and the giant was soon back at work.

## *Philharmonia Chorus*

Ever since Karajan had conducted Beethoven's Ninth Symphony at his second London concert in the late 1940s with the BBC Chorus, which sang deplorably to his ears and mine, I had planned to have my own Philharmonia Chorus to match the quality of the Philharmonia Orchestra. The one man in England capable of training such a chorus, Herbert Bardgett, was tied up with the Huddersfield Chorus and various similar but small bodies in the North and could not undertake a weekly visit to London. The problem obsessed me for years. Klemperer said I would never solve it. Suddenly at lunch with Elisabeth in a restaurant above Lucerne in August 1956 I found the only possible solution; I would cable Wilhelm Pitz, whose work I knew well from Bayreuth, inviting him to Lucerne to discuss an interesting project. He came within two days and agreed to audition possible singers; if we could get a minimum of two hundred good *young* voices, all amateurs—I set low age limits—I would establish the Philharmonia Chorus and he should be its Chorus Master, flying from Aachen once a week for at least one rehearsal, with two months holiday for the chorus while Pitz was in Bayreuth. We started the auditions in September and to our mutual astonishment found nearly all we needed. We were a bit short on real tenors and deep contraltos when we started, but the Ninth went into rehearsal and after a year's intensive work Klemperer conducted the Ninth Symphony with my Philharmonia Orchestra and Chorus singing in impeccable German—two performances—as the climax of the first of his London Beethoven Festivals (1957). It was recorded that November. A distinguished conductor who was staying with me at the

With Maestro George Szell we recorded Strauss, Mozart, and Mahler. Alfred Brendel played the piano obbligato for Mozart's "Ch'io mi Scordi di te?" We listen to the playback (*top*).

Walter traveled constantly—either to record or advise his musical colleagues. At Bayreuth (*top*) he talks with Maestro Hans Knappertsbusch. In Stockholm (*center*) he advises Elisabeth Söderström, the Octavian to my Marschallin, while Goeran Gentele observes. Again in Bayreuth (*bottom*), he listens to a playback of *Die Meistersinger* with Wieland Wagner.

Many famous sopranos came under Walter's charge. Here he helps prepare Joan Sutherland for the role of Donna Anna (*below, left*), Birgit Nilsson as Minnie (*right*), and Maria Callas as Gioconda (*below, right*). Renata Scotto's first recital album (*bottom*) was also under Walter's aegis.

Walter produced all of Callas' best recordings, many of them with her
other great musical mentor, Maestro Tullio Serafin (*above*).

In retirement Walter continued to produce my own recordings (*above,* with Geoffrey Parsons and Dietrich Fischer-Diskau), but there were other pleasures—flowers and cats, for example.

He also accompanied me on my concert tours. Like everyone else, we sometimes had to wait. I took this picture in the train station in Milan.

One of Walter's great pleasures was gardening. We had beautiful ones at all our homes. Here is his very English garden at the Petit Port, near Geneva.

And, of course, our greatest pleasure, the master classes—in New York (*above*), in Trieste (*below*), and many points in between.

time listened to the first pressings of the choral sections and muttered: "Unfortunately . . . too good." Klemperer, Pitz, the Chorus and I were very proud.

In the summer of 1958 I went to Zürich for the first public exhibition of works of art from the incredible Buehrle collection. To my surprise Lotte Klemperer was waiting for me outside my hotel. She was drawn and pale. Hastily she explained that her father had a sudden recurrence of his euphoric state. She evidently knew from experience that these periods could last a long time and perhaps endanger his work.

## Tragedy Again

That autumn Klemperer was to conduct concerts at the Leeds Festival. A couple of days before he was due to arrive Lotte telephoned me to say that he had bronchitis and would have to cancel Leeds, but he would be well in time for the London concerts—one miscellaneous programme and a Beethoven Festival due to start in the last week of October. Daily telephone calls to Zürich were reassuring; the patient was recovering normally. Early one morning, shortly before he was due in London there was a telephone call from his daughter; against doctors' orders her father had been secretly smoking in bed during the night, set the bed clothes on fire and, in an effort to quench the flames, doused himself with the nearest liquid, which happened to be a large bottle of spirits of camphor. Awakened by the smell of burning and camphor she had run to his room and managed to put out the flames but not before her father was terribly burned. He had been rushed into hospital and the situation was grave. The best doctors in Zürich were in attendance but his life was in danger.

Lotte was as brave as her father who was soon talking of fulfilling all his London engagements. The doctors insisted that I must be the person to break it to him that for the first few concerts deputies would have to be found, but that I must give him to believe he would be able to conduct the later concerts. It was a chilling experience to have to lie to this huge, fearless and determined old man now helpless, bandaged and prostrate, knowing perfectly well that even if he recovered he had months of suffering ahead. I asked Karajan and Böhm if they would take over but neither was free any of those dates. Eventually Cluytens agreed to conduct the first concert and Giulini the first concert of the

183

Beethoven cycle. The greatest help came from van Beinum, a man I greatly admired but had never met nor invited to conduct my orchestra. He rearranged his Concertgebouw schedule so that he could, if needed, conduct nearly all the concerts but he could not in any case take over the two performances of the Ninth. Between the concerts I frequently flew to Zürich to reassure Klemperer that he would soon be well again and able to conduct.

The doctors insisted that he must not know he would not be able to conduct the Ninth; they feared he might suffer a relapse. Eventually, about two weeks before the rehearsals for the Ninth were due to begin I had to break it to him that I must engage someone to stand in just in case he did not feel well enough to conduct; would he choose with me from the list of available conductors? Slowly I read out the eleven names; to each one he replied either with a mock-pitying or a scornful "No," once or twice with a weak but strident laugh. At the end of this depressing litany he said, "I have the solution—engage Hindemith!" I explained gently that much as I admired a lot of Hindemith's music, and liked him enormously as a man, I could not do that to the Philharmonia audiences.

I had heard Hindemith conduct the Ninth twice—twice too often for me. Klemperer replied that either Hindemith had been in bad conducting form or I in bad listening form. In any case it would be interesting for the London public to hear how a great composer of the twentieth century conducted the music of a great composer of the nineteenth century. Seeing my reluctance Klemperer, ill as he was, put on a virtuoso performance which convinced me in retrospect that he could have been a great ham-actor. He appealed to me half-tearfully as "the only friend I have, you who have helped me so much, not to refuse what may be the last favour I ask of you." He would not like me to have that on my conscience for the rest of my life. I capitulated and, still against my better judgment, engaged Hindemith.

I had to go to New York but I told Jane Withers to telephone me after Hindemith's first concert as soon as she had collected the opinions of the few people whose judgement I relied on. They were chilling. I was back in London to hear the second performance but crept out of my box shamefully in the middle of the slow movement. A few days later I was in Zürich to see Klemperer. He was obviously much better and, rarely for him, quietly genial.

Klemperer: "My friend and colleague Hindemith had bad criticisms for the Ninth in London."

Legge: "How do you know? You've always said you never read criticisms of your own concert or anyone else's."

Klemperer: "When a man is as ill as I am he reads anything—even musical criticism."

Legge: "It's your fault; you insisted I should engage him. I'll never take your advice about artists again."

Klemperer: "You have been in the musical profession long enough to know that gloating over the misfortunes of colleagues is the only joy left in life."

A month later Peter Diamond beamed to me that he had a good new Klemperer story—against me. He had recently seen the old man, who had said to him, "You know, Herr Diamond, that I have only one real friend in the world—and he's not a Jew and he's not German . . . . he's English . . . . Legge! Do you know what he did to remind the London public how I conduct Beethoven? He engaged Hindemith—think of it, *Hindemith!* to conduct the Ninth Symphony!"

My troubles were not yet over. For the spring of 1959 I had announced that Klemperer would conduct a Mozart cycle of three concerts, a Brahms cycle of four concerts, two miscellaneous programmes and finally the complete *St. Matthew Passion* with the cast that eventually recorded it and sang it at the Festival Hall with him a couple of years later. I had to find other conductors for all these concerts except the *Matthew Passion* which was postponed.

## Harmonious Thirteen

I knew Klemperer personally only from 1951 until the spring of 1964 and for ten years supervised every recording he made except a couple of sessions of the Mozart Horn Concertos with Alan Civil. It was a harmonious cooperation and except on two occasions—both of them at recordings of concertos—we got on well together. We frequently argued, mostly about tempi and balance of texture, but almost invariably came to agreement without more than parry and thrust.

He preferred to record whenever possible whole movements at a stretch and was reluctant to repeat even short passages to edit into a complete take however necessary they might be—mostly because of untidy chording or because, as Sir Henry Wood was wont to say, "Gentlemen, this ensemble ain't ensemble!"

Klemperer's main preoccupations were with form and with clarity of musical structure. Everything thematic had to be in high relief. In general he favoured a big sound and he rarely asked for *pianissimi* such as Toscanini, Furtwängler, and Karajan insisted on. The only two memorable exceptions to this were the opening of the slow movement of the *Eroica* and the cello and bass *unisono* in the last movement of the Ninth. He had little interest in sensuous beauty of sound either in orchestra playing or in voices. Musicianship, rhythm, solidity of sound, steady tempi, accuracy of note-values and clarity of texture were all he asked. Tenderness and sentiment, elegance, grace and charm seem to have been left out from his musical make-up nor did he admire them in other conductors; he was all intellectual power and granite will. In front of the orchestras he had a strong force of suggestion and an almost hypnotic ability to get out of them what he wanted even though in the years we worked together the partial paralysis somewhat limited what he might have expressed with his exceptionally beautiful hands.

His wit was ironical and mocking, often cruel. He usually greeted the news of a distinguished colleague's death with, "So. We are having quite a good year." The one time they met, Callas got the better of him. She went with me to a Klemperer concert and at the end I took her down to meet him.

Klemperer: "I have heard you twice. *Norma,* very good. *Iphigénie*—horrible."
Callas (smiling): "Thank you, Maestro."
Klemperer: "But I am sure Herr Legge will agree to invite you to sing at a concert here with me. What would you like to sing?"
Callas (wreathed in smiles): "The arias from *Iphigénie,* Maestro."

From 1955 onwards I had been sending Wieland Wagner each new Klemperer record as soon as it was published, hoping we could together devise some way of getting Klemperer to conduct in Bayreuth. There was, of course, the difficulty for the physically-handicapped Klemperer to clamber up the steep steps to the rostrum in Bayreuth's orchestral pit but we projected a performance of the Ninth to open a Bayreuth Festival with Klemperer conducting the Philharmonia Orchestra. Unfortunately the Bayreuth musicians refused to play for the Festival unless they played the Ninth.

Some years later Peter Diamond, at that time Director of the Hol-

186

land Festival, engaged Klemperer to conduct and Wieland Wagner to produce *Tristan und Isolde*. That was in 1959. In defiance of his doctor's orders Klemperer, not fully recovered from his burns, still having skin-grafts to repair his wounds, went to Holland to prepare *Tristan*.

He was running a high temperature and after a few days Lotte telephoned me to go over to Holland immediately to induce her father to give up *Tristan*. By the time I arrived he had sensed he could not go on. The two Klemperers, Wieland and I lunched together. Klemperer ate little and seemed to be asleep. Wieland whispered to me across the table that he had something important to discuss. Klemperer, immediately alert, suspiciously insisted on knowing what we were going to talk about. Wieland hedged at first but to placate Klemperer admitted he wanted to discuss with me possible cuts—not for Holland but for Bayreuth—in the second act of *Tristan*: König Marke's long solo, from the dramatic point of view, holds up the action. Klemperer protested: "What do I hear? Wagner's grandson wants to make cuts in his grandfather's work? Horrible! Wait—I have the solution! Marke sings his first bar 'Thatest Du es wirklich?' ('Did you really do it?') to Tristan. Now the cut you want. Marke sings 'You fool! I have to do it, you don't!' Curtain!" Klemperer left for a long convalescence a few days later.

By the end of that August he had sufficiently recovered to conduct the Philharmonia Orchestra in the Lucerne Festival. The euphoric phase had not yet spent itself during his long illness though perhaps it may have helped him through it, even saved his life. We were all so glad that he was restored to physical health that at the first rehearsal in front of the whole orchestra I invited him to become its Principal Conductor for life, which he accepted.

## Don Giovanni

I was now near realizing a long-cherished project for Klemperer to record and afterwards give two concert performances of *Don Giovanni* in October that year. I had collected a jewelled cast of great singers: even for Masetto the young Piero Cappuccilli, now the supreme Italian baritone, was engaged. After two days recording Klemperer suddenly ran a high temperature and his London doctor insisted that he should cancel the recording and the concerts. I was left with the cast contracted for the recording and the concerts which were already nearly sold out three weeks ahead, but no conductor. I appealed to Giulini who hardly knew the opera but agreed to take over.

Heinrich Schmidt from the Vienna Opera and Antonino Tonini from La Scala—my invariable and invaluable musical assistants—and I had all lived with this opera more than half our lives. We promised Giulini that as a team and with that cast we would help him produce a great *Don Giovanni*. Four or five days before the end of the recording Giulini, who had hoped to be released from a broadcast in Holland, learned that the Dutch refused to change the dates: he would be unable to conduct the concert performances but he could finish the recording, except many of the recitatives. Fortunately Colin Davis, who had helped me out during the Mozart cycle that spring, was free and he took over the concerts with great success. I am happy to believe that these concerts born of many crises successfully launched him on his career.

The 1959–60 season then continued without mishap. Klemperer was well enough to fulfil all his further engagements to audiences happily welcoming him after his long illness. That season included the Mozart and Brahms cycles which deputies had conducted for him the previous season. The same summer he went with the Philharmonia Orchestra to the Vienna Festival to conduct a Beethoven cycle. I believe this was the greatest success he ever enjoyed in Vienna, where more than fifty years earlier he had aspired to be a member of Mahler's musical staff.

In 1960 Herbert Graf invited Klemperer to conduct *Fidelio* at the Zürich Opera. Mansouri produced, Jurinac was the Leonore. For Klemperer it was a triumph but thanks to his acrimonious rows with the orchestra they refused to play with him again.

He had his recompense in 1961 when he produced and conducted *Fidelio* at Covent Garden, his début there at the age of 76! Finding a scenic designer to his taste had already given the Covent Garden staff many headaches. His ideas had changed since the Kroll *Fidelio* and it was evident he wanted more conventional, nearly naturalistic, sets, so I suggested Hainer Hill, whose *Elektra* scenery in the East Berlin Opera had impressed me. I showed Klemperer a photograph of it and Hill was engaged. This series of performances was and still is considered a major peak in Covent Garden's post-war history. We agreed to record the opera in 1962 but I insisted on an entirely different cast except for Jon Vickers. We were both stubborn but I won, and with Christa Ludwig, who had never sung the part, Vickers, Berry, Hallstein, Unger and Crass we achieved what I consider Klemperer's best operatic recording.

The *Zauberflöte* performances were less distinguished: Klemperer insisted on having a relation of an old Berlin friend as designer and the man produced sets which looked to me like a provincial monumental mason's junkyard. His third Covent Garden production was *Lohengrin* with Régine Crespin, Rita Gorr, Sandor Konya and others. This was in 1963. He conducted *Fidelio* again at Covent Garden in 1970.

## The Pipe-Smoker

In private life he was usually quiet, stern and unostentatious. He had no interest in luxury and ate sparingly. At times, usually when he was in his euphoric state, he smoked a great deal. Then he often dropped lighted cigarettes or matches still burning on to the floor or blew sparks from his pipe like an old-fashioned railway-engine. In the depressive state he studied and re-studied the works he had known for more than half a century, always seeking new truths, searching for the innermost recesses of the composer's mind and intentions. He was a man of few words but with people he liked he had good manners and for a few flowers, a little present, or some extra attention to his comfort he would invariably telephone to express his thanks.

Although he had been a Roman Catholic for many years before I knew him, his Jewishness was a *Leitmotiv* of his thought, although he always crossed himself half-furtively before going on to the platform at every concert. I once asked him if he was convinced that Mahler was a better composer than Bruckner.

Klemperer: "Of course not."
Legge: "Then why do you play more Mahler than Bruckner?"
Klemperer: "Because Mahler was a Jew and because he got me my first jobs."

Yet after he conducted Mahler Four for the first time in London, I asked him why, considering that both he and Bruno Walter had been close to Mahler, their interpretations of his music were so different. He dis-

189

missed the question with, "Walter's Mahler is too Jewish for me." But the only present Klemperer gave me was an anthology of Jewish humour.

Haftel, the leader and business manager of the Israel Philharmonic Orchestra, told me the following story: Klemperer had a sister living in Israel and visited her at least twice. He was offended that he had not on either occasion been invited to conduct the Israel Philharmonic and he asked Haftel to call on him. The nub of the short meeting was:

Klemperer: "Mr Haftel, I am on my second visit to Israel, I am a well-known Jewish artist and you have never invited me to conduct your orchestra. Why?"

Haftel: "Dr Klemperer, you have chosen to be received into the Roman Catholic Church—so for us you are a heretic."

Klemperer: "But my colleague, Dr Koussevitzky, is also a Jew who was baptised and he has not only conducted your orchestra here, he has also toured with it in the United States."

Haftel: "Yes, but Dr Koussevitzky conducted without fee."

Klemperer: "I am still Jewish enough not to do that."

Like several German Jews I have known, Klemperer was more German than most Germans. Unfortunately I never heard him conduct *Meistersinger* but his broad tempi and the weight as well as the clarity of the counterpoint in his recordings of the Overture, and the heavy-footed accents and the stolid lumpishness of his "Dance of the Apprentices," for me at least, came nearer to what must have been Wagner's own concept than any other performances I have heard. Wieland Wagner was of the same opinion.

This is neither the time nor the place to discuss the reasons for my decisions to resign from EMI and, before the year's notice of my departure had elapsed, to suspend the activities of both the Philharmonia Orchestra and Chorus. I must however say that a recently published statement implying that the dissolution of the orchestra was decided upon without Klemperer knowing beforehand is simply untrue. Two or three days before I invited the orchestra's committee to meet me I sent Klemperer for his approval a copy of the statement I intended to circulate to the press. Jane Withers, the Managing Director of the orchestra, telephoned Lotte Klemperer to ask if Klemperer wished for any alterations. No suggestions or alterations were made.

I still had important recordings planned with Klemperer. *Messiah* we started but did not finish together. I had intended that my last great operatic recording for EMI (the Verdi *Requiem* with Giulini was to follow later) should be *Die Zauberflöte* with a matchless cast. The Beecham version of this work had been my first great operatic recording production in 1937–38, and it has not yet been equalled. Without preliminary warning Klemperer informed me that he would not allow me to attend any rehearsal. He knew perfectly well that I had worked intensively, sometimes for weeks, with singers before such important recordings. I could not and would not involve myself in and take the responsibility for such an important and expensive undertaking without having personally supervised the rehearsals least of all with a conductor whose hearing was by then more evidently impaired. That was the end of our association.

"Immer war Undank Legges Lohn." ["*Ingratitude was always Legge's wage"—a punparaphrase on Loge's famous remark in* Rheingold, *an expression that Walter used often and with good reason.*]

Klemperer is reported to have said after he came to dinner at my house that I was "a very dangerous man." Three years later in Milan I had launched him on the last and longest stage of his career, the one by which he will be best remembered. And I had put him for the first time in his long life on a road which was to provide him and now, for many years to come, his children with a safe and substantial income. I had also induced the West German Government to award him their highest order for distinguished civilians.

I ask myself what his posthumous reputation and influence will be. No one convincingly attempts to adopt his slow tempi and none his austere sound-palette: I hope no one will attempt to copy his slow-motion soundtracks of the skeletons of Mozart's Da Ponte operas. Toscanini's brilliance and intensity, and the early Stokowski's intoxicating sonorities have been models for half a century of younger conductors. Furtwängler, much disputed in his lifetime, is now the idol and the ideal for that generation of young men who were "stars" before they were thirty and still have to find their personal styles valid for themselves and the public.

Klemperer was a lone giant in a period of great contemporaries born between 1885 and 1900. When the best conductors of my generation are dead, the world may have to do without men of Klemperer's quality and devotion to music who have made music live for us.

# 11
# LA DIVINA
## Callas Remembered

*When Walter had heard Maria, he insisted that at the earliest mo-
ment I should hear her in person too. So we went on a pilgrimage to
Parma, where she was singing* Traviata. *She was then still more than
robust and healthy looking, far from the fragile, delicate Violetta of
her later years. The house was already seething with anticipation when
we took our seats. To our amazement the back of the orchestra was
lined with police, firemen, and nurses, anticipating things to come.
And already during the overture when the conductor took a few meas-
ures too fast, a chorus of hissing began. Apart from the conductor,
there was the elder Germont who had a slight frog and several others
who never dared show themselves before the curtain. And even Maria
had a moment's opaqueness on a top note. Still, we all witnessed a
major victory for Callas. As everyone knows, there is no victory in
Italy like being acclaimed in Parma in a Verdi role! Walter and I went
backstage and quite spontanously I said to Maria, "There is no point
in my singing this role again." And I didn't. From then on I tried
to hear her whenever I could, not only in Milan but whenever I
could spare a day or two; and always when Walter recorded her
in Milan. However, I missed the famous* Tosca *recording sessions,
which conflicted with my Hugo Wolf recital in Salzburg that season
with Furtwängler at the piano, which, of course, Walter had to miss.
Nor shall I ever forget the famous Karajan–Visconti–Callas* Lucia *when
I found myself quite hoarse after cheering throughout the entire interval—something I had done only once before, when Toscanini conducted the Philharmonia in London.*

*Walter realized he was going to make a lot of enemies with the
following article, and sure enough, the hate mail arrived by the sackful.
Still in all, it is probably the most objective and truthful analysis*

*of the Callas phenomenon, and one must never forget that Walter had
to threaten to resign from EMI to get them to sign Callas.*

DON'T LET us kid ourselves or allow sudden death at a comparatively early age to distort our judgment of a famous opera singer
who had retired early after a short, meteoric career. The name Callas
was a household word throughout the civilized world. Thanks to an
immediately identifiable voice, her magnetic personality, her many
phonograph records and a constant flow of sensational news and gossip-column publicity, her fame was even greater than Caruso's in his heyday. Let us balance this with Tullio Serafin's considered judgment,
delivered after more than sixty years work with the best singers of
our century: "In my long lifetime there have been three miracles—
Caruso, Ponselle and Ruffo. Apart from these, there have been several
wonderful singers." Though Serafin had been her most important
mentor, her fatherly guide and the main architect of Callas' extraordinary career, he did not rank her among his three miracles; she was
one of his "several wonderful singers." Serafin's words, no doubt unknowingly, echoed Ernest Newman's wise and concise evaluation after
her Covent Garden debut: "She's wonderful, but she is not a Ponselle."

Even though gallery-girls may lynch me for it, either at Lincoln
Center, in the Piazza della Scala or outside Bow Street police station
in London, I must try to put into focus the Callas phenomenon as a
person and as an artist. My justification is that I knew her for more
than twenty-five years and worked closely with her for twelve of them,
producing and mid-wifing all her best recordings from preparation to
published product.

More than enough has been published about her unhappy childhood, quarreling parents, myopia, avoirdupois and deprivations, but
no one has assessed the effects of these disadvantages on her career and
character. Callas suffered from a superhuman inferiority complex. This
was the driving force behind her relentless, ruthless ambition, her
fierce will, her monomaniacal egocentricity and insatiable appetite for
celebrity. Self-improvement, in every facet of her life and work, was
her obsession. When she was first pointed out to me, a year or two
before we met, she was massive, shabbily dressed in a nondescript
tweed coat, and her walk had the ungainly lurch of a sailor who, after
months on rough seas, was trying to adjust himself to terra firma. At
our first meeting I was taken aback by her rather fearsome New York

accent, which may have had a booster from G.I.s when she worked as interpreter for the American forces in Athens. Within months Callas was speaking what the English call the King's English until the BBC murdered it. A gifted linguist, she soon learned good Italian and French. When she had slimmed down from over 200 pounds to less than 140, she became one of the best-dressed women in Milan. Her homes in Verona, Milan and Paris paid silent tribute to her taste and love of order. Attached to every garment in her wardrobe in Milan was a list giving the date she had bought it, what it cost, where, when and in whose company she had worn it. Gloves—each pair in a transparent plastic envelope—and handbags were similarly documented, and every object had its place. These were private reflections of the meticulous care she put into her work.

A woman who worked at the Athens conservatory when Callas was a student there gave me a fascinating picture of her: bulky, shabby, serious, her pockets filled with food, which she consumed voraciously throughout the day. She neither had nor made friends. Invariably the first to arrive and the last to leave the building, when she was not having lessons she attended other classes irrespective of musical subject, listening insatiably and silently, absorbing every facet of musical information that might one day be useful to her. De Sabata later said to me, "If the public could understand as we do how deeply and utterly musical Callas is, they would be stunned."

I was rather late on the Callas bus. Italy was not officially my territory, but I had found and contracted the then unknown Boris Christoff there in 1947 and spent a lot of time with Karajan at La Scala. My first acquaintance with the Callas voice came from early Cetra 78s recorded in 1949, "Casta Diva," "Qui la voce" and the "Morte d'Isotta." At long last, a really exciting Italian soprano! My appetite was further whetted when one of her famous male colleagues described her as "not your type of singer." I knew that gambit: it had been tried on me by jealous colleagues of Kathleen Ferrier, Welitsch, Schwarzkopf and many another. At the earliest opportunity, 1951, I went to Rome when I knew she was singing. My wife and I were staying with a singer with whom Callas had recently had a row, so under the discreet pretext of a business engagement I slipped into the Rome Opera and heard her first act of *Norma*. I telephoned my wife to join me at once for something quite exceptional. She declined: she had just heard the first half of a broadcast of arias by one Maria Callas, and neither wild horses nor the promise of supper at Passetto's could drag her from hearing the second half.

At the end of the performance I went to Callas' dressing room and offered her an exclusive contract with English Columbia. She and her husband, Giovanni Battista Meneghini, were delighted. The negotiations, conducted in the friendliest manner over meals in Verona, at Biffi Scala and Giannino's in Milan, seemed interminable: they lasted well over a year. My ally was Dario Soria, who already knew from his Cetra-Soria experience how essential she was to Angel Records, the label we were preparing to launch in the U.S. under his management. She expected tribute at every meeting, and my arms still ache at the recollection of the pots of flowering shrubs and trees that Dario and I lugged to the Verona apartment. Eventually terms were agreed. I signed a copy of the contract for them to keep, asking for her signature on my own copy. Another snag: The Meneghini-Callases explained they had a superstition that prevented them from signing a contract until two weeks after it had been mutually agreed. I was given *parola d'onore* that the signed copy would be mailed in fifteen days.

When three weeks had passed with no signed contract, I sent a member of our Milan staff to Verona. Three visits and three flowering trees later, my young collaborator—who had been hardened to tough operations as an officer parachuted into the Yugoslav civil war—telegraphed:

PAROLA D'ONORE UNKNOWN IN VERONA STOP ONLY POSSIBLE SOLUTION YOU INCREASE TERMS

Dario and I had to follow his advice, and it was not until July 21, 1952, that I could wearily breathe, "Callas—finalmente mia!" over the signed contract. They had not yet told me she owed Cetra two or three operas under her old contract with them!

Our first recordings together were made in Florence after a series of performances of *Lucia* there with Serafin. The acoustics of the hall our Italian branch had chosen were antimusical and inimical. I decided to make a series of tests of "Non mi dir" with Callas for two purposes—to get the psychological feel of working with her, sensing how receptive she would be to criticism, and to find placings to give at least a decent sound. It was soon clear that she would take suggestions without a murmur. I had found a fellow-perfectionist as avid to prove and improve herself as any great artist I have ever worked with. Ten years later we were to spend the best part of three hours just repeating the last dozen bars of the *Faust* Jewel Song to get a passable end to it. I have never known anybody to have such a will to repeat. She was always so critical; on one occasion we were recording, and she called over the microphone, "Walter, is that all right?" I said, "Maria, it's marvelous, you can go on." "I don't want to know if it's marvelous, is it good?"

We delayed publication of this *Lucia* until after *I Puritani*, made a few weeks later: Angel's first Callas recording had to be a revelation, for her sake and for Angel's reputation for quality, which we had yet to establish. Also, *I Puritani* was the first fruit of EMI's contractual collaboration with La Scala—a double coup—though it was recorded in a Milan basilica.

Early in 1952 I had introduced the Meneghini-Callases to Herbert von Karajan one evening when he was conducting at La Scala. Two minutes of mutual courtesies: Karajan couldn't take his eyes off a huge emerald she was wearing. A year later, during the *Lucia* recording in Florence, I called Karajan to say I was catching the first train to Milan with the answer to Antonio Ghiringhelli's plea that he conduct an Italian opera at La Scala. I pocketed a little spool of tape—the last three minutes of *Lucia*, Act II. The maestro listened reluctantly, then telephoned La Scala to send the score of *Lucia* to his hotel. "I'll stage it myself. Scenery and Scottish costumes raise problems. . . ." "No kilts and sporrans for Callas," I warned him. "Even Tetrazzini, who was eighteen inches shorter than Callas and a bundle of fun, drew the line at wearing her sporran in its traditional position, because she said it looked rude. It would be all right behind, because the audience could think it was her cushion."

Karajan took *Lucia* very seriously, even making excursions through the Walter Scott country to know its architecture, iron-work and light. In 1954 Callas, Di Stefano, Panerai and Karajan excited Scala audiences to frenzy. Karajan was so proud of this production that a year later he took it to West Berlin for a few performances. Walter Gieseking went with me to the first. After the second act he said, "Let's get out of here—I can't stand any more tonic-and-dominant harmony." The promise of rather better music in the last act and a bottle or more of the best burgundy in Berlin induced the great pianist reluctantly to sit it through. At three in the morning I got back to the hotel, where the concierge told me that Mme. Callas and her husband were waiting for me, no matter how late I came home. He let me into their room, where both were sitting up in their beds, woollen undervests visibly projecting above their nightwear (very Italian!), reading Italian illustrateds while they waited for an inquest on the performance. Had she done herself justice? Was her applause louder and longer than anyone else ever had in Berlin? Reassured, they turned on their sides and switched off the lights.

Years later, she flew to London for the dress rehearsal of Sutherland's *Lucia*, insisted we sit with her, had herself photographed with the new prima donna, and then took us off to lunch. Seated, she stated: "She will have a great success tomorrow and make a big career if she can keep it up. But only we know how much greater I am."

The supreme Callas recording was her first *Tosca*, after nearly twenty-five years still unique in the history of recorded Italian opera. Callas had opened the 1951–52 La Scala season with *I Vespri Siciliani*, Victor de Sabata conducting. (During the dress rehearsal attended by critics and invited guests, there was a momentary discrepancy in rubato between Callas and the orchestra. De Sabata stopped immediately and shouted, "Callas—watch me!" Putting on her most seraphic smile, she wagged her forefinger and answered, "No, Maestro, you watch me— your sight is better than mine.") Nine months later we embarked on *Tosca*. De Sabata and I had been friends since 1946 but never recorded together. In those pre-stereo days, effects of distance were more difficult than now. To achieve Tosca's convincing entry, her three calls of "Mario!" were done separately—all from the wings, each one nearer the microphones—and spliced together later. The "Te Deum" took the greater part of two sessions: Tito Gobbi recently reminded me that we had made him sing all his first-act music thirty times, changing the inflections and colors even on individual syllables, before we were satisfied. Callas had arrived in superb voice and, as always in those days, properly prepared. Only for "E avanti a lui tremava tutta Roma" was she put through de Sabata's grinding mill for half an hour—time well spent. We used miles of tape, and when the recording was finished I warned de Sabata that I needed him for a few days to help select what should go into the finished master tape. He replied, "My work is finished. We are both artists. I give you this casket of uncut jewels and leave it entirely to you to make a crown worthy of Puccini and my work."

Callas had that sine qua non for a great career, an immediately recognizable personal timbre. It was a big voice and in her best years had a range of almost three octaves, though the extreme top was sometimes precarious and, as we discovered in trying to record Dalila's "Mon coeur s'ouvre à ta voix," the lower register needed more consistent power than she could sustain. The basic quality was luxurious, the technical skill phenomenal. Callas possessed in fact three different voices, all of which she colored for emotional effect at will—high coloratura, ample, brilliant (and when she chose, dark-colored), admirably agile. Even in the most difficult fioriture there were no musical or technical difficulties in this part of the voice which she could not execute with astonishing, unostentatious ease. Her chromatic runs, particularly downwards, were beautifully smooth and staccatos almost unfailingly accurate, even in the trickiest intervals. There is hardly a bar in the whole range of nineteenth-century music for high soprano that seriously tested her powers, though she sometimes went sharp on sustained high notes or took them by force.

The center of the voice was basically dark-hued, her most expressive range, where she could pour out her smoothest legato. Here she had a peculiar and highly personal sound, often as if she were singing into a bottle. This came, I believe, from the extraordinary formation of her upper palate, shaped like a Gothic arch, not the Romanesque arch of the normal mouth. Her rib cage was also unusually long for a woman of her height. This, together with what must have been her well-trained intercostal muscles, gave her unusual ability to sing and shape long phrases in one breath without visible effort. Her chest voice she used mainly for dramatic effects, slipping into it much higher than most singers with similar range when she felt text or situation would gain by it. Unfortunately it was only in quick music, particularly descending scales, that she completely mastered the art of joining the three almost incompatible voices into one unified whole, but until about 1960 she disguised those audible gear changes with cunning skill.

Her legato line was better than any other singer because she knew that a legato must be like a telegraph wire or telephone wire, where you can see the line going through and the consonants are just perched on it like the feet of sparrows. She used the consonants with great effect, but basically the legato line was held so that you could hear that all the time and were not aware of the interruption of the consonants except for their dramatic purpose.

Callas had an absolute contempt for merely beautiful singing. Although she was preoccupied all her career with bel canto, that is, beautiful singing, she was one of the few Italian artists in my memory who quite deliberately produced significant signs of a particular dramatic intensity or meaning on a syllable or even on a single consonant—sometimes over a long phrase to convey dramatic meaning. She herself often said, "After all, some of the texts we have to sing are not distinctive poetry. I know that to convey the dramatic effect to the audience and to myself I must produce sounds that are not beautiful. I don't mind if they are ugly as long as they are true."

I am afraid that Callas may harm a generation of singers. Young singers try to imitate not her virtues but some of those things that she did deliberately and could only do because of her intelligence and because she knew the dramatic purpose.

Most admirable of all her qualities, however, were her taste, elegance and deeply musical use of ornamentation in all its forms and complications, the weighting and length of every appoggiatura, the smooth incorporation of the turn in melodic lines, the accuracy and pacing of her trills, the seemingly inevitable timing of her portamentos, varying their curve with enchanting grace and meaning. There were innumerable exquisite felicities—minuscule portamentos from one note to its nearest neighbor, or over widespread intervals—and changes of color that were pure magic. In these aspects of bel canto she was supreme mistress of that art.

But . . . can you, dear reader, swear that you have never winced at or flinched from some of her high notes, those that were more like pitched screams than musical sounds? Or those she waved at you like Isolde's scarf, so unsteady they could be mistaken for labored trills? They were brave triumphs of will, but remote from the beauty that the term bel canto implies. A couple of years ago, I asked her what she was doing with her time—"I play and study our records of *Lucia* and *Tosca* and then try to get back to those vocal positions I used then." She would not or could not accept the fact that after fifty no woman can expect to have the upward range and facility she had at thirty. She was particularly interesting about the pirated recordings made in Mexico in 1951 and 1952. "Don't listen to them—they're awful! I was singing like a wildcat. Something must have happened to me between these and our *Lucia, Puritani* and *Tosca*." That something was the contract with La Scala, which she had been hoping and striving for in the four years since her debut in Verona, and the luxury and discipline of working under ideal conditions with de Sabata. She knew she had arrived.

Great directors, particularly Visconti and Zeffirelli, like great conductors, invariably got the best out of her. The challenge of a great conductor and/or stage director curiously paralleled her reactions to a less enthusiastic reception than she expected and felt she deserved after a first act. She would pace her dressing room with a hard glint in her eyes and mutter, "I'll teach those stinkers out there," or sometimes, "Don't worry! When I'm furious I'm always at my best." Then she would sing the rest of the performance with incandescent inner fire and aggressive flamboyance. During several *Sonnambula*s I sat in Ghiringhelli's box watching her move down to the footlights to hurl "Ah, non giunge" into the very teeth of the gallery. The Scala gallery was a vital factor in Meneghini's operations, especially the seats near the proscenium, which he infiltrated with young fans to throw bouquets to his wife when she took curtain calls. One evening the opponents got there first: fewer floral tributes were mixed in the rain of bunches of small vegetables from the gallery. Callas, trading on her well-known myopia, sniffed each bunch as she picked it up; vegetables she threw into the orchestra pit, while flowers were graciously handed to her colleagues. Not even Strehler could have staged that improvised scene better.

Callas and Meneghini had met in Verona when she made her Italian debut, the launching of her world career. She was twenty-three, he twice her age, a partner in a family brickmaking concern, reputedly fairly rich and a shrewd businessman, a contention I could endorse after negotiating her recording contracts. Their relationship, as I saw it, was staid, his attitude to her one of fatherly solicitude. He never showed himself at rehearsals, but until they separated he attended every recording session without listening to a note of hers. He habitually dozed or fell asleep behind a newspaper.

She ran into a patch of vocal difficulties as early as 1954. During the *Forza* recording the wobble had become so pronounced that I told her if we dared publish the records Angel and EMI would have to give away a seasickness pill with every side, which we could not afford. She took this to heart and worked hard on steadying down the wide pulse in her voice. She had several of her best years ahead of her. When I suggested Rosa Ponselle as the person to give her help, she revealingly snapped back, "I won't see that woman—she started off with better material than I did." That was the oft reported evening when Callas, knowing my wife was due in Milan that evening, insisted she have supper with us. Unfounded rumor that I might be looking for a deputy for Callas had magnetized several well-known sopranos, who were buzzing hopefully in and around Biffi Scala, where we habitually ate. Callas walked in as if unconcerned, pecked my wife's cheeks and without sitting down said, "Show me how you sing top A's and B's and make a diminuendo on them. Walter says mine make him seasick." When Schwarzkopf demurred, Callas, ignoring the astonished diners, sang with full voice the notes that were giving her trouble, while Schwarzkopf felt her diaphragm, lower jaw, throat and ribs. Waiters froze in their stride, while guests turned to watch and hear the fun. Within minutes Schwarzkopf was singing the same notes while Callas prodded her in the same places to find out how she kept those notes steady. After twenty minutes or so she said, "I think I've got it. I'll call you in the morning when I've tried it out," and sat down to supper. She did call next day to say it worked, but the recording shows the cure was not complete.

Her lack of humor and comedy were handicaps she rarely overcame. Hers was the brilliance of the diamond, not of the sun; she could blind without warming. Her *Barbiere* Rosinas with Giulini at La Scala woefully lacked humanity, and in my experience only in the recording of that opera in London with Galliera did comedy brush her with its wings. I rank it among her best.

Among Callas' greatest strengths were her power of projection in the theater and communication with audiences, almost animal instincts that excited a public irrespective of her purely vocal form. Apart from her best singing, the asset I most valued was her skill in the use of words: she charged recitatives with rare intensity. Since her stock in trade onstage so often was murder, suicide, infanticide, poison and hate, she curdled much blood in her time. Her humor was more of the dark variety. One Sunday evening during a Commonwealth conference in London, I had booked her favorite table at the Savoy Grill for dinner. Ushered in by the maître d'hotel, we had to cross the full width of the huge room, every table of which was occupied by black potentates and their entourages. Maria whispered to me, "Look round discreetly, they think we are the next course."

Callas was not a particularly lovable character except to her servants and her dressmaker, and of course to the multitudes of admirers who did not know her personally. She could be vengeful, vindictive, malicious in running down people she was jealous of or had taken a dislike to, often without reason. She was ungrateful: for years she refused to work with or even talk to Serafin, who had been her invaluable help and guide since her Italian debut, after he recorded *La Traviata* with Antonietta Stella.

She learned more from Serafin of the qualities that made her what she was than from anybody else. The old man was a great master of that particular sort of repertoire that Callas was to do better than anybody—Rossini, Bellini, Donizetti, Verdi. And nobody else, apart from Toscanini, knew such an enormous amount about singing. After all he had produced—he made—Ponselle.

She was convinced that sooner or later she would quarrel with every friend.

She said to me one day, "You know when we have our quarrel, its going to be hell, because you know how to hurt me and I know how to hurt you." I said to her, "Maria, there is no need for us to quarrel. Why should we ever quarrel?" She said, "People of our strength of will and personality always quarrel eventually."

She quarreled with me because I resigned from EMI, which she claimed I had done solely to ruin her recording career. That did not stop her from begging me, after years of non-communication, to share her Juilliard master classes with her, "because we are the only two people who know what bel canto is, and you can talk."

The Callas-Tebaldi feud was wildly overworked in the press but probably useful to agents and impresarios who played one diva off against the other. There were some tetchy exchanges between them in Brazil, but Tebaldi was always a good humored, equable person and Callas played her cards carefully.

With Ghiringhelli's approval I tried to silence the scandalmongers by getting the two ladies to appear together at La Scala alternating as Norma and Adalgisa (both roles were comfortably within their vocal ranges at that time) and/or in *Die Walküre*—Tebaldi as Sieglinde, Callas as Brünnhilde. Callas was eager (except some indecision as to whether she should insist on doing the first *Norma* or trying to overtrump by singing the second), but Tebaldi charmingly explained that she was past singing *seconda donna*. A pity! I should have enjoyed those rehearsals.

Her breach with Meneghini coincided with the decline of her artistic achievements—or caused it. Her life with him had been built on community of interests, mutual respect, Spartan domestic economy, rigorous self-discipline and hard work. The sumptuous party Onassis gave for them after her first London *Medea*, and the luxury of the first Mediterranean cruise on the *Christina* as fellow guests with Sir Winston and Lady Churchill opened new vistas for Callas—and new ambitions. This suddenly appealed to her as the world she had subconsciously craved—the lap of Croesus in the company of celebrities from every walk of life, without a rival in her own field. What bound Callas and Onassis was the mutual admiration of two fiercely ambitious, proud Greeks who had fought their way up from obscurity and deprivation to preeminence.

There were occasional flashes of the "real" Callas, in the Epidaurus *Medea*, but her career as an important artist lasted hardly thirteen years. Still she fought against declining powers. She lived and danced in Paris and Monte Carlo, where she toyed with the idea of recording, even having her own opera company in a little bandbox theater. She sang at Covent Garden and the Paris Opéra to frenzied audiences and saddened connoisseurs. Concerts with orchestra showed rare flashes of what she had once been. Better to draw a curtain over the last tours, with di Stefano and piano accompaniment.

She was long possessed by the idea of making films, convinced they would widen her public and vastly increase her income. But Onassis was unwilling to finance such an undertaking. Even when she had accepted the fact that she could no longer sing sufficiently well she worked fruitlessly on the idea of using her *Tosca*, *Norma*, and *Lucia* recordings as soundtracks to which she would synchronize her acting. When she finally reached the screen, it was merely as an actress in Pasolini's adaptation of Euripides' *Medea*—a sad but revealing episode in her downward path. I saw an early screening in a cinema not far from La Scala, the theatre she had consistently filled for nearly a decade. The cinema was half-empty, and emptier still at the end of the film.

Her death was sudden, at an age when she ought still to have been singing magnificently. I doubt if she had expected to die so soon, or that she really minded.

# 12

## ERNEST NEWMAN
## AND HUGO WOLF

*Ernest Newman and Hugo Wolf were two inseparable stars in Walter's firmament. He first met Newman when he was a very young man and instantly came under his influence—or spell. Their friendship lasted until Newman's death, but the effects of Newman's philosophy and teaching were always with Walter. They were alike in many ways—no more so than in the fact they were both largely self-taught musically and owed no allegiance to any school or movement. Their friendship was a perfect meeting of minds. When Walter and I married it was in Ernest Newman's house.*

*Walter, of course, was familiar with Newman's writings long before they met and through them took up the cause of Hugo Wolf. I think it is safe to say that Walter was responsible more than any other person for bringing Wolf's remarkable oeuvre to the public.*

ERNEST NEWMAN raised the writing of books about music and the writing of musical criticisms in newspapers—one the function of an author, the other that of a journalist—to great art. No previous or subsequent writer has understood music so *musically,* and no one has writen about it so comprehensibly for "the common man." He had no comparable predecessors in these fields, and it is unlikely that he will be equalled in the foreseeable future. He will have imitators and followers, but no successor.

I have separated the two mainstreams of Newman's writing about music not because he did so himself but because his subconscious awareness of the readers for whom he was writing determined his manner of address. His books were written with immense care and fanatical passion for truth, to inform and stimulate the best minds of his time and of generations to come; his newspaper criticisms of performances, written, so to speak, with a lighter hand, were designed to help, by their wisdom and wit, a larger public of thinking men and women to understand and enjoy music with their minds as well as through their senses. Newman had no use for music as ear ointment.

His mental gifts were prodigious, and he tended and developed them to the end of his life. Learning came easily to him and sat lightly upon him. He had endless intellectual curiosity and a memory, even at ninety, which gave him, for the subjects close to his heart, almost total recall. Less than a week before he died he talked to me for fully half an hour about Nietzsche's lack of moral integrity. The words came from him in sentences as lucid, well-formed, and fine-nerved as any prose he had ever written. He quoted letters and dates which I noted as he talked. The same night I checked the dates and quotations; they were as accurate as if they had been copied. I have never known a man so rich in knowledge, so wise, so well versed in such a wide range of subjects, so quick in perception, or so dispassionate and just in judgment.

As a musician he was entirely self-taught and the shrewd sense of self-preservation which kept him clear of the British schools and colleges of music (which he held in pitying contempt all his life) gave him an independent and international outlook unique among musicians of any nationality. He left Liverpool University intending to enter the Indian Civil Service, but his doctor advised him that the Indian climate would not suit his health. He became a bank clerk. It is strange to think that Ernest Newman's *Gluck and the Opera* (1895)—still one of the most erudite books on the nature of Gluck's reforms—and *A Study of Wagner* (1899) were written by a clerk working by day in the offices of a provincial bank! In later years he spoke with affection of his life in the bank, where his duties made a minimal call on his intelligence, leaving him free to think about music by day, the short working hours giving him long evenings to study and write.

Much of his early writing was on non-musical subjects: philosophy, religion, drama, literature, and even banking. Later he wrote occasionally about boxing, a sport he loved to watch and of which he had had practical experience and some expertise as an amateur. He never missed a big fight. Even in his late sixties he kept himself fit and active with daily spells at the punching ball, and at that time he would race me, a man less than half his age, up or down the large staircase of the

National Liberal Club. At eighty he was still remarkably active, and one evening, demonstrating to my wife the judo art of self-defence, he pitched all hundred-and-ninety pounds of me over his shoulder!

His famous controversies with Bernard Shaw in the *Nation* in 1910 and 1914 on Strauss's *Elektra* and *Josephslegende* had shown that with the rapier he was as swift, and with the broad-sword as hard-hitting, as the great Irishman, but it was not until 1919, when he was fifty and world-famous, that he settled in London as musical critic of the *Observer*. After a year he moved to the *Sunday Times,* where he stayed until he retired a couple of months before his ninetieth birthday. The effect of Newman's regular columns in a national newspaper was electrifying. His *bons mots* were repeated and chortled over in clubs and pubs, and men who could not tell a B flat from a bull's foot read his articles for their style and wit. In his forty years in London, Newman did more than any other man to raise the standard of performances, to broaden the repertoire, and to educate the public.

But for all his brilliance and influence as a journalist, Newman's finest qualities are concentrated in his books. His monumental *Life of Richard Wagner* is one of the great biographies of the world and the summit of his life's work. And if I were asked how the standards of operatic performances could be raised my answer would be to make the study of Newman's *Wagner Nights, Opera Nights,* and *More Opera Nights**
compulsory for producers, conductors, and singers. And audiences.

The admiration and love for Wolf's work remained with Newman to the end of his long life. In an essay published in the *New Witness* in 1918 there is this revealing passage:

> I venture to think that the supreme master of form in music is not Beethoven or Wagner but Hugo Wolf. Nowhere but in Wolf do I find, in work after work, the perfect adaptation of means to end, not a note too few, not a note too many, the idiom and the mode of treatment always varying with the emotional subject, the music always working itself out from the first bar to the last as if under the control of a logical faculty that was never in the least doubt as to its aim and never swerved from the straight pursuit of it. To some people this praise may seem excessive; I can only say that this is my own conviction after some fifteen years' study of Wolf. But Wolf's marvellous

* Published in the United States as *The Wagner Operas, Seventeen Famous Operas,* and *More Stories of Famous Operas,* respectively.

achievements were all on the small scale of the song: a composer who could realize the same formal perfection in the symphony or the opera would be the greatest master of musical form that the world had ever seen.

## Hugo Wolf

Wolf was born in a village in Styria, the southern-most part of Austria, in 1860. He died in 1903 in an asylum. The situation of Wolf's birthplace has an important bearing on our understanding of him because although he was essentially a Germanic composer, he was not a German composer. His father came of a family that had lived in Styria for generations—his mother was of mixed Slavonic and Italian origin. Biographers of Brahms are always at great pains to point out how that composer, as a pure North German, had the brooding melancholy that is peculiar to those sons of the Fatherland born on the North Sea coast.

Wolf's was a southern nature; he loved the sun and fine weather, he was passionate, quick and hot-tempered, gay, witty, highly nervous and yet deeply serious. Already in childhood these characteristics showed themselves. I have copies of his school reports from his sixth year and one sees there already how the land was father of the man. He was intensely affectionate to those he liked and to those who liked him, stubborn and resentful of those whom he felt did not understand him. At the age of seven the family fortunes, which had been reasonably prosperous, suffered a sudden reverse, and Wolf was never in his life to know the feeling of economic security, let alone affluence. His school career was a series of changes from one institution to another, almost invariably because his willful nature brought him into disfavour. At sixteen, after a long and, for a mere boy, astonishingly determined struggle with his family, he was allowed to take up music as a career and went to the Vienna Conservatory, from which he was dismissed after less than two years because of a threat which was made on the life of the principal in the form of a letter which was signed "Hugo Wolf." It has never been definitely settled whether or not he wrote that letter. From the ages of eighteen to twenty-seven Wolf lived in miserable poverty in Vienna, eking out an existence by giving lessons, copying, scoring, and working as a musical critic. His activities as a musical critic brought him into great disfavour with the Brahmsians because, within

207

a few weeks of his appointment, Wolf and his articles had become the talk of Vienna for the violence of his opinions and for these passionate tirades.

During these years, Wolf composed a great deal of music, much of which he destroyed, and some of which has been recently published. It was Wolf's great fortune that, although his temper and his out-spokeness made enemies for him, his remarkable intelligence, his friendliness to those who understood him, and his instinctive culture made him many firm friends. If it had not been for these friends he might well have starved to death, but he found his lifelong friends in a family named Koechert, the richest and most famous jewellers in Vienna, and Friedrich Eckstein, a wealthy young man of Wolf's own age. Through these two sources he quickly found the entry into the most advanced musical circles in Vienna and the finest literary society.

Wolf's family was musical in the way that the families in Austrian villages are musical. His father had wanted to become a professional musician, and he made a lot of music at home with three or four cronies in the village and his own family, most of whom could read and play the piano and two stringed instruments fairly well. But the programmes played on the Sundays and week-day evenings in the Wolf household were hardly the background from which one would expect a great com-poser to develop—fantasias on Gounod's *Faust* and the more popular operas of the period were the diet.

As soon as he reached Vienna, Wolf came under the influence of Wagner, and Wagner remained the predominating influence in his life. The other gods of his musical heaven were Berlioz and Liszt. His out-look that is to say was that of the out-and-out romantic revolutionary. He also had particular affections for *Carmen* and *Don Giovanni*.

He knew the songs of Schubert, Schumann, and Loewe intimately, and he loathed and despised Brahms, not on personal grounds, but because the art of Brahms was antithetical to Wolf's own aesthetic. The better to understand this dislike it is essential to study a little the state of the musical world in Vienna between 1860 and 1900 when the Brahms–Wagner question was a far more vital matter to the inhabitants of Vienna than political questions. Side by side with Wolf's musical development was a taste and understanding of literature unique in the hisory of music. Wolf was never without a book in his hand. He wrote of poetry to all his friends: his letters almost throughout his life contained as many references to poetry and to literature as they did to music, and if we are to understand Wolf at all we must have always at the front of our minds that he had discernment and knowledge of poetry and literature such as no other composer has ever enjoyed. He was intimate not only with a vast mass of German poetry and literature, he read avidly in the classics; he knew Byron, Scott, and Dickens, and he read widely in French literature.

I have recently been permitted to see some letters written when Wolf was only nineteen, in which, in the course of a poem, he had found a reference to a detail of mythology with which he was not familiar. Intending to set this poem to music he went to endless trouble, started up a train of correspondence, amazing in its forensic determination to complete his own mental picture of the background of the poem. And so it was all through his life. When he first discovered the Swabian poet Mörike he set himself to learn all he could about the poet, about his friends, about his circle; so it was with Goethe and Heine and Byron. His avidity was not, however, uncritical; He had the greatest discernment, and from the age of twenty-three onwards he never once set to music a poem that was not in itself a masterpiece of the poet's art.

Hermann Bahr, one of the greatest dramatists and men of letters of his epoch, met Wolf in 1882 and for a while lived with him and two other companions, and he has given several vivid accounts of Wolf's powerful reading of poetry.

> The door would open and Wolf would appear in a very long nightdress, a candle and a book in his hands, very pale, scarcely visible in the grey uncertain light with mysterious gestures, half satirical, half solemn. He coughed shrilly and mocked us. Then he stepped into the middle of the room, swung the candle, and, while we undressed, began to read to us, generally something out of *Penthesilea*. This however had such power that we were silenced, not daring to speak another word, so impressive was he when reading. Like immense black birds the words came rushing and roaring from his pale lips; they seemed to grow till the room was full of their strong and terrible shadows. Suddenly he would burst into laughter again, once more gibe at us, and slowly disappear through the door in his long, long shirt, the flickering candle in his outstretched hand. But we two sat up long, until the dawn came, and were vaguely conscious of something mysterious in the air around us, and knew that a great man had been with us.

209

He shows how those who had heard Wolf recite verses could recognize in his settings of them the same keen sense of verbal values and of rhythmic accentuation.

> Never in my life have I heard such reading. It is impossible to describe it. I can only say this: when he spoke the words, they assumed a prodigious truth, they became corporeal things; we had, indeed, the feeling as if his own body had suddenly become an incarnation of the words, as if these hands, that we saw glimmering in the dim light, no longer belonged to a man, but to the words that we heard. He had, as it were, transubstantiated himself with all his body into the words of the poet. These stood before us, our friend had vanished. Then, wandering about Europe, I heard nothing of him for some time, until his Goethe songs appeared. These struck into the very depths of me; and then I suddenly remembered. Yes, it was the same! The same man as in those nights. Just as that time he sank, as it were, his own existence in that of the words, so that the gleaming hands and the threatening eyes which we saw seemed to be no longer his, but the hands and eyes of the words, which otherwise we should not have noticed, so this music could not have been "added" by a man, but was the natural music of the verses. We had had only imperfect ears, or we should always have heard it; since it is the essential music of these verses, it inheres in them and must always have been in them: he has only made it audible.

Eckstein has told me how, when they were both in their middle twenties they spent their summers by the lakes in the Salzkammergut. Wolf, in a bathing costume, but always with a book or two—one usually of poetry he loved and one in which he had found something he despised—would dance round the recumbent figures of his companions, intoning poetry with a savage glee. If some line particularly annoyed him he would howl and scream and jabber like an infuriated monkey, pouring out abuse and eternal damnation on the head of the accursed bungler who had so misused words. This passion of Wolf's for poetry and this understanding of it is the key to the interpretation of his songs.

At twenty-seven Wolf had written only three or four of the songs on which his fame rests; but suddenly in 1887 he started pouring out a series of masterpieces—sometimes two, sometimes three a day. He neither ate nor slept except from sheer exhaustion; the mood was on him and his pen could hardly keep pace with his mind. All those songs were by one poet, and before the year was out Wolf was working equally furiously on another poet. In the next year it was the same, this time Goethe, and in between these spates of composition were periods in which his mind seemed to lie entirely fallow and in which he felt his own inspiration had died. Fecundity is not rare among some composers. Schubert had it too; but his was not intermittent like Wolf's. In 1840 Schumann wrote nearly as many songs as Wolf did in any one year, but the methods were different, and so that we can properly compare Wolf and the other masters of the German song it is essential for us for a moment to reflect on these differences.

Schubert, the first great song writer, lived in poverty as miserable as Wolf's, but he was a man of little or no literary culture. He seems to have had no discernment in the choice of texts and anyone at all familiar with the German language can only suffer when he reads through a mass of the rubbish which Schubert set to music. Schubert did not soak himself in his poets; his nature was so full of music, so rich in melody, that almost any piece of verse was enough to stimulate his imagination. He read a poem and set it to music and sometimes when one examines his songs one wonders whether he even troubled to read them through. Several of them look as if he read the first verse, cast an eye further down to see that the metrical system was roughly speaking even through the stanzas, and just let the music flow to the general mood of the first stanza. We get a particular instance of this in a song like "Heimliches Lieben."

Next came Brahms. Twenty-seven years older than Wolf but still a contemporary, Brahms was a man of limited literary taste and culture. His ideal was the folk song and he was, throughout his life, even in his songs, more concerned with the music than the words. He preferred the strophic song and advised his pupils to study Schubert in order to see whether a text allowed of strophic handling. In short, Brahms was a typical lower-middle-class German whose taste in poetry had a leaning towards that variety which deals with the various aspects of sorrowful contemplation of unrequited, unhappy, or dead love. The luxury of love-lorn grief was the stock in trade of the nineteenth-century German minor poets—occasionally they would be pert or playful. These sufficed for Brahms and to have attempted to express a greater range of moods than these would have been foreign to his emotional and musical natures.

The history of song has been one long struggle to effect the perfect fusion of music and words, and the claims of these two to play the predominant part in the making of a song.

Only in Wolf have the two found their perfect fusion. Those who do not understand Wolf's mind or Wolf's songs, or who have only a nodding acquaintance with them labour under the delusion and help in the spreading of the fallacy that the peculiar quality of Wolf's songs is the rightness of his accentuation and verbal phrasing, that is to say, that the vocal line declaims with the most punctilious regard for word values. Co-existent with this fallacy is the idea that Wolf was not a melodist. If Wolf had done no more than merely to write a vocal line which did no injustice to his poets and provide those vocal lines with effective accompaniments, the name of Wolf would have been forgotten within a month of the day in which he went into an asylum. The genius of Wolf lay in the fact that each of his songs is entirely suffused not only with the idea and the meaning and spirit of the poem, but with the dramatic and emotional and imaginative content of the poem. In all Wolf's songs every note is of equal importance.

Every note in the voice and the piano parts lives in the particular part of the poem with which it deals. Wolf did not write an independent piano piece and then fit words to it. His mind was not only highly contrapuntal in the ordinary sense of the term, but contrapuntal in a higher sense. His poetic imagination worked at several points hand in hand with his musical imagination. Wolf's songs are not inspired by poems or even settings of poems. They are new manifestations of the poem raised to higher expressive powers by music, just as the finest prose stands high above journalism and as poetry raises the finest thoughts of good prose to new heights of expression. The fallacy that Hugo Wolf was not a melodist is hardly worth discussing. For those simple-minded people who believe that melody simply means square two- or four-bar tunes that can be hummed or whistled or played equally well on any musical instrument, Wolf was not a melodist. His mind was of an entirely different order. The type of melody that people speak loosely of as melody is a tune of the simpler Schubertian or Italian type which may be played equally expressively on any instrument capable of legato. There is no passage in music which an instrument cannot render more perfectly from a technical point of view than a human voice can. The function of the human voice in music is to express words, otherwise there is no excuse for dragging the human voice into music at all. And it is Wolf's particular genius that he understood words as no composer has ever done and that in his songs the maximum of emotional expression co-exists in perfect unity with the greatest concision of form and musical beauty.

Wolf's method in writing a song was not to read a poem and then sit down and put it to music. He lived with and in the poems before he put them to music; he knew them and their emotions and their inflections so thoroughly that they became a part of himself until they were sunk into the depths of his subconscious mind. The period of gestation was a long one with him; he did not, as the conventional view has it, write each song down straight away without alteration.

At almost every public performance of his songs, he first insisted on turning to his audience and reading the poem to them, not in the way that we hear poetry read on the BBC, but with the extraordinary intensity of understanding that seems to have been Wolf's and Wolf's alone. Frequently he would remark with his curious Styrian accent, "Isn't that poem enough to make you cry?" Then, and only then, when the audience had heard the poem, was Wolf prepared to let his song be heard.

For this reason, if for no other, Wolf will never be understood by the British public at large. There are too few people with the energy or will enough to take the trouble of mastering the language. I can only advise those who may be interested that Wolf is worthy of greater sacrifices than that. The first and the last requisite in the performance of Wolf is vividness of imagination, freedom from the silly delusion that music is a gentlemanly calling, complete lack of our natural racial inhibition about the fear of showing one's emotions in public. Wolf was a man who suffered. One has only to see his portraits to realize that, and the fact is established all the more clearly in his songs. He suffered deeply and was torn by pain, and when he rejoiced he could rejoice with the jubilant ecstasy that few men have known.

For the interpreter then to do justice to Wolf he must cast off the shackles of repression and live in an intellectual and emotional world, keener, more alive, more vital, more impassioned than his everyday life. He must transplant himself into a new world and a new world for every song. This is equally true of the pianist. Notation is a clumsy deaf and dumb language, a strange hieroglyphic system. The pianist as much as the singer must enter into Wolf's own imagination, obeying implicitly Wolf's markings and never indulging in the liberty of a rallentando or an accelerando that the composer has not marked.

The rhythm must be crisp and alive, and the pianist must always remember that Wolf described his songs, not as songs for voice with piano accompaniment, but songs for voice and piano. The pianist is as important as the singer, the singer as important as the pianist; the two must think as with one mind. And what is the singer's task? The singer's task is first to achieve a mastery of his vocal material so complete that he can produce in any part of his compass the type of tone which the meaning of the poem demands at that particular point. Vocal technique in itself and in the way that coloratura sopranos use it has no musical value whatever. Technique is merely the means by which a singer can express. Expression is the thing—not expression applied from without, but expression born from within, from within the poem and the music.

It is a popular fallacy that the Lieder singer is a different breed from the opera singer. The function of the Lieder singer is much that of the opera singer—to make vivid in the mind of the listener certain emotions. The tone need not always be beautiful. Appropriate sound to words. The beauty of the German language. Musical phrasing. A beautiful voice not essential.

*Not long ago a British music magazine, reviewing the reissue of one of my Wolf albums, wrote, "The best thing that ever happened to Hugo Wolf was Elisabeth Schwarzkopf." Flattering as this remark was, it should have been, "The best thing that ever happened to Hugo Wolf was Walter Legge." I came to Wolf very early in my career, introduced to his music by the famous pianist Michael Raucheisen. I had sung it in my first recital in Berlin. Walter was, of course, way ahead of me. And he was fortunate that he was able to put his ideas about Wolf into more practical form, with his founding of the Hugo Wolf Society—one of his many innovations in the recording industry. He first took subscriptions and when there were enough to ensure the financial success of a series the recordings were made. Later, during the Philharmonia concerts, Walter saw to it that the meticulous translations of the all-important poems were models of perfection, also in printing and lay-out. More often than not Walter's name should have gone under those translations, for he sat up nights, improving the translator's work. A labour of*

214

*love which the concertgoers were unaware of. Walter's feeling for poetry—English and German—was a great gift. I heard him recite poems from memory with great truth and expression, poems I have never heard from anyone else.*

*Walter's tremendous love for Wolf was like a constant undercurrent. Ernest Newman's widow, Vera, asked him to write the foreword to the American edition of Newman's volume on Wolf and the Hugo Wolf Society of Vienna awarded him the Wolf medallion. Walter's Wolf Society recordings also prove Walter's credos: he was not interested in producing recordings for a quick return; he wanted to make records that would last over decades—simply by their excellence. The Wolf Society recordings with Elena Gerhardt, Hüsch, Ginster, Janssen, Rethberg, Kipnis, et al., were rereleased in 1981 and immediately won a prize, which I was asked to present to EMI. Walter had recorded them fifty years before!*

*I still have the lovely oak table and embossed leather chairs that belonged to Wolf, which Walter acquired in Vienna and brought to our house in London. He also brought a suitcase crammed with Wolf documents and memorabilia, which he gave to Frank Walker for his definitive biography.*

The first volume of the Hugo Wolf Society was published in 1932. Subscribers and critics were unanimously delighted with the records. The inevitable choice of singer and pianist at that time was Elena Gerhardt and Coenraad V. Bos, who were then considered the best Wolf interpreters.

I supervised the recordings myself and interfered with their preconceived ideas quite a lot—an unheard-of intrusion in those days when the attitude of all recording companies was "we invite the best artists into the studio and make the best sound picture of their performances that we can."

Newman, whom I kept daily informed by telephone of the slow progress, sent me a postcard quoting the second *Cophtisches Lied*:

> Du musst steigen oder sinken,
> Du musst herrschen und gewinnen,
> Oder dienen und verlieren,
> Leiden oder triumphieren,
> Ambos oder Hammer sein.

215

> You must rise or sink,
> You must rule and gain,
> Or serve and lose,
> Suffer or triumph,
> Be anvil or hammer.

Intoxicated by this success, I immediately decided to embark on my first venture as an impresario, and with the somewhat nebulous financial assistance of a "public-relations man" who had somehow come into my ken, I launched the London Lieder Club, a curious adventure for a twenty-five-year-old. The recitals were given first in the ballroom of London's Dorchester Hotel, later in the Hyde Park Hotel. Both of these establishments gave us the use of their acoustically excellent ballrooms, each with a couple of hundred seats, in exchange for the right to circularize our subscribers with a prospectus of a special pre-recital dinner. It was all very full-evening-dress snob appeal, but the public came.

I started the series naturally with a Hugo Wolf *Abend* by Gerhardt and Bos—probably the first all-Wolf evening in British history. The soloists on subsequent evenings in the first season included some of the most distinguished singers of the time: Herbert Janssen, Alexander Kipnis, Gerhard Hüsch, and many others, some of whom I forced to sing Wolf for the first time in their lives and to put up with a young Englishman whose command of the German language was poetically fluent—if occasionally Wagnerianly tinged—but was less than vernacular. One famous Viennese bass invited to sing the *Michelangelo Lieder* flatly refused even to look at them unless he were allowed to ensure his personal success by singing "Ol' Man River" (from *Show Boat*) and a group of Negro spirituals! He confessed to me years later that he could not read a note of music. It was at these concerts that I launched Gerald Moore on the career in which he became famous as the best accompanist in the world until his retirement.

The first volume of the Hugo Wolf Society contained nineteen songs; by the time the sixth volume was published, we had reached a hundred and eighteen songs, nearly half of the Lieder output of Wolf's maturity. Apart from Elena Gerhardt the singers I employed to make these Wolf records were Marta Fuchs, Ria Ginster, Tiana Lemnitz, Elisabeth Rethberg, Alexandra Trianti (a Greek soprano who had studied with Maria Ivogün), Karl Erb, Gerhard Hüsch, Herbert Janssen, John McCormack, Helge Roswänge and Friedrich Schorr; the pianists, after Coenraad V. Bos, were Gerald Moore, Hans Udo Müller, Michael

Raucheisen, and Edwin Schneider. Both the Hugo Wolf Society and the London Lieder Club came to an end with the 1939 war but the idea of publishing these deluxe limited editions by subscription and thus expanding the repertoire of music recorded in the best possible way became not only one of the major steps forward in the history of music on record but for the company "big business"!

In London I founded the Philharmonia Concert Society first as a show-window for my new orchestra but expanded the activities of my Concert Society to include subscription series of twentieth-century music, great pianists, chamber music, and, of course, Lieder. Until the Royal Festival Hall was completed in 1953, London was poor in concert halls. The lovely old Queen's Hall had been destroyed during the war and the only hall suitable for concerts was the vast gasometer-like Royal Albert Hall with its ten thousand seats. For recitals and chamber music there was only the Wigmore Hall (it had originally opened with recitals by Busoni and Ysaÿe) with only 550 seats, or the larger but uncomfortable Kingsway Hall, which the public resolutely refused to go to.

There is no doubt in my own mind that the most important factors in the sudden growth of the musical public in London after the last war were the large number of refugees from Austria and Germany who were particularly attracted by the Central European repertoire, the great increase in the repertoire available on gramophone records, and the opening of the Royal Festival Hall with more than 3,000 seats.

I started promoting *Liederabende* at the Wigmore Hall in 1947 when Elisabeth Schwarzkopf, already known through the Wiener Staatsoper's first London visit, made her London debut as a *Liedersängerin*. The programme ranged from Mozart to Richard Strauss with naturally a substantial group of Hugo Wolf. Hans Hotter followed suit. Four years later Dietrich Fischer-Dieskau immediately made a great impact on the London public, first with the two major Schubert song cycles. Schwarzkopf's and Fischer-Dieskau's recitals in the Wigmore Hall were sold out as soon as they were announced, and this encouraged me to believe that in spite of its size the Royal Festival Hall was the only London hall suitable for the potential Lieder public developing in London. It was one of the happiest and proudest days of my life when every one of the more than 3,000 seats was sold out to hear Hugo Wolf's complete *Italienisches Liederbuch* by Elisabeth Schwarzkopf, Dietrich Fischer-Dieskau, and Hermann Reutter. With Irmgard Seefried and *two*

217

pianists, Gerald Moore and Erik Werba, Fischer-Dieskau has repeated this programme in London and elsewhere.

Following Gerhardt's example in appearing with the great conductor Artur Nikisch as her accompanist, I induced Wolfgang Sawallisch to make his London debut (before he had conducted there) in a Wolf recital with Schwarzkopf. Incredible though it sounds Herbert von Karajan in the early 1950s gave a recital with Schwarzkopf, including a large group of Wolf, in Tangiers! At the Salzburg Festival in 1953 the fiftieth-anniversary commemoration of Wolf's death was made by a joint recital with Elisabeth Schwarzkopf and Wilhelm Furtwängler at the great conductor's suggestion.

Today very few songs published in Wolf's lifetime are not available on records. Schwarzkopf and Fischer-Dieskau have recorded nearly all the songs within their ranges; Seefried, Christa Ludwig, Hotter, Walter Berry and Hermann Prey have made important contributions too, and Fischer-Dieskau and Daniel Barenboim have begun recording all Wolf's songs for male voice, including most of the posthumously published songs.

The supreme quality of Hugo Wolf's songs is now acknowledged and attractive to the public not only in England and the German-speaking world but in France, the United States, and Japan. But I cannot avoid asking myself how long this will last. Wolf demands more of his interpreters than any other *Liederkomponist*; not only or always beauty of line and sound but a profounder sensibility, a love and under-standing of the poems he set to music, the submersion of the singer's and pianist's personalities to Wolf's and his chosen poets, an interpreta-tion of his unique imaginative world. In the last forty years all the best Wolf singers have come from opera-houses. If Fritz Wunderlich had lived, he would surely have developed into a great Wolf interpreter; there is, I believe, much to be hoped from Peter Schreier. But other-wise the younger generation does not seem endowed with the qualities of heart and head that Wolf's art demands.

*Walter's extensive correspondence with British musicologist and fellow Wolfian Eric Sams discloses some of his approach to the interpre-tation of the songs of Hugo Wolf.*

*An die Geliebte:* For me this is one of Wolf's supreme achievements. I've slaved with it with the best male German singers both before and after the war hoping to recreate what H. W. had in his mind's ears—unavailingly.

*Zur Warnung:* This is for men only, but so abstemious are our contemporary male vocalists that they don't know what a hangover is. The song needs an old soak like Emil Schipper (who stopped a performance by loudly and copiously vomiting at his first—and last— entry), Chaliapin, Bockelmann, or Andrésen (who fell asleep on the stage before Hagen's "Hier sitzt ich" and had to be prodded to consciousness by a Gibichung standing with his spear behind the scene). Wolf's only recorded experience of alcoholic excess was innocently drinking a bottle of whiskey thinking it was Scotch wine.

*Bei einer Trauung:* This side of Wolf's humor is difficult to project and in my experience has always escaped Fischer-Dieskau's more than Prussian awareness of humour of any sort. I believe it needs a laconic, serious, rueful performance, with the village organ style for the piano part.

*Nun lass uns Frieden schliessen:* Take note of the metronome markings. The song is not in my view as much a love song as it is made to sound in the tempo usually adopted. I take it to be, because of Wolf's fastish tempo, an enchanting, tender, smiling, *wheedle.*

# 13

## HERBERT VON KARAJAN

*The musical colleague to whom Walter felt closest was Herbert von Karajan. Indeed, over the years, he and Walter were often called musical alter egos. Walter was interviewed many times, and sooner or later the subject would turn to Herbert. He was also often asked to write about Herbert and his approach to music and conducting.*

KARAJAN MADE his operatic debut in March 1929 conducting *The Marriage of Figaro* in Ulm, the lowest rung on Germany's operatic ladder. Four years later he conducted the off-stage music for Max Reinhardt's production of Goethe's *Faust* at Salzburg. He learned a lot from Reinhardt's whispered guidance of his principals and he was much impressed by his undisputed authority. Working for Reinhardt convinced Karajan that unity of music and stage presentation can only be achieved when they are controlled by one mind, and when he returned to Ulm he launched himself as producer of the operas he had to conduct.

Karajan did not leave Ulm of his own volition; the director refused to renew his contract because he sensed that the young *condottiere* needed wider scope. In April 1934, the twenty-five-year-old Karajan found himself unemployed. He made his way to Berlin, where he worked as an occasional accompanist at auditions, but otherwise had no prospects. Fortunately Aachen, which had been an important rung in Fritz Busch's career, needed a conductor. It was too late in the season for Karajan to conduct a performance on trial but in desperation he hypnotized the director into giving him an orchestral rehearsal to show what he was made of. Both the local critics who were invited and the orchestra rejected him as too young and inexperienced, but a local big-wig with shrewder judgment forced the issue and Karajan was appointed *Kapellmeister*. A year later he became the youngest *Generalmusikdirektor* in Germany. Aachen's advantages were almost beyond his dreams. But there was a price. He had to join the National Socialist Party. Politics as such never interested Karajan—only musical politics of which he was later to become the supreme master. He made no secret of his affiliation.

I first heard the name of Karajan from the German soprano Tiana Lemnitz in 1938. She told me there was a young conductor in Aachen who was the sort of man I might like to work with. I heard performances of *The Magic Flute* and *Falstaff* and was enormously impressed. Since in those days there was no possibility of recording a young conductor, I didn't bother to meet him; but I told the director of the Berlin Opera, Heinz Tietjen, that I had found a new conductor for him. The wily Tietjen was desperately in need of a new conductor, if not to rival at least to play off against Furtwängler. All the other conductors had left Berlin. On my advice he invited Karajan to conduct guest performances of *Fidelio* and *Tristan*. A newspaper review headlined "The Miracle Karajan" fused the feud between the two conductors, which ended only with Furtwängler's death. While establishing his bridgehead in Berlin, Karajan gently loosened the bonds which tied him to Aachen.

As head of the Berlin Philharmonic, Furtwängler was able to block Karajan's concert activities in Berlin until, with Tietjen's connivance, Karajan decided to use the State Opera Orchestra as a symphonic body and have his own series of concerts. This Berlin period, which lasted only until 1942, built up Karajan's popularity, but in 1940 he had aroused Hitler's personal animosity with his conducting of a performance of *Meistersinger*, which, as usual, he did without a score. The Hans Sachs was the worse for drink and Karajan had evident difficulties in covering up the befuddled singer's lapses of memory and false entries. Hitler left the theatre in a towering rage and refused ever again to attend a performance conducted by Karajan, who further courted official disfavor by marrying Anita Gutermann, who was one-quarter Jewish.

It was in Berlin that Karajan met and established good relations with Victor de Sabata, who was conducting *Aida* and some concerts. After hearing the first act of Karajan's *Tristan*, de Sabata said to Tietjen: "Mark my words. In the next twenty-five years this man will rule the whole world of music and leave his mark on it. Take him as soon and as often as you can." The admiration was mutual and it was through de Sabata's insistence that Karajan conducted concerts at La Scala each year from 1940 to 1943. Karajan and his wife were caught in Milan in 1944. But he made his way to Vienna by acting as interpreter and guide for American military convoys.

When the war ended, I went over to the middle of Europe to re-capture for my company the best established artists and recruit the best new ones. I arrived in Vienna in January 1946, two days after Karajan had given his first concert. He was due to give another on the following Saturday. Although as usual with him the rehearsals were sealed, I managed to get in and I was absolutely astonished at what the fellow could do. The enormous energy and vitality he had was hair-raising. That Saturday morning, the Vienna Philharmonic phoned to tell me that the Russians had forbidden Karajan to appear and the concert had been cancelled. So I rang him up and said that I was awfully sorry to hear about this, and would he like to have lunch with me and talk things over? He said that he was sorry, he was going to sleep but he could see me at 4 o'clock. So at 4 o'clock I went to the appointed address. I knew how difficult it was to get anything in Vienna at that time so I took him a bottle of whiskey, a bottle of gin, and a bottle of sherry. Years after he told me that after I left that evening he divided each of those bottles into thirty portions so that he had one drink for each of the next ninety days but he did not touch them that day. And he stuck to his rule. He has that sort of iron will. He was living in the most uncomfortable conditions on the eighth floor of a block of flats, sharing a room with people he did not know. And we started to talk. I tried to make it a business conversation but he was obviously out for a real chat. He probably had not talked to anybody for a long time. We met almost daily, and the negotiations for the contract went on for about six months. I made several visits to Vienna. He was in no hurry to sign even though he had no money and no work—and no possibility of work—yet he had an inner sense of repose that I have never met in any man in similar circumstances. He then took a house in Salzburg. God knows who paid for it or how it was paid for—and we stayed together. We went to all the rehearsals of the Salzburg Festival and a lifelong friendship was established. We found that we had shared so many common experiences. In 1926, when Toscanini first took La Scala to Berlin we both made the pilgrimage there, he from Salzburg and I from London, just to hear what La Scala sounds were. We had both suddenly found things that we never be-lieved existed in Italian opera. The Toscanini of those days was not the Toscanini that one knows of the operatic records. He was much more flexible, much warmer than the old-man-in-a-hurry he became in the last years. Also, without knowing each other, we had sat in the pit for Toscanini's rehearsals in Bayreuth and watched the great man at work. In 1926 there came out a series of records by Stokowski, Toscanini, and Mengelberg which gave people of Karajan's generation and mine an entirely new concept of sound.

Our collaboration became the foundation on which Karajan's great fame and fortune were built. In September 1946, defying the American and French military authorities' fiat that the ban on Karajan's conducting included recording, EMI started making records with him. At the first session we did not get a note recorded—he was really out to show what he could do with the Vienna Philharmonic. There is a charming story of the first time Karajan was allowed to conduct at the Academy in Vienna. He had had two years tuition and at the end-of-term concert he was given the Mozarteum Orchestra to show what he could do. He sent everybody out but the cellos and then proceeded to use his twenty minutes to show how he could make those six cellos play the little bit in the *William Tell* Overture for six solo cellos.

His theory about young conductors is that there is no point in putting a young conductor with a first-class orchestra. He said to me a dozen times that the only way with a younger conductor is to put him in front of a tenth-rate orchestra and let him try and make them play like a sixth-rate orchestra—then he is really beginning to learn his craft.

We took an enormous time to get his first record out of him. Then he did the Beethoven Eighth and then the big things started. Next year we did the Brahms *Requiem,* which was one of Toscanini's favorite records, the Beethoven Fifth, and some Strauss waltzes. In 1947, he made his debut with the Philharmonia at the Albert Hall with Dinu Lipatti—the Strauss *Don Juan,* the Schumann Piano Concerto with Lipatti, and the Beethoven Fifth. On the morning of the concert he had his last rehearsal, which lasted probably not more than eight minutes. He said, "I want to know how much fortissimo I can expect tonight. Give me the last two chords of the Beethoven Fifth with all the force of which you are capable, but still to retain an absolutely beautiful sound, but the maximum of force." The stick came down like a whiplash and he did that about twenty times until he really had the maximum that he knew he could expect—because until then he had not let them play a fortissimo. All the rehearsals had been, "Keep the dynamics down, we'll wait for the occasion and then—now, I want to know what you have, now show them." And it came out.

The concerts were enormously successful, but the following season he gave two more London concerts and the audiences were appalling. At one, we did the Beethoven Ninth with quite good soloists, Schwarz-kopf, Schock, a Canadian mezzo whose name I've forgotten (but it doesn't matter about the mezzo in the Ninth because if you hear her she's bad!), and Boris Christoff as the bass. But I think there were rather more people on the platform than there were in the audience. For the second concert the ticket sales were so bad that we changed the programme and ended with *Bolero*; but there were still only about a couple of hundred people in the house.

Karajan knows the psychology of an orchestra I think probably better than anybody else. He is a man who does everything with the greatest economy of his time. He spends a great deal of thought pre-paring everything, trying out the effect of different sorts of beat on an orchestra—to make everything clear to the orchestra with the minimum of effort. It's a great experience to watch him rehearse, to see him take a piece for the first time with an orchestra—usually with an or-chestra he knows. He just reads it straight through and then corrects. And I have never heard him raise his voice at a rehearsal. Hardly a word spoken: the whole thing done visually. He knows exactly what he wants and he has this strange quiet authority. As he has said to me many times, "If I don't raise my voice, they'll listen to what I say, and the less I speak, the more important each word is." He's extremely patient at rehearsals. He never loses his temper. I have never once seen any sign of ill-will or temper or dissatisfaction from him. But I have heard him make some very good jokes with orchestras, wittier than those of most conductors. Once at the Lucerne Festival, there was a not very good bassoon player who liked to talk a lot. One evening Karajan and I had been out motor-boating on the lake of Lucerne, and heard for the first time in our lives the alphorn, which is the most magical sound if you hear it carried over the water from a distance. Next morn-ing Karajan greeted the orchestra and said, "Last night I heard an alphorn for the first time. Is there anybody here who plays it?" And this inferior bassoon player stood up and said rather pompously that it was obligatory in the curriculum of all Swiss schools. Karajan said, "Pity it's not the bassoon."

Karajan has an enormous natural musical instinct but he doesn't leave it to that alone. Everything is thought out ahead. The whole thing is treated as a campaign, just as his whole career has been. It was the recordings that made him famous. He more than any other conductor, except perhaps Stokowski, was really made by gramophone recordings, and I don't know a man who is not professionally engaged in the record business who studies records as he does. He will listen to every bar of any colleague of fame, just to see if there is a nuance that pleases him, a way of doing things, or a way of not doing things. He's like a magpie when he comes to the house to stay. He goes through all the piles of new records, takes them up in his room and plays bits through. "Listen, what do you think of this?" "Have you heard Munch's tempo for that bit of *La Mer*? Quite extraordinary. We must try that out some time." "I am not ashamed to admit that's where I got that from and that's where I got that from." He knows by heart I should think everybody's metronome mark for every stage.

Many people have asked me about the so-called Karajan sound. It is exquisitely polished, free of anything that is unbeautiful, of great brilliance, and can jump to fortissimo without the click of an attack. Every phrase which can be begun beautifully is begun as beautifully as he knows how. At Aachen, and Ulm before, he spent a great deal of time working with choruses. And also being an athlete, he knows the value of breathing, so all his phrasing is based on the fact that he has to breathe with the players and breathe with the singers. Any singer who has ever worked with him will tell you that he is, from the point of singers in opera, incomparable. He mouths the words so that they can read the text from his lips. He breathes with them, anticipates every difficulty, and nurses them through. He sticks with them like chewing gum to a heel. Probably from Richard Strauss's example he knows that clarity of text is the *sine qua non* of operatic performance and he accompanies *pianissimo* and *parlando* passages with the softest translucent cushion of orchestral sound even, when necessary, in scores as complex as *Elektra*. So highly developed is his instinct for clarity of texture and so intimate his knowledge of his scores that even in the most compactly orchestrated episodes in Wagner and Strauss he can give the orchestra what seems full rein without obscuring the polyphony or covering or overtaxing his singers. He has taught his players not only to listen to each other but to listen to the stage. One of his most characteristic gestures is turning his head in the direction of the player or singer with an important solo phrase, pointing to them with the first finger of his left hand and hushing the rest of the orchestra with his other three fingers.

Karajan takes the time to get it as he wants it, and he knows that what players need is an indication of where a beat ends and where the next one begins. The line never stops, its tempo is constant unless he wants to move faster or to slow down. That is why he gets such beautifully smooth playing, with never an ugly entrance. We worked together for years on the theory that no entrance must start without the string vibrating and the bow already moving, and when you get a moving bow touching an already vibrating string, you get a beautiful entry. But if either of those bodies is not alive and already moving, you get a click, and Karajan has calculated all that. No other man has worked out so exactly the psychology of players, their needs, and what he must do to get exactly the result he wants. He told me that it took him twenty years before he knew really how to conduct.

Tape has produced false standards. I began tending away from it a bit toward the end of my career. No singer can sing as well as their records sound. Occasionally you get odd bits—for example, the first four minutes of *Rosenkavalier*. Karajan walked in, no rehearsal, no attention to the microphone. "Good morning, let's begin—ready?" He played it straight through, down to Octavian's first words and then said, "Let's listen to it." I said, "Do you think the horns are loud enough—you see what Strauss has written? Let's really get them to do what he meant." He said "All right, if you want to do it again, we'll do it, but I'm satisfied." And by ten past ten, we'd done the first four minutes of *Rosenkavalier* without a splice! However, on the Mozart B-flat Divertimento with the Philharmonia we spent ten sessions. It was a piece Bruno Walter used to have as one of his showpieces in Vienna, but Karajan said he had never heard it in tune. In those days the gramophone industry was more prosperous than it is now, and after three sessions, Parikian who was leading the orchestra at that time came to me and said, "I'm sorry, but will you tell Mr. von Karajan that we cannot play this piece." So I said, "You come in and tell him yourself." Karajan said, "Huh—a little modesty is quite welcome. Er, we will go on."

At the end of that session I was getting a bit desperate. I knew that Toscanini had recorded this piece, but the recording had not been published. I got hold of a set of lacquers before lunchtime, and when Karajan came in I said, "Well, listen, I've had a lacquer cut of what we've done this morning. Let's compare it with Toscanini's record." And Toscanini was so appallingly out of tune that Karajan just laughed ribaldly and said, "Huh, what are you complaining about? At least we're better than the old man is!"

I've known no conductor who's so interesting to talk to, on so many aspects of music. His mind is full of it, but his mind is full of all sorts of things. He's interested in nuclear science, motor cars, flying, boating. When water-skiing first came to Europe, we were sitting in a boat at Lucerne, and there was somebody giving a demonstration. I said to him, "Why don't you have a shot at that?" He said, "No, I want to watch it." And he sat watching this man for an hour and a half without a word. Then he said, "Now I'll try." He got on the water-skis and from his observation knew everything that was necessary. He fell only once. Simply by the power of concentration and will, having observed the mistakes that others had been making, and a demonstration, he mastered that particularly practical skill. He built his career up with equal skill. He knew that as long as Furtwängler lived his way would be blocked. But he said to me, "We are not worried, we have time."

Furtwängler's death in 1954 and three months later the sad farce of Böhm's resignation from his four-month directorship of the newly rebuilt Vienna State Opera had cleared the path to the fulfillment of Karajan's immediate ambitions. In six years he had unostentatiously, in his concerts, recordings, and tours with the Philharmonia Orchestra, and his operatic performances at La Scala, staked his claim and made himself the inevitable choice for both Berlin and Vienna. And the road to Salzburg was open again. Within months he had the best part of musical life in Europe in his hands. Berlin gave him a contract for life, almost unlimited subventions, absolute authority, and the inner satisfaction of being the acknowledged heir to the lineage of von Bülow, Richard Strauss, Nikisch, and Furtwängler. This galvanized him into making the Berlin Philharmonic the best in the world. He quickly moulded it into the audible manifestation of his own musical personality. He gave it new delicacy and power, precision and flexibility, transparency, brilliance and deep sonority, and the ability to adapt itself to a wide variety of musical styles. In Berlin, as in Salzburg, Karajan's ideas were the determining factor in the design of the platform and auditorium of the new hall in which he was to work. Unorthodox seating focuses every eye on the conductor, but for many ears, his and the orchestra's work sounds better in some other halls. Less than a year after his Berlin contract was signed, Vienna announced his appointment to the State Opera.

In retrospect Karajan's eight-year reign at the Vienna Opera will probably rank even higher than Mahler's. He transformed a complacent national institution into the world's most prestigious opera house. His activities as a regisseur often caused heated dispute, but his conducting (forty or more performances a year) won almost unstinted praise and admiration. There were inevitable troughs in standards when he was absent from Vienna—there have never been enough great singers and conductors to maintain gala quality ten months a year, but the general level was high. Ministerial interventions, political cross-currents, factions, and irresponsible gossip have long plagued Austrian musical life but rarely so intensely as during the Karajan era. The Austrian newspapers, with the constance of the weathercock and the modesty of the peacock, to use Ernest Newman's admirable phrase, made hay and headlines of every wisp of gossip at the whims and prejudice of every scribbler—and the dictates and politics of their papers' financial backers. Karajan was induced to withdraw his first resignation from Vienna, but made what seemed the unique and unaccountable tactical blunder in his career: he insisted on the appointment of Egon Hilbert as his co-director. Karajan despised Hilbert and Hilbert hated Karajan. Most probably he was bored by the job and saw no stimulating future in it. His resignation in 1964 was final.

Karajan's participation in the Salzburg Festivals has also had an embattled history. He had been engaged for both the 1946 and 1947 Festivals but the delay in his denazification reduced his participation to directing the conductors and producers from the auditorium during rehearsals. In 1948 he conducted two operas and two concerts. My attempt to arrange an armistice between Furtwängler and Karajan was a disaster. The rivals, with their wives and myself, dined in a *chambre séparée* in a Salzburg hotel, and vowed eternal friendship. Early next morning, Furtwängler summoned Egon Hilbert, then director of the Festival, and dictated a contract undertaking to conduct every year at Salzburg on condition that Karajan should be excluded from Salzburg as long as Furtwängler lived. He agreed to Karajan's being allowed to conduct the two concerts in 1949 for which he was already engaged. Only days later did Karajan discover how he had been duped. During his seven-year exile from Salzburg he conducted at Bayreuth, but the clash of his and Wieland Wagner's conceptions and egocentricities ruled out further collaboration. In 1956 Karajan was appointed Artistic Leader (he always rejected the title Director although he exercised its functions and privileges) of the Salzburg Festival and in 1957 returned to conduct and produce *Fidelio* and his own *Falstaff* staging transposed from La Scala. Since then, under varying titles— and sometimes without, because he often used timely resignation to gain future advantages—he has been the autocrat of the Salzburg festivals.

It is likely that Karajan had already conceived his next major move in Salzburg when he insisted on the extraordinary width, thirty-three meters, of the proscenium opening in the new Grosses Festspielhaus, which he inaugurated in July 1960. Early in 1965 there were rumors which found their way into the press that Karajan had agreed with Herbert Graf of Geneva and Rudolf Bing of the Metropolitan to produce The Ring in Geneva, then take it lock, stock, barrel, and casts to the Met. Privately Graf and Bing denied all knowledge of the project but neither at the time made public contradictions. Suddenly during the Salzburg Summer Festival, Karajan launched his rocket: he would establish Easter Festivals in Salzburg starting in 1967 at which he would produce and conduct The Ring, financing the whole project himself.

It was a masterpiece of ruseful planning, a paramilitary operation in organization and coordination. He covered the expenses of musical preparation and rehearsals by recording for one company or another (DGG for The Ring) the operas he intended to produce at the next Festival: tapes of the recordings were given to the singers well in advance of rehearsals so that they could constantly remind themselves of tempi, rubati, and verbal inflections. In that way he radically reduced the attendances of orchestra and casts at his invariably long lighting and stage rehearsals. He used his own recordings and amateur stand-ins to set and light the singers' movements. He had his own Berlin Philharmonic, unsullied by operatic routines, and the works played in the interspersed orchestral concerts were safely in the Berliners' repertoire.

For concerts Karajan has a vast repertoire of all the important works the international public likes to hear, naturally based on the German and Austrian classics from Bach to Richard Strauss, with a comparatively high percentage of choral works. This was extended to works he never performed in public by the demands of his multitudinous recording commitments. He has recorded much of the symphonic repertoire of Beethoven, Brahms, Richard Strauss, and the last three Tchaikovsky symphonies two, three, even four times. There are, however, strange lacunae in his repertoire. He conducts almost no Handel, very few Haydn symphonies, only the later symphonies of Mozart, the last two Schubert, the Bruckner symphonies from No. 4 to No. 9, and some Mahler. Apart from Sibelius and Shostakovitch and two major works of Bartok, music by contemporaries rarely appears in his programmes, although Orff's *Carmina Burana* has been one of his warhorses in Berlin, and a carefully prepared *Belshazzar's Feast* in Vienna moved William Walton to tears and privately to say that he could not believe he had ever been capable of writing such marvellous music. It may have been pique at Stravinsky's rumored disapproval of his recording of *Sacre du Printemps* that urged Karajan astonishingly to record at great expense of time and care an album of the New Viennese School—Schönberg, Berg, and Webern. Stravinsky's primitive savagery was probably foreign to Karajan's preoccupation with beauty but he probed the neurasthenia of Schönberg and his successors in recordings which reveal entirely new aspects of the music and the clarity and profundity of his own musical perception. He has woven fascinating beauty and made musical sense out of what under the hands of two generations of conductors has seemed willful, even senseless cacophony—and gave cohesion to Webern's wispy fragmentations. Over the years his interpretations have varied little in tempo, texture, and form, probably because he did not play a work until he had convinced himself how it should sound.

The basic quality of every interpretative artist depends on the degree to which he has identified himself with the composer's spirit and intentions, but each interpreter inevitably leaves the fingerprints of his musical personality and predilections on them. The enduring validity and, on listening to his records, the satisfaction that Karajan brought to music is his musical integrity. He does not attempt to impose a philosophy nor preach a personal *Weltanschauung*.

Most of the scores Karajan has used have been my property, but they are returned with never a mark on them—not a sign of a mark, not a dog-eared page. He studies his scores propped up on his elbows in bed or lying like a relaxed Siamese cat on a floor. I have watched him observing how Siamese cats relax themselves and he has learned even from them how to relax his body completely so that the mind is absolutely free to do what it wants. He never makes a mark of any kind in a score but absorbs, memorizes and hears in his mind's ears what the printed notes convey to him as what the composer intended, and how beautifully it can be realized. For many years he conducted all his concerts with closed eyes, disconcerting for the players until they got used to it, and it would seem depriving himself of one of his most powerful means of communication. He was satisfied, however, that with his eyes shut he could "see" the score more clearly in his mind's eye, and that by not seeing the orchestra playing he could better hear and adjust the niceties of balance.

He has a dowser's instincts for musical styles. Sibelius considered him his best interpreter, "the only one who plays what I meant." No other non-Italian and no Italian conductor except his seniors Toscanini, de Sabata, and Serafin can be compared with him in the Italian operas he specializes in.

It is pointless to discuss the mechanics of Karajan's conducting technique: what he does with his arms, hands, and fingers is the distillation of a lifetime's experience of how to make his intentions explicit by the most economical gestures. His physical movements are instinctive extensions of his musical mind and he has developed a sixth sense alert to anticipate and correct any likely or possible error. In rehearsal his body is relaxed, his mind intensely concentrated: he is sparing of words and speaks very quietly to make the orchestra listen—except Italian orchestras, "a noise-loving lot who don't take you seriously unless you bawl at them." His power of communication to both performers and audience is hypnotic. Once we were in Berlin and he gave a couple of master classes for the students at the Academy and we were talking about the difficulty the youngsters had in getting chords together, and he said, "Well, I will show you. I'll bet you five marks that I can get the wind in first, the brass in first, the strings in first, and I will get them together and I won't warn them. They will know nothing at all, simply that by the upbeat I will throw them and then get them together." And he did it. I merely said which I wanted in first and he got them in first. Just by a hair's breadth, but it was not together. Karajan has the ability to hypnotize, the power of communication to make an orchestra give that sound that he wants, because, after all, sound comes from gesture basically. The basic sound a conductor makes comes from the nature of his gesture. What is a conductor's gesture? It's merely the prolongation of his musical will. It's his means of communication, it's the nearest it can be to tactile. But I think every great conductor, or every conductor who has achieved what we call greatness, has that power of communication. Because what is conducting? It's the power of communication by the hands of a musical idea, and nothing else.

231

# 14

# THE
# RETIREMENT YEARS

*It was difficult to watch the discrepancy between Walter's brain—
to the end in Olympic condition—and his body, which after his heart
attack in 1967 was not able to keep pace, although his bearing never
gave in.*

*For a man who all his life had been in his office at 9:00, would re-
cord from 10:00 until 6:30 with a business lunch squeezed in, perhaps
a dinner break until 8:00 and then would keep on recording until 11:00,
it was difficult to comprehend that he now needed an afternoon nap.
Grudgingly Walter realized he had to slow down.*

*As far as the recording industry was concerned amazingly few offers
came, now that he was no longer an exclusive EMI producer. Perhaps
other companies did not cherish the idea of inviting an expensive shark
into their midst. (Walter's exactitude, his keen ear, and his passion for
perfection were not only well known but perhaps feared.) Though
most artists welcomed those qualities, the business side of the recording
industry saw Walter's perfectionism only in terms of precious overtime.*

*One offer that did come was from RCA; they wanted to know if
Walter were interested in recording Massenet's Thaïs, starring Anna
Moffo. Walter thought a bit, then said if they would get a French chorus
(as no English chorus could do it justice) and record the whole thing
in their Paris studios, he would consider it. "Let me look at the score;
it's been ages since I've seen it. Then I'll let you know." I went to
Patelson's Music Shop, near Carnegie Hall, to buy the score, and that
night he re-read the entire opera in our suite at the Regency Hotel.*

*Walter liked the idea of Anna doing Thaïs. He had produced her
first album of Italian arias, then chose her as Nanetta for the Karajan
Falstaff and as Susanna to my Contessa. We both have always loved
Anna and watched her career with parental pride. Now, Walter was
told, she was in a sort of vocal crisis. More reason to try and help her*

as much as he could. Next day he told RCA he would like to have a crack at it. Nothing ever happened. There were many personnel changes at RCA right then; no one ever said "it's off"—but then no one had ever said "it's on." It gradually fizzled into nothing. I learned from Anna later that she was never told that Walter had been asked, let alone that he had agreed, to produce Thaïs. As things turned out, it was a pity for all concerned. So this, except for all the recordings Walter still did with me, was his one and only "might have been."

But there came other projects: Wexford, that tiny jewel of a festival, could have been enchanting, but Walter's heart attack intervened. The creation of the new musical school in Paris would have been perfect. And the revamping of the Casals Festival in Puerto Rico interested Walter greatly, but it did not come off. It might have been for financial reasons, but more probably it was artistic differences. There were people venturing the opinion that Walter's bad heart would have prevented his seeing through any of these projects. Rubbish! Given the chance he would have mastered them superbly.

Perhaps the most interesting of the plans was the French National School of Style and Interpretation in Singing. The project foundered when the government changed and the minister who had sought Walter's counsel found himself out of a job. But for a time it seemed that Walter and I would be going to France to help found the new music school. His plan included enlisting the aid of such colleagues as Maria Callas, Birgit Nilsson, Monserrat Caballé, Magda Olivero, Peter Pears, Geoffrey Parsons, Martin Isepp, Heinrich Schmidt, Antonino Tonini, Gabriel Bacquier, Michel Sénéchal, Nicolai Gedda, Günther Rennert, Peter Brook, and many others who were preeminent in their particular fields.

With his usual thoroughness the plan not only set forth the curriculum—which covered every aspect of the vocal art, opera, oratorio, and song—but even gave minute instructions, such as how many typewriters we would need in the office and even the size of the students' lockers.

In a letter to Eric Sams, Walter said:

You'll be amused to hear that the French Minister of Cultural Affairs has asked my wife and me to be the Directors of a new "School of Style and Interpretation" in Paris. He has been here to visit us and we have meetings with his technical consultants and advisers on 25th and 26th in Paris. They propose to place at our disposal an architecturally valuable old theatre, restore it, and equip it with sound-proof studios and all the facilities I asked for in a long memorandum on the topic. If it materializes I shall need tons of Benzedrine, the glands of jungles of monkeys, and vast buttocks to take the multitudinous injections of all the rejuvenating hormones known to modern geriatry.

Keep this absolutely to yourself until I tell you that everything is signed, but the prospects are considered sufficiently good for the Ministry to advise us to look for a house in or near Paris. The anticipated opening date is October 1976.

*Walter's view of the musical scene in France was not a charitable one, but he felt that the situation was salvageable and discussed it at great length with André Tubeuf, to whom he offered advice and encouragement when Tubeuf was appointed to the Ministry of Culture with the task of putting music back onto its feet in that country. Walter modestly said, "May I advance a few theories or suggestions?"*

THERE IS so much to do! For nearly fifty years I have visited Paris every year—except during the war—and despaired of hearing even one really first-class performance either in the Opéra or in the now-alas-defunct Opéra-Comique. The only ones that have remained pleasantly in my mind have been those conducted by Furtwängler in the years of the Paris Exhibition—a *Gastspiel* of the Berlin Opera, though the main reason for my visit was the incredibly wonderful van Gogh exhibition.

In all these years musical life in Paris and, I believe, the whole of France has been undermined and, to use a very English phrase, is "sick unto death" by the diseases of amateurism, nepotism, ignorance, lack of organization and an overriding patriotic provincialism. And since the war the rise to power of a very strong musico-political party—the homosexuals.

I believe that the Opéra in Paris should be a National Theatre. It seems—and this has always been confirmed by the sales of operatic records in France—that the French prefer to hear opera sung in French. However, I feel that for two periods each season of about eight to ten weeks, when both the good Parisian public and tourists with the money to pay for exceptional performances are in Paris, there should be performances, a minimum of four each week, by international casts of the highest quality giving the masterpieces of opera of all periods—from Gluck to Puccini, Strauss, and the end of the great period of operatic creation. I will consider Mozart separately. All these performances should be in the original language: I managed to record an excellent *Boris* in Paris in Russian, which proves it can be done, but not with the comprimarii and chorus singing in French!

WAGNER     I believe that Wagner should be represented in every season—the complete Ring twice every second year. The intervening years always two of the following: *Meistersinger, Tristan, Lohengrin, Tannhäuser.* I do not know how the Parisian public reacts to *Parsifal*—if they like it, two performances in each of The Ring year.

Over seven years the following repertoire should be produced new and kept in the repertoire for both the international seasons and the rest of the season:

GLUCK     *Orphée, Iphigenia in Tauris, Iphigenia in Aulis, Alceste.* I feel strongly that these productions should be in scenery and costumes either exact reproductions of those given in Gluck's time or severely classical—not modern stylized.

BERLIOZ     In my experience the French do not really admire Berlioz but *Les Troyens* (both parts) should be done if one can find the casts. I do not believe it possible to make *Benvenuto Cellini* or *Béatrice et Bénédict* successes. And I do not believe in spending money to play to empty seats. Ever!

BEETHOVEN     *Fidelio.* Ideally in a smaller theatre but it makes its effect in any theatre if it is well done.

STRAUSS     *Der Rosenkavalier.* Every second or third year in German in the "luxury" periods. In the general season in French.
*Elektra.* This depends on the availability of the exceptional voices needed. I would suggest this be kept only for the "luxury" seasons every third or fourth year.
*Salome.* As *Elektra* but perhaps also in French during the rest of the year according to demand.
*Die Frau ohne Schatten.* Paris has new and, I believe, beautiful scenery and costumes. Every second year. I do not believe it can be adequately translated into French

235

or any language because the symbolism is almost incomprehensible in German!

*Capriccio.* Only possibility is to borrow a first-class German or Austrian company with scenery and costumes. I have not much faith in the other Strauss operas as far as Paris is concerned. But for *Ariadne* see next paragraph.

MOZART        Only *Zauberflöte* is practicable or possible in the Paris Opéra. What one needs is a more intimate theatre with 1,000–1,400 seats and a charming atmosphere for Mozart. The lovely Versailles theatre is too far out and has awful acoustics. The Marigny I used to love but it is probably too small. The Odéon? The pit holds 34 players, which is ideal for the Da Ponte operas, for *Ariadne,* and for a range of lighter operas—*Barbiere, L'Elisir d'Amore, Don Pasquale, La Fille du Régiment,* a lot of Offenbach, some Auber but rather small for Johann Strauss and Smetana's *Verkaufte Braut* and *Zwei Witwen* (which Strauss himself, told me is "the best comic opera since *Così*—except *Rosenkavalier* and *Ariadne*").

BIZET         In my view both *Carmen* and *Pêcheurs de Perles* should be done in the smaller house but the wide popularity of *Carmen* I suppose condemns it to the big theatre.

But in all this thinking about the repertoire for a small house the most important matter is STYLE in musical performance, in settings, in *Regie.* Never let anyone play down to the public. Educate the public to what used to be and still is latent in the French nation and nature: TASTE and ELEGANCE!

VERDI         *Rigoletto, La Traviata, Il Trovatore, Aida, Otello* and perhaps *Don Carlos* must all be in the permanent repertoire of the Opéra, international casts in the "luxury" seasons in Italian (*Carlos* in French always), the others in French in the rest of the season.

MEYERBEER     I am afraid of him at the moment because of the scarcity of singers and the need of elaborate staging.

PUCCINI     *Bohème, Butterfly, Tosca* as permanent plats du jour in
            Italian in the "luxury" periods, otherwise in French.
            Leave the others except perhaps *Manon Lescaut* and
            *Gianni Schicchi*, which would make a good double bill
            with *Carmina Burana*.

*Faust, Cavalleria,* and *Pagliacci* are, I suppose, essential. About Massenet I do not dare express opinions: *Manon* is, I suppose, essential and
*Thaïs* deserves the occasional revival for a decade or so.

## Staging and Costumes

Owing to the present mania for *Regie* and decor, which is a cancer on
operatic life, much too much money is being spent on these two aspects
of opera. This disease, this tyranny must be broken. If I had an opera
house I would not produce *any* opera unless I were sure that each
production would yield 80 to 100 performances. Otherwise the ex-
penditure is disproportionate to the possible receipts.

## Opera in the Provinces

I do not know how many of the French provincial opera houses are
still functioning. Certainly Lyon, Bordeaux, Marseille, Toulon, Monte
Carlo. Lille? Toulouse? Nice? Cannes? In any case I would put them
all together, knock the directors on the heads or dismiss them if necessary and make an arrangement by which all the provincial theatres
are under one director who gives each theatre the same repertoire and
scenery and soloists in rotation, each theatre temporarily (except Monte
Carlo, Nice, Cannes, Toulon, which are close enough to use one and the
same orchestra and chorus) using its local orchestral forces and chorus.
This is probably cheaper. This whole complex should be an "école de
perfection" preparing the best young French native singers and orchestral
players for eventually taking their places in Paris. This is your work and
duty because you are the only Frenchman I know who has the
knowledge, the taste, the love, the distinction of mind, the integrity necessary to achieve the Renaissance of Opera in France. And to do it
economically!

*In 1969 we went to Montreux, where Walter received a special
award for his contributions to the art of recording. It was a happy oc-*

*casion, made even more so by the presence of Leopold Stokowski,*
*whose recordings in the 1920s had so influenced the young Walter*
*Legge. Walter's speech was vintage Legge.*

Since my retirement I have lived the life of a Trappist monk, so I
hope you will forgive me if I express myself *in tempo lento e molto*
*nervoso.*

I am deeply grateful for the honour the jury of the Prix Mondial du
Disque has conferred on me. It is, I am ashamed to say, the first time I
have been honoured in this way. So far the only recognition I have received of my achievements such as they are have been a gravestone-like
inscription in the hall of the Salzburg Mozarteum and the jealousy and
dislike of many of my ex-colleagues in the musical profession—and of
that I am proud.

In England it is rare for anyone working in the arts to be honoured
by a diploma, a medal, or a title. In musical England such honours are
confined to Beatles and to composers on reaching the age of sixty or so.
British conductors are almost invariably knighted between the age of
fifty and sixty: it is a sort of occupational risk.

But, as my teacher and friend Ernest Newman said when I asked
him why he had declined a knighthood: "I am particular about the
company I keep." Or, as Groucho Marx replied to the secretary of one
of New York's most exclusive clubs which had invited him to become
a member: "I would not think of joining a club that would have a man
like me as a member."

But here, in Montreux, I am in excellent company. I had never
hoped to find myself honoured in the most distinguished company of
Leopold Stokowski.

Stokowski's influence in improving the standards of orchestral recording cannot be overestimated. It was his first series of electrical
recordings with the Philadelphia Orchestra that gave to millions of
people who had never heard a real orchestra in their lives their first
experience of something like the sound of a great orchestra. I attribute
the vast proliferation of symphony orchestras in the United States in
the last forty years to Stokowski, who gave to people who lived two or
three thousand miles from the nearest symphony orchestra first the
taste, then the need of helping to establish orchestras in their own
communities.

Ladies and gentlemen, the past is past and cannot be altered, except by historians. Therefore if you will be patient with me for two or three minutes, I would like to talk to you about the present state of recording and its possible future.

The fact that I resigned from EMI has not in any way reduced my love for gramophone records or my interests in the gramophone industry. It has, if anything, increased it. Often I sit at my desk and make out lists of the records which I regret not having made!

Early this year I was in New York and, as usual, talked with the big boys in nearly all the leading American companies. When I asked one of them, "How's business?," he answered, "Lousy! What we all ought to do is to stop making records for three years and concentrate on selling what we already have in the catalogue."

That would be a radical—too radical—solution. But I feel that many of the major recording companies have in recent years been making too many records and advertising them too little, or hardly at all. Only the comparatively small public which reads the specialist magazines like *High Fidelity, Gramophone, Phono Forum* or *Hifi Stereophonie* really knows what records are being published each month. I have been living in Switzerland for more than five years and in all that time no record dealer has sent me a list of new or recently published records nor made the slightest effort to induce me to buy a record—not even the dealers who service my reproducing equipment and tune my piano. And this weakness in the selling of records is worldwide. It is only the large record clubs which advertise on a substantial scale, and what they advertise is almost entirely well-proven best-sellers.

The bitter truth of the record trade is the decreasing percentage of so-called classical sales in relation to the so-called pops. The tendency for the last ten years has been for the classical sales to represent a decreasing percentage—expressed in hard figures from over 6 percent to under 5 percent of the total amount of money the public spends or records.

I hope that in giving you a few economic facts about the record industry I have not made you believe that money has been my major concern in recording or that it has been a vital factor in my thinking or my way of working. I was in HMV and, after their merger with Columbia, in EMI for nearly forty years, at the heart of record-making. I learned very early that although profit is what the business directors want, the only way to satisfy this aim of theirs is to make exceptionally good records.

I have often been accused of being a perfectionist—I am. Only a week ago Tito Gobbi reminded me that I had made him sing the last minutes of the first act of *Tosca*—the Te Deum—forty times before I was satisfied. But that *Tosca* is and will probably be for generations to come the standard by which other recordings and performances of *Tosca* will be judged and found wanting.

There is a lady here who for the last twenty-three years has enthusiastically aided and abetted me in this search for perfection. We have never exchanged cross words on this subject—and I think she looks well on it, particularly when you remember that she has been married to me for much the greater part of that time.

Now I want to put to you and to the major recording companies a proposal which could have only a beneficial effect on their sales. My scheme is simply this: that all the major recording companies—listen how carefully I am naming them alphabetically—Columbia Records, Deutsche Grammophon, EMI, Philips, and RCA Victor should pool all the artists they have under exclusive contracts for the purpose of making each year a series of eight or ten major recordings.

All the five companies must agree on repertoire, soloists, orchestra, conductor and, of course, the hall in which the records should be made and all five companies shall record simultaneously with their own technical staff and equipment. Each recording should be published on the same day in every important country. Each company should be free to advertise as it likes, but only from a mutually agreed date.

From the point of view of all the companies, there would be an enormous saving of costs, and each company would exert itself to a hitherto unprecedented degree to make the best recording. I know from long experience how major recordings I have made have been handicapped by artists essential to my work being tied to one company or another.

The companies would profit substantially by much reduced expenses in recording, even if they gave—as they would have to do—royalties to the orchestras, even for operatic works. But each of them would have a de luxe product otherwise out of their reach.

At first I would restrict the repertoire to opera and the few major choral works. I hope this proposal will meet with your approval and that of the five great companies. I am sure it would find favour with the record-buying public.

240

It is particularly in the field of opera that this scheme would be invaluable. Considering the enormous number of recordings of opera made since Dario Soria started his Cetra-Soria series, it is surprising how few operatic recordings are really worth their places in the catalogues. Furtwängler's *Tristan und Isolde* will probably never be equalled. Nor *Tosca* conducted by de Sabata with Callas, di Stefano, and Gobbi, all at their best.

But think of the sins of omission! George Szell, one of the supreme Mozart conductors of the twentieth century, has not recorded one Mozart opera, nor as far as I can remember has he recorded *any* complete opera. Karajan, who is demonstrably one of the best if not the uniquely great Verdi conductor, has not recorded a Verdi opera since he parted company with EMI. And some of the greatest performances of his life, *Lucia* and his miraculous *La Bohème* have not been recorded. And Giulini, the only great Italian conductor of Italian opera, has not recorded even one opera by an Italian composer.

The purpose of my scheme is to repair these omissions and ensure that in the next eight or ten years there will be at least fifty supreme recordings of the major works in the operatic repertoire.

The only possible obstacle to the proper realization of this scheme of mine is that John Culshaw and I would have to be induced to return to record-making because, as far as I can see, we two have no successors!

*At the reception afterward, someone asked Walter if there had been recordings he still would have liked to make. "Hundreds," he replied. "For example, the complete Beethoven and Mozart trios, quartets, and quintets with 1st violin, David Oistrakh; 2nd violin, Igor Oistrakh; viola, Barshai; and cello, Rostropovitch." He also mentioned Verdi's Otello, for which, because of contractual reasons, it was impossible in the early stereo era to get an ideal cast together. And besides there was no even satisfactory Iago. "It is only now that one has come on the scene. But why should I give away my ideas?—I may yet return to producing records."*

*I overhead this and my heart sank. He would never again be able to do the thing he did better than anyone else: produce records. But ten years later, after he had gone, I took heart. There he was: furiously and beseechingly raising the Heavenly Choirs to the standard of the old Philharmonia Chorus!*

# Epilogue

"Die Zeit, die ist ein sonderbar Ding," says the Marschallin. Yes, time is a strange thing. But she also says in that marvellous rôle, "Jedes Ding hat seine Zeit." Each thing has its time.

And so with our lives and careers. Walter's and mine. When the cruel time had come and we both knew that my concert career could last only a few more years, I became concerned what Walter's life would be when he no longer needed to refine and improve and worry about my recitals. He, I am sure, although we never talked about it, worried what would fill my time when I would no longer have to dash from airport to airport and from concert hall to concert hall. A kind fate intervened: an offer from Peter Mennin, head of the Juilliard School of Music in New York, to conduct master classes together.

We accepted happily, for it meant that Walter would have a stimulating and exciting time and would be able to pass on his vast knowledge—so far tapped only in the recording studio—to young singers, and I would find out if I could teach. I was also apprehensive—for Walter, who up to then had not been a "performer," and also for myself. It is one thing to be able to sing out—quite another to speak up.

Walter, as I found out while preparing this book, accepted those classes because he felt that making the plunge with him would prepare me for a future when I would be alone. As usual he was right. His presence and support in those first classes (and the subsequent ones in San Francisco, Bloomington, and Ann Arbor, as well as in Italy and Canada) showed me that a new extension of my life lay ahead. More, that handing on our knowledge to all those young, gifted people was a challenging, exhausting, and exciting task, which by now I find easy. The two years after Walter's death were so filled with teaching that I had no time to feel alone.

And finally it has dawned on me, that this new life of mine is—I suppose—Walter's last gift. . . .

# A Selected Discography

ALAN SANDERS

WALTER LEGGE supervised some 3,500 recordings of separate works, large and small. A complete discography is clearly beyond the scope of this book, so I have prepared a limited survey based on the list produced by Mr. Legge in which he set out the recordings of which he was most proud.

Thus, in this discography will be found the prewar Lieder recordings Walter Legge made for the HMV "Society" albums, the recordings of Sir Thomas Beecham made between 1934 and 1940, wartime recordings made by John McCormack, the series of operettas, the postwar Herbert von Karajan recordings, and of course the records made by Mr. Legge's wife, Elisabeth Schwarzkopf. Also represented are such artists as Callas, Flagstad, Furtwängler, Gieseking, Lipatti, and Klemperer.

Details of unpublished recordings are not provided, and published recordings bear the principal UK and US record numbers only. Tape and cassette recordings are not listed, and, by and large, reissues, arranged in a format different from the original issue are excluded. Dedicated students of discographies need not despair at these various omissions; all this information and much more is contained in a complete discography of all Walter Legge's recordings which will be published elsewhere.

The role of the record producer has only recently been recognized at its true importance, and in many cases, particularly among the early recordings, I have had to rely on the memories of Mr. Legge's colleagues and friends rather than documentation, which does not exist. The help given to me in my quest for information has been generous indeed, yet to the extent that human memory is fallible, so may this discography also be fallible in occasionally crediting Mr. Legge with a recording he perhaps did not supervise or in omitting a recording that he did produce. But all care has been taken to make this information as accurate as possible.

The discography is in general arranged chronologically session by session. Each group of sessions is headed by—from left to right—the date of the recording, its location, and a note of the artists taking part. When a work was recorded over a number of different dates these dates have been grouped together to show the progress of the recording sessions at a glance. In the case of 78-r.p.m. recordings, only the dates of the takes accepted for publication have been given: in the case of recordings emanating from tape it is more difficult to disentangle published from unpublished takes and for the most part it has been necessary to include all relevant session dates. When more than one session involving different groups of artists took place on the same day, only the differences of personnel are noted: the date heading is usually not changed. Conversely, when the same artists recorded in the same location over several dates, only the change of date is noted.

Underneath the main heading is set out a description of the work or works recorded, and finally to each work or group of works are appended the published record or set numbers. These numbers are arranged to give, as applicable, details firstly of 78-r.p.m. issues, then long-playing records, next extended-play 45-r.p.m. discs, and lastly standard play 45-r.p.m. versions. In each category UK numbers are given first, then US numbers. In the few cases where a record has been published only outside the UK and the USA a number relating to the actual country of publication is provided.

The locations of recording venues outside London are given in full. London recordings usually took place in the EMI Abbey Road Studios or in Kingsway Hall. The venues of some Berlin recordings are not known.

The symbol † denotes a recording which was only partly supervised by Walter Legge. In these cases it may be assumed that Mr. Legge approved the final result on tape or disc before publication.

My grateful thanks are due to Peter Andry, Anthony Locantro, Robert Dockerill, and John Watson of EMI. Without their help and that of other staff members this discography would not have been possible. I should also like to thank four former EMI staff members, J. David Bicknell, Anthony Griffith, Elaine Divall, and Elizabeth Wicks, all of whom have provided much invaluable advice and assistance. In addition I am grateful for help provided by Jane Withers, previously managing director of The Philharmonia Orchestra, Andrew Cornall of the Decca Record Company, Anthony Pollard and Malcolm Walker of *Gramophone* magazine, Eric Hughes of the British Institute of Recorded Sound, Roxy Bellamy of CBS Records, Hilary Sheard of Polygram Classics, Nancy Crozier, Gerhard Hüsch, Geoffrey Parsons, Mrs. John Tobin, and Isabella Wallich. I am also indebted to Margaret Pacy for much help and advice in the preparation of the manuscript. Michael Gray's *Beecham: A Centenary Discography* (1979) has been an invaluable source.

## RECORD COMPANY PREFIXES

General Symbols: LP—Long-playing record; EP—7-inch extended-play 45-r.p.m. record; SP—7-inch standard-play 45-r.p.m. record; 78—78-r.p.m. record. Unless otherwise indicated the prefix refers to a 12-inch, 33⅓-r.p.m. LP of UK origin.

| | |
|---|---|
| A | US Columbia EP set mono |
| AL | US Columbia 10-inch LP mono |
| ALP | HMV mono |
| AN | EMI Angel mono |
| ASD | HMV stereo |
| BLP | HMV 10-inch LP mono |
| CFP | EMI Classics for Pleasure stereo |
| COLH | HMV Great Recordings of the Century mono |
| DB | HMV 12-inch 78 |
| EG | German Electrola 10-inch 78 |
| EHA | US RCA Victor EP set mono |
| EHB | US RCA Victor EP set mono |
| EL | US Columbia EP set mono |
| ENC | EMI Encore mono |
| ESL | Columbia EP stereo |
| GR | US Angel set mono |
| GDR | US Capitol set mono |
| H | EMI World Records mono |
| HLM | HMV Treasury mono |
| HQM | HMV mono |
| IR | Irish HMV 10-inch 78 |
| LB | Columbia 10-inch 78 |
| LC | International Columbia 10-inch 78 |
| LCT | US RCA Victor mono |
| LHMV | US RCA Victor mono |

| | |
|---|---|
| LV | Austrian Columbia 10-inch 78 |
| LX | Columbia 12-inch 78 |
| M | US Columbia 12-inch 78 set |
| M-digit-X | US CBS set mono/stereo |
| MFP | EMI Music for Pleasure mono |
| ML | US Columbia mono |
| OC | EMI World Records mono |
| OH | EMI World Records mono |
| RL | US Columbia mono |
| RLS | HMV mono set |
| SAN | EMI Angel stereo |
| SAX | Columbia stereo |
| SBO | Columbia 10-inch stereo |
| SCB | Columbia SP |
| SCD | Columbia SP |
| SDX | Columbia Delius Society 12-inch 78 |
| SEL | Columbia EP mono |
| SH | EMI World Records mono/stereo |
| SHB | EMI World Records set mono |
| SL | US Columbia set mono |
| SLPM | International Polydor stereo |
| SLS | HMV stereo/electronic stereo set |
| SMFP | EMI Music for Pleasure stereo |
| SOC | EMI World Records stereo/electronic stereo |
| ST | EMI World Records stereo/electronic stereo |
| SXDW | HMV two-record stereo/electronic stereo set |
| SXL | Decca stereo |
| SXLP | HMV Concert Classics stereo |
| T | EMI World Records mono |
| THS | US Vox Turnabout mono |
| TV | US Vox Turnabout mono |
| WDM | US RCA Victor SP set |
| WFS | Unicorn mono |
| WHMV | US RCA Victor SP set |
| X | US Columbia two-record 78 set |
| XLP | HMV Concert Classics mono |
| 3-000 | US Columbia 10-inch mono |
| 10-0000 | US Victor 10-inch 78 |
| 12-0000 | US Victor 12-inch 78 |
| 7P | HMV SP mono |
| 7R | HMV SP mono |
| 7EB | HMV EP mono |
| 7ER | HMV EP mono |
| 33C | Columbia 10-inch mono |
| 33CX | Columbia mono |
| 1900 and | |
| 2000 | US Victor 10-inch 78 |
| 2726-000 | International Polydor stereo |
| 3500 | US Angel mono/stereo set |
| 6000 | US Seraphim mono/stereo set |
| 12000D | US Columbia 12-inch 78 |
| 15000 | US Victor 12-inch 78 |
| 17000D | US Columbia 12-inch 78 |
| 35000 | US Angel mono/stereo |

60000 US Seraphim mono/stereo
60000D and
70000D US Columbia 12-inch 78
76000 CBS stereo
30000000 US CBS Odyssey mono/electronic stereo disc/set

1. The numbers of records in Victor and US Columbia 78-r.p.m. sets are not given, since each record bears the set number. Victor sets published in manual sequence bear the prefix M; sets published in the conventional automatic sequence, e.g. sides 1/12, 2/11, 3/10 etc., have the prefix DM; and sets published in the unconventional automatic sequence, e.g. sides 1/7, 2/8, 3/9 etc., have the prefix AM.

Columbia two-record sets have the prefix X in manual sequence and MX in automatic sequence; sets of three records and above have the prefix M for manual sequence, MM for automatic sequence—Columbia had no unorthodox automatic sequences. In all cases the set number remains the same.

2. Some Angel and Seraphim stereo LP issues have the prefix S.

3. In Angel and Seraphim album sets the set numbers have a prefix or a suffix, e.g. 3577C/L, which denotes that it is a three-record set with libretto.

### 1932

**May 28.** EMI Studio 1. Schorr (baritone), London Symphony/Heger. WOLF: Prometheus (78: DB1829. LP: Set RLS759).

**May 31.** EMI Studio 3. McCormack (tenor), Schneider (piano). WOLF: Ganymed; Beherzigung (78: DB1830. LP: COLH123, Set RLS759).

**Sept. 26–27.** Beethovensaal, Berlin. Trianti (soprano), Bos (piano). WOLF: Die Spröde; Die Bekehrte (78: DB1828. LP: Set RLS759). Mögen alle bösen Zungen; Köpfchen, Köpfchen, nicht gewimmert (78: DB2047. LP: Set RLS759). Wer rief dich denn?; Mein Liebster hat zu Tische mich geladen; Schweig' einmal still; Klinge, klinge, mein Pandero; Bitt' ihn, o Mutter (78: DB2048. LP: Set RLS759).

**Sept. 29.** Beethovensaal, Berlin. Janssen (baritone), Bos (piano). WOLF: Harfenspieler I and II (78: DB1825. LP: Set RLS759). Anakreons Grab; Coptisches Lied II; Harfenspieler III (78: DB1826. LP: Set RLS759).

**Oct. 25.** Beethovensaal, Berlin. Hüsch (baritone), Bos (piano). WOLF: Benedeit die sel'ge Mutter; Der Mond hat eine schwere Klag' erhoben; Schon streckt' ich aus im Bett (78: DB2049. LP: Set RLS759). Epiphanias; Genialisch Treiben; Der Rattenfänger (78: DB1827. LP: Set RLS759).

**Nov. 17.** EMI Studio 3. Trianti (soprano), Bos (piano). WOLF: Blumengruss; Gleich und gleich; Frühling übers Jahr (78: DB1828. LP: Set RLS759). Erstes Liebeslied eines Mädchens; Nixe Binsefuss (78: DB2047. LP: Set RLS759).

### 1933

**May 11.** EMI Studio 3. Kipnis (bass), Bos (piano). WOLF: Um Mitternacht; Fühlt meine Seele (78: DB2046. LP: Set RLS759, 60163). Grenzen der Menschheit (78: DB2050. LP: Set RLS759, 60163). Wohl denk' ich oft; Alles endet, was entstehet (78: DB2045. LP: Set RLS759).

### 1934

**Apr. 9, 22.** EMI Studio 1. London Philharmonic/Beecham. DELIUS: Paris—Song of a great city (78: SDX1–3, Set M305. LP: Set SHB32).

**May 23, 25.** EMI Studio 3. Kipnis (bass), Wolff (piano). WOLF: Geselle, woll'n wir uns in Kutten hüllen?; Heb' auf dein blondes Haupt; Nun lass uns Frieden schliessen; Wir haben beide lange Zeit geschwiegen. (78: DB2373. LP: Set RLS759, 60163). Sterb' ich, so hüllt in Blumen meine Glieder (78: DB2374. LP: Set RLS759, 60163). Wie glänzt der helle Mond (78: DB2707. LP: Set RLS759, 60163).

**June 24.** EMI Studio 1. London Philharmonic/Beecham. BIZET: La jolie fille de Perth—suite (78: LX317–8, Set X28. LP: SHB55).

**Sept. 19, 21.** Beethovensaal? Berlin. Hüsch (baritone), Müller (piano). WOLF: Dass doch gemalt all' deine Reize wären; Und willst du deinen Liebsten sterben sehen?; Wenn du mich mit den Augen streifst; Heut' Nacht erhob ich mich; Ein Ständchen Euch zu bringen (78: DB2372. LP: Set RLS759).

**Sept. 21.** Beethovensaal? Berlin. Rethberg (soprano), Bos (piano). WOLF: Wohl kenn' ich Euren Stand; Man sagt mir; Wenn du, mein Liebster (78: DB2370. LP: Set RLS759). Wie lange schon war immer mein Verlangen; Du sagst mir; Ich liess mir sagen; Was soll der Zorn; Ich esse nun mein Brot; Wie soll ich fröhlich sein (78: DB2369. LP: Set RLS759). Mühvoll komm' ich und beladen (78: DB2703. LP: Set RLS759).

**Sept. 22.** Beethovensaal? Berlin. Janssen (baritone), Bos (piano). WOLF: Gebet; Auf ein altes Bild; An die Geliebte (78: DB2705. LP: Set RLS759).

**Oct. 3–5.** Live recordings taken at the Leeds Festival. Leeds Festival Chorus, London Philharmonic/Beecham. HANDEL: Israel in Egypt—But as for His people; Moses and the Children of Israel (78: LX378, 68412D). Israel in Egypt—The Lord is a man of war (78: LB20, 17044D). SIBELIUS: The Tempest—Incidental music, Op. 109. Caliban's Song; Canon; Oak Tree; Humoresque (78: 68409D). MOZART: Mass in C minor, K427—Kyrie (Labbette, soprano) (78: LB19, 17050D). Mass in C minor, K427—Qui tollis (78: LX370, Set X54). BORODIN: Prince Igor—Polovtsian Dances (78: LX369–70, Set X54. LP: Set SHB100).

**Oct. 8.** EMI Studio 1. Szigeti (violin), London Philharmonic/Beecham. MOZART: Violin Concerto No. 4 in D, K218 (78: LX386–8, Set M224. LP: ML4533, Set M6X31513).

**Oct. 11.** Beethovensaal? Berlin. Hüsch (baritone), Müller (piano). WOLF: Gesegnet sei, durch den die Welt entstund; Ihr seid die Allerschönste; Hoffätig seid Ihr, schönes Kind (78: DB2371. LP: Set RLS759).

**Oct. 20.** EMI Studio 1. London Philharmonic/Beecham. ROSSINI: Guillaume Tell—overture (78: LX339–40, Set X60. LP: SH313). La gazza laddra—overture (78: LX353, 68301D. LP: SH313).

**Nov. 2.** Electrola Studios, Berlin. Kipnis (bass), Bos (piano). WOLF: Wie viele Zeit verlor' ich; Was für ein Lied (78: DB2374. LP: Set RLS759, 60163).

**Nov. 12.** Electrola Studios, Berlin. Hüsch (baritone), Müller (piano). SCHUBERT: Der Wanderer, D493; Der Musensohn, D764 (78: EG3201. LP: Set SHB65). BRAHMS: Wie bist du, meine Königin, Op. 32, No. 9; Feldeinsamkeit, Op. 86, No. 2 (78: EG3308, EG6779).

**Nov. 14.** EMI Studio 1. London Philharmonic/Beecham. DELIUS: Eventyr. (78: SDX4–5, Set M305. LP: Set SHB32). HANDEL (arr. BEECHAM): The Gods go a-begging—Musette; The Origin of Design—Minuet (78: LX340, Set X60).

**Dec. 4, 11.** EMI Studio 1. London Philharmonic/Beecham. DELIUS:

Koanga—Closing Scene (London Select Choir) (78: SDX6, Set M305. LP: Set SHB32. EP: SEL1700).

**Dec. 11.** DELIUS: Hassan—Intermezzo and Serenade (78: SDX7, Set M305. LP: Set SHB32).

**Dec. 13–14.** Electrola Studios, Berlin. Ginster (soprano), Raucheisen (piano). WOLF: Mein Liebster singt am Haus; O wär dein Haus; Gesegnet sei das Grün (78: DB2370. LP: Set RLS759). Mir ward gesagt; Mein Liebster ist so klein; Ich hab' in Penna (78: DB2371. LP: Set RLS759). Ein Stündlein wohl vor Tag; Elfenlied (78: DB2707. LP: Set RLS759).

### 1935

**Jan. 23.** EMI Studio 3. Ginster (soprano), Moore (piano). WOLF: Trau nicht der Liebe; Sie blasen zum Abmarsch (78: DB2704. LP: Set RLS759).

**Jan. 31, Feb. 2 and 5.** EMI Studio 3 (also March 22 in Berlin). Hüsch (baritone), Müller (piano). SCHUBERT: Die schöne Müllerin, D795 (78: DB2429–36. LP: SH295).

**Feb. 5.** EMI Studio 3. Hüsch (baritone), Müller (piano). WOLF: Auf dem grünen Balkon; Treibe nur mit Lieben Spott (78: DB2703. LP: Set RLS759).

**Feb. 8.** EMI Studio 3. (also March 5, 7–8, 11 in Electrola Studios, Berlin). Hüsch (baritone), M. Kilpinen (piano). KILPINEN: Lieder um der Tod, Op. 62, Nos. 1–6; Lieder der Liebe, Op. 61, Nos. 1, 2, 4, 5; Spielmannslieder, Op. 77, Nos. 4, 5, 8; Elegie an die Nachtigall, Op. 21, No. 1; Vergissmeinnichte, Op. 39, No. 3; Venezianisches Intermezzo, Op. 79, No. 4; Marienkirche zu Danzig im Gerüst, Op. 79, No. 7; Mondschein; Der Skiläufer (78: DB2594–8).

**Mar. 22, Apr. 3, 17.** EMI Studio 1. London Philharmonic/Beecham. ROSSINI (arr. RESPIGHI): Rossiniana (78: LX391–2, Set X56. LP: SH313).

**Apr. 3, 17 and July 16.** DVORAK: Slavonic Rhapsody, Op. 45, No. 3. (78: LX402–3, Set X55).

**Apr. 17.** DVORAK: Legend, Op. 59, No. 3 (78: LX403, Set X55, 12902D).

**June 7.** EMI Studio 3. Kipnis (bass), Moore (piano). WOLF: Der Musikant; Der Soldat I; Der Schreckenberger; Coptisches Lied I. (78: DB2708. LP: Set RLS759, 60163).

**July 16.** EMI Studio 1. London Philharmonic/Beecham. WAGNER: Lohengrin—Act 3 Prelude (78: LX482, Set X63, 72635D).

**July 16 and Feb. 28, 1936.** WAGNER: A Faust Overture (78: LX481–2, Set X63. LP: HLM7154).

**Aug. 23.** PROKOFIEV: Violin Concerto No. 1 in D, Op. 19 (Szigeti, violin). (78: LX433–5, Set M244. LP: HLM7016, ML4533, Set M6X31513).

**Oct. 4.** DELIUS: Summer Night on the River (78: LB44, 17087D. LP: Set SHB32).

**Oct. 4 and February 28, 1936.** HAYDN: Symphony No. 99 in E flat (78: LX505–7, Set M264. LP: Set RLS734).

**Nov. 4.** Electrola Studios, Berlin. Janssen (baritone), Raucheisen (piano). WOLF: Verborgenheit; Denk' es, o Seele!; Bei einer Trauung (78: DB2706. LP: Set RLS759). Biterolf; Seufzer (78: DB2704. LP: Set RLS759).

# A Selected Discography

**Nov. 25 and Dec. 9.** EMI Studio 1. Perli (soprano), Andreva (soprano), Nash (tenor), Brownlee (baritone), Easton (bass), London Philharmonic/ Beecham. PUCCINI: La bohème—Act 4 (78: LX523–6, Set M274. LP: HQM1234).

**Nov. 26 and Dec. 14.** EMI Studio 1. Heifetz (violin), London Philharmonic/Beecham. SIBELIUS: Violin Concerto in D, Op. 47 (78: DB2791–4, Set M309. LP: SH207, LCT1113, 60221. SP: Set WCT1113).

**Dec. 11, Jan. 3, 1936.** EMI Studio 3. Petri (piano). BEETHOVEN: Piano Sonata No. 32 in C minor, Op. 111 (78: LX491–3, Set M263).

**Dec. 12.** BACH (arr. PETRI): Minuets in G, BWV841–3 (78: LX508, 69153D).

**Dec. 12; Jan. 3, 1936.** LISZT: Mazeppa, G52 No. 4 (78: LX483).

**Dec. 14.** EMI Studio 1. London Philharmonic/Beecham. SIBELIUS: Scènes historiques—No. 1, Festivo, Op. 25 (78: LX501, 68590D).

**Dec. 20.** EMI Studio 3. Petri (piano). SCHUBERT (arr. LISZT): Soirées de Vienne, G212 (78: LX469, 68504D).

**Dec. 20; Jan. 2, 1936.** BIZET (arr. BUSONI): Carmen Fantasia (78: LX462).

## 1936

**Jan. 2.** EMI Studio 3. Petri (piano). SCHUBERT (arr. TAUSIG): Andantino varié in B minor (78: LX764, 69249D).

**Jan. 3.** GLUCK (arr. SGAMBATI): Orpheus ed Euridice—Mélodie (78: LX508, 69153).

**Jan. 29–30.** EMI Studio 3. Hüsch (baritone), Müller (piano). SCHUMANN: Dichterliebe, Op. 48 (78: DB2940–2).

**Feb. 26.** EMI Studio 1. London Philharmonic/ Beecham. BIZET: L'arlésienne—Suite No. 1 (78: LX541–2, Set X69. LP: Set SHB55).

**Feb. 28.** BIZET: L'arlésienne—Suite No. 2, Farandole (78: LX614, 68882D).

**Mar. 14 and 24.** BRAHMS: Symphony No. 2 in D, Op. 73 (78: LX515–9, Set M265. LP: Set RLS733).

**Apr. 3.** PUCCINI: La bohème—Donde lieta uscì (Perli, soprano) (78: LX526, Set M274, 72638D. LP: HQM1234).

**Apr. 3, Nov. 2.** DELIUS: Sea Drift (Brownlee, baritone, London Select Choir) (78: SDX8–11, Set M290, LP: Set SHB32).

**June 9.** EMI Studio 3. Petri (piano). BEETHOVEN: Piano Sonata No. 27 in E minor, Op. 90 (78: LX544–5, Set X71).

**June 10.** BEETHOVEN: Piano Sonata No. 24 in F sharp minor, Op. 78 (78: LX576, 68939D. LP: HQM1112).

**June 11.** GOUNOD (arr. LISZT): Waltz from Faust, G142 (78: LX520, 69031D. LP: HLM7008).

**June 15.** EMI Studio 3. Kipnis (bass), Moore (piano). BRAHMS: Vier ernste Gesänge, Op. 121 (78: DB2995–8, Set M522. LP: HQM1101, HLM7040). Erinnerung, Op. 63 No. 2 (78: DB2994, Set M522. LP: HQM1198, 60124).

**June 19.** EMI Studio 1. London Philharmonic/Beecham. WAGNER: Die Meistersinger von Nürnberg—Act 1 Prelude (78: LX557, 68854D). BIZET: L'arlésienne—Suite No. 2, Minuet (78: LX614, 68882D). OFFENBACH:

Les contes d'Hoffmann—Barcarolle; Entr'acte; Duet; Act 1 Intermezzo (78: LX530, 68692D. LP: Set SHB55).

**June 26, July 2.** EMI Studio 3. Kipnis (bass), Moore (piano). BRAHMS: Von ewiger Liebe, Op. 43, No. 1 (78: DB2994, Set M522. LP: HQM1198, 60124). Verrat, Op. 105, No. 5; An die Nachtigall, Op. 46, No. 6 (78: DB2999, Set M522. LP: HQM1198, 60124). Ein Sonnette, Op. 14, No. 4; Sonntag, Op. 47, No. 3 (78: DB2996, Set M522. LP: HQM1198, 60124). O wüsst' ich doch den Weg zurück, Op. 63, No. 8 (78: DB2997, Set M522. LP: HQM1198, 60124). Die Mainacht, Op. 43, No. 2 (78: DB2995, Set M522). Ständchen, Op. 106, No. 1; Vergebliches Ständchen, Op. 84, No. 4 (78: DB2998, Set M522. LP: HQM1198, 60124).

**Sept. 28.** EMI Studio 1. London Philharmonic/Beecham. DELIUS: Over the hills and far away (78: SDX12–13, Set M290. LP: Set SHB32). Fennimore and Gerda—Intermezzo. (78: SDX11, Set M290. LP: Set SHB32).

**Oct. 2.** DELIUS: In a Summer Garden (78: SDX13–14, Set M290. LP: Set SHB32).

**Oct. 3, Nov. 27, Dec. 18.** BEETHOVEN: Symphony No. 2 in D, Op. 36 (78: LX586–9, Set M302. LP: Set RLS734).

**Oct. 6.** MENDELSSOHN: A Midsummer Night's Dream, Op. 61—Wedding March; Nocturne (78: LX574, 68888D). NICOLAI: Die lustigen Weiber von Windsor—overture (78: LX596, Set M552, 68938D).

**Nov. 10.** Electrola Studios, Berlin. Janssen (baritone), Raucheisen (piano). SCHUBERT: Ständchen, D957; SCHUMANN: Die beiden Grenadiere, Op. 49, No. 1 (78: DB3024, 15379).

**Nov. 12.** EMI Studio 3. Fuchs (soprano), Moore (piano). WOLF: Storchenbotschaft (78: DB3324. LP: HQM1072, Set RLS759). Mignon I (78: DB3322. LP: Set RLS759).

**Nov. 27.** EMI Studio 1. London Philharmonic/Beecham. BERLIOZ: Overture, le carnaval romain, Op. 9 (78: LX570, 68921D, Set M552. LP: Set SHB100). WEBER: Der Freischütz—overture. (78: LX601, 68986D).

**Dec. 18.** HAYDN: Symphony No. 93 in D (78: LX721–3, Set M336. LP: Set RLS734).

*1937*

**Feb. 4; Sept. 2.** MOZART: Symphony No. 40 in G minor, K550 (78: LX656–8, Set M316. LP: Set SHB20, ML4674, THS65022–6).

**Feb. 15.** EMI Studio 3. Petri (piano). BEETHOVEN: Piano Sonata No. 14 in C sharp minor, Op. 27, No. 2 (78: LX602–3, Set X77).

**Feb. 16.** BUSONI: Fantasia after J. S. Bach in memory of my father (78: LX640, 69127D. LP: HQM1112). Indianisches Tagebuch (78: LX617, 69010D. LP: HQM1112). LISZT: Concert Study No. 3 in D flat—Un sospiro (78: LX603, Set X77. LP: HQM1112). 12 études d'exécution transcendente—No. 9, Ricordanza, G139 (78: LX846, 72792D. LP: HQM1112, 3–123).

**Feb. 18.** VERDI (arr. LISZT): Rigoletto—Concert Paraphrase, G219 (78: LB39, 17106D).

**Mar. 4.** BRAHMS: Variations on a theme of Paganini, Op. 35 (78: LX628–9, Set X80).

# A Selected Discography

**Mar. 22.** EMI Studio 1. London Philharmonic/Beecham. BRAHMS: Tragic Overture, Op. 81 (78: LX638–9, Set X85). MOZART: Le nozze di Figaro—overture (78: LX639, Set X85, 69058D, 71606D. LP: ALP1870, Set SHB20, Set 3621, THS65022–6).

**Apr. 20.** Electrola Studios, Berlin. Fuchs (soprano), Raucheisen (piano). WOLF: Neue Liebe (78: DB3324. LP: Set RLS759). Mignon III (78: DB3322. LP: Set RLS759).

**May 20.** EMI Studio 3. Janssen (baritone), Moore (piano). WOLF: Der einst, der einst; Alle gingen, Herz, zur Ruh'; Tief im Herzen trag' ich Pein; Zur Ruh', zur Ruh' (78: DB3325. LP: Set RLS759). STRAUSS: Zueignung, Op. 10, No. 1 (78: DA1591).

**May 24.** EMI Studio 3. Weber (bass), Moore (piano). WOLF: Ritter Kurts Braufahrt; Der Sänger; Die Geister am Mummelsee (LP only: Set RLS759).

**June 10.** EMI Studio 3. Janssen (baritone), Moore (piano). SCHUMANN: Widmung, Op. 25, No. 1; Die Lotosblume, Op. 27, No. 7 (78: DA1569, 1931). STRAUSS: Traum durch die Dämmerung, Op. 29, No. 1 (78: DA1581, 1930). Allerseelen, Op. 10, No. 8 (78: DA1591).

**June 15.** WOLF: Komm', o Tod (78: DB3326. LP: Set RLS759). Wo wird einst (LP only: Set RLS759). STRAUSS: Die Nacht, Op. 10, No. 3 (78: DA1581, 1930). BRAHMS: Nicht mehr zu dir zu gehen, Op. 32, No. 2; Minnelied III, Op. 71, No. 5; Wie bist du, meine Königin, Op. 32, No. 9 (78: DB3941).

**Aug. 27.** Electrola Studios, Berlin. Hüsch (baritone), Moore (piano). SCHUBERT: Schwanengesang, D957—Nos. 7, 10, 12, 14 (LP only: Set SHB65).

**Aug. 29.** Electrola Studios, Berlin. Roswaenge (tenor), Moore (piano). WOLF: Der Feuerreiter; Kein Meister fällt von Himmel (78: DB3321. LP: Set RLS759).

**Aug. 29.** Electrola Studios, Berlin. Fuchs (soprano), Moore (piano). WOLF: Geh', Geliebter, geh' jetzt (78: DB6813. LP: Set RLS759).

**Aug. 31.** Electrola Studios, Berlin. Erb (tenor), Moore (piano). WOLF: An den Schlaf; Lebewohl; Ach, im Maien war's; Herz, verzage nicht geschwind (78: DB3323. LP: Set RLS759). Jägerlied; Der Gärtner; Auftrag; Der Scholar; Der verzweifelte Liebhaber; Unfall (78: DB6812. LP: Set RLS759). Nimmersatte Liebe (78: DB6813. LP: Set RLS759).

**Oct. 12.** EMI Studio 1. London Philharmonic/Beecham. SIBELIUS: Four Legends, Op. 22—The Return of Lemminkainen (78: DB3355–6, Set M446. LP: SH133, THS65059).

**Oct. 12, Nov. 1.** SCHUBERT: Symphony No. 8 in B minor, D759 (78: LX666–8, Set M330. LP: Set RLS733).

**Oct. 13.** HANDEL (arr. BEECHAM): The Gods go a-begging—Minuet; Hornpipe (78: LX756, Set M360, 72637D).

**Oct. 13; Nov. 14, 1938.** WAGNER: Tannhäuser—overture (78: LX768–9, Set X123).

**Oct. 14.** Electrola Studio A, Berlin. Lemnitz (soprano), Raucheisen (piano). WOLF: In der Frühe; St Nepomuks Vorabend; Wiegenlied im Winter (LP only: Set SHB47, Set RLS759). Schlafendes Jesuskind (LP only: Set SHB47). Wiegenlied im Sommer (78: DB3326. LP: Set SHB47).

**Nov. 1.** EMI Studio 1. London Philharmonic/Beecham. WAGNER: Der fliegende Holländer—overture (78: LX732–3, Set X107).

**Nov. 1, Dec. 10.** SIBELIUS: The Tempest, Op. 109—Incidental music. (78: DB3356–7, Set M446).

**Nov. 5.** Electrola Studios, Berlin. Fuchs (soprano), Raucheisen (piano). SCHUBERT: Gretchen am Spinnrade, D118; Erlkönig, D328. (78: DB3361).

**Nov. 8–10, 12–13; Feb. 24, Mar. 2, 1938.** Beethovensaal, Berlin. Lemnitz (soprano), Beilke (soprano), Berger (soprano), Roswaenge (tenor), Hüsch (baritone), Strienz (bass), etc. Berlin Philharmonic/Beecham. MOZART: Die Zauberflöte (78: DB3465–83, Sets M541–2. LP: ALP1273–5, SH158–60, Set LCT6101, TV4111–3, THS65078–80. SP: Set WCT56).

**Nov. 30.** EMI Studio 1. London Philharmonic/Beecham. MOZART: Symphony No. 29 in A, K201 (78: LX687–9, Set M333. LP: Set SHB20, THS65022–6).

**Dec. 10.** SIBELIUS: Symphony No. 4 in A minor, Op. 63 (78: DB3351–5, Set M446. LP: SH133, THS65059).

**Dec. 16; Feb. 1, 1938.** BERLIOZ: La damnation de Faust, Op. 24—Menuet des follets; Danse des sylphes; Marche hongroise (78: LX702–3, Set X94. LP: Set SHB55).

**Dec. 20.** BERNERS: The Triumph of Neptune—suite (Alva, baritone). (78: LX697–8, Set X92).

### 1938

**Jan. 6–7, 31.** DELIUS: Appalachia (BBC Chorus) (78: SDX15–19, Set M355. LP: Set SHB32).

**Feb. 1.** SIBELIUS: Finlandia, Op. 26 (78: LX704, 69180D).

**Feb. 1, Oct. 3.** MENDELSSOHN: Overture, The Hebrides, Op. 26 (78: LX747, 69400D, Set M552).

**Feb. 11.** DELIUS: A Mass of Life—Prelude to Part 2, No. 3 (LP only: SHB32). Koanga—La Calinda (78: SDX21, Set M355. LP: Set SHB32. EP: SEL1700). Whither; The Violet; I Brasil: Klein Venevil (Labbette, soprano) (LP only: Set SHB32).

**Mar. 22:** EMI Studio 3. Janssen (baritone), Moore (piano). SCHUBERT: Die Winterreise, D911—No. 20, Der Wegweiser; No. 21, Das Wirtshaus (78: DB3496).

**June 1.** EMI Studio 3. Petri (piano). SCHUBERT (arr. LISZT): Der Lindenbaum, G346 No. 7 (78: LX753, 72632D, Set X136).

**June 1, Sept. 29.** BUSONI: Sonatina (Ad usum infantis) (78: LX806, 69736D).

**June 3.** BRAHMS: Variations and Fugue on a theme of Handel, Op. 24 (78: LX734–6, Set M345).

**June 28.** EMI Studio 1. London Philharmonic/Beecham. DELIUS: Hassan—Closing Scene (van der Gucht, tenor, Royal Opera House Chorus) (78: SDX20, Set M355. LP: Set SHB32. EP: SEL1700).

**July 18.** WAGNER: Tannhäuser—Entry of the Guests. (78: LX733, Set X107, 72635D). DELIUS: Irmelin—Prelude (78: SDX21, Set M355. LP: Set SHB32).

## A Selected Discography

**July 18, Oct. 3.** WEBER: Oberon—overture (78: LX746, 69410D. LP: Set SHB100).

**Sept. 2.** EMI Studio 1. Petri (piano), London Philharmonic/Heward. LISZT: Piano Concerto No. 2 in A, G45 (78: LX737–9, Set M362). LISZT: Fantasia on themes from Beethoven's Ruins of Athens, G42 (78: LX752–3, Set X136).

**Sept. 27.** EMI Studio 3. Petri (piano). SCHUBERT (arr. LISZT): Gretchen am Spinnrade, G343, No. 8. (78: LX739, 69554D, 72632D). BUSONI: Albumblatt No. 3; Elegy No. 2—All' Italia (78: LX792, 69761D. LP: HQM1112).

**Oct. 3.** EMI Studio 1. London Philharmonic/Beecham. BORODIN: Prince Igor—Polovtsi March (78: LX769, Set X123, 72638D).

**Oct. 4.** MOZART: Symphony No. 31 in D, K297 (78: LX754–6, Set M360. LP: Set SHB20, THS65022–6).

**Nov. 14.** SIBELIUS: In Memoriam—Funeral March (78: DB3890, Set M658. LP: SH133, THS65059).

**Nov. 14** (July 7, 1939, Kingsway Hall). SIBELIUS: En Saga (78: DB3888–9, Set M658. LP: SH207).

**Nov. 15.** SIBELIUS: Kuolema, Op. 44—Valse triste. (78: DB3893, Set M658). The Tempest, Op. 109—Prelude (78: DB3894, Set M658). The Bard, Op. 64 (78: DB3891, Set M658. LP: SH133, THS65059).

**Nov. 16–17.** EMI Studio 3. Janssen (baritone), Moore (piano). WOLF: Der Musikant; Der Freund. (78: DA1672). Sonne der Schlummerlosen; Fussreise; Lied eines Verliebten; Keine gleicht von allen Schönen; Schlafendes Jesuskind. (LP only: Set RLS759). SCHUBERT: Schwanengesang, D957—No. 4, Ständchen; No. 13, Der Doppelgänger. (78: DB5797).

**Nov. 25.** EMI Studio 1. (July 4, 1939, Kingsway Hall). London Philharmonic/Beecham. MOZART: Symphony No. 35 in D, K385 (78: LX851–3, Set M399. LP: Set SHB20, ML4770, THS65033–5, THS65022–6).

**Dec. 15; Jan. 11, 1939.** Kingsway Hall. London Philharmonic/Beecham. SCHUBERT: Symphony No. 5 in B flat, D485 (78: LX785–8, Set M366. LP: Set RLS733, ML4771).

**Dec. 21; Jan. 11, Feb. 13, 1939.** MOZART: Symphony No. 36 in C, K425 (78: LX797–800, Set M387. LP: Set SHB20, ML4770, THS65022–6).

### 1939

**Jan. 18, Feb. 13, July 4.** HAYDN: Symphony No. 104 in D (78: LX856–8, Set M409. LP: ML4771).

**Feb. 13.** DEBUSSY: Prélude a l'après-midi d'un faune (78: LX805, 69600D. LP: Set SHB55).

**Apr. 12.** EMI Studio 1. London Philharmonic/Beecham. BIZET: Carmen—Suite (78: LX823–4, Set X144. LP: Set SHB55).

**Apr. 12** (July 7, Kingsway Hall). GRIEG: Peer Gynt, Op. 46—Suite No. 1 (78: LX838–9, Set X180).

**June 23** (July 7, Kingsway Hall). SIBELIUS: Pelleas and Melisande—Incidental Music, Op. 46 (78: DB3892–3, Set M658).

**Nov. 27.** SUPPE: Morning, Noon and Night in Vienna—overture (78: LX865, 71439D).

Nov. 27; Jan. 4, 1940. MOZART: Don Giovanni—overture (78: LX893, Set M552. LP: Set SHB20, THS65022–6).

Nov. 28. MENDELSSOHN: Overture, Ruy Blas, Op. 95 (78: LX879, 70352D). J. Strauss II: Waltz, Frühlingsstimmen, Op. 410 (78: LX867, 70338D).

Nov. 30. ROSSINI: Semiramide—overture (78: LX884–5, Set X215. LP: SH313).

Nov. 30, Dec. 19. CHABRIER: Rapsodie, España (78: LX880, 71250D. LP: Set SHB55).

Nov. 30. EMI Studio 3. McCormack (tenor), Moore (piano). O'CONNOR: The Old House (78: DA1715. LP: COLH124. SP: 7P238). THAYER: A Child's Prayer (78: DA1715. SP: 7P238). TRAD. (arr. HUGHES): The Star of the County Down (78: DA1718. LP: COLH124. EP: 7EB6029. SP: 7P211). MURRAY: I'll walk beside you (78: DA1718. LP: BLP1084. SP: 7P211).

Dec. 7, 19. EMI Studio 1. London Philharmonic/Beecham. TCHAIKOVSKY: Francesca da Rimini, Op. 32 (78: LX887–9, Set M447).

Dec. 18; Jan. 4, 1940. TCHAIKOVSKY: Symphony No. 5 in E minor, Op. 64 (78: LX869–73, Set M470. LP: Set RLS733).

### 1940

January 3–4. FRANCK: Symphony in D minor (78: LX904–8, Set M479. LP: Set RLS733).

Jan. 4. GRETRY: Zémir et Azor—Air de Ballet (78: LX885, Set X215, 72637D. LP: Set SHB55).

Jan. 12, Mar. 26. MOZART: Piano Concerto No. 12 in A, K414 (Kentner, piano) (78: LX894–6, Set M544. LP: Set SHB20).

Mar. 19, Apr. 5. MOZART: Symphony No. 39 in E flat, K543 (78: LX927–9, Set M456. LP: Set SHB20, ML4674, THS65022–6).

Mar. 19, 21. MOZART: Symphony No. 38 in D, K504 (78: LX911–3, Set M509. LP: Set SHB20, THS65022–6).

Mar. 26, Apr. 5. MOZART: Symphony No. 34 in C, K338 (78: LX920–2, Set M548. LP: Set SHB20, ML4781, THS65022–6).

Apr. 2. HANDEL (arr. BEECHAM): Suite, The Faithful Shepherd (78: LX915–7, Set M458).

Apr. 12. EMI Studio 1A. McCormack (tenor), Orchestra/Goehr. LEHAR (arr. STOTHART): Balalaika—The magic of your love (78: DA1730). HARLINE: Pinocchio—When you wish upon a star; Little Wooden-Head (78: DA1729).

May 2. CHOPIN (arr. MILLER): So deep is the night (78: DA1730. LP: MFP1090). NEVIN: Mighty lak' a rose (78: DA1740. LP: MFP1090). TREVELSA: My Treasure (78: DA1740).

June 19. EMI Studio 3. McCormack (tenor), Moore (piano). MARTINI: Plaisir d'amour (78: DA1829. LP: MFP1090). PERGOLESI (attrib.): Tre giorni son che Nina (LP only: COLH123, H110). SOMERSET: Echo (78: DA1741). RASBACH: Trees (78: DA1741. LP: MFP1090).

July 11. WOODFORD-FINDEN: Four Indian Love Lyrics—Nos. 3 and 4 (78: DA1746, 2169). M. ARNE: The lass with the delicate air (EP: 7ER5054). E. PURCELL-COCKRAM: Passing by (LP: COLH124. EP: 7ER5054).

**Aug. 9.** TRAD. (arr. SCHNEIDER): Oft in the stilly night (78: IR1043. LP: COLH124). MOORE (arr. SCHNEIDER): The Meeting of the Waters (78: DA1752, 10–0041. LP: COLH124). BOULTON (arr. SOMERVELL): The Gentle Maiden (78: IR1043. LP: COLH124). TRAD. (arr. HUGHES): The Bard of Armagh (78: DA1752. LP: COLH124).

**Oct. 25.** GRUBER (arr. WOODGATE): Silent night, holy night; TCHAIKOVSKY: Legend–Christ in His garden, Op. 54, No. 5 (78: DA1755). TRAD.: All thro' the night; GOSS: See amid the winter snow (78: DA1756). GERALD CARNE: Faith (78: DA1803).

**Dec. 17.** GOUNOD: There is a green hill far away (78: DA1773). MOZART (arr. MCCORMACK): Oh! What bitter grief is mine (78: DA1828). MALASHKIN: O could I but express in song (78: DA1829).

**Dec. 19.** SOMERVELL: Since first I saw your face (78: IR1060). TRAD. (arr. MOORE): Ye banks and braes (78: DA1762. LP: COLH124). BOULTON (arr. LAWSON): Maiden of Morven (78: DA1762). EASTHOPE MARTIN: The light of the sunset glow (78: DA1770).

### 1941

**Jan. 28.** EMI Studio 3. McCormack (tenor), Moore (piano). RAY: God keep you in my prayer (78: DA1770). TRAD.: At the mid hour of night (78: IR1044). TRAD.: Down by the Sally Gardens (78: DA1788). COLERIDGE-TAYLOR: She rested by the broken brook (78: DA1778. LP: HQM1176).

**Mar. 6.** BACH: Cantata No. 4—Jesus Christ the Son of God (78: DA1773). BACH: Cantata No. 147—Jesu, joy of man's desiring (78: DA1786). SOMERVELL: The street sounds to the soldiers' tread; White in the moon the long road lies (78: DA1834). VAUGHAN WILLIAMS: Silent Noon (78: DA1776. LP: COLH126). SOMERVELL: Loveliest of trees (78: DA1776).

**May 29.** HAYDN WOOD: The village that nobody knows (EP: 7ER5054). HANDEL (attrib.): Cantata con stromenti—Praise ye the Lord (78: DA1786. LP: HQM1176).

**June 25.** VAUGHAN WILLIAMS: Linden Lea; BAX: The White Peace (78: DA1791. LP: HQM1176). TRAD. (arr. HUGHES): She moved thro' the fair (78: DA1813. LP: COLH124).

**Aug. 26.** TRAD. (arr. KEEL): The Green Bushes (LP: COLH124. EP: 7ER5054). TRAD. (arr. MOLLOY): Bantry Bay (78: DA1813). TRAD. (arr. ROBERTON): Maureen (EP: 7ER5054).

**Sept. 17.** MOORE: Our finest hour (78: DA1803).

**Oct. 6.** PENN: Smilin' thro'; MAUD VALERIE WHITE: The Devout Lover (78: DA1805). MURRAY: Will you go with me? HAYDN WOOD: A rose still blooms in Picardy (78: DA1806).

**Nov. 6.** PARRY: Jerusalem (78: DA1817).

**Dec. 3.** TRAD. (arr. HAYNES): Off to Philadelphia (78: IR1056. LP: COLH124). RUBINSTEIN: Come back my love; GERALD CARNE: Here in the quiet hills (78: DA1809).

**Dec. 23.** BERLIN: God bless America; TRAD. (arr. JOHNSON): The Battle Hymn of the Republic (78: DA1808).

1942

**May 26.** CASE: By the lakes of Killarney (78: IR1044). MOORE: Love thee, dearest, love thee (78: IR1056. LP: COLH124). WOLFE: Children's Prayer in Wartime (78: DA1817).

**Aug. 10.** L. SMITH: One love forever; D. GREGORY MASON: Say a little prayer (78: DA1820).

**Sept. 10.** MOZART: Ave verum corpus, K618 (78: DA1828). An Chloë, K524 (LP: COLH123).

1944

**Aug. 3–4, 25.** Bedford Grammar School. BBC Symphony/Boult. ELGAR: Symphony No. 2 in E flat, Op. 63 (78: DB6190–5).

1945

**Jan. 2–5.** Corn Exchange, Bedford. BBC Symphony/Boult. HOLST: The Planets, Op. 32/H125 (78: DB6227–33. LP: LHMV1002. SP: Set WHMV1002).

**Aug. 29.** EMI Studio 3. Schumann (soprano), Moore (piano). WOLF: In der Frühe; In dem Schatten meiner Locken; Mausfallen-Sprüchlein (78: DA1862. LP: COLH102, H102). HAYDN: She never told her love (78: DA1850).

**Aug. 30.** MOZART: Abendempfindung, K523 (LP: COLH154). Das Veilchen, K476 (78: DA1854. LP: COLH154). HAYDN: The Sailor's Song (78: DA1850. LP: HQM1072) SCHUBERT: Dass sie hier gewesen!, D775 (78: DA1854. LP: COLH131, HQM1240).

**Nov. 21.** EMI Studio 1. Neveu (violin), Philharmonia/Süsskind. SIBELIUS: Violin Concerto in D minor, Op. 47 (78: DB6244–7. LP: ALP1479, Set RLS739, 35129).

**Nov. 26.** EMI Studio 1A. Schumann (soprano), Moore (piano). SCHUBERT: Rosamunde, D797—Romanze (78: DA1852. LP: COLH131). Die Forelle, D550 (78: DA1852. SP: 7P290). WOLF: Auch kleine Dinge (78: DA1860. LP: COLH102, H102).

**Nov. 27.** WOLF: Nimmersatte Liebe (LP: COLH102, H102).

1946

**Mar. 26, Aug. 13.** EMI Studio 3. G. Neveu (violin), J. Neveu (piano). RAVEL: Tzigane (78: DB6907–8. LP: ALP1520, Set RLS739. EP: 7ER5099).

**June 4.** EMI Studio 3. Schnabel (piano). MOZART: Rondo in A minor, K511 (78: DB6298. LP: COLH305, HQM1142, 60115).

**June 5; June 5, 1947.** MOZART: Sonata No. 12 in F, K 332 (LP only: COLH305).

**June 5, 7.** EMI Studio 1. Schnabel (piano), Philharmonia/Dobrowen. BEETHOVEN: Piano Concerto No. 4 in G major, Op. 58 (78: DB6303–6. LP: COLH4, LCT1131, Set GR4006).

**June 6.** BEETHOVEN: Piano Concerto No. 2 in B flat, Op. 19 (78: DB6323–6. LP: COLH2, Set 6043, Set GR4006).

**June 18.** EMI Studio 1. Schumann (soprano), Moore (piano). SCHUBERT: Das Mädchen, D652 (78: DA1864. LP: COLH131). An mein

## A Selected Discography

Klavier, D342 (78: DA1864. LP: COLH131, HQM1240). WOLF: Und willst du deinen Liebsten sterben sehen? (78: DA1860. LP: COLH102, H102).

**Aug. 12.** EMI Studio 3. G. Neveu (violin), J. Neveu (piano). RAVEL: Pièce en forme de habañera (78: DA1871. LP: Set RLS739. EP: 7ER5099). SCARLATESCU: Bagatelle (78: DA1871. LP: Set RLS739). FALLA: La vida breve—Danse espagnole (78: DA1865. LP: Set RLS739).

**Aug. 13.** CHOPIN (arr. RODIONOV): Nocturne No. 20 in C sharp minor, Op. posth. (78: DB6908. LP: Set RLS739). DINICU (arr. HEIFETZ): Hora staccato (78: DA1865. LP: Set RLS739).

**Aug. 14.** SUK: Four Pieces, Op. 17 (78: DB6359–60. LP: ALP1479, Set RLS739).

**Aug. 16–18.** EMI Studio 1. Neveu (violin), Philharmonia/Dobrowen. BRAHMS: Violin Concerto in D, Op. 77 (78: DB6415–9. LP: COLH80, Set RLS739).

**Aug. 18.** CHAUSSON: Poème, Op. 25 (LP: ALP1520, Set RLS739).

**Sept. 13–15.** Musikvereinsaal, Vienna. Vienna Philharmonic/Karajan. BEETHOVEN: Symphony No. 8 in F (78: LX988–90. EP: Set EL51).

**Sept. 15–17, 19.** SCHUBERT: Symphony No. 9 in C, D944. (78: LX1138–43. LP: ML4631).

**Oct. 9.** EMI Studio 3. Schumann (soprano), Moore (piano). †SCHU-MANN: Frauenliebe und -leben, Op. 42. (78: DB9567–9. LP: SH157).

**Oct. 18–19.** Brahmssaal, Vienna. Vienna Philharmonic/Karajan. MOZART: Symphony No. 33 in B flat, K319 (78: LX1006–8, Set M778. LP: ML54370, ML4370).

**Oct. 21.** MOZART: Le nozze di Figaro—overture (78: LX1008, Set M778).

**Oct. 21–22.** MOZART: Serenade No. 13, K525 (78: LX1293–4. LP: ML54370, ML4370).

**Oct. 23.** Brahmssaal, Vienna. Schwarzkopf (soprano), Vienna Philharmonic/Karajan. MOZART: Die Entführung aus dem Serail—Martern aller Arten (LP only: Set RLS763).

**Oct. 26.** Brahmssaal, Vienna. Schwarzkopf (soprano), Hudez (piano). SCHUBERT: Seligkeit, D433; Die Forelle, D550 (78: LB77. LP: Set RLS763).

**Oct. 28–29.** Musikvereinsaal, Vienna. Vienna Philharmonic/Karajan. TCHAIKOVSKY: Overture, Romeo and Juliet (78: LX1033–5).

**Oct. 29–30.** J. STRAUSS II: Die Zigeunerbaron—overture (78: LX1009).

**Oct. 30.** J. STRAUSS II: Kaiserwalzer, Op. 437 (78: LX1021. LP: AL28). Künstlerleben, Op. 316 (78: LX1012. LP: AL28. EP: SEL1503). Waltz— An der schönen, blauen Donau, Op. 314 (78: LX1118. SP: SCD2144).

**Oct. 31.** Musikvereinsaal, Vienna. Schwarzkopf (soprano), Vienna Philharmonic/Krips. MOZART: Die Entführung aus dem Serail—Welcher Kummer (78: LX1249. LP: Set RLS763, ML4649).

**Nov. 1.** Brahmssaal, Vienna. Schwarzkopf (soprano), with ensemble. BACH: Cantata No. 208—Schafe können sicher weiden. (78: LX1051. LP: ML4792, 60013).

**Nov. 2.** Brahmssaal, Vienna. Schwarzkopf (soprano), Vienna Philharmonic/Krips. MOZART: Il re pastore—L'amerò sarò costante (Sedlak, violin) (78: LX1096. LP: Set RLS 763). HANDEL: L'allegro, il penseroso ed il moderato—First and chief on golden wing; Sweet Bird (78: LX1010).

**Nov. 6.** Brahmssaal, Vienna. Hotter (baritone), Nordberg (piano). SCHUBERT: Der Wanderer, D493; Schwanengesang, D957—No. 13, Der Doppelgänger. (78: LX1004. LP: HQM1030).

**Nov. 7.** SCHUMANN: Die beiden Grenadiere, Op. 49, No. 1; Wer machte dich so krank?, Op. 35, No. 11; Alte Laute, Op. 35, No. 12 (78: LX997).

### 1947

**Feb. 20.** EMI Studio 3. Lipatti (piano). SCARLATTI: Sonata in D minor, L413 (78: LB113. LP: 33CX1386, Set RLS749, ML2216). CHOPIN: Nocturne No. 8 in D flat, Op. 27, No. 2 (78: LB63. LP: HQM1248, Set RLS749, ML4732. EP: SEB3511, Set A1085).

**Feb. 21.** EMI Studio 3. E. Fischer (piano). BRAHMS: Ballade in G minor, Op. 118, No. 3; Rhapsody in G minor, Op. 79, No. 2 (78: DB6437). Intermezzo in B flat minor, Op. 117, No. 2; Intermezzo in E flat, (78: DB6478).

**Mar. 1, 4.** EMI Studio 3. Lipatti (piano). CHOPIN: Piano Sonata No. 3 in B minor, Op. 58 (78: LX994–6. LP: 33CX1337, HQM1163, Set RLS749, ML4721, 32160369).

**May 27–28.** EMI Studio 1. Schnabel (piano), Philharmonia/Galliera. BEETHOVEN: Piano Concerto No. 5 in E flat, Op. 73 (78: DB6692–6. LP: COLH5, Set GR4006).

**May 30.** BEETHOVEN: Piano Concerto No. 3 in C minor, Op. 37 (LP only: COLH3, Set GR4006).

**June 2.** EMI Studio 3. Schnabel (piano). WEBER: Invitation to the Dance, J260 (78: DB6491. LP: HQM1142, 60115).

**June 3.** SCHUMANN: Kinderscenen, Op. 15 (78: DB6502–3).

**June 4.** BRAHMS: Rhapsody in G minor, Op. 79, No. 2 (78: DB6504. LP: HQM1142, 60115). Intermezzo in E flat, Op. 117, No. 1; Intermezzo in A minor, Op. 116, No. 2 (78: DB6505. LP: HQM1142, 60115).

**Sept. 18–19.** EMI Studio 1. Lipatti (piano), Philharmonia/Galliera. GRIEG: Piano Concerto in A minor, Op. 16 (78: LX1029–32. LP: 33C1040, XLP30072, HLM7046, ML4525, 32160141).

**Sept. 24.** EMI Studio 3. Lipatti (piano). LISZT: Années de pèlerinage, Book 2, G74—No. 5, Sonetto del Petrarca, No. 104 (78: LB68. LP: HQM1163, Set RLS749, ML2216. EP: SEB3501). CHOPIN: Waltz No. 2 in A flat, Op. 34, No. 1 (78: LX1032. LP: HQM1248, Set RLS749).

**Sept. 26.** EMI Studio 1. Schwarzkopf (soprano), Philharmonia/Krips. MOZART: Don Giovanni—In quali eccessi . . . Mi tradi, quell'alma ingrata (78: LX1210, 72640D. LP: Set RLS763. EP: SEL1511).

**Sept. 26–27.** EMI Studio 1. Schwarzkopf (soprano), Seefried (soprano), Philharmonia/Krips. HUMPERDINCK: Hänsel und Gretel—Dance Duet; Sandman's Song; Evening Prayer (78: LX1036–7. LP: Set RLS763).

**Sept. 27.** EMI Studio 3. Lipatti (piano). SCARLATTI: Sonata in E major, L23 (78: LB113. LP: 33CX1386, HQM1163, Set RLS749, ML2216).

**Oct. 2.** EMI Studio 3. Schwarzkopf (soprano), Moore (piano). MOZART: Männer suchen stets zu naschen, K433 (78: LB73. LP: ML4649).

# A Selected Discography

T. ARNE: Love's Labour Lost—When daisies pied; The Tempest—Where the bee sucks (78: LB73. LP: Set RLS763).

Oct. 10. EMI Studio 1. E. Fischer (piano), Philharmonia/Krips. MOZART: Piano Concerto No. 25 in C, K503 (78: DB6604-7. LP: LHMV1004, THS65094. SP: Set WHMV1004).

Oct. 20-22, 27-29. Musikvereinsaal, Vienna. Schwarzkopf (soprano) Hotter (baritone), Gesellschaft der Musikfreunde, Vienna Philharmonic/ Karajan. BRAHMS: Ein deutsches Requiem, Op. 45 (78: LX1055-64. LP: Set SL157).

Oct. 27-28, Nov. 3. Musikvereinsaal, Vienna. Vienna Philharmonic/ Karajan. STRAUSS: Metamorphosen (78: LX1082-85).

Nov. 3-6, Dec. 10-12, 14. Musikvereinsaal, Vienna. Schwarzkopf (soprano), Höngen (contralto), Patzak (tenor), Hotter (baritone), Gesell-schaft der Musikfreunde, Vienna Philharmonic/Karajan. BEETHOVEN: Symphony No. 9 in D minor (78: LX1097-1105. EP: Set EL51).

Nov. 10-12, 17; Feb. 15, 1949. Musikvereinsaal, Vienna. Vienna Philharmonic/Furtwängler. BEETHOVEN: Symphony No. 3 in E flat, Op. 55 (78: DB6741-7).

Nov. 10, 19, 26, Dec. 3. Brahmssaal, Vienna. Vienna Philharmonic/ Furtwängler. MOZART: Serenade No. 10 in B flat, K 361 (78: DB6707-11. LP: WFS10).

Nov. 17-20. Musikvereinsaal, Vienna. Vienna Philharmonic/Furt-wängler. BRAHMS: Symphony No. 1 in C minor, Op. 68 (78: DB6634-39. LP: COLH97).

Nov. 25. BEETHOVEN: Overture, Coriolan, Op. 62 (78: DB6625).

Dec. 3. Brahmssaal, Vienna. Vienna Philharmonic/Karajan. MOZART: Adagio and Fugue, K546 (78: LX1076. LP: ML54370, ML4370).

Dec. 8. Musikvereinsaal, Vienna. Vienna Philharmonic/Karajan. REZNICEK: Donna Diana—overture (78: LX1402. LP: ML5141. SP: SCD2075, SCB112).

Dec. 9. STRAUSS: Der Rosenkavalier—Presentation of the Rose (Schwarz-kopf, soprano; Seefried, soprano) (78: LX1225-6. LP: SH286, Set RLS763, ML2126).

Dec. 13. Brahmssaal, Vienna. Vienna Philharmonic/Karajan. MOZART: Maurische Trauermusik, K477 (78: LX1155, 72846D).

## 1948

Mar. 10. EMI Studio 1. Flagstad (soprano), Philharmonia/Braithwaite. GRIEG: Eros, Op. 70, No. 1 (78: DA1879. LP: LM99. SP: Set WDM1533). En Svane, Op. 25, No. 2 (78: DA1879. LP: LM99, HQM1057. SP: Set WDM1533).

Mar. 18. EMI Studio 3. G. Neveu (violin), J. Neveu (piano). DEBUSSY: Violin Sonata (LP only: ALP1520, Set RLS739).

March 26. EMI Studio 1. Flagstad (soprano), Philharmonia/Furt-wängler. WAGNER: Götterdämmerung—Immolation Scene (78: DB6792-4. LP: LHMV1024. SP: Set WHMV1024).

Mar. 31. EMI Studio 1. Flagstad (soprano), Höngen (contralto), Phil-harmonia/Dobrowen. WAGNER: Tristan und Isolde—Isolde's Narration and Curse (78: DB6748-9. LP: HQM1138, LM1151).

**Apr. 1.** EMI Studio 1. Flagstad (soprano), Philharmonia/Dobrowen. WAGNER: Tannhäuser—Elisabeth's Prayer (78: DB6795, 12–1062).

**Apr. 3.** EMI Studio 1. Flagstad (soprano), Philharmonia/Braithwaite. GRIEG: Ved Rundarne, Op. 33, No. 9 (78: DA1992. LP: LM99. SP: Set WDM1533). Den Sarede, Op. 33, No. 3; En Drøm, Op. 48, No. 6 (78: DB21020). Tak for dit Rad, Op. 21, No. 4 (78: DB21020. LP: HQM1057).

**Apr. 9–10.** EMI Studio 1. Lipatti (piano), Philharmonia/Karajan. SCHUMANN: Piano Concerto in A minor, Op. 54 (78: LX1110–3. LP: 33C1001, XLP30072, HLM7046, ML2195, ML4525, 32160141).

**Apr. 12.** EMI Studio 1. Schwarzkopf (soprano), Philharmonia/Braithwaite. VERDI: La traviata—Act 1 finale (78: LX1079).

**Apr. 17.** EMI Studio 1. Lipatti (piano). CHOPIN: Barcarolle, Op. 60 (78: LX1437. LP: 33CX1386, HQM1163, Set RLS749, ML4721). RAVEL: Miroirs—No. 4, Alborada del gracioso (78: LB70. LP: 33CX1386, HQM1163, HLM7008, Set RLS749, ML2216. EP: SEB3501).

**May 25–26.** EMI Studio 1A. Flagstad (soprano), Moore (piano). WAGNER: Wesendonck Lieder (78: DB6749 and 6841–2. LP: 60046).

**May 26.** GRIEG: Med en vandlilje, Op. 25, No. 4; Prinsessen (78: DA1957. LP: HQM1057).

**May 26 and 28.** Kingsway Hall. Schwarzkopf (soprano), Philharmonia/ Süsskind. MOZART: Exsultate, jubilate, K165 (78: LX1196–7. LP: ML4649, 60013).

**May 27.** Kingsway Hall. Flagstad (soprano), Philharmonia/Süsskind. GRIEG: Varen, Op. 33, No. 2 (78: DA1904. LP: LM99. EP: 7EB6011. SP: Set WDM1533). GLUCK: Orfeo ed Euridice—Che farò (78: DB6913. LP: HQM1057. SP: 7R164).

**May 29.** EMI Studio 1. Flagstad (soprano), Philharmonia/Braithwaite. GRIEG: Von Monte Pincio, Op. 39, No. 1 (LP: LM99. EP: 7EB6011. SP: Set WDM1533). (orch. GUNSTROM): Guten, Op. 33, No. 1 (78: DA1992. LP: LM99. SP: Set WDM1533). PURCELL: Dido and Aeneas— Thy hand Belinda . . . When I am laid in earth (78: DB6913. LP: HQM1057. SP: 7R164).

**May 30.** EMI Studio 1A. Flagstad (soprano), Moore (piano). GRIEG: Mens jeg venter, Op. 60, No. 3; Langs ei Aa, Op. 33, No. 5; Efteraarsstormen, Op. 18, No. 4; Fyremaal, Op. 33, No. 12 (LP: 60045. EP: 7EB6007).

**June 15–16.** EMI Studio 3. Schnabel (piano). BACH: Chromatic Fantasia and Fugue in D minor, BWV903 (78: DB9511–2).

**June 16.** MOZART: Sonata No. 16 in B flat, K570 (78: DB6839–40. LP: COLH305, HQM1142, 60115).

**June 17–18.** EMI Studio 1. Schnabel (piano), Philharmonia/Süsskind. MOZART: Piano Concerto No. 20 in D minor, K466 (LP: LHMV1012, THS65046. SP: Set WHMV1012). †Piano Concerto No. 24 in C minor, K491 (LP: LHMV1012, THS65046. SP: Set WHMV1012).

**July 3.** EMI Studio 1. Flagstad (soprano), Philharmonia/Braithwaite. BIZET: Agnus Dei; HANDEL: Xerxes—Ombra mai fù (78: DB6791).

**Nov. 4, 6, 8–10; Jan. 21, 1949.** Musikvereinsaal, Vienna. Vienna Phil-

A Selected Discography

harmonic/Karajan. TCHAIKOVSKY: Symphony No. 6 in B minor, Op. 74 (78: LX1234–9. LP: 33CX1026, ML4299).
**Nov. 6.** Brahmssaal, Vienna. Schwarzkopf (soprano), Vienna Philharmonic/Karajan. PUCCINI: Gianni Schicchi—O mio babbino caro (78: LB85. LP: Set RLS763. EP: SEL1575).
**Nov. 11, 15–17.** Musikvereinsaal, Vienna. Vienna Philharmonic/Karajan. BEETHOVEN: Symphony No. 5 in C minor, Op. 67 (78: LX1330–3. LP: 33CX1004, RL3068).
**Nov. 23.** J. STRAUSS II: Waltz, Geschichten aus dem Wienerwald, Op. 325 (78: LX1274).
**Nov. 30.** J. STRAUSS II: Die Fledermaus—overture (78: LX1546. SP: SCD2101). PUCCINI: Manon Lescaut—Act 3 Intermezzo (78: LX1208. SP: SCD2084, SCB109).
**Dec. 7–8; Feb. 17, 1949.** Musikvereinsaal, Vienna. Vienna Philharmonic/Furtwängler. MOZART: Symphony No. 40 in G minor, K550 (78: DB6997–9. LP: ALP1498, XLP30104, LHMV1010. SP: Set WHMV1010).

### 1949
**Jan. 21.** Musikvereinsaal, Vienna. Vienna Philharmonic/Karajan. J. STRAUSS II; Perpetuum mobile, Op. 257 (78: LB128. SP: SCD2111). MASCAGNI: Cavalleria rusticana—Intermezzo (78: LX1208. SP: SCD2084, SCB109).
**Feb. 15.** Musikvereinsaal, Vienna. Vienna Philharmonic/Furtwängler. MENDELSSOHN: Overture, The Hebrides, Op. 26 (78: DB6941. LP: ALP1526, XLP30097. SP: 7R102).
**Feb. 16–17.** WAGNER: Siegfried Idyll (78: DB6916–7. LP: XLP30108, WFS2–3, LHMV1049, Set 6024).
**Feb. 23.** WAGNER: Götterdämmerung—Siegfried's Rhine Journey (78: DB6949–50. LP: ALP1016, COLH307, LHMV1049).
**Mar. 3.** Musikvereinsaal, Vienna. Schwarzkopf (soprano), Vienna State Opera Orchestra and Chorus/conductor unknown. GRUBER: Stille Nacht; TRAD.: O Tannenbaum (78: LC32). TRAD.: O du Fröhliche, o du Selige; TRAD.: Es ist ein Rose entsprungen (78: LC33).
**Mar. 16.** Musikvereinsaal, Vienna. Schwarzkopf (soprano), Vienna Philharmonic/Böhm. PUCCINI: Turandot—Tu che di gel sei cinta (78: LB85).
**Mar. 30–31, Apr. 4.** Musikvereinsaal, Vienna. Vienna Philharmonic/Furtwängler. WAGNER: Der fliegende Holländer—overture (78: DB6975–6. LP: XLP30108, WFS2–3, Set 6024).
**Mar. 30 and Apr. 2.** BRAHMS: Variations on a theme of Haydn, Op. 56a (78: DB6932–4. LP: ALP1011, LHMV1010. SP: Set WHMV1010).
**Mar. 31.** WAGNER: Die Walküre—Walkürenritt (78: DB6950. LP: XLP30108, WFS2–3, LHMV1049, Set 6024. EP: Set EHA17. SP: 7P206, 7R141).
**Apr. 1.** MOZART: Serenade No. 13 in G, K525 (78: DB6911–2. LP: ALP1498, XLP30104, LHMV1018. SP: Set WHMV1018).
**Apr. 1 and 4.** WAGNER: Die Meistersinger von Nürnberg—Act 1 Prelude (78: DB6942–3. LP: XLP30108, WFS2–3, LHMV1049, Set 6024).

**Apr. 4.** WAGNER: Die Meistersinger von Nürnberg—Dance of the Apprentices (78: DB6943. LP: XLP30108, WFS2–3, LHMV1049. EP: Set EHA17. SP: 7P206, 7R141). BRAHMS: Hungarian Dances—No. 2 in D minor, No. 3 in F (78: DB6934, DB9402). No. 1 in G minor (78: DB6976, DB9727. EP: Set EHA17).

**May 30.** EMI Studio 3. E. Fischer (piano). BRAHMS: Piano Sonata No. 3 in F minor, Op. 5 (78: DB21213–5. LP: BLP1017, LHMV1065. SP: Set WHMV1065).

**May 30–31.** SCHUMANN: Fantasia in C, Op. 17 (78: DB6959–61. LP: LHMV1065. SP: Set WHMV1065).

**May 31.** BACH: Fantasia in C minor, BWV906 (78: DB21182. LP: COLH45).

**June 4.** EMI Studio 1. Flagstad (soprano), Svanholm (tenor), Philharmonia/Böhm. WAGNER: Die Walküre—Todesverkündigung (78: DB6962–3. LP: HQM1138).

**June 5.** WAGNER: Tristan und Isolde—Love Duet. (Shacklock, contralto). (78: DB21112–4. LP: LM1151. SP: Set WDM1550).

**June 20.** EMI Studio 1A. Flagstad (soprano), Downes (viola), Moore (piano). BRAHMS: Gestillte Sehnsucht, Op. 91, No. 1; Geistliches Wiegenlied, Op. 91, No. 2 (78: DA1932–3. LP: 60046. EP: 7EB6012, Set EHA18).

**Oct. 1.** EMI Studio 3. Hotter (baritone), Moore (piano). SCHUBERT: Ueber allen Gipfeln, D768; Der du von dem Himmel, D224 (78: LX1261. LP: HQM1030).

**Oct. 2.** SCHUBERT: An die Musik, D547; Meeres Stille, D216; Im Frühling, D882 (78: LX1305). SCHUBERT: Am Bach im Frühling, D361 (78: LX1261).

**Oct. 13.** EMI Studio 1A. Schumann (soprano), Moore (piano). SCHUBERT: Nur wer die Sehnsucht kennt, D877, No. 4; So lasst mich scheinen, D877, No. 3 (LP: COLH131).

**Oct. 18.** Musikvereinsaal, Vienna. Vienna Philharmonic/Karajan. JOSEF STRAUSS: Waltz, Sphärenklänge, Op. 235 (78: LX1250. EP: SEL1505). J. STRAUSS II: Tritsch-Tratsch Polka, Op. 214 (78: LB128. SP: SCD2111). J. STRAUSS II: Galop, Unter Donner und Blitz, Op. 324 (78: LV15).

**Oct. 18, 21–22, 24, 27, Nov. 8, 10.** BRAHMS: Symphony No. 2 in D, Op. 73 (LP: 35007).

**Oct. 20.** JOSEF STRAUSS: Transactionen-Walzer, Op. 184 (78: LX1257. EP: SEL1505). J. STRAUSS II: Waltz, Wein, Weib und Gesang, Op. 333 (78: LX1402. SP: SCD2075, SCB112).

**Oct. 20, 26, Nov. 10.** Brahmssaal, Vienna. Vienna Philharmonic/Karajan. MOZART: Symphony No. 39 in E flat, K543 (78: LX1375–7. LP: RL3068).

**Oct. 24.** Musikvereinsaal, Vienna. Vienna Philharmonic/Karajan. JOSEF STRAUSS: Delirien Walzer, Op. 212 (78: LX1303).

**Oct. 24, Nov. 10.** J. STRAUSS II: Waltz, Wiener Blut, Op. 354 (78: LX1321. EP: SEL1503).

**Nov. 2.** Musikvereinsaal, Vienna. Vienna State Opera Chorus, Vienna Philharmonic/Karajan. WAGNER: Tannhäuser—March and Entry of the Guests. (78: LX1347).

**Nov. 3.** WAGNER: Lohengrin—Bridal Chorus; Act 3 Prelude (78:

A Selected Discography

LX1360). WAGNER: Die Meistersinger von Nürnberg—Wach auf!; Da zu dir der Heiland kam (78: LX1258). WAGNER: Der fliegende Holländer—Introduction to Act 3; Sailors' Chorus (78: LX1440).
**Nov. 18, 21–22.** Kingsway Hall. Philharmonia/Karajan. BALAKIREV: Symphony in C (78: LX1323–8. LP: 33CX1002, XLP60001).
**Nov. 22, 28.** ROUSSEL: Symphony No. 4 in A, Op. 53 (78: LX1348–51. LP: XLP60003).
**Nov. 29, 30.** BARTOK: Music for strings, percussion and celesta (78: LX1371–4. LP: ML4456).

### 1950

**Jan. 18–19.** Musikvereinsaal, Vienna. Vienna Philharmonic/Furtwängler. BEETHOVEN: Symphony No. 7 in A, Op. 92 (78: DB21106–10. LP: LHMV1008, Set 6018. SP: Set WHMV1008).
**Jan. 19–21.** SCHUBERT: Symphony No. 8 in B minor, D759 (78: DB21131–3. LP: XLP30104, LHMV1020. SP: Set WHMV1020).
**Jan. 21, 23–24.** STRAUSS: Tod und Verklärung, Op. 24 (78: DB21169–71. LP: HQM1137, LHMV1023, 60094. SP: Set WHMV1023).
**Jan. 24. J. STRAUSS II:** Kaiserwalzer, Op. 437 (78: DB21174. LP: ALP1526, XLP30106).
**Jan. 25, 30.** BEETHOVEN: Symphony No. 4 in B flat, Op. 60 (78: DB21099–103).
**Jan. 31.** WAGNER: Götterdämmerung—Siegfried's Funeral March (78: DB6946. LP: LHMV1049. EP: Set EHB2).
**Feb. 1.** WAGNER: Die Meistersinger von Nürnberg—Act 3 Prelude (LP: XLP30108, WFS2–3). WEBER: Oberon—overture (78: DB21104. LP: ALP1526, XLP30090, LHMV1020. SP: Set WHMV1020).
**Feb. 1.** Brahmssaal, Vienna. Vienna Philharmonic/Furtwängler. TCHAIKOVSKY: Serenade for Strings in C, Op. 48—Waltz (78: DB21173. LP: ALP1526. EP: 7ER5001. SP: 7R134).
**Feb. 2.** TCHAIKOVSKY: Serenade for Strings in C, Op. 48—finale. (78: DB21172. LP: ALP1526. EP: 7ER5001, Set EHA9. SP: 7R140). SCHUBERT: Rosamunde, D797—Ballet Music No. 2; Entr'acte No. 3 (78: DB21192. LP: XLP30106, LHMV1020. SP: 7R121, Set WHMV1020).
**Feb. 3. J. STRAUSS II –JOSEF STRAUSS:** Pizzicato Polka (78: DB21173. LP: XLP30106. EP: 7ER5001. SP: 7R134).
**Mar. 24.** Kingsway Hall. Hotter (baritone), Philharmonia/Bernard. BACH: Cantata No. 82 (78: LX1290–2. LP: ML4792).
**May 6.** EMI Studio 1. Schwarzkopf (soprano), Philharmonia/Dobrowen. CHARPENTIER: Louise—Depuis le jour. (LP only: Set RLS763).
**May 16.** EMI Studio 1. E. Fischer, D. Matthews, R. Smith (pianos), Philharmonia/E. Fischer. BACH: Concerto for three keyboards in C, BWV1064 (78: DB21180–2. LP: ALP1103, LHMV1004. SP: Set WHMV1004).
**June 6.** EMI Studio 3. Schnabel (piano). SCHUBERT: Impromptu in C minor, D899, No. 1 (78: DB21320. LP: BLP1007, LHMV1027. SP: Set WHMV1027). SCHUBERT: Impromptu in E flat, D899, No. 2 (78: DB21335. LP: BLP1007, HQM1142, LHMV1027, 60115. SP: Set WHMV1027).

June 7. SCHUBERT: Impromptu in G major, D899, No. 3 (78: DB21335. LP: BLP1007, HLM7008, LHMV1027. SP: Set WHMV1027).

June 7–8. SCHUBERT: Impromptu in A flat, D899, No. 4 (78: DB21351. LP: BLP1007, HQM1142, LHMV1027, 60115. SP: Set WHMV1027).

June 8–9. SCHUBERT: Impromptu in F minor, D935, No. 1 (78: DB21382. LP: BLP1030, LHMV1027. SP: Set WHMV1027).

June 9. SCHUBERT: Impromptu in A flat, D935, No. 2 (78: DB21500. LP: BLP1030, LHMV1027. EP: 7ER5042, Set EHA4. SP: Set WHMV1027).

June 17–21, Oct. 23–27, 31. Musikvereinsaal, Vienna. Schwarzkopf (soprano), Seefried (soprano), Jurinac (soprano), Höngen (contralto), Kunz (baritone), London (bass-baritone), etc., Vienna State Opera Chorus, Vienna Philharmonic/Karajan. MOZART: Le nozze di Figaro (LP: 33CX1007–9, Set SL114).

June 25. EMI Studio 1. Flagstad (soprano), Philharmonia/Süsskind. BACH: St Matthew Passion—Erbarme dich, mein Gott (78: DB21237. LP: HQM1057. SP: 7R126).

June 30. EMI Studio 1A. Flagstad (soprano), Moore (piano). BACH (arr. DØRUMSGAARD): Komm', süsser Tod (78: DB21490. LP: LHMV1070). LÖHNER (arr. DØRUMSGAARD): O Ewigkeit! (78: DB21490). CARISSIMI (arr. DØRUMSGAARD): Soccorretemi ch'io moro (78: DA2008). J. W. FRANCK (arr. DØRUMSGAARD): Sei nur still; Auf, auf zu Gottes Lob (78: DA2008. LP: LHMV1070).

July 3–6, 8–9, 11–12. Studio 2, Radio Geneva. Lipatti (piano). CHOPIN: Waltzes—Nos. 1–14 (78: LX1341–6. LP: 33CX1032, HLM7075, ML4522, 32160058E. EP: Set A1085).

July 6. BACH (arr. KEMPFF): Flute Sonata No. 2 in E flat—Siciliana (78: LB109. LP: 33CX1386, HQM1210, Set RLS749, ML4633, 32160320E. EP: SEL1631. SP: SCD2110).

July 6 and 10. BACH (arr. HESS): Cantata No. 147—Jesu, joy of man's desiring (78: LB109. LP: 33CX1386, HQM1163, Set RLS749, ML4633, 32160320E. EP: SEL1631. SP: SCD2110).

July 9. MOZART: Piano Sonata No. 8 in A minor, K310 (78: LX8788–9. LP: 33C1021, 33CX1499, HQM1210, Set RLS749, ML4633, 32160320E). BACH: Partita No. 1 in B flat, BWV825 (78: LX8744–5. LP: 33C1021, 33CX1499, HQM1210, Set RLS749, ML4633, 32160320E).

July 10. BACH (arr. BUSONI): Nun komm' der Heiden Heiland; Ich ruf' zu dir, Herr Jesu Christ (78: LX1427. LP: 33CX1386, HQM1210, Set RLS749, ML4633, 32160320E. EP: SEL1631. SP: SCD2142).

July 11. CHOPIN: Mazurka No. 32 in C sharp minor, Op. 50, No. 3 (78: LX1346. LP: 33CX1386, HQM1248, Set RLS749, ML4721).

Oct. 6. Kingsway Hall. Schwarzkopf (soprano), Philharmonia/Gellhorn. BACH: Cantata No. 51—Jauchzet Gott in allen Landen (78: LX1334–6. LP: ML4792, 60013).

Oct. 13. EMI Studio 1. Schwarzkopf (soprano), Ensemble/Gellhorn. BACH: Cantata No. 68—Mein gläubiges Herz (78: LX1336. LP: ML4792).

## A Selected Discography

**Oct. 16, 22.** EMI Studio 1A. Schwarzkopf (soprano), Medtner (piano). MEDTNER: The Muse, Op. 29, No. 1; So tanzet, Op. 15, No. 5; The Waltz, Op. 32, No. 5 (78: LX1425). Einsamkeit, Op. 18, No. 3; Praeludium, Op. 46, No. 1; Winternacht, Op. 46, No. 6 (78: LX1426). The Rose, Op. 29, No. 6; When roses fade, Op. 36, No. 3; Im Vorüberge-hen, Op. 6, No. 4; Elfenliedchen, Op. 6, No. 3 (78: LX1423). Meerstille, Op. 15, No. 7; Glückliche Fahrt, Op. 15, No. 8; Die Quelle; Sellstbetrug, Op. 15, No. 3 (78: LX1424).

**Oct. 18.** EMI Studio 1. Schwarzkopf (soprano), Philharmonia/Galliera. PUCCINI: La bohème—Donde lieta uscì (78: LB110. LP: Set RLS763. EP: SEL1575. SP: SCD2141, SCB101). Turandot: Signore, ascolta (78: LB110. LP: Set RLS763. SP: SCB101). Madama Butterfly—Un bel dì, 78: LX1370. LP: Set RLS763. EP: SEL1575. SP: SCD2076, SCB102).

**Oct. 19.** BEETHOVEN: Fidelio—Ach war ich schon (78: LX1410. SP: SCD2114). VERDI: La traviata—Addio del passato (78: LX1370. LP: Set RLS763. EP: SEL1575. SP: SCD2076, SCB102). BIZET: Carmen—Je dis que rien ne m'épouvante (78: LX1410. SP: SCD2114).

**Nov. 2–3, 6–9, 13–16, 20–21.** Musikvereinsaal, Vienna. Seefried (soprano), Lipp (soprano), Loose (soprano), Dermota (tenor), Klein (tenor), Kunz (baritone), Weber (bass), etc., Gesellschaft der Musik-freunde, Vienna Philharmonic/Karajan. MOZART: Die Zauberflöte (LP: 33CX1013–5, Set SLS5052, Set SL115).

### 1951

**Jan. 4, 8–11.** Musikvereinsaal, Vienna. Vienna Philharmonic/Furt-wängler. TCHAIKOVSKY: Symphony No. 4 in F minor, Op. 36 (78: DB21376–81. LP: ALP1025, ENC109, WFS7, LVT1018, LHMV1005. SP: Set WHMV1005).

**Jan. 11.** CHERUBINI: Anacreon—overture (78: DB21493. LP: ALP1498).

**Jan. 11–12, 17.** HAYDN: Symphony No. 94 in G major (78: DB21506–8. LP: ALP1011, LHMV1018. SP: Set WHMV1018).

**Jan. 17.** SCHUBERT: Rosamunde—overture, D644 (LP: XLP30097).

**Jan. 18.** NICOLAI: Die lustigen Weiber von Windsor—overture (78: DB21502. LP: ALP1526, XLP30097, LHMV1020. EP: Set EHA9. SP: Set WHMV1020).

**Jan. 24.** SMETANA: Má Vlast—Vltava (78: DB9787–9. LP: BLP1009, XLP30106, LHMV1023. SP: Set WHMV1023). SCHUMANN: Manfred, Op. 115—overture (78: DB9787–9. LP: BLP1009, XLP30097, LHMV1023. SP: Set WHMV1023).

**Feb. 19–20.** EMI Studio 1. E. Fischer (piano), Philharmonia/Furt-wängler. BEETHOVEN: Piano Concerto No. 5 in E flat, Op. 73 (78: DB21315–9. LP: ALP1051, LHMV4, THS65072, HLM7027).

**Apr. 3.** EMI Studio 3. Schwarzkopf (soprano), Moore (piano). TRAD.: Gsätzli; Die Beruhigte; O du liebs Angeli; Maria auf dem Berge (78: LB112).

**May 21.** EMI Studio 1A. Hotter (baritone), Moore (piano). WOLF: Der Tambour; Ob der Koran von Ewigkeit sei?; So lang man (78: LB141).

**May 22.** WOLF: Anakreons Grab; Schon streckt ich aus; Ein Ständchen euch zu bringen (78: LB142). BRAHMS: Mit vierzig Jahren, Op. 94, No. 1; Feldeinsamkeit, Op. 86, No. 2 (78: LX1403).

**June 6 and 11.** Kingsway Hall. Gieseking (piano), Philharmonia/Karajan. GRIEG: Piano Concerto in A minor, Op. 16 (78: LX1503–6. LP: 33C1003, ML4431, ML4885).

**June 7.** FRANCK: Symphonic Variations (78: LX8937–8. LP: ML4431, ML4536, ML4885).

**June 8 and 9.** BEETHOVEN: Piano Concerto No. 5 in E flat, Op. 73 (LP: 33CX1010, ML4623, 32160029).

**June 9 and 11.** BEETHOVEN: Piano Concerto No. 4 in G, Op. 58 (78: LX1443–6. LP: 33C1007, ML4535, 32160371).

**June 10.** MOZART: Piano Concerto No. 23 in A, K488 (78: LX1510–3. LP: 33C1012, ML4536, 32160371).

**June 12–13.** EMI Studio 1. Flagstad (soprano), Svanholm (tenor), Philharmonia/Sebastian. WAGNER: Siegfried—Act 3, Closing Scene (LP: BLP1035, HQM1138, LHMV1024. SP: Set WHMV1024).

**June 20.** Kongresshalle, Zürich. Gieseking (piano). BRAHMS: Rhapsody in B minor, Op. 79, No. 1 (78: LX1561. LP: Set 6117). Rhapsody in G minor, Op. 79, No. 2; Intermezzo in E major, Op. 116, No. 4 (78: LX1586. LP: Set 6117). MENDELSSOHN: Lied ohne Worte No. 30 in A major, Op. 62, No. 6 (78: LB139).

**June 21.** SINDING: Rustle of Spring, Op. 32, No. 3 (78: LB139). BRAHMS: Seven Piano Pieces, Op. 116 (LP: 33CX1255, 35028, Set 6117).

**July 27, Aug. 5, 16, 19, 21, 24.** Recordings of rehearsals and performances at Festspielhaus, Bayreuth. Schwarzkopf (soprano), Malaniuk (mezzo-soprano), Unger (tenor), Hopf (tenor), Kunz (baritone), Edelmann (bass), Dalberg (bass), etc., Bayreuth Festival Chorus and Orchestra/Karajan. WAGNER: Die Meistersinger von Nürnberg (78: LX1465–98. LP: 33CX1021–5, Set SL117, Set 6030).

**July 29.** Recording of live performance at reopening of the Festspielhaus, Bayreuth. Schwarzkopf (soprano), Höngen (contralto), Hopf (tenor), Edelmann (bass), Bayreuth Festival Chorus and Orchestra/Furtwängler. BEETHOVEN: Symphony No. 9 in D minor, Op. 125 (LP: ALP1286–7, Set RLS727, COLH78–9, Set LM6043, Set GR4003, Set 6068).

**Aug. 12.** Recording of live performance at Festspielhaus, Bayreuth. Varnay (soprano), Rysanek (soprano), S. Björling (baritone), Bayreuth Festival Orchestra/Karajan. WAGNER: Die Walküre—Act 3 (78: LX1447–54. LP: 33CX1005–6, Set SL116).

**Sept. 16.** EMI Studio 1. Schwarzkopf (soprano), Weber (bass), Philharmonia/Schüchter. WAGNER: Tristan und Isolde—Tod denn Alles! (78: LX8892).

**Sept. 22, 28.** EMI Studio 3. Gieseking (piano). DEBUSSY: Suite bergamasque (78: LX8898–9. LP: ML4539, 35067, 60210, 32360021).

**Sept. 22–23.** DEBUSSY: Préludes—Book 1 (LP: ML4537, 32360021).

**Sept. 23–24, 30.** DEBUSSY: Préludes—Book 2 (LP: ML4538, 32360021).

**Sept. 24, 27.** DEBUSSY: Pour le piano (LP: 33CX1137, 35065).

**Sept. 25.** SCARLATTI: Sonata in D minor, L413 (78: LB136. LP: ML4646). Sonata in D major, L424 (78: LB144. LP: ML4646). Sonata

*A Selected Discography*

in C major, L443 (LP: ML4646). HANDEL: Suite No. 5 (78: LX1532. LP: ML4646).

**Sept. 25–26.** SCHUMANN: Carnival, Op. 9 (LP: ML4772).

**Sept. 26, 28–29.** BACH: Partita No. 6 in E minor, BWV830 (LP: ML4646).

**Sept. 26–27.** DEBUSSY: Children's Corner (LP: 33C1014, ML4539, 35067, 32360021).

**Sept. 28.** SCHUMANN: Kinderscenen, Op. 15 (78: LX8913–4. LP: 33C1014, ML4540, 35321).

**Sept. 29.** DEBUSSY: Arabesques Nos. 1 and 2 (78: LX1556). SCHUBERT: Moments musicaux, D780. No. 1 in C; No. 4 in C sharp minor (78: LX1588). No. 2 in A flat; No. 3 in F minor (78: LX1589). No. 5 in F minor; No. 6 in A flat (78: LX1591). SCARLATTI: Sonata in E minor, L275 (78: LB136. LP: ML4646). Sonata in E major, L23 (78: LB144. LP: ML4646).

**Oct. 3–5, 7.** EMI Studio 3. Fischer-Dieskau (baritone), Moore (piano). SCHUBERT: Die schöne Müllerin, D795 (78: DB21388–95. LP: ALP1036–7, Set LHMV6).

**Oct. 5.** BEETHOVEN: An die ferne Geliebte, Op. 98 (78: DB21347–8. LP: ALP1066, LHMV1046. EP: Set EHA5. SP: Set WHMV1046).

**Oct. 6.** SCHUBERT: Schwanengesang, D957-No. 8, Der Atlas; No. 9, Ihr Bild (78: DA2049. LP: ALP1066). No. 12, Am Meer; No. 13, Der Doppelgänger (78: DB21491, DB21586. LP: ALP1066). No. 10, Das Fischermädchen; No. 11, Die Stadt (78: DA2045. LP: ALP1066). Nos. 8, 10, 12–13 (LP: LHMV1046. SP: Set WHMV1046).

**October 7.** SCHUMANN: Die beiden Grenadiere, Op. 49, No. 1 (78: DB21350. LP: LHMV1046. SP: Set WHMV1046). Mondnacht, Op. 39, No. 5 (78: DB21517. LP: LHMV1046. SP: Set WHMV1046). SCHUBERT: Nacht und Träume, D827 (78: DB21517). Erlkönig, D328 (78: DB21350). Du bist die Ruh', D776; Ständchen, D889 (78: DB21349).

**Oct. 15–16, Nov. 30, Dec. 1–2.** Mermaid Theatre (**Mar. 15, 27–28, 1952,** EMI Studio 1), Flagstad (soprano) Schwarzkopf (soprano), Mandikian (soprano), Hemsley (baritone), etc., Mermaid Singers and Orchestra/Jones. PURCELL: Dido and Aeneas (LP: ALP1026, SH117, LHMV1007, 60346. SP: Set WHMV1007).

**Nov. 10.** EMI Studio 1. Hotter (baritone), Philharmonia/Weldon. HANDEL: Giulio Cesare—Dall' ondoso periglio (78: LX1538). Joshua—Soll ich im Mamres Segens au'm; Samson—Wie willig trägt mein Vaterherz (78: LX1516).

**Nov. 11–12.** EMI Studio 1A. Hotter (baritone), Moore (piano). BRAHMS: Vier ernste Gesänge, Op. 121 (78: LX8933–4).

**Nov. 28–30; Apr. 26, 29, May 5, 8, 1952.** Kingsway Hall. Philharmonia/Karajan. BEETHOVEN: Symphony No. 7 in A, Op. 92 (LP: 33CX1035, T535, Set SLS5053, 35005).

**Nov. 29.** EMI Studio 1. Schwarzkopf (soprano), Moore (piano). SCHUMANN: Der Nussbaum, Op. 25, No. 3; Aufträge, Op. 77, No. 5 (78: LB122). MOZART: Die Zauberer, K472. (78: LB118).

**Nov. 29 and Dec. 2.** arr. BRAHMS: Deutsche Volkslieder—No. 6, Da unten im Tale. (78: LB118).

**Nov. 30, Dec. 1; Apr. 26, July 31, 1952.** Kingsway Hall. Philharmonia/ Karajan. HANDEL (arr. HARTY): Water Music—Suite (78: LX8945–6. LP: 33CX1033, 35004).

**Dec. 1; July 28–29, 1952.** SIBELIUS: Symphony No. 5 in E flat, Op. 82 (LP: 33CX1047, 35002).

**Dec. 3.** STRAUSS: Don Juan, Op. 20 (78: LX8920–1. LP: 33CX1001).

**Dec. 4.** STRAUSS: Till Eulenspiegels lustige Streiche, Op. 28 (78: LX8908–9. LP: 33CX1001).

*1952*

**Apr. 28.** EMI Studio 1. Flagstad (soprano), Moore (piano). SCHUBERT: Du bist die Ruh', D776; Die Allmacht, D852 (78: DB21596).

**Apr. 28, May 2; May 28, 1955.** Kingsway Hall. Philharmonia/Karajan. MOZART: Divertimento No. 15 in B flat, K287 (LP: 33CX1511, 35562).

**May 1.** EMI Studio 1. Flagstad (soprano), Moore (piano). SCHUBERT: Frühlingsglaube, D118; Im Abendrot, D799 (78: DB21554).

**May 1, 8, July 25, 31; June 19, Aug. 1, 18, 1953.** Kingsway Hall. Philharmonia/Karajan. TCHAIKOVSKY: Symphony No. 5 in E minor, Op. 64 (LP: 33CX1133, 35055).

**May 3, 5.** STRAVINSKY: Jeu de cartes (LP: XLP60003).

**May 5, 7, July 26, 28, 31.** BRAHMS: Symphony No. 1 in C minor, Op. 68 (LP: 33CX1053, 35001).

**June.** The precise dates of these sessions are no longer known. Kingsway Hall. Flagstad (soprano), Thebom (mezzo-soprano), Suthaus (tenor), Schock (tenor), Evans (tenor), Fischer-Dieskau (baritone), etc., Chorus of Royal Opera House, Philharmonia/Furtwängler. WAGNER: Tristan und Isolde (LP: ALP1030–5, HQM1001–5, Set LM6700, Set 3588).

**June 23.** Kingsway Hall. Flagstad (soprano), Philharmonia/Furtwängler. WAGNER: Götterdämmerung—Immolation Scene (LP: ALP1016, HQM1057, LHMV1072).

**June 23; Mar. 10, 1954.** EMI Studio 3. Fischer-Dieskau (baritone), Moore (piano). SCHUMANN: Liederkreis, Op. 39 (LP: BLP1068, LM6036).

**July 1.** Kingsway Hall. Schwarzkopf (soprano), Philharmonia/Pritchard. MOZART: Don Giovanni—Batti, batti (78: LB145. LP: 33CX1069, T583, 35021. EP: SEL1511). Le nozze di Figaro—Voi che sapete (LP: 33CX1069, T583, 35021).

**July 2.** MOZART: Don Giovanni—Vedrai, carino (78: LB145. LP: 33CX1069, T583, 35021. EP: SEL1511). Le nozze di Figaro—Non so più (LP: 33CX1069, T583, 35021). Giunse alfin il momento . . . Deh, vieni, non tardar (LP: 33CX1069, T583, Set RLS763, 35021).

**July 4.** MOZART: Don Giovanni: Crudele? . . . Non mi dir (LP: 33CX1069, T583, Set RLS763, 35021. EP: SEL1515). Le nozze di Figaro—Porgi amor (LP: 33CX1069, T583, Set RLS763, 35021).

**July 6–21.** Théâtre des Champs-Elysées, Paris. Lebedeva (soprano), Zareska (mezzo-soprano), Gedda (tenor), Christoff (bass), Borg (bass), etc., Choeurs Russes de Paris, Orchestre Nationale/Dobrowen. MUSSORGSKY (rev. RIMSKY-KORSAKOV): Boris Godunov (LP: ALP1044–7, SLS5072, Set LHMV6400, Set GDR7164, Set 6101. SP: Set WHMV6400).

July 29–31. Kingsway Hall. Philharmonia/Karajan. SIBELIUS: Finlandia, Op. 26 (78: LX1593. LP: 33CX1047, 35002. SP: SCD2115).

July 30–31, Dec. 1. TCHAIKOVSKY: The Nutcracker—Suite, Op. 71A (LP: 33CX1033, 35004).

Sept. 9. Kingsway Hall. Schwarzkopf (soprano), Philharmonia/Pritchard. MOZART: Le nozze di Figaro—E Susanna non vien . . . Dove sono (LP: 33CX1069, 35021, T583, Set RLS763).

Sept. 11. EMI Studio 1A. Schwarzkopf (soprano), Moore (piano). BACH: Anna Magdalena Notenbuch—No. 25, Bist du bei mir, BWV508; MOZART: Abendempfindung, K523 (78: LX1580).

Sept. 16. Kingsway Hall. Schwarzkopf (soprano), Philharmonia/Pritchard. MOZART: Idomeneo—Zeffiretti lusinghieri (LP: 33CX1069, T583, 35021. EP: SEL1515).

Sept. 27. EMI Studio 1A. Schwarzkopf (soprano), Moore (piano). WOLF: Wiegenlied im Sommer; Mausfallen-Sprüchlein (78: LX1577).

Oct. 3. Kingsway Hall. Schwarzkopf (soprano), Chorus of the Royal Opera House, Covent Garden, Hampstead Parish Church Choir, Philharmonia/Pritchard. GRUBER (arr. SALTER): Silent night, holy night; TRAD. (arr. SALTER): The First Nowell (78: LB131. SP: SCD2112).

Oct. 4–7. EMI Studio 1A. Schwarzkopf (soprano), E. Fischer (piano). SCHUBERT: Auf dem Wasser zu singen, D774; An Silvia, D891; An die Musik, D547; Nachtviolen, D752; Die junge Nonne, D828; Nähe des Geliebten, D162; Das Lied im Grünen, D917; Der Musensohn, D764; Gretchen am Spinnrade, D118; Wehmut, D772; Ganymed, D544; Im Frühling, D882 (LP: 33CX1040, ALP3843, 35022).

Nov. 7. Musikvereinsaal, Vienna. Chorus and Orchestra of the Vienna Musikfreunde/Karajan; also—

Nov. 23, 28–30; July 16, 1953. EMI Studio No. 1, Schwarzkopf (soprano), Höffgen (contralto), Gedda (tenor), Rehfuss (baritone), Philharmonia/Karajan. BACH: Mass in B minor, BWV232 (LP: 33CX1121–3, T854–6, Set RLS746, Set 3500).

Nov. 19, 24, Dec. 1. Kingsway Hall. Philharmonia/Karajan. TCHAIKOVSKY: Swan Lake, Op. 20—Ballet Suite (LP: 33CX1065, 35006).

Nov. 20–22, Dec. 1. BEETHOVEN: Symphony No. 3 in E flat, Op. 55 (LP: 33CX1046, 35000, T532, Set SLS5053).

Nov. 24, Dec. 1. TCHAIKOVSKY: The Sleeping Beauty, Op. 66—Ballet Suite (LP: 33CX1065, 35006).

Nov. 28–29; July 17, 21–22, 1953. BARTOK: Concerto for Orchestra (LP: 33CX1054, 35003).

Dec. 8–9. EMI Studio 1. Flagstad (soprano), Moore (piano). FREYLINGHAUSEN (ed. DØRUMSGAARD): Es ist vollbracht; BOHM (ed. DØRUMSGAARD): Geh' ein, mein Lieb, in deine Kammer; J. S. BACH (ed. DØRUMSGAARD): Liebster Herr Jesu; C. P. E. BACH (ed. DØRUMSGAARD): Preis sei dem Gotte; J. S. BACH (ed. DØRUMSGAARD): O finstre Nacht (LP: LHMV1070).

### 1953

Apr. 16–19, 21. Kingsway Hall. Schwarzkopf (soprano), Loose (soprano), Gedda (tenor), Kunz (baritone), O. Kraus (baritone), Niessner (baritone), Schmidinger (bass), etc., BBC Chorus, Philharmonia/Ackermann. LEHAR: Die lustige Witwe (LP: 33CX1051–2, Set SXDW3045, Set 3501).

**Apr. 17, 19–21, 28.** Kingsway Hall. Schwarzkopf (soprano), Loose (soprano), Gedda (tenor), Kunz (baritone), O. Kraus (baritone), etc., BBC Chorus, Philharmonia/Ackermann. LEHAR: 'Das Land des Lächelns (LP: 33CX1114–5, Set SXDW3044, Set 3507).

**May 3–5, 7–8.** EMI Studio 3. Hotter (baritone), Moore (piano). WOLF: Three Michelangelo Lieder; Coptische Lieder; Harfenspieler Lieder; Grenzen der Menschheit; Prometheus; Geselle, woll'n wir uns in Kutten hüllen (LP: 33CX1162, 35057).

**June 20, July 15.** Kingsway Hall. Philharmonia/Karajan. BEETHOVEN: Egmont, Op. 84—overture (LP: 33CX1136, Set SLS5053, 35097). Overture, Coriolan, Op. 62 (LP: 33CX1227, Set SLS5053, 35196).

**June 27, 29–30, July 1–2, 16.** Kingsway Hall. Schwarzkopf (soprano), Felbermayer (soprano), Grümmer (soprano), Ilosvay (mezzo-soprano), Schürhoff (mezzo-soprano), Metternich (baritone), etc., Loughton High School and Bancroft's School Choirs, Philharmonia/Karajan. HUMPERDINCK: Hänsel und Gretel (LP: 33CX1096–7, OC187–8, Set SLS5145, Set 3506).

**July 4, 8, 10, 16.** Kingsway Hall. Philharmonia/Karajan. TCHAIKOVSKY: Symphony No. 4 in F minor, Op. 36 (LP: 33CX1139, 35099).

**July 6–7.** SIBELIUS: Symphony No. 4 in A minor, Op. 63 (LP: 33CX1125, 35082).

**July 9–10.** BEETHOVEN: Symphony No. 6 in F, Op. 68 (LP: 33CX1124, T534, Set SLS5053, 35080).

**July 13–14.** BEETHOVEN: Overture, Leonore No. 3, Op. 72b (LP: 33CX1136, Set SLS5053, 35097).

**July 14–15.** SIBELIUS: Tapiola, Op. 112 (LP: 33CX1125, 35082).

**July 16–17.** RAVEL: Rapsodie espagnole (LP: 33CX1099, 35081).

**July 17.** CHABRIER: España (LP: 33CX1335, 35327. EP: SEL1528).

**July 20–22.** DEBUSSY: La mer (LP: 33CX1099, 35081).

**July 21.** WALDTEUFEL: Waltz, Les patineurs, Op. 183 (LP: 33CX1335, 35327. EP: SEL1528).

**Aug. 1.** EMI Studio 3. Gieseking (piano). MOZART: Piano Sonata No. 1 in C, K279 (LP: 33CX1242, 35072, Sets 6047–9). Piano Sonata No. 2 in F, K280 (LP: 33CX1160, 35070, Set 3511, Sets 6047–9). Piano Sonata No. 3 in B flat, K281 (LP: 33CX1315, 35074, Set 3511, Sets 6047–9). Piano Sonata No. 4 in E flat, K282 (LP: 33CX1142, 35069, Set 3511, Sets 6047–9).

**Aug. 2.** MOZART: Piano Sonata No. 5 in G, K283 (LP: 33CX1345, 35075, Set 3511, Sets 6047–9).

**Aug. 2–3.** MOZART: Piano Sonata No. 6 in D, K284 (LP: 33CX1271, 35073, Set 3511, Sets 6047–9).

**Aug. 3.** MOZART: Piano Sonata No. 8 in A minor, K310 (LP: 33CX1160, 35070, Set 3511, Sets 6047–9). Piano Sonata No. 7 in C, K309 (LP: 33CX1428, 35077, Set 3511, Sets 6047–9).

**Aug. 10–14, 16, 18–21.** La Scala, Milan. Callas (soprano), di Stefano (tenor), Mercuriali (tenor), Gobbi (baritone), Calabrese (bass), Luise

(bass), etc., La Scala Chorus and Orchestra/de Sabata. PUCCINI: Tosca
(LP: 33CX1094–5, Set SLS825, Set 3508).

**Aug. 22–23.** EMI Studio 1. Gieseking (piano), Philharmonia/Rosbaud.
MOZART: Piano Concerto No. 25 in C, K503 (LP: 33CX1235, 35215).

**Aug. 23–24.** MOZART: Piano Concerto No. 20 in D minor, K466 (LP:
33CX1235, 35215).

**Sept. 25.** Town Hall, Watford. Schwarzkopf (soprano), Philharmonia/
Ackermann. STRAUSS: Vier letzte Lieder (LP: 33CX1107, Set RLS751,
35084).

**Sept. 26.** STRAUSS: Capriccio—closing scene (LP: 33CX1107, Set
RLS751, 35084).

**Nov. 10.** EMI Studio 1. **Nov. 23.** Kingsway Hall. Philharmonia/Karajan.
BRITTEN: Variations on a theme of Frank Bridge, Op. 10 (LP: 33CX1159,
XLP60002, 35142).

**Nov. 11.** EMI Studio 1. **Nov. 23.** Kingsway Hall. VAUGHAN WILLIAMS:
Fantasia on a theme of Thomas Tallis (LP: 33CX1159, XLP60002, 35142).

**Nov. 12–13, 23.** Kingsway Hall. Philharmonia/Karajan. BEETHOVEN:
Symphony No. 2 in D, Op. 36 (LP: 33CX1227, T531, Set SLS5053,
35196).

**Nov. 13, 16.** BEETHOVEN: Symphony No. 4 in B flat, Op. 60 (LP:
33CX1278, T533, Set SLS5053, 35023).

**Nov. 17–18.** MOZART: Sinfonia Concertante, K297b (Sutcliffe, oboe, B.
Walton, clarinet, James, bassoon, Brain, horn) (LP: 33CX1178, XLP60004,
35098).

**Nov. 18.** MOZART: Serenade No. 13 in G, K525 (LP: 33CX1178,
35098).

**Nov. 21.** BEETHOVEN: Symphony No. 1 in C, Op. 21 (LP: 33CX1136,
T531, Set SLS5053, 35097).

### 1954

**Jan. 4–7, 9–11.** EMI Studio 1A. Schwarzkopf (soprano), Moore (piano).
BACH: Anna Magdalena Notenbuch—Bist du bei mir, BWV508; GLUCK:
La recontre imprévue—Einem Bach der fliesst; arr. BRAHMS: Deutsche
Volkslieder—No. 33, Och mod'r ich well en ding han; No. 6, Da unten im
Tale; WOLF: Mausfallen-Sprüchlein; Wiegenlied im Sommer; STRAUSS: Hat
gesagt, Op. 36, No. 3; Schlechtes Wetter, Op. 69, No. 5; MOZART: Der
Zauberer, K472; Abendempfindung, K523; BRAHMS: Vergebliches Ständ-
chen, Op. 84, No. 4; SCHUMANN: Aufträge, Op. 77, No. 5; Der Nussbaum,
Op. 25, No. 3; SCHUBERT: Litanei, D343; Die schöne Müllerin, D795—
No. 7, Ungeduld; BEETHOVEN: Wonne der Wehmut, Op. 83, No. 1 (LP:
33CX1044, 35023. All items except the Beethoven in Set RLS763).

**Mar. 5.** Kingsway Hall. Fischer-Dieskau (baritone), Philharmonia/
Schüchter. WAGNER: Tannhäuser—Als du in kühnem Sange; Blick ich
umher; O du mein holder Abendstern. (EP: 7ER5033).

**Mar. 31.** EMI Studio 3. Gieseking (piano). MOZART: Six German Dances
with Trios, K509; Eight Minuets with Trios, K315A; Incomplete Sonata,
K400 (LP: 33CX1453, 35078, Sets 6047–9). Kleiner Trauermarsch,
K453A (LP: 33CX1160, 35070, Sets 6047–9).

**Apr. 23–May 3.** La Scala, Milan. Callas (soprano), Cavallari (soprano),

Stignani (mezzo-soprano), Filippeschi (tenor), Caroli (tenor), Rossi-Lemeni (bass), etc., La Scala Chorus and Orchestra/Serafin. BELLINI: Norma (LP: 33CX1179–81, Set SLS5155, Set 3517, Set 6037).

**May 4, 14.** EMI Studio 1. E. Fischer (piano), Philharmonia/E. Fischer. †BEETHOVEN: Piano Concerto No. 4 in G, Op. 58 (LP: BLP1067).

**May 18–21, 26, 28, 31, Sept. 25.** Kingsway Hall. Schwarzkopf (soprano), Köth (soprano), Sinclair (contralto), Gedda (tenor), Kunz (baritone), Prey (baritone), Ferenz (bass), Chorus and Philharmonia/Ackermann. J. STRAUSS II: Der Zigeunerbaron (LP: 33CX1329–30, Set SXDW3046, Set 3566).

**May 21–22, 26–28, 31.** Kingsway Hall. Schwarzkopf (soprano), Köth (soprano), Gedda (tenor), Dönch (baritone), Kunz (baritone), Pernerstorfer (bass), etc., Chorus and Philharmonia/Ackermann. J. STRAUSS II (arr. MÜLLER): Wiener Blut (LP: 33CX1186–7, Set SXDW3042, Set 3519).

**May 24–29.** EMI Studio 1. Hotter (baritone), Moore (piano). †SCHUBERT: Die Winterreise, D911 (LP: 33CX1222–3, XLP30102–3, Set 3521, Set 6051).

**May 25–28, 31, Sept. 25.** Kingsway Hall. Schwarzkopf (soprano), Gedda (tenor), Klein (tenor), Kunz (baritone), Dönch (baritone), Chorus and Philharmonia/Ackermann. J. STRAUSS II: Eine Nacht in Venedig (LP: 33CX1224–5, Set SXDW3043, Set 3530).

**May 29–30.** EMI Studio 1A. Hotter (baritone), Moore (piano). †SCHUBERT: Schwanengesang, D957 (LP: 33CX1269, XLP30102–3, 35219, Set 6051).

**June 12–17.** La Scala, Milan. Callas (soprano), di Stefano (tenor), Monti (tenor), Gobbi (baritone), Panerai (baritone), etc., La Scala Chorus and Orchestra/Serafin. LEONCAVALLO—I pagliacci. (LP: 33CX1211–2, Set SLS819, Set 3527, Set 3528).

**June 18–22, 25–27.** La Scala, Milan. Schwarzkopf (soprano), Dominguez (mezzo-soprano), di Stefano (tenor), Siepi (bass), etc., La Scala Chorus and Orchestra/de Sabata. VERDI: Missa da Requiem (LP: 33CX1195–6, Set 3520).

**June 30, July 1–2, 5–7.** Kingsway Hall. Schwarzkopf (soprano), Streich (soprano), Seefried (soprano), Schock (tenor), Cuénod (tenor), Unger (tenor), Dönch (baritone), Philharmonia/Karajan. STRAUSS: Ariadne auf Naxos (LP: 33CX1292–4, Set RLS760, Set 3532).

**July 7–9, 21.** Kingsway Hall. Philharmonia/Karajan. BERLIOZ: Symphonie fantastique, Op. 14 (LP: 33CX1206, 35202).

**July 13.** Kingsway Hall. **July 14–17, 19.** EMI Studio 1. Schwarzkopf (soprano), Otto (soprano), Merriman (mezzo-soprano), Simoneau (tenor), Panerai (baritone), Bruscantini (baritone), etc., Chorus and Philharmonia/ Karajan. MOZART: Così fan tutte (LP: 33CX1262–4, SOC195–7, Set 3522).

**July 22–24.** Kingsway Hall. Philharmonia/Karajan. BIZET: Carmen— Act 4 Entr'acte; MASCAGNI: L'amico Fritz—Act 3 Intermezzo; GRANADOS: Goyescas—Intermezzo; LEONCAVALLO: I pagliacci—Intermezzo; PUCCINI: Manon Lescaut—Intermezzo; MASSENET: Thaïs—Méditation (Parikian, violin); VERDI: La traviata—Act 3 Prelude; MUSSORGSKY: Khovantchina—

## A Selected Discography

Act 4 Entr'acte; OFFENBACH: Les contes d'Hoffmann—Barcarolle; MASCAGNI: Cavalleria rusticana—Intermezzo; KODALY: Háry János—Intermezzo (LP: 33CX1265, 35207).

**July 23.** WEINBERGER: Schwanda the Bagpiper—Polka (LP: 33CX1335, 35327).

**Aug. 31, Sept. 1, 3–8.** La Scala, Milan. Callas (soprano), Gardino (mezzo-soprano), Gedda (tenor), de Palma (tenor), Stabile (baritone), Rossi-Lemeni (bass), Calabrese (bass), etc. La Scala Chorus and Orchestra/ Gavazzeni. †ROSSINI: Il turco in Italia (LP: 33CX1289–91, Set SLS5148, Set 3535, Set 6095).

**Sept. 20.** Town Hall, Watford. Schwarzkopf (soprano), Philharmonia/ Karajan. BEETHOVEN: Ah! perfido, Op. 65 (LP: 33CX1278, 35203). Fidelio—Abscheulicher! Wo eilst du hin? (LP: 33CX1266, 35231).

**Sept. 27–29, Oct. 6.** Kingsway Hall. Schwarzkopf (soprano), Felbermayer (soprano), Gedda (tenor), Metternich (bass), Berry (bass), Philharmonia/Matačić. STRAUSS: Arabella—extracts (LP: 33CX1226, 33CX1897, OH199, Set RLS751, 35094).

**Nov. 5–6, 8.** Kingsway Hall. Philharmonia/Karajan. VERDI: Aida—Act 2 Ballet Music; WAGNER: Tannhäuser—Venusberg Music; PONCHIELLI: La gioconda—Dance of the Hours; MUSSORGSKY: Khovantchina—Dance of the Persian Slaves; BORODIN: Prince Igor—Dance of the Polovtsian Maidens; Polovtsian Dances (LP: 33CX1327, 35307).

**Nov. 9–10.** Kingsway Hall. Philharmonia/Karajan. BEETHOVEN: Symphony No. 5 in C minor, Op. 67 (LP: 33CX1266, T533–4, Set SLS5053, 35231).

**Nov. 13–14.** EMI Studio 1. D. Oistrakh (violin), Philharmonia/Martinon. †LALO: Symphonie espagnole, Op. 21 (LP: 33CX1246, XLP30109, 35205, 60332).

**Nov. 26–27.** Kingsway Hall. D. Oistrakh (violin), Philharmonia/Khachaturian. KHACHATURIAN: Violin Concerto (LP: 33CX1303, 35244).

**Dec. 7–9, 11.** EMI Studio 3. Gieseking (piano). DEBUSSY: Etudes (LP: 33CX1261, 35250).

**Dec. 9–10.** DEBUSSY: Préludes, Book 2 (LP: 33CX1304, Set RLS752, 35249).

**Dec. 10.** RAVEL: Menuet antique (LP: 33CX1352, Set 3341).

**Dec. 10–11.** RAVEL: Sonatine (LP: 33CX1351, Set 3341).

**Dec. 11.** RAVEL: Pavane pour une infante défunte (LP: 33CX1352, Set 3341).

**Dec. 12, 14–15.** †RAVEL: Le tombeau de Couperin (LP: 33CXS1350, Set 3341).

**Dec. 12, 15.** †RAVEL: Jeux d'eau (LP: 33CX1352, Set 3341, 60210).

### 1955

**Apr. 13–14, 16.** EMI Studio 1A. Schwarzkopf (soprano), Gieseking (piano). MOZART: Der Zauberer, K472; Als Luise die Briefe, K520; Das Veilchen, K476; An Chloë, K524; Abendempfindung, K523; Ridente la Calma, K152; Die Zufriedenheit, K349; Im Frühlingsanfang, K597; Die kleine Spinnerin, K531; Das Kinderspiel, K598; Das Traumbild, K530;

Oiseaux, si tous les ans, K307; Dans un bois solitaire, K308; Die Alte, K517; Das Lied der Trennung, K519; Sehnsucht nach dem Frühling, K596 (LP: 33CX1321, ASD3858, 35270).

**Apr. 15–16.** EMI Studio 1A. Gieseking (piano), Sutcliffe (oboe), James (bassoon), Walton (clarinet), Brain (horn). MOZART: Piano Quintet, K452 (LP: 33CX1322, 35303).

**Apr. 18–20.** Kingsway Hall. Schwarzkopf (soprano), Sinclair (contralto), Lewis (tenor), Philharmonia/Walton. WALTON: Troilus and Cressida— excerpts (LP: 33CX1313, OH217, 35278).

**Apr. 26–30.** Kingsway Hall. Schwarzkopf (soprano), Streich (soprano), Gedda (tenor), Christ (tenor), Krebs (tenor), Kunz (baritone), Dönch (baritone), Chorus and Philharmonia/Karajan. J. STRAUSS II: Die Fleder-maus (LP: 33CX1309–10, Set RLS728, Set 3539).

**May 12.** EMI Studio 3. Fischer-Dieskau (baritone), Moore (piano). SCHUBERT: Rastlose Liebe, D138; Anflösung, D807; Nachtviolen, D752; Geheimes, D719; Der Wanderer an den Mond, D870; Todtengräbers Heimweh, D842; Der Kreuzzug, D932 (LP: ALP1295, 35624).

**May 17–19.** Kingsway Hall. Philharmonia/Karajan. †BRAHMS: Varia-tions on a theme by Haydn, Op. 56a (LP: 33CX1349, SXLP30513, 35299).

**May 18–19.** †SCHUBERT: Symphony No. 8 in B minor, D759 (LP: 33CX1349, SXLP30513, 35299).

**May 19.** Salle Colonialle, Brussels. D. Oistrakh (violin), Yampolsky (piano). BRAHMS: Violin Sonata No. 3 in D minor, Op. 108 (LP: 33CX1580, 35331).

**May 19–20.** Kingsway Hall. Philharmonia/Karajan. †BEETHOVEN: Symphony No. 8 in F, Op. 93 (LP: 33CX1392, T536–7, Set SLS5053, Set 3544).

**May 20, July 9.** J. STRAUSS II–JOSEF STRAUSS: Pizzicato Polka (LP: 33CX1393, 35342. EP: SEL1568).

**May 21, 23–24, 27, June 18.** †TCHAIKOVSKY: Symphony No. 6 in B minor, Op. 74 (LP: 33CX1377).

**May 24–25.** BRAHMS: Symphony No. 2 in D, Op. 73 (LP: 33CX1355, 35218, SXLP30513).

**May 25, 27, July 7.** †J. STRAUSS II: Waltz, Künstlerleben, Op. 316 (LP: 33CX1393, 35342).

**May 25–27.** EMI Studio 1A. Schwarzkopf (soprano), Seefried (so-prano), Moore (piano). †DVORAK: Moravian Duets, Op. 32 (LP: 33CX1331, 35390).

**May 27.** CARISSIMI: Lungi o moi; Il mio core; A pie d'un verde alloro; E pur vuole; Detesta la cative sorte in amore. MONTEVERDI: Io son pur vezzosetta pastorella; Ardo o scoprir; O bel pastor; Tornata o cari baci (LP: 33CX1331, 35290).

**July 4–5.** Kingsway Hall. Philharmonia/Karajan. SIBELIUS: Symphony No. 6 in D minor, Op. 104 (LP: 33CX1341, 35316).

**July 5–6.** SIBELIUS: Symphony No. 7 in C, Op. 105 (LP: 33CX1341, SXLP30430, 35316).

**July 6–8.** JOSEF STRAUSS: Delirienwalzer, Op. 212. J. STRAUSS II: Waltz, An der schönen, blauen Donau, Op. 314; Kaiserwalzer, Op. 437; Der Zigeunerbaron—overture (LP: 33CX1393, 35342).

# A Selected Discography

**July 6–8.** J. STRAUSS II: Tritsch-Tratsch Polka, Op. 214 (LP: 33CX1335, 35327).

**July 8–9.** OFFENBACH: Orfée aux enfers—overture; J. STRAUSS I: Radetzky March, Op. 228; J. STRAUSS II: Galop, Unter Donner und Blitz, Op. 324; SUPPE: Leichte Kavallerie—overture; CHABRIER: Marche joyeuse (LP: 33CX1335, 35327).

**July 10, October 10–11.** MOZART: Symphony No. 39 in E flat, K543 (LP: 33CX1361, 35323, 35739).

**July 24–29.** Musikvereinsaal, Vienna. Schwarzkopf (soprano), Höffgen (contralto), Haefliger (tenor), Edelmann (bass), Gesellschaft der Musikfreunde, Philharmonia/Karajan. BEETHOVEN: Symphony No. 9 in D minor, Op. 125 (LP: 33CX1391–2, T536–7, Set SLS5053, Set 3544).

**July 28.** Musikvereinsaal, Vienna. Gesellschaft der Musikfreunde, Philharmonia/Karajan. MOZART: Ave verum corpus, K618. (LP: 33CX1741, SAX2389, SXLP30161, 35948).

**Aug. 1–6.** La Scala, Milan. Callas (soprano), Villa (soprano), Danielli (mezzo-soprano), Gedda (tenor), Borriello (baritone), etc., La Scala Chorus and Orchestra/Karajan. PUCCINI: Madama Butterfly (LP: 33CX1296–8, Set SLS5015, Set 3523).

**Aug. 29–30.** EMI Studio 3. Gieseking (piano). †BEETHOVEN: Sonata No. 17 in D minor, Op. 31, No. 3 (LP: 33CX1417, 35352).

**Sept. 3, 5, 8–14, 16.** La Scala, Milan. Callas (soprano), Lazzarini (mezzo-soprano), Gerbino (mezzo-soprano), Ercolani (tenor), di Stefano (tenor), Gobbi (baritone), Dickie (baritone), Zaccaria (bass), etc., La Scala Chorus and Orchestra/Serafin. VERDI: Rigoletto (LP: 33CX1324–6, Set SLS5018, Set 3537).

**Oct. 3–4, Dec. 17.** Kingsway Hall. Philharmonia/Klemperer. †BEETHOVEN: Symphony No. 3 in E flat (LP: 33CX1346, Set SLS873, 35328).

**Oct. 5–6, Dec. 17.** †BEETHOVEN: Symphony No. 7 in A, Op. 92 (LP: 33CX1379, Set SLS873, 35330).

**Oct. 6–7, Dec. 17.** †BEETHOVEN: Symphony No. 5 in C minor, Op. 67 (LP: 33C1051, Set SLS873, 35329).

**Oct. 11–12; June 18, 1956.** Kingsway Hall. Philharmonia/Karajan. MUSSORGSKY (orch. RAVEL): Pictures at an Exhibition (LP: 33CX1421, SAX2261, SXLP30445, Set SLS5019, 35430).

## 1956

**Feb. 16.** EMI Studio 1. D. Oistrakh (violin), Yampolsky (piano). MOZART:Violin Sonata No. 32 in B flat, K454 (LP: 33CX1415, 35356).

**Feb. 16–17.** TARTINI: Sonata in G minor (LP: 33CX1415, 35356).

**Feb. 18, 28.** SUK (arr. KOCIAN): Love Song, Op. 7 No. 1; KODALY (arr. FEIGIN): Three Hungarian Folk Dances; WIENIAWSKI: Légende, Op. 17; ZARZYCKI: Mazurka in G, Op. 26; DEBUSSY (arr. POULENC): Clair de lune; FALLA (arr. KOCHANSKI): Suite populaire espagnole—No. 6, Jota; TCHAIKOVSKY: Valse-Scherzo, Op. 34; YSAYE: Extase, Op. 21 (LP: 33CX1466, SAX2253, 35354, 60259).

**Feb. 24–25.** Kingsway Hall. D. Oistrakh (violin), Philharmonia/Malko. TANAYEV: Concert Suite, Op. 28 (LP: 33CX1390, Set SLS5004, 35355).

**Feb. 29, Mar. 2–3.** Kingsway Hall. D. Oistrakh (violin), Fournier (cello). Philharmonia/Galliera. BRAHMS: Double Concerto in A minor, Op. 102 (LP: 33CX1487, SAX2264, SXLP30185, 35353).

**Apr. 3–4, 6–8.** EMI Studio 1. Schwarzkopf (soprano), Moore (piano). WOLF: Philine; Mignon 1 and 2; Frühling übers Jahr; Gleich und gleich; Epiphanias; Ganymed; St Nepomuks Vorabend (LP: 33CX1657, SAX2333, Set SLS5197).

**Apr. 8–14, 19, May 15, 19.** SIBELIUS: Schwarze Rosen, Op. 36, No. 1; Schilf, schilf, säusle, Op. 36, No. 4; STRAUSS: Wiegenlied, Op. 41, No. 1; DVORAK: Gypsy Songs, Op. 55, No. 4, Songs my mother taught me; WOLF: Elfenlied; In dem Schatten; HAHN: Si mes vers avaient des ailes; MENDELSSOHN: Auf Flügeln des Gesanges, Op. 34, No. 2; TRAD.: Gsätzli; MARTINI: Plaisir d'amour: TRAD. (arr. GOUNOD): O, du liebs Angeli; GRIEG: Ich liebe dich, Op. 5, No. 3; TRAD.: Drink to me only with thine eyes; A. JENSEN: Murmelndes Lüftchen, Op. 21; GRIEG: Farmyard Song, Op. 61, No. 3; TCHAIKOVSKY: Nur wer die Schnsucht kennt, Op. 6, No. 6 (LP: 33CX1404, SAX2265, 35383). Stereo versions omit Schilf, schilf, säusle.

**Apr. 27.** Kingsway Hall. Schwarzkopf (soprano), Philharmonia/Süsskind. WAGNER: Tannhäuser—Elisabeth's Greeting; Elisabeth's Prayer (LP: 33CX1658, SAX2300, Set SXDW3049, 35806).

**Apr. 27–28.** WEBER: Der Freischütz—Wie nähet mir der Schlummer . . . Leise, leise; Und ob die Wolke (LP: 33CX1658, SAX2300, Set SXDW3049, 35806).

**Apr. 28.** WAGNER: Lohengrin—Einsam in trüben Tagen (LP: 33CX1658, SAX2300, Set SXDW3049, 35806).

**May 11–12, 14–15.** Town Hall, Watford. Schwarzkopf (soprano), Hoffman (soprano), Gedda (tenor), Unger (tenor), Prey (baritone), Czerwenka (bass), etc., Chorus, Philharmonia/Leinsdorf. †CORNELIUS: Der Barbier von Bagdad (LP: 33CX1400–1, Set 3553).

**May 19–21, 31.** EMI Studio 1A. Hotter (baritone), Moore (piano). BRAHMS: Wie Melodien zieht es mir, Op. 105, No. 1; Sonntag, Op. 47, No. 3; Minnelied, Op. 71, No. 5; Komm' bald, Op. 97, No. 5; Botschaft, Op. 47, No. 1; Wir wandelten, Op. 96, No. 2; Sapphische Ode, Op. 94, No. 4; In Waldeseinsamkeit, Op. 85, No. 6; Ständchen, Op. 106, No. 1; O wüsst ich doch, Op. 63, No. 8; Wenn du nur zuweilen lächelst, Op. 57, No. 2; †Verrat, Op. 105, No. 5; †Sommerabend, Op. 85, No. 1; †Mondenschein, Op. 85, No. 2; †Wie bist du, meine Königin, Op. 32, No. 9 (LP: 33CX1448, 35497).

**May 22–26.** EMI Studio 1. Schwarzkopf (soprano), Christ (tenor), Cordes (baritone), Frick (bass), Wieter (bass), Kusche (bass), etc., Philharmonia/Sawallisch. ORFF: Die Kluge (LP: 33CX1446–7, SAX2257–8, Set 3551, Arabesque 8021–2).

**June 21–23, 25–29.** Kingsway Hall. Schwarzkopf (soprano), Moffo (soprano), Merriman (mezzo-soprano), Barbieri (mezzo-soprano), Alva (tenor), Spataru (tenor), Ercolani (tenor), Gobbi (baritone), Panerai (baritone), Zaccaria (bass), etc., Chorus and Philharmonia/Karajan. VERDI: Falstaff (LP: 33CX1410–2, SAX2254–6, Set SLS5037, Set SLS5211, Set 3552).

**Aug. 3–4, 6–9.** La Scala, Milan. Callas (soprano), Barbieri (mezzo-soprano), di Stefano (tenor), Ercolani (tenor), Panerai (baritone), Zaccaria (bass), etc., La Scala Chorus and Orchestra/Karajan. VERDI: Il trovatore (LP: 33CX1483–5, Set SLS869, Set 3554).

**Aug. 20–25, Sept. 3–4, 12.** La Scala, Milan. Callas (soprano), Moffo (soprano), Ricciardi (tenor), di Stefano (tenor), Panerai (baritone), Spatafora (baritone), Zaccaria (bass), Badioli (bass), etc., La Scala Chorus and

# A Selected Discography

Orchestra/Votto. PUCCINI: La bohème (LP: 33CX1464-5, Set SLS5059, Set 3560).

**Oct. 17.** EMI Studio 3. Gieseking (piano). SCHUMANN: Waldscenen, Op. 87—No. 7. Vogel als Prophet; SCRIABIN: Poème, Op. 32, No. 1 (LP: 33CX1761, 35488).

**Oct. 18.** CHOPIN: Barcarolle in F sharp minor, Op. 60 (LP: 33CX1526). Berceuse in D flat, Op. 57; SCRIABIN: Prelude in E, Op. 15, No. 4 (LP: 33CX1751, 35488).

**Oct. 18-19.** BEETHOVEN: Sonata No. 8 in C minor, Op. 13 (LP: 33CX1488, SXLP30129, 35025).

**Oct. 19.** BEETHOVEN: Sonata No. 9 in E, Op. 14, No. 1; Sonata No. 10 in G, Op. 14, No. 2 (LP: 33CX1519, SAX2259, 35652).

**Oct. 19-20.** BEETHOVEN: Sonata No. 11 in B flat, Op. 22 (LP: 33CX1498, 35653).

**Oct. 20.** BEETHOVEN: Sonata No. 19 in G minor, Op. 49, No. 1; Sonata No. 20 in G, Op. 49, No. 2 (LP: 33CX1488, SXLP30129).

**Oct. 20-21.** BEETHOVEN: Sonata No. 12 in A flat, Op. 26 (LP: 33CX1603).

**Oct. 21-22.** BEETHOVEN: Sonata No. 13 in E flat, Op. 27, No. 1 (LP: 33CX1519, SAX2259, 35652).

**Oct. 22.** BEETHOVEN: Sonata No. 14 in C sharp minor, Op. 27, No. 2 (LP: 33CX1519, SAX2259, SXLP30129, 35025, 35652. EP: ESL6253). Sonata No. 15 in D, Op. 28 (LP: 33CX1603).

**Oct. 29-30.** Kingsway Hall. Philharmonia/Klemperer. BRAHMS: Symphony No. 2 in D, Op. 73 (LP: 33CX1517, SAX2362, ASD2706, SXLP30238, Set SLS804, 35532, Set 3614).

**Oct. 29, 31, Nov. 1; Mar. 28-29, 1957.** BRAHMS: Symphony No. 1 in C minor, Op. 68 (LP: 33CX1504, SAX2262, ASD2705, SXLP30217, Set SLS804, 35481, Set 3614).

**Nov. 1; Mar. 27-28, 1957.** BRAHMS: Symphony No. 4 in E minor, Op. 98 (LP: 33CX1591, SAX2350, ASD2708, SXLP30214, Set SLS804, 35546, Set 3614).

**Dec. 12-15, 17-22.** Kingsway Hall. Schwarzkopf (soprano), Stich-Randall (soprano), Ludwig (mezzo-soprano), Meyer (contralto), Majkut (tenor), Kuen (tenor), Edelmann (bass), Waechter (baritone), etc., Chorus and Philharmonia/Karajan. STRAUSS: Der Rosenkavalier (LP: 33CX1492-5, SAX2269-72, Set SLS810, Set 3563).

**Dec. 14.** Kingsway Hall. Schwarzkopf (soprano), Philharmonia/Schmidt. SMETANA: Die verkaufte Braut—Endlich allein . . . Wie fremd und tot (LP: SAX5286, Set SXDW3049, 36434).

**Dec. 22.** Kingsway Hall: **Apr. 28, 1957.** EMI Studio 1. Peter Ustinov (narrator). Philarmonia/Karajan. PROKOFIEV: Peter and the Wolf, Op. 67 (LP: 33CX1559, SAX2375, 35638).

### 1957

**Jan. 7-8.** Grünewald Church, Berlin. Berlin Philharmonic/Karajan. WAGNER: Tannhäuscr—overture; Tristan und Isolde—Prelude and Liebestod (LP: 33CX1496, 35482).

**Feb. 18-19.** WAGNER: Die Meistersinger von Nürnberg—overture (LP: 33CX1496, 35482).

**Mar. 3-6, 8-9.** La Scala, Milan. Callas (soprano), Ratti (soprano),

Cossotto (mezzo-soprano), Monti (tenor), Ricciardi (tenor), Zaccaria (bass), Morresi (bass), La Scala Chorus and Orchestra/Votto. BELLINI: La sonnambula (LP: 33CX1469–71, SLS5134, Set 3568, Set 6108).

**Mar. 16–20.** EMI Studio 1. Kuen (tenor), Peter (baritone), Hotter (baritone), Graml (baritone), Schmitt-Walter (baritone), Lagger (bass), Christ (narrator), etc., Chorus and Philharmonia/Sawallisch. ORFF: Der Mond (LP: 33CX1534–5, Set 3567).

**Mar. 27.** Kingsway Hall. Philharmonia/Klemperer. BRAHMS: Symphony No. 3 in F, Op. 90 (LP: 33CX1536, SAX2351, SXLP30255, Set SLS804, 35545, Set 3614).

**Mar. 29.** BRAHMS: Tragic Overture, Op. 81 (LP: 33CX1517, SAX2362, SXLP30238, Set SLS821, Set SLS804, 35532, Set 3614). Academic Festival Overture, Op. 80 (LP: 33CX1536, SAX2351, SXLP30255, Set SLS804, 35545, Set 3614).

**Apr. 28.** EMI Studio 1. Philharmonia/Karajan. L. MOZART: Cassation in G, movements 3, 4, and 7 [HAYDN: Toy Symphony] (LP: 33CX1559, SAX2375, SXLP30161, Set SLS839, 35638).

**May 23–25.** Grünewald Church, Berlin. Berlin Philharmonic/Karajan. †BRUCKNER: Symphony No. 8 in C minor (LP: 33CX1586–7, T772–3, ST772–3, Set SXDW3024, Set 3576).

**May 25–26, June 1, 30, July 1.** EMI Studio 1. Schwarzkopf (soprano), Chorus and Philharmonia/Mackerras. TRAD. (orch. MACKERRAS): I saw three ships; FRANCK: Panis angelicus; TRAD.: O du fröhliche; HUMPERDINCK (arr. MACKERRAS): Weihnachten; TRAD.: Von Himmel Hoch; TRAD.: In dulce jubilo; TRAD. (arr. MACKERRAS): Easter Alleluia; GRUBER: Stille Nacht; arr. BRAHMS: Volkeskinderlieder—No. 4, Sandmännchen; TRAD.: Maria auf dem Berge; GLUCK: In einem kühlen Grunde; TRAD.: O come all ye faithful; TRAD. (arr. MACKERRAS): The First Nowell (LP: 33CX1482, ASD3798, 35530, 36750).

**May 26, 29, June 3.** EMI Studio 3. A. Fischer (piano). SCHUMANN: Fantasia in C, Op. 17 (LP: 33CX1664).

**May 29, June 1–2; June 2, 1958.** BEETHOVEN: Piano Sonata No. 8 in C minor, Op. 13 (LP: 33CX1593, 35569).

**June 1.** SCHUMANN: Carnival, Op. 9 (LP: 33CX1664).

**June 3 and 4.** BEETHOVEN: Piano Sonata No. 21 in C, Op. 53 (LP: 33CX1593, 35569).

**June 8–10.** EMI Studio 1. Schwarzkopf (soprano), Moore (piano). WOLF: Kennst du das Land?; Die Bekehrte; Anakreons Grab (LP: 33CX1657, SAX2333, Set SLS5197, 35909).

**June 11.** SCHUBERT: Heidenröslein, D257 (LP: 33CX5268, SAX5268, 36345).

**July 2–5.** Kingsway Hall. Schwarzkopf (soprano), Philharmonia/Ackermann. SIECZYNSKY: Wien, du Stadt meiner Träume; LEHAR: Der Zarewitsch—Einer wird kommen; Der Graf von Luxembourg—Hoch, Evoë Angèle; Heut noch werd' ich Ehefrau; J. STRAUSS II (arr. BENATZKY): Casanova—The Nun's Chorus; Laura's Song; ZELLER: Der Vogelhändler—Ich bin die Christel von der Post; Schenkt man sich Rosen in Tirol; HEUBERGER: Der Opernball—Im chambre separée; SUPPE: Boccaccio—Hab' ich nur deine Liebe; LEHAR: Giuditta—Meine Lippen, sie küssen so heiss; ZELLER: Der Obersteiger—Sei nicht bös; MILLÖCKER: Die Dubarry—Was ich im Leben beginne; Ich schenk' mein Herz (LP: 33CX1570, SAX2283, ASD2807, 35696).

# A Selected Discography

**July 9–13, 15.** La Scala, Milan. Callas (soprano), Schwarzkopf (soprano), Nessi (tenor), Fernandi (tenor), Ercolani (tenor), de Palma (tenor), Boriello (baritone), Zaccaria (bass), etc., La Scala Chorus and Orchestra/ Serafin. PUCCINI: Turandot. (LP: 33CX1555–7, Set RLS741, Set 3571).

**July 18–20, 22, 24–27.** La Scala, Milan. Callas (soprano), Cossotto (mezzo-soprano), di Stefano (tenor), Formichini (tenor), Tattone (tenor), Fioravanti (baritone), Calabrese (bass), Forti (bass), etc., La Scala Chorus and Orchestra/Serafin. PUCCINI: Manon Lescaut (LP: 33CX1583–5, Set RLS737, Set 3564, Set 6089).

**Sept. 2–7, 9–11.** Kingsway Hall. Schwarzkopf (soprano), Moffo (soprano), Ludwig (mezzo-soprano), Gedda (tenor), Christ (tenor), Fischer-Dieskau (baritone), Hotter (baritone), Waechter (baritone), etc., Philharmonia/Sawallisch. STRAUSS: Capriccio (LP: 33CX1600–02, OC230–2, Set 3580).

**Oct. 4–5.** Kingsway Hall. Philharmonia/Klemperer. BEETHOVEN: Symphony No. 2 in D, Op. 36 (LP: 33CX1615, SAX2331, ASD2561, Set SLS788, 35658, Set 3619).

**Oct. 7–8.** BEETHOVEN: Symphony No. 6 in F, Op. 68 (LP: 33CX1532, SAX2260, ASD2565, Set SLS788, 35711, Set 3619).

**Oct. 21–22.** BEETHOVEN: Symphony No. 4 in B flat, Op. 60 (LP: 33CX1702, SAX2354, ASD2563, Set SLS788, 35661, Set 3619).

**Oct. 28–29.** BEETHOVEN: Symphony No. 1 in C, Op. 21 (LP: 33CX1554, SAX2318, ASD2560, Set SLS788, 35657, Set 3619).

**Oct. 29–30.** BEETHOVEN: Symphony No. 8 in F, Op. 93. (LP: 33CX1554, SAX2318, ASD2560, Set SLS788, 35657, Set 3619).

**Oct. 30–31, Nov. 21–23.** Lovberg (soprano), Ludwig (mezzo-soprano), Kmentt (tenor), Hotter (baritone), Philharmonia Chorus. BEETHOVEN: Symphony No. 9 in D minor, Op. 125 (LP: 33CX1574–5, SAX2276–7, Set SLS790, Set SLS788, Set 3577, Set 3619).

**Nov. 11, 13–14, 17–18, 20.** EMI Studio 1. Ludwig (mezzo-soprano), Moore (piano). BRAHMS: Sapphische Ode, Op. 94, No. 4; STRAUSS: Allerseelen, Op. 10, No. 8; MAHLER: Des Knaben Wunderhorn—No. 6, Des Antonius von Padua Fischpredigt; No. 7, Rheinlegendchen; Rückert Lieder—No. 4, Ich bin der Welt; BRAHMS: Die Mainacht, Op. 43, No. 2; Liebestreu, Op. 3, No. 1; Der Schmied, Op. 19, No. 4; WOLF: Gesang Weylas; Auf einer Wanderung; SCHUBERT: Fischerweise, D881; Die Allmacht, D852; STRAUSS: Die Nacht, Op. 10, No. 3 (LP: 33CX1552, 35592, 60034).

**Nov. 14.** EMI Studio 1A. Hotter (baritone), Moore (piano). SCHUMANN: Die beiden Grenadiere, Op. 49, No. 1; SCHUBERT: Im Frühling, D882; SCHUMANN: Liederkreis, Op. 24—No. 5, Mondnacht; STRAUSS: Ach, weh mir unglückhaftem Mann, Op. 24 No. 4; WOLF: Anakreons Grab (LP: 33CX1661, 35583).

**Nov. 28–29.** ?Grünewald Church, Berlin. Berlin Philharmonic/Karajan. HINDEMITH: Symphony, Mathis der Maler (LP: 33CX1783, SAX2432, 35949).

**Nov. 28–29, Jan. 6–7, May 18–20, 1958.** DVORAK: Symphony No. 9 in E minor, Op. 95 (LP: 33CX1642, SAX2275, Set SLS839, ASD2863, 35615).

A Selected Discography

1958

Jan. 9. Kingsway Hall. Philharmonia/Karajan. BERLIOZ: Overture, Le carnaval romain (LP: 33CX1548, SXLP30450, Set SLS5019, 35613).

Jan. 9–10. LISZT (arr. MULLER-BERGHAUS): Hungarian Rhapsody No. 2 in C sharp minor, G359 (LP: 33CX1571, SAX2302, Set SLS5019, 35614, 37231).

Jan. 9, 18. WEBER (orch. BERLIOZ): Invitation to the Dance, Op. 65 (LP: 33CX1571, SAX2302, Set SLS5019, 35614, 37550). BERLIOZ: La damnation de Faust, Op. 24—Marche hongroise (LP: 33CX1571, SAX2302, Set SLS5019, 37231, 35614).

Jan. 10, 13. RESPIGHI: The Pines of Rome (LP: 33CX1548, SXLP30450, Set SLS5019, 35613).

Jan. 11. EMI Studio 1A. Schwarzkopf (soprano), Moore (piano). WOLF: Die Spröde; Mignon III; Blumengruss (LP: 33CX1657, SAX2333, Set SLS5197, 35909).

Jan. 12–13. RACHMANINOV: To the children, Op. 26, No. 7; TRAD. (arr. WEATHERLEY): Danny Boy (LP: 33CX5268, SAX5268, 36345).

Jan. 13–16, 18. Kingsway Hall. Philharmonia/Karajan. OFFENBACH (arr. ROSENTHAL): Movements from Gaieté Parisienne (LP: 33CX1588, SAX2274, SXLP30224, Set SLS5019, ST1084, 35607).

Jan. 14–15. BIZET: L'arlésienne—Suites 1 and 2 (LP: 33CX1608, SAX2289, Set SLS5019, ST1044, 35618).

Jan. 16. SIBELIUS: Kuolema, Op. 44—Valse triste (LP: 33CX1571, SAX2302, Set SLS5019, 35614). BIZET: Carmen—Suite No. 1 (LP: 33CX1608, SAX2289, ST1044, Set SLS839, 35618).

Jan. 17. LISZT: Les préludes, G97 (LP: 33CX1548, SXLP30450, Set SLS5019, 35613, 37231).

Jan. 17–18. TCHAIKOVSKY: Overture, 1812, Op. 49 (LP: 33CX1571, SAX2302, Set SLS839, 35614, 37232).

Jan. 18. ROSSINI: Guillaume Tell—Passo a tre; Coro tirolese (LP: 33CX1588, SAX2274, ST1084, 35607, 37231). GOUNOD: Faust—Ballet Music (LP: 33CX1588, SAX2274, ST1084, SXLP30224, Set SLS839, 35607).

Feb. 28, Mar. 1, 10. EMI Studio 1. A. Fischer (piano), Philharmonia/ Sawallisch. †MOZART: Piano Concerto No. 21 in C, K467 (LP: 33CX1630, SXLP30124).

March 1–2, 10. †MOZART: Piano Concerto No. 22 in E flat, K482 (LP: 33CX1630, SXLP30124).

April 1–3, 5–7; Dec. 19, 21, 23, 1959. EMI Studio 1. Schwarzkopf (soprano), Moore (piano). WOLF: Das italienisches Liederbuch (LP: 33CX1714, SAX2366, 35883).

May 9–10, 12. EMI Studio 1A. D. Oistrakh (violin), Knushevitsky (cello), Oborin (piano). BEETHOVEN: Piano Trio No. 6 in B flat, Op. 97 (LP: 33CX1643, SAX2352, SMFP2117, 35704).

May 10. EMI Studio 1. D. Oistrakh (violin), Knushevitsky (cello), Oborin (piano), Philharmonia/Sargent. BEETHOVEN: Triple Concerto in C, Op. 56 (LP: 33C1062, SBO2753, SXLP20081, 35697).

May 13, 16. EMI Studio 1A. D. Oistrakh (violin), Knushevitsky (cello),

# A Selected Discography

Oborin (piano). SCHUBERT: Piano Trio No. 1 in B flat, D898 (LP: 33CX1627, SAX2281, 35713).

**May 18–20.** Grünewald Church, Berlin. Berlin Philharmonic/Karajan. SMETANA: Mà Vlast—Vltava (LP: 33CX1642, SAX2275, ASD2863, Set SLS839, 35615, 37232).

**May 22.** EMI Studio 1. D. Oistrakh (violin), Philharmonia/D. Oistrakh. MOZART: Violin Concerto No. 3 in G, K216 (LP: 33CX1660, SXLP30086, 35714).

**May 25.** EMI Studio 1. Schwarzkopf (soprano), Ludwig (mezzo-soprano), Philharmonia/Wallberg. WAGNER: Lohengrin—Euch luften (LP: 33CX1658, SAX2300, Set SXDW3049, 35806).

**Sept. 12–16.** Musikvereinsaal, Vienna. Schwarzkopf (soprano), Ludwig (mezzo-soprano), Gedda (tenor), Zaccaria (bass), Gesellschaft der Musikfreunde, Philharmonia/Karajan. BEETHOVEN: Missa solemnis, Op. 123 (LP: 33CX1634–5, ST914–5, Set SLS5198, Set 3595).

**Sept. 16–17.** Musikvereinsaal, Vienna. Philharmonia/Karajan. MOZART: Symphony No. 38 in D, K504 (LP: 33CX1703, SAX2356, T1032, ST1032, 35739).

**Oct. 18.** EMI Studio 1. Ludwig (mezzo-soprano), Philharmonia/Boult. MAHLER: Lieder eines fahrenden Gesellen (LP: 33CX1671, SAX2321, T703, ST703, 60026).

**Oct. 19.** EMI Studio 1. Ludwig (mezzo-soprano), Philharmonia/Vandernoot. MAHLER: Kindertotenlieder (LP: 33CX1671, SAX2321, T703, ST703, 60026).

**Nov. 8, 10.** Salle Wagram, Paris. D. Oistrakh (violin), French National Radio Orchestra/Cluytens. BEETHOVEN: Violin Concerto in D, Op. 61 (LP: 33CX1672, SAX2315, SXLP30168, Set SLS5004, 35780).

## 1959

**Jan. 1–2.** Kingsway Hall. Philharmonia/Karajan. TCHAIKOVSKY: Swan Lake, Op. 20—Suite (LP: SAX2306, SXLP30200, Set SLS839, 35740).

**Jan. 2–3.** MASCAGNI: L'amico Fritz—Act 3 Intermezzo; LEONCAVALLO: I pagliacci—Intermezzo (LP: SAX2294, Set SLS5019, 35793). TCHAIKOVSKY: The Sleeping Beauty, Op. 66—Suite (LP: SAX2306, SXLP30200, Set SLS839, 35740).

**Jan. 3.** PUCCINI: Manon Lescaut—Act 3 Intermezzo; VERDI: La traviata—Act 3 Prelude (LP: SAX2294, Set SLS5019, 35793).

**Jan. 3, 5.** GRANADOS: Goyescas—Intermezzo (LP: SAX2294, Set SLS5019, 35793). MUSSORGSKY (arr. RIMSKY-KORSAKOV): Khovantchina—Act 4 Entr'acte (LP: SAX2294, SXLP30445, 35793).

**Jan. 5–6.** SIBELIUS: Finlandia, Op. 26 (LP: 33CX1750, SAX2392, Set SLS5019, 35922, 37232).

**Jan. 6.** OFFENBACH: Les contes d'Hoffmann—Barcarolle; SCHMIDT: Notre Dame—Intermezzo (LP: SAX2294, Set SLS839, 35793). BERLIOZ: Les Troyens—Royal Hunt and Storm (with chorus) (LP: SAX2294, Set SLS5019, 35793).

NB: There is some doubt as to the extent to which Walter Legge supervised the above Karajan sessions.

**Apr. 22–23.** Kingsway Hall. Schwarzkopf (soprano), Philharmonia/ Rescigno. VERDI: Otello—Emilia, te ne prego; Piangeo cantando (with Elkins, mezzo-soprano); Ave Maria plena di grazia. (LP: 33CX5286, SAX5286, Set SXDW3049, 36434).

**Apr. 24.** PUCCINI: Gianni Schicchi—O mio babbino caro; La bohème— Si mi chiamano Mimi (LP: 33CX5286, SAX5286, Set SXDW3049, 36434).

**May 3–5.** EMI Studio 1A. Ludwig (mezzo-soprano), Moore (piano). MAHLER: Rückert Lieder—No. 1, Ich atmet' einer linden Duft; No. 2, Liebst du um Schönheit; No. 5, Um Mitternacht. Des Knaben Wunderhorn —No. 1, Der Schildwache Nachtlied; No. 4, Wer hat dies Liedlein erdacht; No. 5, Das irdische Leben; No. 9, Wo die schönen Trompeten blasen; No. 10, Lob des hohen Verstandes. Lieder und Gesänge aus der Jugendzeit—No. 6, Um schlimme Kinder; No. 7, Ich ging mit Lust (LP: 33CX1705, SAX2358, 60070).

**May 3–4.** SCHUMANN: Frauenliebe und -leben, Op. 42 (LP: 33CX1693, SAX2340).

**May 6.** BRAHMS: Zigeunerlieder, Op. 103; Vergebliches Ständchen, Op. 84, No. 4; Auf die Nacht in der Spinnstub'n, Op. 107, No. 5; Am jungsten Tag, Op. 95, No. 6; Ständchen, Op. 106, No. 1 (LP: 33CX1693, SAX2340).

**June 4.** Kingsway Hall. Philharmonia/Giulini. RAVEL: Alborada del gracioso (LP: 33CX1694, SAX2341, SXLP30198, 35820).

**June 8–10.** †RAVEL: Daphnis et Chloé—Suite No. 2 (LP: 33CX1694, SAX2341, SXLP30198, 35820).

**June 25.** EMI Studio 1A. Ludwig (mezzo-soprano), Moore (piano). BRAHMS: Feldeinsamkeit, Op. 86, No. 2. (LP: 33CX1693, SAX2340). MAHLER: Lieder und Gesänge aus der Jugendzeit—No. 1, Frühlingsmorgen; No. 3, Hans und Grete (LP: 33CX1705, SAX2358, 60070).

**June 25–27, 29–30, July 1–2.** Kingsway Hall. Lipp (soprano), Martini (soprano), Scheyrer (soprano), Ludwig (mezzo-soprano), Terkal (tenor), Dermota (tenor), Kunz (baritone), Berry (bass), Waechter (baritone), etc., Philharmonia and Philharmonia Chorus/Ackermann. J. STRAUSS II: Die Fledermaus (LP: 33CX1688–9, SAX2336–7, Set 3581).

**September 4–11.** La Scala, Milan. Callas (soprano), Cossotto (mezzo-soprano), Companeez (contralto), Ferraro (tenor), Ercolani (tenor), Cappuccilli (baritone), Vinco (bass), Monreale (bass), Forti (bass), etc., La Scala Chorus and Orchestra/Votto. PONCHIELLI: La gioconda (LP: 33CX1706–8, SAX2359–61, Set SLS5176, Set 3606, Set 6031).

**Sept. 16–19, 21–25, 27.** Kingsway Hall. Schwarzkopf (soprano), Moffo (soprano), Cossotto (mezzo-soprano), Ercolani (tenor), Taddei (baritone), Cappuccilli (baritone), Waechter (baritone), Vinco (bass), etc., Philharmonia and Philharmonia Chorus/Giulini. MOZART: Le nozze di Figaro (LP: 33CX1732–5, SAX2381–4, SLS5152, Set 3608).

**Oct. 7–15, Nov. 23–24.** EMI Studio 1. Schwarzkopf (soprano), Sutherland (soprano), Sciutti (soprano), Alva (tenor), Taddei (baritone), Cappuccilli (baritone), Waechter (baritone), Frick (bass), etc., Philharmonia and Philharmonia Chorus/Giulini. MOZART: Don Giovanni (LP: 33CX1717–20, SAX2369–72, SLS5083, Set 3605).

**Oct. 22–24.** EMI Studio 1. Philharmonia/Klemperer. BEETHOVEN: Symphony No. 5 in C minor, Op. 67 (LP: 33CX1721, SAX2373, ASD2564, Set SLS788, 35843, Set 3619).

**Oct. 29, Nov. 11–13.** BEETHOVEN: Symphony No. 3 in E flat, Op. 55 (LP: 33CX1710, SAX2364, ASD2562, SXLP30310, Set SLS788, 35853, Set 3619).

**Dec. 30–31.** Grünewald Church, Berlin. Berlin Philharmonic/Karajan. HANDEL: The Water Music—Suite. MOZART: Serenade No. 13 in G, K525 (LP: 33CX1741, SAX2389, Set SLS839, SXLP30161, 35948).

### 1960

**Feb. 23–24.** Kingsway Hall. Philharmonia/Klemperer. WAGNER: Tannhäuser—overture; Der fliegende Holländer—overture (LP: 33CX1697, SAX2347, Set SLS5075, SXLP30436, 36187, Set 3610).

**Feb. 27.** WAGNER: Götterdämmerung—Siegfried's Funeral March; Lohengrin—Act 3 Prelude (LP: 33CX1698, SAX2348, Set SLS5075, 36188, Set 3610).

**Feb. 29—March 1.** Grünewald Church, Berlin. Berlin Philharmonic/ Karajan. TCHAIKOVSKY: Symphony No. 4 in F minor, Op. 36 (LP: 33CX1704, SAX2357, T872, ST872, SXLP30433, 35885). MOZART: Symphony No. 29 in A, K201 (LP: 33CX1703, SAX2356, ST1032, 35739).

**Mar. 1–2.** Kingsway Hall. Philharmonia/Klemperer. WAGNER: Die Meistersinger von Nürnberg—overture (LP: 33CX1698, SAX2348, Set SLS5075, 36187, Set 3610). WAGNER: Tristan und Isolde—Prelude and Liebestod (LP: 33CX1698, SAX2348, Set SLS5075, 36188, Set 3610).

**Mar. 2–3.** †WAGNER: Rienzi—overture (LP: 33CX1697, SAX2347, Set SLS5075, SXLP30436, 36187, Set 3610).

**Mar. 8.** WAGNER: Die Meistersinger von Nürnberg—Dance of the Apprentices; Entry of the Masters (LP: 33CX1698, SAX2348, Set SLS5075, 36188, Set 3610).

**Mar. 10.** WAGNER: Die Walküre—Walkürenritt (LP: 33CX1820, SAX2464, SXLP30528, Set SLS5075, 35947).

**Mar. 26–27, 29–30.** EMI Studio 1 and Kingsway Hall. Philharmonia/ Karajan. ROSSINI: La gazza ladra—overture; Semiramide—overture; La scala di seta—overture; Guillaume Tell—overture; Il barbiere di Siviglia— overture; L'italiana in Algeri—overture (LP: 33CX1729, SAX2378, SXLP30203, 35890).

**Mar. 28–29.** Kingsway Hall. Philharmonia/Karajan. SIBELIUS: Symphony No. 2 in D (LP: 33CX1730, SAX2379, SXLP30414, 35891).

**May 22–24; May 9–10, 16, 31, 1962.** EMI Studio 1. A. Fischer (piano), Philharmonia/Klemperer. †SCHUMANN: Piano Concerto in A minor, Op. 54 (LP: 33CX1842, SAX2485).

**May 24; May 10, 1962.** LISZT: Piano Concerto No. 1 in E flat, G124 (LP: 33CX1842, SAX2485).

**June 17–19.** Salle Wagram, Paris. D. Oistrakh (violin), French National Radio Orchestra/Klemperer. BRAHMS: Violin Concerto in D, Op. 77 (LP: 33CX1765, SAX2411, SXLP30264, Set SLS5004, 35836).

**Sept. 5–12.** La Scala, Milan. Callas (soprano), Vincenzi (soprano),

Ludwig (mezzo-soprano), Corelli (tenor), de Palma (tenor), Zaccaria (bass), La Scala Chorus and Orchestra/Serafin. BELLINI: Norma (LP: 33CX1766–8, SAX2412–4, Set SLS5186, Set 3615).

Sept. 20–21, 23. Kingsway Hall. Philharmonia/Karajan. SIBELIUS: Symphony No. 5 in E flat (LP: 33CX1750, SAX2392, SXLP30430, 35922).

Sept. 21. VERDI: Aida—Act 2 Ballet Music (LP: 33CX1774, SAX2421, 35925, 37250). SUPPE: Leichte Kavallerie—overture (LP: 33CX1758, SAX2404, T838, ST838, CFP40368, Set SLS839, 35926, 37231).

Sept. 21, 23. WALDTEUFEL: Waltz, Les patineurs, Op. 183 (LP: 33CX1758, SAX2404, SXLP30224, T838, ST838, CFP40368, Set SLS839, 35926, 37250).

Sept. 22. BORODIN: Prince Igor—Dance of the Polovtsi Maidens; Polovtsian Dances (LP: 33CX1774, SAX2421, SXLP30445, Set SLS5019, 35925, 37232).

Sept. 22–23. PONCHIELLI: La gioconda—Dance of the Hours (LP: 33CX1774, SAX2421, Set SLS5019, 35925, 37250). WAGNER: Tannhäuser—Venusberg Music (LP: 33CX1774, SAX2421, 35925).

Sept. 23. MUSSORGSKY: Khovantchina—Dance of the Persian Slaves (LP: 33CX1774, SAX2421, Set SLS839, SXLP30200, SXLP30445, 35925). CHABRIER: Marche joyeuse (LP: 33CX1758, SAX2404, T838, ST838, CFP40368, Set SLS5019, 35926, 37250). WEINBERGER: Schwanda the Bagpiper—Polka (LP: 33CX1758, SAX2404, T838, ST838, CFP40368, Set SLS5019, 35926). OFFENBACH: Orfée aux enfers—overture (LP: 33CX1758, SAX2404, T838, ST838, CFP40368, Set SLS839, 35926). CHABRIER: Rapsodie España (LP: 33CX1758, SAX2404, T838, ST838, CFP40368, Set SLS839, 35926).

Sept. 24. J. STRAUSS II: Tritsch-Tratsch Polka, Op. 214 (LP: 33CX1758, SAX2404, T838, ST838, CFP40368, 35926). Galop, Unter Donner und Blitz, Op. 324 (LP: 33CX1758, SAX2404, T838, ST838, CFP40368, 35926, 37231). J. STRAUSS I: Radetzky March, Op. 228 (LP: 33CX1758, SAX2404, T838, ST838, CFP40368, Set SLS839, 35926, 37232).

Oct. 25, Nov. 19, Dec. 3. Kingsway Hall. Philharmonia/Klemperer. BEETHOVEN: Symphony No. 7 in A, Op. 92 (LP: 33CX1769, SAX2417, ASD2566, Set SLS788, 35945, Set 3619).

Nov. 21, 25–26; Jan. 3–4, Apr. 14–15, May 10–12, Nov. 28, 1961. Kingsway Hall and EMI Studio 1. Pears (tenor), Fischer-Dieskau (baritone), Berry (bass), Case (baritone), Gedda (tenor), Kraus (baritone), Schwarzkopf (soprano), Evans (baritone), Ludwig (mezzo-soprano), Baker (mezzo-soprano), Brown (tenor), Watts (contralto), Boys of the Hampstead Parish Church Choir, Chorus and Philharmonia/Otto Klemperer. †BACH: St Matthew Passion, BWV244 (LP: 33CX1799–1803, SAX2446–50, Set SLS827, Set 3599).

### 1961

Jan. 2, Mar. 21, 23, 25–26, May 4–6, 8. Kingsway Hall. Schwarzkopf (soprano), Fischer-Dieskau (baritone), Philharmonia and Philharmonia Chorus/Klemperer. BRAHMS: Ein Deutsches Requiem, Op. 45 (LP: 33CX1781–2, SAX2430–1, Set SLS821, Set 3624).

# A Selected Discography

**Jan. 15–18, 20, 30.** EMI Studio 1A. Schwarzkopf (soprano), Moore (piano). WOLF: Singt mein Schatz wie ein Fink; Du milchjunger Knabe; Mausfallen-Sprüchlein; Wandl' ich in dem Morgentau; Morgentau; Wie glänzt der helle Mond; Der Spinnerin; Das Vöglein; Wiegenlied im Winter; Sonne der Schlummerlosen; Der Schäfer (LP: 33CX1946, SAX2589, Set SLS5197, 36308).

**Apr. 6–7, 10, 25.** Kingsway Hall. Schwarzkopf (soprano), Philharmonia/Klemperer. MAHLER: Symphony No. 4 (LP: 33CX1793, SAX2441, ASD2799, 35829).

**June 13–15.** EMI Studio 1. A. Fischer (piano). †BEETHOVEN: Sonata No. 32 in C, Op. 111 (LP: 33CX1807, SAX2435).

**Oct. 24, Nov. 13–14, 22.** Kingsway Hall. Philharmonia/Klemperer. WAGNER: Das Rheingold—Entry of the Gods into Valhalla; Siegfried—Forest Murmurs; Parsifal—Act 1 Prelude; Götterdämmerung—Siegfried's Rhine Journey (LP: 33CX1820, SAX2464, SXLP30528, Set SLS5075, 35947).

**Nov. 22–24, Mar. 15 and 24, 1962.** Kingsway Hall. Schwarzkopf (soprano), Rössl-Majdan (contralto), Philharmonia and Philharmonia Chorus/Klemperer. MAHLER: Symphony No. 2 (LP: 33CX1829–30, SAX2473–4, Set SLS806, Set 3634).

**Nov. 28–30.** EMI Studio 1. Ludwig (mezzo-soprano), Parsons (piano). SCHUBERT: Der Musensohn, D764; Ave Maria, D839; Der Tod und das Mädchen, D531; Litanei, D343; Erlkönig, D328 (LP: SAX5272).

*1962*

**Feb. 6–10, 12–15, 17, 19.** Kingsway Hall. Hallstein (soprano), Ludwig (mezzo-soprano), Vickers (tenor), Unger (tenor), Crass (bass), Berry (bass), Frick (bass), Philharmonia and Philharmonia Chorus/Klemperer. BEETHOVEN: Fidelio (LP: 33CX1804–6, SAX2451–3, SLS5006, Set 3625).

**Feb. 20.** EMI Studio 1. Ludwig (mezzo-soprano), Parsons (piano). SCHUBERT: Frühlingsglaube, D686 (LP: SAX5272).

**March 21–23.** Kingsway Hall. Ludwig (mezzo-soprano), Philharmonia/Klemperer. BRAHMS: Alto Rhapsody, Op. 53 (Philharmonia Chorus) (LP: 33CX1817, SAX2462, ASD2391, Set SLS821, 35923). WAGNER: Wesendonck Lieder (LP: 33CX1817, SAX2462, ASD2391, 35923). WAGNER: Tristan und Isolde—Liebestod (LP: 33CX1817, SAX2462, 35923).

**July 2–7, 9, 12.** Kingsway Hall. Schwarzkopf (soprano), Steffek (soprano), Gedda (tenor), Equiluz (tenor), Waechter (baritone), etc., Philharmonia and Philharmonia Chorus/Matačić. LEHAR: Die lustige Witwe (LP: AN101–2, SAN101–2, SLS823, Set 3630).

**Sept. 10–15, 17–18.** Kingsway Hall. Schwarzkopf (soprano), Steffek (soprano), Ludwig (mezzo-soprano), Kraus (tenor), Taddei (baritone), Berry (bass), etc., Philharmonia and Philharmonia Chorus/Böhm. MOZART: Così fan tutte (LP: AN103–6, SAN103–6, Set SLS5028, Set SLS901, Set 3631).

**Dec. 3–4, 7.** EMI Studio 1. Schwarzkopf (soprano), Moore (piano). WOLF: Tretet ein, hoher Krieger; Hochbeglückt in deiner Liebe; Das Köhlerweib ist trunken; Als ich auf dem Euphrat schiffte; Nimmer will ich dich

285

verlieren; Wiegenlied im Sommer (LP: 33CX1946, SAX2589, Set SLS5197, 36308).

Dec. 12. WAGNER: Wesendonck Lieder—No. 5, Träume (LP: SAN255).

### 1963

Sept. 16–21, 23–27; Apr. 7, 1964. Kingsway Hall. Schwarzkopf (soprano), Ludwig (mezzo-soprano), Gedda (tenor), Ghiaurov (bass-baritone), Philharmonia and Philharmonia Chorus/Giulini. VERDI: Missa da Requiem. (LP: AN133–4, SAN133–4, Set SLS909, Set 3649).

### 1964

Feb. 17–19. Kingsway Hall. Ludwig (mezzo-soprano), Philharmonia/ Klemperer. MAHLER: Rückert Lieder—Nos. 1, 4, 5 (LP: ASD2391).

Feb. 19–22. †MAHLER: Das Lied von der Erde (LP: AN179, SAN179, Set 3704).

Dec. 7. EMI Studio 1. Schwarzkopf (soprano), Moore (piano). SCHUBERT: Der Jüngling an der Quelle, D300 (LP: 33CX5268, SAX5268, 36345).

### 1965

Aug. 22–27. Evangelisches Gemeindhaus, Berlin. Schwarzkopf (soprano), Moore (piano). arr. WOLF-FERRARI: Quando a letto vo' la sera; Dimmi, bellino mio; Com'io ho da dare; Dio ti facesse star tanto digiuno; Vo'fa' 'na palazzina alla marina; Giavanottino che passi per via; Viovanetti, cantate ora che siete; Vado di notte come fa la luna. SCHUBERT: Seligkeit, D433; Die Forelle, D550; Der Einsame, D800; Liebe schwärmt auf allen Wegen, D239. WOLF: Die Zigeunerin; Wenn du zu den Blumen gehst. DEBUSSY: Mandoline (LP: 33CX5268, SAX5268, 36345). SCHUMANN: Zwei Venezienisches Lieder—Leis' rudern hier, Op. 25, No. 17; Wenn durch die Piazetta, Op. 25, No. 18. SCHUMANN: Widmung, Op. 25, No. 1 (LP: 33CX5268, SAX5268, 36345, ASD3124). SCHUMANN: Wie mit innigstem Behagen, Op. 25, No. 9 (LP: ASD2634, 36752).

Aug. 28–30, Sept. 6–11. Evangelisches Gemeindhaus, Berlin. Schwarzkopf (soprano), Fischer-Dieskau (baritone), Moore (piano). BRAHMS: Deutsche Volkslieder, Nos. 1–42 (LP: AN163–4, SAN163–4, Set 3675).

Sept. 1–3. Grünewald Church, Berlin. Schwarzkopf (soprano), Berlin Radio Symphony/Szell. STRAUSS: Vier letzte Lieder; Zueignung, Op. 10, No. 1; Freundliche Vision, Op. 48, No. 1; Die heiligen drei Könige, Op. 56, No. 6; Muttertändelei, Op. 43, No. 2; Waldseligkeit, Op. 49, No. 1 (LP: 33CX5258, SAX5258, ASD2888, 36347).

Sept. 12–13, Apr. 10–17, 1966; Sept. 27–Oct. 3, 1967. Evangelisches Gemeindhaus, Berlin. Schwarzkopf (soprano), Fischer-Dieskau (baritone), Moore (piano). WOLF: Das italienisches Liederbuch (LP: SAN210–1, Set 3703).

### 1966

Jan. 14. New York City. Schwarzkopf (soprano), Gould (piano). STRAUSS: Lieder der Ophelia, Op. 67—Nos. 1–3 (LP: 76983, Set M2X35914).

# A Selected Discography

**Apr. 21–29.** Evangelisches Gemeindhaus, Berlin. Schwarzkopf (soprano), Parsons (piano). MAHLER: Rückert Lieder—No. 1, Ich atmet' einen linden Duft; Des Knaben Wunderhorn—No. 6, Des Antonius von Padua Fischpredigt; No. 10, Lob des hohen Verstandes. STRAUSS: Ach, was Kummer, Op. 49, No. 8; Wer lieben will, Op. 49, No. 7; Meinem Kinde, Op. 37, No. 3. WOLF: Verborgenheit; Nimmersatte Liebe; Selbstgestandnis. SCHUBERT: An mein Klavier, D342; Erlkönig, D328 (LP: ASD2404, 36545).

**Sept. 16–17.** Kingsway Hall. Schwarzkopf (soprano), London Symphony/Galliera. TCHAIKOVSKY: Eugene Onegin—Tatiana's Letter Scene (LP: SAX5286, Set SXDW3049, 36434).

**Dec. 16–17, Jan. 2–10, 1967.** Berlin. Schwarzkopf (soprano), Fischer-Dieskau (baritone), Moore (piano). WOLF: Das Spanisches Liederbuch (LP: SLPM139329–30, 2726 071).

## 1967

**Feb. 20.** Royal Festival Hall, London. Live recording, farewell concert of Gerald Moore. Schwarzkopf (soprano), de los Angeles (soprano), Fischer-Dieskau (baritone), Moore (piano). SCHUBERT: Der Einsame, D800; Nachtviolen, D752; Abschied, D957; Im Abendrot, D799 (Fischer-Dieskau, Moore). BRAHMS: Sapphische Ode, Op. 94, No. 4; Der Gang zum Liebchen, Op. 48, No. 1; Vergebliches Ständchen, Op. 84, No. 4 (de los Angeles, Moore). WOLF: Kennst du das Land; Sonne der Schlummerlosen; Das verlassene Mägdlein; Die Zigeunerin (Schwarzkopf, Moore). MOZART: Ecco quel fiero istante, K436; Più non si trovano, K549 (Schwarzkopf, de los Angeles, Fischer-Dieskau, Moore). ROSSINI: La regata veneziana; La pesca; Duetto buffo di due gatti (Schwarzkopf, de los Angeles, Moore). HAYDN: An den Vetter; Daphnens einziger Fehler (Schwarzkopf, de los Angeles, Fischer-Dieskau, Moore). SCHUMANN: In der Nacht, Op. 74, No. 4; Vier Duette, Op. 78—No. 1, Tanzlied; No. 2, Er und sie; No. 3, Ich denke dein (Schwarzkopf, Fischer-Dieskau, Moore). MENDELSSOHN: Ich wollt' meine Lieb'ergosse sich, Op. 63, No. 1; Gruss, Op. 63, No. 3; Lied aus "Ruy Blas", Op. 77 No. 3. Drei Volkslieder—No. 2, Abendlied; No. 3, Wasserfahrt (de los Angeles, Fischer-Dieskau, Moore). SCHUBERT (arr. MOORE): An die Musik, D547 (Moore). (LP: AN182–3, SAN182–3, Set 3697).

**Oct. 24–28.** Evangelisches Gemeindhaus, Berlin. Schwarzkopf (soprano), Parsons (piano). WOLF: Lebe wohl; Mozart: Das Veilchen, K476; Mein Wunsch, K539; SCHUMANN: Die Kartenlegerin, Op. 31, No. 2; STRAVINSKY: Pastorale; MUSSORGSKY: In dem Pilzen; TCHAIKOVSKY: Pimpinella, Op. 38, No. 6 (LP: ASD2404, 36545).

**Oct. 28.** STRAUSS: Lieder der Ophelia, Op. 67—Nos. 1–3 (LP: ASD2634, 36752).

## 1968

**Mar. 8–9, 11–12.** Kingsway Hall. Schwarzkopf (soprano), Fischer-Dieskau (baritone), London Symphony/Szell. MAHLER: Des Knaben Wunderhorn, Nos. 1–10, 13, 14. (LP: SAN218, 36547).

**Mar. 10–14, 18.** Kingsway Hall. Schwarzkopf (soprano), London Sym-

phony/Szell. MOZART: Alma grande e nobil core, K578; Vado ma dove?
. . . O Dei, K583; Ch'io mi scordi di te? . . . Non temer, K505 (Brendel,
piano); Nehmt meinem Dank, K383. STRAUSS: Meinem Kinde, Op. 37, No.
3; Ruhe, meine Seele, Op. 27, No. 1; Wiegenlied, Op. 41, No. 1; Morgen,
Op. 27, No. 4; Das Rosenband, Op. 36, No. 1; Das Bächlein, Op. 88, No. 1;
Winterweihe, Op. 48, No. 4. (LP: ASD2493, 36643).

**Oct. 20–27.** Evangelisches Gemeindhaus, Berlin. Schwarzkopf (soprano),
Parsons (piano). LISZT: Die drei Zigeuner, G320; MAHLER: Lieder und
Gesänge aus der Jugendzeit—No. 6, Um schlimme Kinder artig zu machen.
GRIEG: Ich liebe dich, Op. 5, No. 3; Mit einer Wasserlilie, Op. 25, No. 4;
Letzter Frühling, Op. 33, No. 2. SCHUBERT: Hänflings Liebeswärbung,
D552; Ach, um deine feuchten Schwingen, D717; Was bedeutet die Bewe-
gung?,D720. CHOPIN: 17 Polish Songs, Op. 74—No. 1, Mädchens Wunsch;
No. 16, Litauisches Lied. LOEWE: Kleiner Haushalt, Op. 71 (LP: ASD2634,
36752).

### 1970

**Aug. 27–31, Sept. 1–8.** MOZART: Der Zauberer, K472; Abendempfindung, K523. BRAHMS: Wie Melodien zieht es mir, Op. 105, No. 1; Immer
leiser wird mein Schlummer, Op. 105, No. 2; Der Jäger, Op. 95, No. 4;
Liebestreu, Op. 3, No. 1; Ständchen, Op. 106, No. 1; Vergebliches Ständchen, Op. 84, No. 4. arr. BRAHMS: Deutsche Volkslieder—No. 4, Sandmännchen. WOLF: Im Frühling; Auf ein Christblume. GRIEG: Erstes Begeg-
nen, Op. 21, No. 1; Zur Rosenzeit, Op. 48, No. 5; Mit einer Primula veris,
Op. 26, No. 4; Lauf der Welt, Op. 48, No. 3. STRAUSS: Die Nacht, Op. 10,
No. 3; Wiegenliedchen, Op. 49, No. 3 (LP: ASD2844).

**Sept. 22–30; Mar. 1–10, 1973.** WOLF: An eine Aeolsharfe; Denk'es, o
Seele; Keine gleicht von allen Schönen; Der Gärtner; An den Schlaf; Auf
einer Wanderung; Begegnung; Sonne der Schlummerlosen; Auftrag. SCHU-
BERT: Gretchen am Spinnrade, D118; Wehmut, D772; Meeres Stille,
D216; An Silvia, D891; Erntelied, D434. SCHUMANN: Der Nussbaum, Op.
25, No. 3 (LP: ASD3124).

### 1974

**Jan.** SCHUMANN: Frauenliebe und -leben, Op. 42; Liederkreis, Op. 39
(LP: ASD3037, 37043).

### 1977

**Jan. 5–7, 13–17.** Rosslyn Hill Chapel, Hampstead. Schwarzkopf (soprano), Parsons (piano). WOLF: Lebe wohl!; Das verlassene Mägdlein;
Fussreise; Auf ein altes Bild; Jägerlied; Heimweh; Bei einer Trauung; Selbst-
geständnis; Storchenbotschaft; Nimmersatte Liebe; Elfenlied; Nixe Binsefuss
(LP: SXL6943).

### 1979

**Jan. 2–3, 6, 9–10.** Sofiensaal, Vienna. Schwarzkopf (soprano), Parsons
(piano). WOLF: Mausfallen-Sprüchlein; LOEWE: Die wandelnde Glocke,
Op. 20, No. 3; GRIEG: Ein Schwann, Op. 25, No. 2; BRAHMS: Mädchen-
lied: Am jüngsten Tag, Op. 95, No. 6; Blinde Kuh, Op. 58, No. 1; Therese,
Op. 86, No. 1 (LP: SXL6943).

# Index

# Index